D0482256

Why Not Creation?

Selected Articles from the
CREATION RESEARCH SOCIETY QUARTERLY
Volumes I through V (1964-1968)

WALTER E. LAMMERTS, *Editor*

PRESBYTERIAN AND REFORMED PUBLISHING CO.
1970

Library of Congress Catalog Card No. 78-133085
Printed in the United States of America

Contents

CONTENTS

V

Introduction

The best way of giving the history of the Creation Research Society is to simply reprint pertinent parts of my introduction to the 1964 Annual. By way of orientation it should be stated that this was written in the spring of 1964. The meeting referred to was the joint meeting of the Evangelical Theological Society and the American Scientific Affiliation held at Asbury College in Wilmore, Kentucky, June 19-21, 1963. The one at the home of Dr. John Grebe was a few days later. The following is then the introduction to the 1964 Annual:

"My own interest in the continuing dialogue between those scientists who believe in evolutionary concept and those who are creationists began about six years ago when my older daughter, Karen, brought home a high school textbook in which the statement was made that 'all scientists now accept the fact of evolution as basic to their study of nature.' When she asked me if this was true I told her that I certainly did not agree, and patiently explained to her a few of the many evidences which make the evolution theory invalid. About three years later my younger daughter, Camilla, showed me three high school textbooks making essentially the same statement.

"By this time I began to wonder if perhaps I might be the sole remaining intellectual dinosaur surviving in an otherwise completely enlightened age of mammals. Inquiry at our local church revealed that not one of the five scientists holding responsible positions at the Lawrence Radiation Laboratory had any use for the theory; they were all creationists. Thus encouraged, I contacted a number of Fellows of the American Scientific Affiliation and soon found that several of them such as William J. Tinkle, now retired but formerly Professor of Genetics at Anderson College, were still creationists.

"We then set up a Creation Research Committee, or 'team of ten' as Tinkle called it, for mutual exchange of ideas. By this time Henry M. Morris and John C. Whitcomb had published their now famous book, *The Genesis Flood*. The many facts so well presented by them have re-established Biblical catastrophism as an intellectually sound alternative explanation of geological and geographical facts.

"The two concepts of creation and catastrophism are so closely interwoven that our Creation Research Committee decided to start a

Creation Research Society. The statement of belief to which we all subscribed was first drawn up by our committee while attending a joint meeting of the Evangelical Theological Society and the American Scientic Affiliation at Asbury College in Wilmore, Kentucky. It was then amended at a meeting of the northern group in the home of John J. Grebe, physical research chemist, in Midland, Michigan.

"Our aim is a rather audacious one, namely the complete re-evaluation of science from the theistic viewpoint. Actually Christian men of science have allowed themselves to be dominated by a certain code, i.e., all *legitimate* scientific inquiry must proceed on the basis of appealing only to processes and forces and reaction rates now in operation. This idea is all right as a way of stating either in words or mathematical symbols the natural processes and laws we observe or detect. As a result great progress has been made in such sciences as chemistry and physics and even biology, particularly genetics and medicine. The increasingly successful application of engineering principles has led successively to the exploitation of power from coal, oil, electricity and finally in a fantastic way nuclear energy. Equally startling is the resulting expense and danger to the taxpayer! However, many scientists have mistakenly come to the conclusion that these laws express the totality of nature. Accordingly the wonderful adaptations everywhere so clearly pointing to design are popularly credited vaguely to Nature and spoken of as being the result of evolution by natural selection. Rarely does one see the phrase 'as we gaze at the beauty of this rose we marvel at the glory of God whose creation it is.'

"It is our hope to publish from time to time *original* research. Though we have no hope of convincing our agnostic and atheistically-minded scientific colleagues of the barren and worn out nature of evolution concepts, we expect they will read our annual and quarterlies in order to get much needed *new* information published for the first time.

"Our theistic evolutionary-minded friends may also see that their position is illogical. Our atheistic colleagues are at least logical in their basic assumptions, i.e., that the universe is eternal though ever changing and that *present* rates and kinds of *naturally* occurring processes are adequate to explain it. If so, what need is there of postulating the theory of a personal God?

"Mainly, however, it is our hope the educators, pastors, theologians, and laymen may see that we can, with better logic, postulate a personal

God who created this universe by the conversion of His energy (a part of it) into mass and therefrom very rapidly brought into being the marvelous order we see both in the inorganic and organic realms. The tasks involved in reorganizing the many fields of science in line with this concept are many. Creationists have too long been merely negative in their thrust, indicating the weaknesses of the evolution concepts, but offering little in its place. As will be clearly shown by Henry M. Morris, this world shows such clear evidence of degeneration and catastrophy that one marvels how so many of our scientific colleagues have been blinded. To paraphrase the words of our great President, the late and beloved John F. Kennedy, we cannot hope in one lifetime to complete the structure of a truly theistic science, but let us begin.

"This first annual of our Creation Research Society is then presented as a beginning of the task ahead."

Five years have gone by since then and it has been my privilege to edit four more Annuals and fifteen quarterlies. The response to our requests for really worthwhile articles by our scientists and active members has been most heartening. Last winter Dr. John Whitcomb and President Henry Morris decided that it would be very useful to publish selected, representative articles in one volume. The board of directors unanimously voted approval of this idea and appointed me to make the selections and edit this book.

As I write this introduction the Apollo 11 flight has just been successfully concluded. Over eighty pounds of rock samples were taken from the surface of the moon. In the July 18, 1969, issue of *Time* Magazine we read on page 23, "Some scientists, assuming that the moon was created when the earth was, some 4.5 billion years ago, calculated that about 10 trillion tons of meteors have fallen on the lunar surface." Also it is stated on page 21, "Perhaps most intriguing is what the moon may reveal about the earth's murky infancy. The earth was formed some 4.5 billion years ago, but the slow relentless process of its evolution wiped out all traces of its earliest years; the oldest known terrestrial rocks date back to about 3.3 billion years. 'What happened during the missing 1.2 billion years?' wonders astronomer Robert Jastrow, director of NASA's Goddard Institute for Space Studies in New York."

They hope for an answer to this question from a study of the approximately 80 pounds of lunar rock collected. Not the slightest suggestion is made in all of these discussions of the moon flight that these age estimates are entirely based on theory. Possibly Dr. Jastrow might be interested in reading chapter 4 on radioactivity dating.

On the strength of concepts developed in this fascinating chapter I venture to predict that the 10 trillion tons of meteors will not be found or even a small percentage of this amount. Also not a vestige of evidence for life on the moon either now or in the past will be found.

It will be most interesting to see which line of thinking will prove correct as the study of this expensive collection of rocks and dust goes on. Meanwhile this volume presents the thinking of a significant minority group of scientists who reject the evolution theory because it simply is not supported by the facts of nature. Many of us also doubt the validity of radioactive dating. We are well aware that many problems yet remain unsolved and it is toward this task that our new editor, Dr. George Howe, invites continued contributions of worthwhile articles.

Walter E. Lammerts
Editor
P.O. Box 496
Freedom, Calif. 95019
July 21, 1969

Chapter I

Philosophical and Theological Background

1

THE PHILOSOPHY OF SCIENCE IN RELATION TO CONCEPTS OF CREATION VS. THE EVOLUTION THEORY

John W. Klotz, Ph.D.*

I should probably begin by defining what I mean by evolution. I do not equate evolution with change. It is obvious that change has taken place in the past and is taking place today. Organisms become extinct; new species develop. I am not suggesting a static world in which the species on our time level have existed unchanged since creation; nor does Scripture teach this.

By evolution I mean the idea that life came into existence by purely natural process according to the principles which we find operative on our time level, that given the conditions which existed in the primitive world life might come into existence today, that no special supernatural activity or intervention was necessary, that all of the forms of life we know today have descended from a single, or at most a few, common ancestors, and that man is descended from animal ancestors.

It is my conviction that life came into existence by God's almighty power in a miraculous way that does not lend itself to scientific description or scientific study and examination, that life from the beginning existed in a wide variety of forms, some relatively simple, others extremely complex, and that all human beings are the descendants of Adam and Eve, who were not the descendants of animals.

I believe that the observational evidence gives no more support to evolution than it does to special creation. I believe there are observations which fit the theory of evolution better than they do special creation, but I also believe there are observations which do not fit the theory of evolution.

---

*Concordia Senior College, Fort Wayne, Indiana

In order to see evolution in its proper perspective it might be desirable to explore first the nature of the scientific method, how the scientist proceeds, what his objectives are, what his assumptions are, and what he believes that he achieves. Modern science is a relatively new phenomenon. It developed when the logical methods of the Greeks were wedded to the experimental methods of the alchemists and metalurgists. The Greeks were competent individuals and in a real sense competent scientists, but they failed to employ some of the techniques of modern science, particularly the experimental method, and consequently did not make the progress that modern science has made.

Let us recognize at the outset that science has contributed immensely to the society of which we are members. No Christian can be anti-scientific, for science has been a means God has employed in bringing blessings to us. Science is a gift of God. Through it God has enabled us to exercise greater control of the environment than He has given to any previous generation. To reject evolution is not to reject science.

Controlled Experimentation in Science

The chief technique of the scientist today and the technique which he has used successfully in developing modern science has been the experimental method. If we examine the science of the ancient Greeks and modern science, this seems to be the only significant difference. The Greeks were certainly our peers and possibly even our superiors in their intellectual equipment; they made careful observations, but they failed to use the technique of the controlled experiment, for thy were prejudiced against the use of experimentation.

It is generally agreed that controlled experiments are of critical importance in the progress of science today. Ideally the experiment enables the investigator to assign a given effect to a given cause. He is able to eliminate causes which are irrelevant and in this way he seeks to determine the correctness of the explanation which his theory presents.

It is at once obvious that experimentation can only be used with phenomena on our time level. It is simply impossible to conduct controlled experiments regarding the past. This is also true of direct observation. Since evolution is supposed to be a process requiring long periods of time, it is not possible to observe changes of the magnitude required for the development of the higher categories. And it is in this area—the past—that the difference of opinion between those who accept special creation and evolution arises. Dr. Conant discussed this in his *Science and Common Sense* (page 259ff) and calls attention to the fact that there is no basic controversy between science and the Church on our time level. He says that these controversies deal chiefly with the phenomena of the past. I am convinced that the reason for this is the impossibility of using experimentation and direct observation in discussing most aspects of the theory of evolution. We simply do not have available to any appreciable extent these very important tools and resources. We cannot test the theory and therefore we lack the reasonable certainty we have in dealing with phenomena on our time level.

The Scientific Method

How does the scientist work? In most cases he begins by gathering his facts. He may do this by carrying on observations or he may set up experiments of discovery which will assist him in "getting the facts." After he has gathered his facts, he arranges them in a logical order through correlation, classification, mathematical manipulation, and the like. Next comes the great leap of the scientific method, the formation of a hypothesis or a theory. Once the scientist has gathered his facts, he tries to relate them and to explain them. This is the function of a hypothesis or a theory—to relate facts to one another and to explain them.

After the theory or hypothesis has been formulated the scientist works deductively and asks himself this question: If my theory is correct, what are the logical consequences of the theory? He then proceeds to test these logical consequences by means of a second type of experiment, an experiment of confirmation. If his experiments confirm his theory or hypothesis, he is happy. If they do not, he restructures his theory or hypothesis to fit these additional observations which he has made.

It is at once evident that the scientist deals with two kinds of "things"—facts and theories. A theory is never a fact, and it cannot be a fact. This does not mean that theories are unimportant; they are of the utmost importance. Evolution cannot be dismissed because "it is only a theory." As a matter of fact it is generally agreed that progress in science comes not by gaining new facts but by developing new theories. Theories are also of immense practical importance. George Washington died because of a wrong theory. He lived at a time when disease was explained according to the humoral theory and it was thought that disease was due to imbalances in the humors, one of which was the blood, and he was treated accordingly, with fatal results. Let me say then that while I would argue evolution is not a fact, I am not saying it is unimportant.

Characteristics of a Good Theory

What are the criteria by which we judge the adequacy of a theory? It is generally agreed (1) that a theory must be testable by experimentation, (2) that it must be fruitful, and (3) that it must make possible predictions. Gruenberger, in his discussion of the scientific method,[1] lists the various criteria, putting these three first and indicating points that are to be assigned to the different criteria. The fact of the matter is that the theory of evolution does not meet these three most important criteria.

The theory of evolution cannot be checked by experimentation and direct observation.

In addition, it cannot be used to predict to any greater degree than the theory of special creation. Very often evolutionists point to the similarities either in structure or in physiology that can be predicted from the theory of evolution. But it is possible to predict these same similarities from what we might call the theory of special creation. There are at least as many instances in which predictions from the theory of evolution break down as there are instances when the predictions from special creation break down.

In addition the theory of evolution has not been particularly fruitful in stimulating biological research. It has stimulated some research but not nearly so much as some of the other theories.

Therefore, the theory of evolution fails to meet three of the most important criteria for a good theory: capability of being examined by controlled experimentation, predictability, and fruitfulness.

Assumptions of Science

The scientist makes a number of assumptions and imposes a number of limitations upon himself. One of his assumptions is that of uniformity. He assumes that the natural laws and principles which he discovers in his laboratories hold throughout time and space. He believes that matter is the same everywhere in the universe and behaves in the same way. He also assumes that matter has always been constituted in the same way and has always behaved in the same manner throughout time. He assumes that this has been true of the past and that it will be true of the future.

Actually it is only by making this assumption that the scientist is able to work at all. Were he to assume that matter did not obey the same general laws and principles there would be no point in his carrying out his work. If matter were erratic and chaotic, if the scientific laws and principles which we have been able to discover do not hold throughout time and space there would be little purpose in carrying out the scientific enterprise.

At the same time we must recognize that the principle of uniformity is an assumption and nothing more. What is even more interesting is that some scientists and philosophers of science have been inclined to question it. William S. Beck says,

> When all is said and done there seems to be evidence that even the "laws of nature" are changing. Modern physics suggests the possibility that changes are taking place in the speed of light and in the rates of chemical reactions. In other words the universe is changing, and it becomes hazardous to attempt calculations concerning the very remote past and future. It appears that eternal natural stability is as improbable as its psychological corollary, eternal truth. This should worry no one except the seeker of eternal certainty. It may turn out that fundamental change and uncertainty are the nearest things we have to eternal principles.[2]

Closely associated with the principle of uniformity is the principle of uniformitarianism. Uniformitarianism started among the geologists. Perhaps its greatest exponent was Charles Lyell, who argued that the present is the key to the past. His particular interest was the rate of deposit of sedimentary rock and the formation of the various rock strata. He was arguing against the theory of catastrophism promulgated by a number of his contemporaries who believed that the rock strata and the fossils which they contained were the products of sudden catastrophies rather than of slow gradual processes. Lyell argued that the strata were the products of the gradual processes which he and other geologists were able to observe on their own time level. Lyell greatly influenced Darwin.

Actually uniformitarianism is something different from uniformity. It deals with rates rather than with fundamental physical processes and Beck points out there is good reason for believing that rates at which processes take place may change. Uniformitarianism has come under considerable attack among geologists since the end of World War II. Norman Newell of the American Museum of Natural History was recently quoted as saying,

Geology suffers from a great lack of data and in such a situation any attractive theory that comes along is taken as gospel. That is the case with uniformitarianism. Geology students are taught that "the present is the key to the past" and they, too, often take it to mean that nothing ever happened that isn't happening now. But since the end of World War II, when a new generation moved in we have gathered more data and we have begun to realize that there were many catastrophic events in the past, some of which happened just once.

Dr. Newell went on to say,

I am in favor of junking both of the terms, catastrophism and uniformitarianism, completely. They are just too confusing.[3]

The scientist assumes that his senses do not deceive him, that the picture they present is true and correct. Once more it would appear that this is a reasonable assumption and one that is necessary for the existence of any body of scientific knowledge. It does not necessarily follow that the interpretation of these observations is correct. It is important that we recognize this in considering the evidences for evolution.

Sometimes the argument is advanced that evolution must be true since there are so many evidences which seem to support the theory of evolution and God would certainly not deceive us. It is argued that if we deny evolution in the light of its acceptance by unbiased observers we are implying that God is a god who plays cat and mouse games with us, teasing and tormenting us with things which appear to us to be true but which are not. Actually the situation is somewhat different.

True, God does not deceive us, but we may misinterpret the evidence of our sense organs. The fault lies not with God but rather with the limitations of the human mind. Who would argue that God is a god who deceives because He created a world which appeared for thousands of years to be geocentric but which seems actually to be heliocentric. Would we say that God deceived because the world which He created appeared to the best scientists of the day to be geocentric? Rather would we not argue that the men who studied the solar system were deceived because of the limitations of the human mind?

Hanson, in writing on "Galileo's Discoveries in Dynamics," says something quite similar:

Facts are always facts about or with respect to or set out in terms of some theoretical framework. Should the framework deliquesce, the objects, processes, and facts will dissolve conceptually. Where are the "facts" of alchemy, of the phlogiston theory? Or must we grant that no observations ever really supported such frameworks of ideas? . . . They are actually once-descriptive references whose supporting rationale has disappeared. Their articulators were, in their way, dedicated empiricists, groping, struggling, to delineate *the facts* concerning intricacies of a near incomprehensible world. May not the solid acquisitions of our own laboratory performances yet grow pale before the chilling winds of new doctrine—doctrine opposed to our presently accepted theories?[4]

Perhaps "the facts" which are supposed to support evolution are not so overwhelmingly impressive after all.

Paradigms in Science

In this connection it is worth calling attention to a recent article by E. G. Boring, Professor Emeritus of Psychology at Harvard.[5] Boring speaks of changing paradigms in science. Paradigms are essentially fundamental hypotheses or points of view. He cites as an example of a paradigm the Ptolomaic point of view which was supplanted by the heliocentric system of Copernicus; and the creationist point of view which was opposed by evolution. He says that paradigms are fundamental to the thinking of men until something better comes along. They work best for the time being, and their influence is profound. However, he points out, they are not permanent and inevitably they are replaced by another paradigm.

Now what I am saying is that science on any time level does not have the certainty which is popularly assigned to it. Science is an ever-changing thing and the fundamental paradigms—and evolution is one of these—are likely to be replaced, even though at the time they may seem permanent and may answer many questions and provide many explanations.

Science and Faith

Many people make much of the fact that acceptance of special creation is based on faith, whereas the acceptance of the theory of evolution, they believe, is based on observation. We must recognize that all science is based on a great deal of faith—faith in the correctness of basic scientific assumptions, faith in the integrity of other scientists, faith in the accuracy of their observations. It is not true that the Christian walks by faith and the scientist by sight. It is very obvious that also the scientist walks much of the way by faith. Aldous Huxley writes,

All science is based upon an act of faith—faith in the validity of
the mind's logical processes, faith in the ultimate explicability of
the world, faith that the laws of thought are laws of things. In
practice, I repeat, if not in theory, such conceptions are fundamental to all scientific activity. For the rest, scientists are oppor-
tunists. They will pass from a commonsense view of the world
to advanced idealist theories, making use of one or the other according to the field of study in which they are at work. Unfortunately, few scientists in these days of specialization are ever
called upon to work in more than one small field of study. Hence
there is a tendency on the part of individual specialists to accept
as true particular theories which are in fact only temporarily convenient.[6]

The Objectivity of Science

Another point that requires comment is the supposed objectivity of
science. The scientist is often pictured as a cold, unemotional, objective person who accepts facts and lets the chips fall where they
may. Yet Boring insists that scientists cling tenaciously to conceptual
schemes even in the light of mounting evidence against them. He has
coined the term "egoism" for this trait. He says that while the very
life blood of scientific progress is change, scientists form an emotional
attachment to the hypotheses and theories which they have come to
accept. There is a pride of authorship, a fearsome loyalty to the conceptual schemes which the individual espouses. The longevity of a
pet theory is directly proportional, he says, to the hero status of its
proponent; yet in the course of time, all conceptual schemes are
doomed either to be modified or replaced completely.

Boring is not alone in his point of view. James B. Conant says, "The
notion that a scientist is a cool, impartial, detached individual is, of
course, absurd. The vehemence of conviction, the pride of authorship,
burn as fiercely among scientists as among any creative writers." [7]

Now I am not trying to deny that this happens to theologians; I am
simply trying to point out that contrary to the popular image of the
objective scientist, it happens also to scientists.

Emotionalism in Evolution

The theory of evolution is one in which there has been a great deal
of emotion, and consequently it has been difficult to discuss the theory
objectively. Charges and counter-charges flew in the late 19th century when Darwin presented his Origin of Species. Darwin, the mild-
mannered man that he was, was deeply disturbed by the controversy

that his theory raised. When the theory was discussed at the Oxford meeting of the British Association for the Advancement of Science in 1860, Darwin was not even present because he did not want to become embroiled in the controversy which he knew a discussion of his theory was bound to arouse. Unfortunately it was a British bishop who assumed the responsibility for attacking the theory, and what is even more unfortunate, he chose to attack personally Thomas Huxley, who in Darwin's absence found himself cast in the role of apologist for the theory. Instead of discussing the theory and the evidence for and against it, he chose to attack Huxley personally and to ridicule him.

Later the teaching of evolution was forbidden by law in some of the states of the United States. Most of these laws were passed at the insistence of churches and churchmen. When the Tennessee law which forbade the teaching of evolution in the public schools of the state came under attack and John Scopes was arrested for teaching evolution in the schools of Dayton, Tennessee, it was a Christian layman, William Jennings Bryan, who assumed the responsibility of prosecuting Scopes.

Bryan was poorly prepared for the task; he had not tried a case for 25 years. Moreover, he was critically ill at the time and died five days after the conclusion of the trial. He assumed a very grave responsibility in agreeing to represent the Church, and did a poor job in the role which he accepted. Both these episodes reflected unfavorably on the Church. The Church was placed in the position of using personal attacks and the authority of the state to interfere with science and to hamper the search for scientific truth. Consequently any attack on evolution, even today, raises a red flag and resurrects the controversies of the past. It is very difficult to get an objective discussion of evolution; the subject continues to be an emotional one. Personally, I believe this has been one of the most unfortunate aspects of the whole creation-evolution controversy.

Lest anyone think that only the evolutionists have been the victims of emotionalism and personal attacks it is only necessary to consider what happened in the state of Washington about five years ago. Dr. John M. Howell, Supervisor of Curriculum Guides and Courses of Study for the state of Washington, was asked to express his opinion of evolution in a letter addressed to him by a freshman at the University of Puget Sound who was writing a theme on Darwinism. His answer, in which he expressed doubts as to the correctness of the theory, and in which he states that acceptance of evolution implied a denial of the Bible, was published in the student newspaper. As a result Howell lost his job and found himself shifted to another position in the state Department of Education.

It will not be possible for us to analyze in detail all of the so-called "evidences" for evolution. Suffice it to say there are many observed facts which can be interpreted as indicating relationship, but these same facts can also be interpreted as indicating a single general plan or pattern such as one would expect in a scheme in which life came into being in a wide variety of forms.

Similarity and Descent

The general argument employed is that similarity is evidence of descent from a common ancestor. This represents a slight modification of a common everyday observation, but a modification which is significant. It is readily observable that siblings tend to resemble one another in their external appearance, but it does not follow that individuals who resemble one another are closely related by descent. We all know instances of individuals who resemble one another to such a degree that they might well be taken for identical twins but whose common ancestor is either completely unknown or found only in the far distant past.

Moreover there is evidence which casts doubt on the assumption that similarity is the function of descent from a common ancestor. The phenomenon of parallel mutations is a well-known one. This is the occurrence by mutation of similar characteristics in different species. For instance, the fruit fly, *Drosophila melanogaster* and *Drosophila simulans,* two separate species, have both experienced mutations of eye color to prune, to ruby, and garnet; of body color to yellow; of bristle shape to forked and boxed; of wings to cross veinless, vesiculated, and rudimentary. It might be assumed by those who regard similarity as proof of descent from a common ancestor that two flies, both of which have ruby eyes, have inherited this trait from a common ruby-eyed ancestor, but this is not necessarily the case. The same type of mutation has occurred in both species, and the two ruby-eyed flies may not be related at all.

This phenomenon of parallel mutations is not confined to *Drosophila.* It is a wide-spread phenomenon and has been clearly established in a number of forms. It is often argued that parallel mutations are indeed evidence of close relationship since the fact that they occur indicates similar genetic material which is capable of such parallel mutations. Thus it is argued that the phenomenon of parallel mutations, instead of being a problem for evolution, is actually evidence for it. Dobzhansky cautions against such a line of argumentation, pointing out that similarities do not necessarily indicate similar genetic material. He says,

> But here is a caveat—phenotypically similar, or mimetic mutants are produced also at different, fully complementary and not even linked genes within a species. Among the classic mutants in *Drosophila melanogaster* there are several non-allelic but visibly similar changes of the eye color, the eye surface, the bristle shape, etc. A few of these mimetic genes may conceivably have arisen through the reduplication of the same ancestral genes. But for the majority such a supposition is quite gratuitous. Our powers of observation are limited, and what to our eyes are phenotypically similar changes may actually be due to different genes.[8]

Later Dobzhansky says, "The presence of homologous organs is, then, not necessarily evidence of persistence of identical, similar, or even homologous genes. The genetic system which brings about the development of an eye in a fish is probably quite different from that of an eye in a bird or in a man."

He goes on to say: "What has been said above concerning organs applies as well to their chemical constituents and to enzymes. To an evolutionist, the fact that certain enzymes are widely distributed in most diverse organisms is very impressive. But to conclude that these chemical constituents are produced everywhere by the same genes is going far beyond what is justified by the evidence."

Actually the evolutionist selects his similarities. Those that fit his theory are presented as evidences for evolution, those similarities which do not fit with the theory of evolution are cited as examples of parallel evolution and convergence, that is, the development of similar traits by organisms who are not closely related. For instance, there are many resemblances between the duckbill, or platypus, an Australian monotreme, and the ordinary duck. If these were related by supposed evolutionary descent, I am sure that these resemblances would be regarded as due to descent from a common ancestor. But since they are not supposed to be closely related these evidences are completely ignored.

There are also many instances in which resemblances do not fit the supposed phylogenetic evidence. Sanger *et al* are quoted as saying that, on the basis of insulin composition, sperm whales are identical with pigs and are quite different from sei whales.[9]

In studying hemoglobin similarities, Buettner—Janusch and Hill, find some unusual similarities in hemoglobin. They find, for instance, that hemoglobin of the Ceboidea—the New World monkeys—appears to resemble human hemoglobin rather closely. This, they say, is most interesting for the Ceboidea are not closely related to man. They appear, they say, as a completely distinct lineage in the Miocene deposits of South America. The authors believe that this similarity is due to convergence.[10]

To cite just one more example, an extraordinarily powerful neurotoxin called Tarachatoxin has recently been isolated in crystalline form from the eggs of various western American newts as well as in newt eggs and embryos. It is very different chemically and pharmacologically from other known salamander toxins. This toxin, however, is identical to a toxin which occurs in the Japanese fugu or puffer fish. Thus this substance appears to occur in only one family of the amphibia and in one sub-order of the fishes. It is highly questionable whether this is evidence of a descent from a common ancestor.[11] Instances of this sort could be multiplied.

The Mechanism of Evolution

Let us turn now to a discussion of the mechanism for the changes which evolution requires. Darwin postulated a variation in living organisms on which natural selection worked, selecting the fit to survive and killing off those that were not fit. To this day, evolutionists have not developed what to my way of thinking is a satisfactory explanation for the mechanism whereby the variation postulated by Darwin could arise. Darwin himself did not deal with this problem; he apparently was unacquainted with Mendel's work or at least did not appreciate its importance and developed a rather bizarre and far-fetched theory for the origin of variation.

Today, two methods are suggested for these changes: (1) chromosomal changes or chromosomal aberrations and (2) gene changes or mutations. Chromosomal changes do not appear to be of very much importance in providing the variation required by progressive evolution. Chromosomal changes have only a very slight chance of survival because they upset a great deal the delicate balance of the gene complex. The most favorable type of chromosomal change, so far as the possibility of survival is concerned, is probably polyploidy, but this is regarded as an evolutionary dead end. Cameron says that ultimately polyploids succumb because they cannot go back to the diploid condition, and their gradual change of genetic variation seems to be hampered by the high number of chromosomes.[12]

Strict autopolyploids—polyploids derived from a single ancestor—are rare in nature.[13] Polyploidy in general, according to Ehrlich and Holm, is generally disadvantageous in the long range view. They believe, however, that because they are extremely common in both plants and animals, they must result in a selective advantage. (An example of a rather common type of circular reasoning.)

The other chromosomal changes are either so lethal that they can hardly be of any importance in progressive evolution, or they actually decrease the genetic material. In aneuploidy, for instance, usually there is a decrease rather than an increase in chromosome number, which would hardly provide for the increase in genetic material that progressive evolution would presumably require.

Mutation as a Mechanism

So far as mutation is concerned, evolutionists will have to agree that there are many, many unsolved problems. One of the really critical problems is the fact that most mutations are either lethal, semi-lethal, or subvital and in the ordinary course of events will be eliminated by the very natural selection which is postulated as the guiding factor of evolution. It is usually argued that natural selection works with those mutations which are favorable. While this is theoretically possible, it would certainly increase substantially the amount of time required for evolution. Some evolutionists feel that even the billions of years postulated by evolutionists are not enough for evolution if this is to be the guiding factor.

Even favorable mutations are likely to be eliminated. Fisher calculates that out of 10,000 mutations which have a one percent selective advantage, 9,803 will eventually be eliminated. This means that only 197 out of 10,000 favorable mutations can be expected to survive.

Generally, evolutionists have felt that most mutations important in evolution have had an even smaller advantage, which would increase the probability of extinction. This poses a real dilemma. Large changes with large selection coefficients (which would provide for relatively rapid evolution) would probably upset the delicate balance of the gene complex and would be lethal for this reason. Consequently, evolutionists believe that small changes are the only possible mechanism, a point of view with which Ehrlich and Holm disagree.

Small changes, however, are so time consuming that they are unlikely to provide the diversity needed by progressive evolution. This dilemma has still not been solved.

Another problem of evolution is the fact that the changes provided by mutation do not necessarily bring about sterility which is necessary presumably in the development of new species.

Nor do they provide the kind of changes that progressive evolution needs. Carson says: "One of the great dilemmas that modern evolutionary theory has had to face is the fact that most of the mutations found repeatedly, for instance, within populations of different *Drosophila* species, do not constitute the kind of differences which distinguish species." [14] If this is the case they certainly do not provide the kind of change required by progressive evolution.

The Evolution of Man

Another problem area for the evolutionist is the evolution of man. There is a wide gap between man and the anthropoids in spite of the emphasis that is often placed on the similarities between man and the anthropoids, and progress in studying the evolution of man has been very slow. This is all the more remarkable in the light of the fact that there is considerable interest in man's evolution and consequently considerable incentive to study this area.

One of the problems has been the paucity of fossil material. While fossils in general are very common, and while we have a great many fossils of various organisms, the number of human and prehuman fossils is very limited. Evolutionists explain this on the basis of the fact that man is believed to have been a tropical organism who very early in his history practiced earth burial. Under these circumstances we are likely to have very few fossils. But the fact of the matter is that we do have some fossils from non-tropical areas which would indicate that man was found in these regions.

This paucity of fossils has resulted in a real problem. Dobzhansky says, "Investigators often submit to the temptation of speculating on the basis of scanty bone fragments (and it goes without saying, virtually all finds are fragmentary)." [15] Herberer says, "Despite all progress made by primate paleontology, especially since the end of World War II, documentation is still sparse and more material is greatly needed; that is, any reconstruction must use the methods of comparative morphology and physiology." [16]

As indicated above, most of the fossils are quite fragmentary.

Often the entire find consists of a skullcap or a piece of lower jaw or even a few teeth. Much of the classification has been done on brain box size. At first glance this seems to be a very valid method of determining relative evolutionary development, but the fact of the matter is that it does not work out quite so easily. Bennett, Diamond, Krech, and Rosenweig say,

> In the 19th century the measurement of the size and weight of the brains of men [was] made in an effort to discover differences that might relate to the degree of intellectual attainment. The first results were encouraging, since men of distinction were usually found to have larger brains than those of inferior intellect. Gradually it was realized, however, that men of different stations in life often differed in health and nutrition as well as in intellect and that the former factors might affect brain weight. There were also striking exceptions to the general relation—idiots with larger brains and geniuses with smaller brains. The hypothesis of an intrinsic relation between brain size and cerebral exercise or ability was therefore generally abandoned. In its place there were suggestions of more subtle factors involving neural inter-connections, or chemical changes in the brain. The difficulty of working with such factors discouraged research, and the problem largely reverted to the speculative realm.[17]

Skerlj raises many of the same objections when he says, "Brain size does not seem to me a proper measure since we know in modern man the variability goes from 800 to 2000 cc. and covers all the range from Java to modern man. Furthermore why not mention the Neanderthalers who had on the average a somewhat larger brain size than modern man." [18]

Actually the evidence for human evolution is not nearly as conclusive as one would be led to believe from the number of named forms. The fact of the matter is there are far more named forms than are justified. Dobzhansky says, "A minor but rather annoying difficulty for a biologist is the habit human paleontologists have of flattering their egos by naming each find a new species, if not a new genus. This causes not only a needless cluttering of the nomenclature but is seriously misleading because treating as a species what is *not* a species beclouds some important issues." [19]

Another writer says,

> High physical and dental variability in given species of man and apes has long been known, but it is clear that this has not been taken into account by the majority of past and recent describers of fossil Hominoids. Beginning with Mayr in 1950, taxonomists

have drawn attention to the extreme over-splitting of the known
varieties of Pleistocene Hominoids. Since the late 19th century
this erroneous approach to taxonomy has produced approximately 30 genera and almost countless species.

At the other extreme from this taxonomy prolixity, stand such
workers as Mayr and Dobzhansky who, drawing on their knowledge of modern speciation, have adduced evidence for a single
line of but a few species successive through time in this particular
lineage. To alter their view it would only be necessary to demonstrate the occurrence of two distinguishable species of Hominoids
in a single zone of one site, but despite much discussion of possible contemporaneity, in my opinion such contemporaneity has
not been satisfactorily established. There is fair morphological evidence that there were two species of *Australopithicus* but their
synchronous existence has not been confirmed by finds at the
same level in one site.[20]

Concluding Remarks

In conclusion, it would seem to me that evolution is far from
"proved." The scientific method is, itself, limited to approximations
and reasonable certainty. In studying evolution we do not have the
major tool of modern science, experimentation. We must recognize
that scientists, too, are human, that they are emotional, and that they
are conservative in the sense that they like to keep the theories they
have come to accept. Evolution presents a great many problems.

True, there are many evidences and observations which seem to
support the idea of evolution, but there are also many which do not
fit in with the general Darwinian scheme. Fair-minded evolutionists—
and most evolutionists are fair-minded—have come to recognize
this. Ehrlich and Holm ask,

Is our current explanation of evolutionary process without a
flaw? Hardly; even the most sanguine evolutionist would admit
there is much to learn. The fine theoretical structure of population genetics has not been thoroughly tested in natural populations—although the broad outlines of the spreading processes
seem to be understood adequately, no general mathematical
treatment has been possible, and many of the details are ob-
scure.[21]

Mayr says,

Yet in spite of all these advances numerous unsolved problems
remain. Let me single out only four aspects of natural selection
which raise doubt in my troubled mind. 1) The selection of
genes vs. the selection of genotypes. Selection places a consid-

erable strain upon populations. Too rapid a rate of simultaneous selection against too many genes might eliminate the entire population. 2) The measure of fitness. It is crucial to find an objective yardstick. "Is it not a basic error of methodology to apply such a generalized technique as mathematics to a field of unique events such as organic evolution?" 3) The population as a unit of selection. 4) Reproduction success. Natural selection may be defensless against certain genes.[22]

Mayr quotes Lerner as saying, "What we have learned so far about natural selection is obviously only the beginning. What remains to be learned is immeasurably more."

Ehrlich and Holm say,

> The most obvious aspect of evolutionary theory that may be at least partially explained as a reaction to the Bishop Wilberforce approach has been the development of a rather stringent orthodoxy. This orthodoxy is easily detected in the compulsion of biologists to affirm *belief* in evolution (rather than to accept it as a highly satisfactory theory) and to list *proofs* that evolution has occurred. It is, of course, a matter of debate as to where healthy conservatism leaves off and dogma begins. Suffice it to say that the discipline is at least close enough to the danger area to call for some critical reexamination of its basic tenets.[23]

Elsewhere Ehrlich and Holm say,

> The strong urge to believe in present evolutionary theory, which is so evident among workers in the field, seems to stem partly from a very common human error, the idea that one of a number of current explanations *must* be correct. One usually finds the theory of evolution being contrasted with that of special creation, a one-sided contest to say the least. The demonstration that the idea of special creation is scientifically meaningless does not however "prove" that the theory of evolution is correct. Current faith in the theory is reminiscent of many other ideas which at one time were thought to be self-evidently true and supported by all available data—the flat earth, the geocentric universe, the sum of the angles of a triangle equalling 180 degrees. It is conceivable, even likely, that what might facetiously be called a non-Euclidean theory of evolution will be developed. Perpetuation of today's theory as dogma will not encourage progress toward more satisfactory explanations of observed phenomena.[24]

Sylvio Fiala writes,

> With all due recognition to the greatness of Darwin's achievement, we cannot remain blind to the fact that not a single step

in the evolutionary mechanism has been clarified. Evolution means primarily an increase in the content of information in the case of DNA, but natural selection means only the elimination of error in information or mutation (in the most favorable case, only a modification of the information), not an increase in the quantity of information. Correcting a misspelled word or substituting one word for another is, after all, something quite different from writing down a sentence, an article, a whole book.[25]

It would seem to me premature to reject the clear account of Genesis in favor of this theory. The evidence is not so overwhelming that reason insists on this approach.

NOTES AND REFERENCES

1. Fred J. Gruenberger, "A Measure for Crackpots," *Science*, vol. 145, p. 1414.
2. William S. Beck, *Modern Science and the Nature of Life* (New York: Harcourt, Brace, 1957), p. 170.
3. Quoted in *Newsweek*, December 23, 1963, p. 48.
4. Norwood Russell Hanson, "Galileo's Discoveries in Dynamics," *Science*, vol. 14, p. 472f.
5. Edwin G. Boring, "Cognitive Dissonance: Its Use in Science," *Science*, vol. 145, pp. 680-685.
6. Aldous Huxley, *Ends and Means* (London: Chatta, 1938), p. 258.
7. James B. Conant, *Modern Science and Modern Man* (New York: Columbia, 1952), p. 67.
8. Th. Dobzhansky, "Evolution of Genes and Genes in Evolution," *Cold Spring Harbor Symposia on Quantative Biology*, vol. 24, p. 22.
9. Sanger *et al.* Quoted by George Gaylord Simpson, "Organisms and Molecules in Evolution," *Science*, vol. 146, p. 1537.
10. John Buettner-Janusch and Robert L. Hill, "Molecules and Monkeys, *Science*, vol. 147, p. 8410.
11. H. S. Mosher, F. A. Fuhrman, H. D. Buckwald, and H. G. Fischer, "Tarichatoxin—Tetrodotoxin: A Potent Neurotoxin," *Science*, vol. 144, p. 1100.
12. Thomas Cameron (ed.), *Evolution, Its Science and Doctrine* (Toronto: University of Toronto Press, 1960), p. 121.
13. Paul Ralph Ehrlich and Richard W. Holm, *The Process of Evolution* (New York: McGraw-Hill, 1963), p. 190.
14. Hampton L. Carson, "Genetic Conditions Which Promote or Retard Species," *Cold Spring Harbor Symposia on Quantitative Biology,* vol. 24, p. 95.
15. Th. Dobzhansky, *Mankind Evolving* (New Haven: Yale University Press, 1962), p. 171.
16. G. Heberer, "The Descent of Man and the Present Fossil Record," *Cold Spring Harbor Symposia on Quantitative Biology,* vol. 24, p. 235.
17. Edward L. Bennett, Marian C. Diamond, David Krech, and Mark R.

Rosenzweig, "Chemical and Anatomical Plasticity of Brain," *Science*, vol. 146, p. 610.
18. Bozo Skerlj, "Discussion," *Cold Spring Harbor Symposia on Quanitative Biology*, vol. 24, p. 215.
19. Dobzhansky, *Mankind Evolving*, p. 171.
20. Elwyn L. Simons, "Some Fallacies in the Study of Hominoid Phylogeny," *Science*, vol. 141, p. 880.
21. Ehrlich and Holm, *op. cit.*, p. 310.
22. *Ibid.*, p. 5ff.
23. Ernst Mayer, "Where Are We?" *Cold Spring Harbor Symposia on Quantitative Biology*, vol. 24, p. 1.
24. Ehrlich and Holm, *op. cit.*, p. 310.
25. Sylvio Fiala, "Letter," *Science*, vol. 135, p. 975.

2

THE GENESIS ACCOUNT OF CREATION

ARTHUR F. WILLIAMS, D.D.*

There are certain areas of biblical interpretation in which Christians find themselves in serious disagreement. One of these is the Genesis account of creation. Some interpret the record *literally,* believing each of the six days to have been cycles of 24 hours, on the sixth of which God created man in His own image by divine fiat from the dust of the earth. They believe that God breathed into man's nostrils the breath of life and he became a living soul. They, likewise, believe that this occurred at a time not longer than a few thousand years ago. Others interpret the entire record of creation "parabolically," and insist that the six days represent a vast period of time, extending into millions or billions of years. The evidence for these opposing views will be examined together with the theological implications involved.

Does It Make Any Difference?

Some regard the issue as peripheral and of such trivial importance as to be unworthy of debate. Others regard the day-age theory as merely an attempt to accommodate the Word of God to the prevailing scientific philosophy. They believe that it opens the door to further compromises with the world in its antagonism to the credibility of Scripture. This article presents evidence in support of the literal interpretation of the Genesis account of creation, which requires us to believe each of the six days was comparable to our own. The day-age theory, though espoused by some men who are sincere Christians, is fraught with dangerous consequences to the Christian faith. This question is not merely academic, as some assert, but it directly affects biblical theology.

For instance, if there is textual justification for interpreting each of the six days of Genesis parabolically or figuratively, what defense can be offered for not doing the same with the language descriptive

*Cedarville College, Cedarville, Ohio

of God's creation of man in Genesis 2:7? Are we to understand that there was a literal garden in which God planted "the tree of life" and the "tree of the knowledge of good and evil," or is this to be understood figuratively? And what about the record of God's creation of woman? Did God literally cause a deep sleep to fall upon Adam, and did He literally take one of his ribs from which He made woman, or is this, too, to be regarded as figurative? Are we to understand that a literal serpent was the diabolical instrument in the temptation of Eve, or should this also be interpreted parabolically? And further, what are we to understand from the language concerning the curse which God is said to have pronounced upon the serpent? Was this literal, and did it affect the posture of the serpent, or are we to take this figuratively, too? Such questions demand an answer. Where does the figurative or parabolic end and sober history begin? Or are we at liberty to treat the entire record as "mythological" as neo-orthodoxy does? In the light of the confusion which presently prevails in Christendom concerning origins, it is not surprising that some young people who were students at a certain Christian college asked their pastor, "Don't you think we could just forget the first eleven chapters of Genesis and still be Christians?" The issue is not so peripheral as some would lead us to believe. The first chapters of Genesis must be regarded as the seed plot of the entire Bible, and if we err here, there is reason to believe that those who come under false interpretations of the Genesis account of creation will sooner or later become involved in error in other areas of divine revelation. It is our conviction that once the interpretation of the six days of creation which makes them extended periods of perhaps millions of years in duration is accepted, the door is opened for the entire evolutionary philosophy. In saying this, we do not mean to imply that all who hold to the day-age theory are evolutionists. We do insist, however, that such a view can be maintained only by an acceptance of the mental construct known as the geologic column, which is based upon the assumption of evolution.

Why Such Divergent Conclusions?

How is it that men who claim to believe the Bible to be the very Word of God can arrive at such contradictory conclusions? Why is it that some believe in a relatively recent creation fully accomplished in six solar days, while others believe the earth with life upon it is billions of years old, and that each of the six days was of undetermined duration? The answer is to be found in the method of Bible interpretation employed. There is no more important discipline for the Bible exegete than a painstaking study of sound principles of biblical hermeneutics.

By What Method Is Scripture to Be Interpreted?

One of the first and most important steps in any exegesis of Scripture is to determine the purpose of the writer and the literary nature of the book. Some books of the Bible are historical; some are poetic; others are prophetic in character. Figures of speech abound in poetic literature, but they are recognized as such and the reader is mentally prepared to adjust his thinking to the real concept so beautifully expressed in figurative terms. Our Lord made much use of the parable as a means of conveying truth more understandingly to the minds of those whose hearts were open to receive divine instruction. When He did use this method of communication, however, He always made it clear that it was parabolic and not to be understood literally.

The exegete must decide if the text of Genesis is poetic, prophetic, or historical. It is my contention as a professional student of hermeneutics that the five books of Moses must be classified as historical. The first three chapters of Genesis are just as truly historical as the remainder of the book. Therefore, we are not prepared to find parables in such a record of sober history.

One of the recognized dangers of Bible interpretation is that of "eisegesis," or reading into the texts of Scripture meanings which they did not originally possess. There are certain important rules of hermeneutics which must be faithfully observed if one is to be preserved from error. Consideration must be given to the cultural context in which the Word of God was communicated. We endeavor to discover what the words which the Holy Spirit prompted the writer to employ meant, both to the writer and also to the people to whom this revelation was to be given. With this rule in mind let us consider the record of creation as given through Moses to the nation Israel.

What did the word *yom* (day) mean to Moses and to Israel in the day in which the books of Moses were written? I am sure that all will agree that neither Moses nor the people of his day had any knowledge of the science of geology or of the theories which had been advanced to account for geological phenomena. Therefore, we are not justified in attributing to Moses a meaning of the word "day" which later use may have given to the word in an entirely different context.

The word "day" in our English Bibles occurs a total of 396 times in the five books of Moses. They are distributed as follows: 72 times in Genesis; 76 in Exodus; 64 in Leviticus; 81 in Numbers, and 103 in Deuteronomy. In every instance, with the exception of Genesis 32:24, the word "day" is a translation of the Hebrew word *yom*. Since this is true, it becomes necessary to find out what the word *yom* meant to Moses and to the people of Israel, to whom this revelation was given. Let us not be guilty of reading into the word a meaning which later use may have given to it in an entirely different context.

In the Genesis account of creation the word "day" occurs 14 times, always a translation of the Hebrew word *yom*. Those who hold to the day-age theory ask us to give the word "day" a meaning which it has nowhere else in the five books of Moses. Such a meaning (that of an indefinite period of time), we are told, has for its justification the cultural significance of the word *yom* in the thinking of Moses and that of the children of Israel. One might very properly inquire why the cultural meaning of the word *yom* should be so very different in the Genesis account of creation from that which it obviously had in all the other writings of Moses.

As if the consistent significance of the word *yom* throughout the writings of Moses were not enough to establish the meaning of the English word "day," God added statements which are difficult to interpret otherwise. ". . . God divided the *light* from the *darkness*. And God called the light *Day*, and the darkness he called *Night*. And the *evening* and the *morning* were the first day." In the light of cultural considerations of hermeneutics, can anyone honestly believe that these terms as used in the Genesis account of creation had a meaning almost infinitely removed from the meaning which they had elsewhere in the writings of Moses? The word "day" would have had no meaning to Moses or to his contemporaries other than that which was limited by reference to the sun. It would be impossible to prove from Scripture that the Israelites in the days of Moses had any concept of a "day" in terms of millions or billions of years. The evidence arising from serious consideration of the cultural meaning of the word *yom* as used by Moses and understood by the Israelites is wholly on the side of a 24-hour day in the Genesis account of creation. Such a view is consistent with its meaning as used by Moses throughout his writings.

In the twentieth chapter of Exodus we read, beginning at verse 8, "Remember the sabbath day to keep it holy. Six days shalt thou labour, and do all thy work: But the seventh day is the sabbath of the Lord thy God: in it thou shalt not do any work. . . . For in six days the Lord made heaven and earth, the sea, and all that in them is, and rested the seventh day: wherefore the Lord blessed the sabbath day, and hallowed it." An examination of this passage and also another similar passage in Exodus 31:17 must be considered in any interpretation of the Genesis account of creation. Did Moses enjoin upon Israel the observance of the seventh day, attaching to it the concept of from sunset to sunset, while at the same time wishing to convey the idea that the six days in which God created were periods of one million years or more? Did Moses mean that the six days are to correspond with the geological column of the evolutionary paleontologist? Such an interpretation would require a rendering such as the following: "Six days shalt thou labour and do thy work: But the seventh day is the sabbath of the Lord thy God. . . . For in six million years the Lord made heaven and earth, the sea, and all that in them is. . . ."

The Meaning of the Word "Day"

The root meaning of the Hebrew word *yom*, translated "day" throughout the writings of Moses, according to Strong, is " 'to be hot,' a day (as the warm hours) whether literally from sunrise to sunset, or from one sunset to the next." That the word is also used figuratively is readily acknowledged, but when so used, Strong says, "It is defined by an associated term." An illustration of this would be "the day of the Lord." Those who insist that the six days of Genesis One should be interpreted parabolically claim "proof" for this method of interpretation on the basis of its use in Genesis 2:4, which reads, "These are the generations of the heavens and of the earth when they were created, in *the day* that the Lord God made the earth and the heavens. . . ." Since the word "day" is used in Genesis 2:4 with obvious reference to all time involved in creation we are told, "Thus *incontestably* the usage of 'day' in Genesis 2:4 is parabolic."

Now every student of Scripture recognizes the fact that the word "day" is used to designate a period of time of varying lengths.

When Zephaniah speaks of "the day of the Lord" (1:7) we have no reason to think of his use of the word "day" as a period limited to 24 hours. Nor when Peter speaks of the same period are we justified in concluding that "the day of the Lord" is to be limited to 24 hours. But we are not justified in assuming that because Peter tells us "one day is with the Lord as a thousand years, and a thousand years as one day" that the word "day" has no time signification. The duration of time indicated by the use of the word "day" must be determined by the context in which it is found.

Now those who hold to the day-age theory of creation insist that the use of the word "day" in Genesis 2:4 proves that the use of the same word in Genesis One must refer to a period of undetermined length. That such "proof" is open to question we shall endeavor to demonstrate. Not all Hebrew scholars agree with this conclusion. Regarding the day-age interpretation, Dr. Bernard Ramm says, "The problem of the meaning of *yom* is not fully decided as to whether it can mean period or not. The word is one which has many uses as we have already indicated. We are not presently persuaded that it can be stretched so as to mean *period* or *epoch* or *age* as such terms are used in geology. Though not closing the door on the age-day interpretation of the word *yom*, we do not feel that lexicography of the Hebrew language will as yet permit it."

Leupold, a recognized Hebrew scholar, says:

> In the interest of accuracy it should be noted that within the confines of this one verse, Genesis 1:5, the word "day" is used in two different senses. "Day" (yom) over against "night" (layelah) must refer to the light part of the day, roughly, a twelve hour period. When the verse concludes with the statement that the first "day" (yom) is concluded, the term must mean a twenty-four hour period . . . to make this statement refer to two parts of a long geologic period; the first part of a kind of evening; the second a kind of morning; both together a kind of long period, runs afoul of three things: first, that "evening" nowhere in the Scripture bears this meaning; secondly, neither does "morning"; thirdly, "day" never means "period."

There ought to be no need of refuting the idea that *yom* means period. Reputable dictionaries like Buhl, B D B or K W know nothing of this notion. Hebrew dictionaries are our primary source of reliable information concerning Hebrew words. Commentaries with critical leanings utter statements that are very decided in this instance. Says Skinner: "The interpretation of *yom* as aeon, a favorite resource of harmonists of science and revelation, is opposed to the plain sense of the passage and has no warrant in Hebrew usage." Dillman remarks: "The reasons advanced by ancient and modern writers for construing these days to be longer periods of time are inadequate." If it is claimed that some works can with difficulty be compressed within twenty-four hours, like those of the third day or the sixth, that claim may well be described as a purely subjective opinion. He that desires to reason it out as possible can assemble fully as many arguments as he who holds the opposite opinion. Or if it be claimed that "the duration of the seventh day determines the rest" let it be noted that nothing is stated about the duration of the seventh. This happens to be an argument from silence, and therefore it is exceptionally weak. Or again, if it be claimed that "the argument of the fourth (our third) commandment confirms this probability" we find in this commandment even stronger confirmation of our contention. Six twenty-four hour days followed by one such day of rest alone can furnish a proper analogy for our laboring six days and resting on the seventh day; *periods* furnish a poor analogy for *days*. Finally, it is contended that our conception contradicts one school of thought in the field of geology. But this is a school of thought which we are convinced is hopelessly entangled in misconceptions which grow out of attempts to co-ordinate the actual findings of geology with an evolutionistic conception of what geology should be, and so is for the present thrown into a complete misreading of the available evidence, even as history, anthropology, Old Testament studies and many other sciences have been derailed and mired by the same attempt."

It is interesting to note that even Dr. Edward John Carnell admits that the "Genesis account implies an act of immediate creation, but the same account implies that God made the world in *six literal days*." But having made this admission he then proceeds to state what he cannot prove: "And since orthodoxy has given up the literal-day theory out of respect for geology, it would certainly forfeit no principle if it gave up the immediate-creation theory out of respect for paleontology. The two seem to be quite parallel." This statement in its entirety is most significant. First, it tells us that Dr. Carnell and others like him who still want to be regarded as orthodox *have given up the literal-day theory out of respect for geology*, not out of respect for the text of God's Word. Secondly, it tells us what logically follows from an abandonment of sound biblical exegesis, namely, the *giving up of the immediate-creation theory out of respect for paleontology.* Nor have we any reason to conclude that this is the end of "giving up" out of respect for the intellectual world of our day. Consistency makes certain demands of us, either for the truth or against it. What Dr. Carnell has failed to prove is that "orthodoxy has given up the literal-day theory." He does not, and cannot, speak for "orthodoxy." He is a representative of that school of thought which Dr. Harold John Ockenga of Park Street Congregational Church in Boston designates as "neo-evangelicalism." These men have surrendered the plain teachings of God's Word "out of respect for geology and paleontology." One cannot help wondering what the final outcome of such a surrender may be. There is not a miracle in the entire Bible which can be substantiated by the empirical methods of modern science. Will such men, or their children, find it necessary to surrender the doctrine of the virgin birth and the bodily resurrection of Christ out of respect for biology and physics? That evangelical scholars are increasingly surrendering to the theory of evolution should become evident from a quotation in an article in the *Journal of the American Scientific Affiliation* entitled, "The Evolution of Evangelical Thinking on Evolution," by J. Frank Cassel, a recent president of the ASA (Dec. 1959, p. 27):

> Thus, in 15 years we have seen develop in the A.S.A. a spectrum of belief in evolution that would have shocked all of us at the inception of this organization. Many still reserve judgment, but few, I believe, are able to meet Dr. Mixter's challenge of, "Show me a better explanation."

When once an attempt is made to harmonize the Word of God with "the consensus of modern scholarship" it is difficult to terminate the compromise of Scripture which such accommodation requires.

It is our conviction that we have a parallel use of the word "day" in the seventh chapter of Numbers to that in Genesis one and two. In Numbers 7:1, 2, we read, "And it came to pass on the day that Moses had fully set up the tabernacle, and had anointed it, and sanctified it. . . . That the princes of Israel . . . offered." In verse 10 we read, "And the princes offered for dedication of the altar in *the day* that it was anointed, even the princes offered their offering before the altar." In the verses which follow we read what Nahshon offered on "the first day" (v. 12); what Nethaneel offered "on the second day" (v. 18); and what Eliab offered "on the third day" (v. 24). Each of the twelve princes offered, one on each of twelve days. Then in verse 84 we read, "This was the dedication of the altar, *in the day* when it was anointed, by the princes of Israel." There appears to be no more justification for the idea that the word in Genesis 2:4 is used parobolically than in Numbers 7:84. In both instances we have first a record of details which occurred in "days" of 24 hours' duration, and then we have the same word used *comprehensively* of what has been previously set forth in detail. Such a use of the word "day" is not peculiar to the Hebrews; we use the word similarly today without confusion. A biographer of Lincoln may state the day of his birth and the day of his marriage, the day of his inauguration and the day of his death, etc., and then when summing up the details of his life may say, "Now in Lincoln's *day* there were no automobiles, radios, or television." No one would think such a biographer was using the word "parabolically." Rather, he would be using it comprehensively. And this is exactly what we find in Genesis 2:4. After the writer has informed us as to what transpired on each of six days, he sums up God's creative acts by saying, "These are the generations of the heavens and of the earth when they were created, *in the day* that the Lord God made the earth and the heavens."

To insist that the word "day" is used parabolically in Genesis One and Two is implicit with danger in the exegesis of Scripture. Parabolic interpretation is not justified by the language and it opens the door for parabolic interpretation of other details in the early chapters of Genesis. This would rob Genesis of all historical significance and leave the reader uncertain as to where the parabolic ends and sober history begins. When we read such expressions as "light" and "darkness, "night'" and "day," "evening" and "morning" in connection with the six days of Genesis One, we would very naturally conclude that such days were similar to our own. We have failed to find a single example of the use of the word "day" in the entire Scriptures where it means other than a period of 24 hours when modified by the use of a numerical adjective. Doctors Morris and Whitcomb state,

> Therefore, we must approach a study of the work of the six days of creation strictly from the perspective of scriptural revelation, and not at all from that of a projection of present natural processes into the past. It is precisely this sort of illegitimate projection which has led to the theory of evolution and to the various theological devices that have been conceived for harmonizing it with the Biblical revelation. Since God's revealed Word describes this creation as taking place in six "days" and since there apparently is no contextual basis for understanding these days in

any symbolic sense, it is an act of both faith and reason to accept them, literally, as real days.

The Appeal to Science

Those who argue for the day-age theory of creation appeal to the science of geology for confirmation. We are told that sedimentary rocks have been laid down in certain areas to depths of seven miles or more. Of necessity, this would require millions of years for their formation. I do not profess to be an authority on geology, but I do favor a literal interpretation of the biblical record over that of current scientific opinion to the contrary. Is there any place on God's footstool where sedimentary rocks can be found for a depth of seven miles? Is it not true that this claim is based upon a method of *correlation which assumes evolution as the starting point?* We are told that "in 1815 William Smith observed that each layer had a characteristic *assemblage of fossils, and by comparing the fossils in various strata* in England he could establish the relative sequence of these strata. The subsequent refinement of this technique has become one of the most powerful tools for dating which the modern geologist has." There is no doubt but that this last statement is true. Now if this method of dating the rocks is "one of the most powerful tools for dating which the modern geologist has," it will not be necessary to examine his weaker ones. It is strange that anyone who repudiates the theory of evolution should place any confidence in such a method of dating. It is based in its entirety upon the assumption of evolution. Modern geology is based upon the assumption that sedimentary rocks in which the prevailing fossils are primitive must have been deposited earlier than rocks with fossil remains of higher forms of life. Rocks are examined in various parts of the world and classified as to their age, not on the basis of their relation to layers above and beneath, but on the basis of their predominant fossil enclosures. "The refinement" of a method which is basically false does not enhance its validity!

No one should form conclusions as to the age of the earth or life by quoting from the pen of fallible men. It is interesting to note, however, that not all "scholarship" is on the side of the day-age theory or "progressive creation."

Dr. Walter E. Lammerts, for example, received his Ph.D. from the University of California, taught at UCLA, and is now Director of Research at the Germain Seed Company, Livermore, California. Along with more than 300 other scientists, many listed in American

Men of Science, he is a member of the Creation Research Society. Some months ago the editor of *The Progress Summary* became interested in the evasion of some neo-evangelical scholars as to the age of man. He stated that the maximum age of man, biblically, is not more than 10,000 years and asked Dr. Lammerts for his opinion from the standpoint of his scientific research. His answer, as quoted below, is the most responsible and fascinating statement we have ever read on this subject for it goes far beyond the mere question of the age of man.

> Regarding the question you asked in your second paragraph, I am in complete accord with Dr. Henry Morris, particularly as regards not only the age of man, but the earth, our stellar system and in fact, the universe. As a matter of fact, were it not for my belief in the truth and literal interpretation of the Genesis account, I would have great difficulty in believing that the earth was even 6,000 years old! However, there seems to be no doubt but that people would live for vastly longer periods of time, i.e., almost a thousand years in the days before the Flood. Accordingly, I am willing to grant this extreme age for the earth and universe. Actually from the strictly scientific point of view, most of the surface features of the earth give the appearance of being far younger. The reason for this, I presume, is that as the number of years from the time of the Flood increase, the amount of erosion and other geological actions decrease. Accordingly, most of our rivers, mountains, and other features of the earth give the impression of being quite young, geologically speaking.

The prevailing uniformitarian concept in scientific circles is that the processes now operative in the world are the same as have been active from time immemorial. I believe this to be purely an assumption. There is abundant evidence of great cataclysms in past ages which cannot possibly be accounted for in the theory of uniformity. It is incredible on the theory of uniformity that fossil forms of tropical plant and animal life could have been formed in such a state of preservation and on such a scale as those which have been found in northern Siberia. What convulsions of nature account for such phenomena we may not yet fully know, but that such have occurred cannot be honestly denied. The theory that the earth must be billions of years old is based in part upon the method of determining the age of rocks by the evidence supplied in the decay of Uranium 238 to form lead. Since this rate of decay is measurably slow, it is assumed that the formation of lead has required billions of years. But is it not pure assumption to insist that this is the only way lead has come into existence? Is it not possible, and even probable, that God created quantities of lead at the same time He created Uranium 238? It as also been argued that since some distant stars are millions of light years removed from the earth, it has required an almost incredible period of time for their light to become visible. But this, too, is an assumption. God who created the stars could cause their light to become visible on earth at the instant of their creation. It is my conviction that the creative acts of God were instantaneous, and created organisms were mature. God did not create Adam as an infant, but as a mature man. I am not willing, on the basis of the currently accepted geological column or on the basis of radioactive dating, to accept the conclusions that the earth is billions of years old and that life upon it has existed for a vast period of time.

Do the Rocks Prove "Progressive Evolution"?

The fact remains that sedimentary rocks do not exhibit such an orderly sequence as the evolutionary geologist would have us believe. There are vast areas of the earth's crust in which the fossil record is embarrassing to the evolutionist. Rocks with relatively primitive fossil forms are found on top of rocks with fossil remains of higher forms of life. In the face of such evidence the evolutionist resorts to a marvelous explanation. He tells us that the rocks on top (with fossil forms of primitive life) are really older than those beneath them, and their present location is due to immense lateral thrusts! Great areas of rock of earlier deposition allegedly were upraised and then moved laterally over more recent sedimentary deposits. Such areas have been examined which cover thousands of square miles! Now the credulous are asked to believe the above explanation since the rocks *must exhibit* evolutionary development from the simple to the more complex. The entire theory upon which evolutionary geology is built rests upon the assumption that the age of the rocks must be determined on the basis of the state of life development as exhibited by their fossil remains. Thus the geologic column which originated with William Smith and was refined by evolutionary scholars has become "one of the most powerful tools for dating which the modern geologist has."

Evolution Theorists and the Genesis Flood

All evolutionists insist that the earth and the universe came into being millions, if not billions, of years ago. The geological column is predicated upon the theory of uniformitarianism. It makes no provisions for cataclysms, which might produce in a relatively short period of time what the evolutionary geologist can account for only on the basis of millions of years. Evolutionary geologists repudiate the literal interpretation of the Genesis account of creation and rather than accepting the plain statements of Scripture, some writers attempt to disprove the universality of the flood by appealing to evolutionary geology. Everyone who believes that the Bible is the very Word of God must decide for himself whether he will interpret the phenomena of nature by the simple statements of Scripture, or interpret Holy Scripture by the theories of modern scientists.

Unacceptable Alternatives

Now if one is to accept this method of dating, there are only two possible conclusions which can be drawn. One must accept the evolutionary concept of creation, either naturalistic or theistic, or what some scholars call "progressive creation." Unlike evolution, progressive creation credits God with creating by divine fiat something new on each of the six "days"—some new forms of life unrelated biographically to preceding forms of life. Now if "progressive creation" is to be accepted it would seem that more than six days would be required. The evolutionary geological column is divided into major eras designated by such terms as archeozoic, proterozoic, mesozoic, and cenozoic, each of which is subdivided into vast periods of time. If we were to accept the day-age theory of creation it could seem that the Genesis record has ceased to have any historic significance. Genesis covers not more than a few hours of the billions of years which the theory seeks to establish.

The Question of Authority

An interpretation is not necessarily substantiated just because it is approved by a long list of eminent scholars. With all due respect to such scholarship it is still our very basic statement of faith that the Bible is our *sole* authority in all matters of faith and practice. The careful student will not allow himself to be persuaded by a long list of illustrious names. The Bible repeatedly refers to the record of creation, and invariably speaks of it as the work of God accomplished in "six days." Agnostic scientists work on the *a priori* assumption that all phenomena of nature are to be explained in terms of present day observable physico-chemical laws. Either consciously or subconsciously, they are prejudiced in favor of this viewpoint.

In contrast, we work on the *a priori* assumption that all the phenomena of nature are to be explained in terms of God's creative power and design. The so-called "laws" of nature are God at work providentially maintaining His original creation.

Implications of the Genesis Flood

The language of Scripture represents the flood of Noah as both anthropologically and geologically universal. Yet, even within the ranks of professing Christians are many who appear to be more disposed to accept the conclusion of evolutionary scientists than they are to believe the plain statement of God's Word. I believe that many of the geological phenomena observable in the world today have had their origin in the Genesis flood. Some argue, however, that the flood was only local or at best only "anthropologically" universal. It is my contention that if the Genesis flood was only local, several deductions are logically inevitable. First, we must conclude that the language of Scripture is susceptible to meanings which are not obvious to average intelligence. Secondly, God's bow in the cloud has ceased to have the significance which He attached to it when He said, "I do set my bow in the cloud, and it shall be for a token of a covenant between me and the earth." By this covenant God promised never again to destroy the earth with a flood. It cannot be denied that local floods have devastated vast areas of the earth from the days of Noah until today, but there has been no universal flood since Noah's day. Thirdly, the warning which God has given to the world through the Apostle Peter has ceased to have any significant meaning if the flood was local in character. Peter refers to it as of such universal destructiveness as to foreshadow the universal judgment of God upon an unrepentant world in the day of the Lord's wrath.

The Intellectual Trend of Our Day

It is not within our province to judge the motives of men, but it appears to us that in our day there are those who *disdain to be called "fundamentalists"* and who brand *all who are willing to be identified by such a designation as naive, unscientific,* and *reactionary.* There are some who insist that one's views with reference to the "days" of creation should not be made a test of *spirituality,* but they do not seem to object to its being made a test of *mentality*. Regardless of how he may be evaluated by the so-called "intellectual world" of our day, one must rest upon the statement of Holy Scriptures, interpreting them *literally*, unless the context requires otherwise. So-called "conclusions of scholarship" should not be regarded as infallible. The statements of God's Holy Word should be accepted with a reverence not granted to the writings of any man, however learned he may be. In the future, the discrepancies between "science" and the Bible will be completely resolved. Those who have placed implicit confidence in the theories of scientists will regret that they have tried to make the Bible "acceptable" to unregenerate intellectuals.

Chapter 2
Theories of the Origin of the Universe

EXAMINING THE COSMOGONIES —
A HISTORICAL REVIEW

GEORGE MULFINGER*

Making plausible guesses as to the origin of the universe is evidently a challenging pastime. Given a generous supply of matter in a simple "undifferentiated" form, the known laws of nature, and almost infinite time, the object of the game is to derive the present state of the physical world. One of the rules, unfortunately, is that no intervention on the part of a divine Creator can be tolerated. In refusing to retain God in their thinking, cosmogonists have "taken away the key of knowledge" and condemned their efforts to failure.

No system of evolutionary cosmology, once it has been given an adequate length of time to demonstrate its worth, has survived. In the final analysis, the only statements on the subject of origins that will weather the test of time are those set down by "holy men of God . . . as they were moved by the Holy Ghost" (II Peter 1:21).

The history of astronomy furnishes a convincing demonstration of the fickleness and transitoriness of man's best thinking in this realm. The various theories discussed in this paper are presented in two chronological sequences—one for the solar system and one for the universe in general. While this is by no means a complete listing, it does include what appear to be the major highlights in the historical panorama from Copernicus to the present time.

THE SOLAR SYSTEM
The Cartesian Hypothesis (1644)

In 1644 René Descartes, in his *Principles of Philosophy*, set forth a rather bizarre conception of the development of the physical world.

*Faculty member at Bob Jones University, Greenville, S. C.; pursuing Ph.D. program at Syracuse University.

He regarded the universe as a vast system of vortices originally set in motion by God, and then left to run spontaneously.[1]

As they age, the structures within each vortex gradually merge from one type to another. Stars decay to form comets. Comets in turn degenerate into planets, while terrestrial matter arises from the decay of planets.

Although this might on the surface sound like the second law of thermodynamics in action, it most decidedly was not. To Descartes there were no irreversible processes or entropic degradations in the system, for the "quantity of motion" remained constant.[2]

Newton was anything but favorably impressed with this type of thinking. In a letter to Richard Bentley he stated that "the Cartesian hypothesis . . . can have no place in my system and is plainly erroneous." As evidence to refute it he cited the fact that comets always leave the sun with a speed equal to that of their approach. There is never any indication that a cometary orbit is in the process of degenerating into a planetary orbit.

Were the planets derived from former comets, he noted, they would have highly disorganized eccentric orbits and would not have the coplanar arrangement of the planets as we know them. It is gratifying to see Newton, perhaps the greatest genius in the history of science, holding high the banner of the creationist position:

> It is plain that there is no natural cause which could determine all the planets, both primary and secondary, to move the same way and in the same plane . . . ; this must have been the effect of counsel. Nor is there any natural cause which could give the planets those just degrees of velocity, in proportion to their distances from the sun and other central bodies, which were requisite to make them move in such concentric orbs about those bodies.

He also found it remarkable that the solar system contains but one luminous body and that all the others are "opaque": "I know of no reason but because the Author of the system thought it convenient." [3]

Swedenborg's Nebular Hypothesis (1734)

Emanuel Swedenborg, the brilliant founder of the cult known as the "Church of the New Jerusalem," outlined a scheme to account for the origin of the solar system in his *Principia*, published in 1734. This effort preceded Kant's hypothesis by several years and undoubtedly influenced it.[4]

Swedenborg conjectured that what is now the solar system was once a rapidly rotating nebula. As it cooled and contracted, its speed of rotation progressively increased. There was eventually enough force available to expel a large ring of material. Nuclei of condensation formed within the ring that subsequently developed into planets, while the dense central mass became the sun.

Swedenborg did not take credit for originating this idea; he claimed to have received it in spiritualistic communications from inhabitants of the moon and distant planets.[5] Objections to this and other early nebular hypotheses will be taken up under the discussion of Laplace.

Kant's Nebular Hypothesis (1755)

In 1755 the German philosopher Immanuel Kant attempted to develop the idea that the solar system evolved from a tenuous gas spread uniformly throughout a vast region of space. As it contracted by gravitational forces the cloud began to rotate.

This process continued, with the rate of rotation increasing as more and more material gravitated toward the center of the system. After a time the cloud became almost disc-shaped as a result of "centrifugal force."

While this was happening the heavier elements were attracting the lighter elements from the regions around them, forming increasingly larger aggregations of material, the most sizable of which appeared in the center of the system to become the sun. Continual collisions reduced the number of outer particles and formed them into more or less separate rings. The rings eventually coalesced into planets with orbits around the sun. Q.E.D.!

It has been said that Kant, though a self-styled expert on the entire universe, never once in his lifetime strayed from the city of Königsberg, Prussia. But this in no way limited his ambitions or his confidence. With the lack of humility that is so characteristic of cosmogonists in general he boasted, "Give me matter and I will construct a world out of it." [6]

There are several objections to this hypothesis from a scientific standpoint.[7] The first problem is that gravitational forces alone would not cause the rotation he envisioned. (Swedenborg and Laplace were shrewd enough to *begin* with a rotating system.) But Kant resorted to the use of repulsive forces as well as attractive. There seems to be little or no justification for this additional assumption.

Secondly, the diffuse material in the cloud would not condense into solid particles in the manner postulated. This fact has been very troublesome even to more recent nebular hypotheses. Finally, there are problems concerning the fine structure of the solar system which will be discussed more fully in connection with Laplace's hypothesis.

Buffon's Collision Hypothesis (1779)

Georges Louis Leclerc de Buffon, the noted French naturalist, sought to account for the existence of the earth by a celestial accident. In his *Epochs of Nature*, which appeared in 1779, he theorized that a passing comet tore a quantity of material from the sun. This material cooled and formed the earth.

The idea was not well received either in scientific or in theological circles. It is said to have been too speculative for the scientists and too radical for the theologians of the day. Today our knowledge of the structure of comets, though still far from complete, makes it clear that they are not nearly massive enough to cause an event of such a magnitude.

It has been estimated that there are some 20 billion comets in the solar system having a *total* mass of only one-tenth the earth's mass.[8] And of course, even if the idea were correct, there remains the problem of the origin of the comet and the sun.

Laplace's Nebular Hypothesis (1796)

Laplace's Nebular Hypothesis of 1796 holds a rather unique place in the history of cosmogony. Its acceptance was probably more widespread and long-lived than was that of any other "scientific" hypothesis down through the years. And even in the present century, after the disenchantment of the scientific world with the Planetesimal Hypothesis (to be described below) had reached proportions that rendered it untenable, there was a general reversion to the Laplacian type of thinking.

Laplace began with a hot, slowly rotating nebula. As it cooled it contracted and increased in rotational speed. Eventually it assumed the form of a rapidly rotating disc with a thin rim of material on the edge moving too fast to be held by gravitational attraction. This material, after being ejected from the nebula, coalesced to form the outermost planet of the solar system.

Further contraction and ejection of rings formed planets at various distances from the center of the cloud, while the material remaining in the center became the sun. Satellites (moons) were accounted for by rotational eddies in the rings that repeated the overall process on a smaller scale.

This hypothesis was readily and warmly received by many who were of an anti-religious turn of mind. Not anxious to "stare a gift horse in the teeth," they failed to scrutinize it closely, and the defects that later became only too apparent were all but overlooked for almost a century.

Among objections to the hypothesis, the following seem to be the most prominent:

1. The sun is rotating much too slowly to have been formed by a system that was continually contracting and speeding up. Stated another way, the planets have far too much angular momentum in comparison to the sun.[9]

2. The gaseous rings would have dispersed into space rather than condensing into planets.

3. The earth does not appear to have an "original crust" such as the hypothesis would demand.[10]

4. A number of stubborn peculiarities about the solar system militate against any such simple sweeping hypothesis. Some of these are the retrograde motions of 11 of the 32 known satellites, the highly inclined orbits of the asteroids and comets, and the retrograde rotations of Venus and Uranus.[11]

Ironically, Laplace's hypothesis, originally based on a mathematical approach to the question of origins, was, in the final analysis, torn down by mathematical scrutiny, beginning with the penetrating analysis of a well-known Christian man of science, James Clerk-Maxwell. "He disappointeth the devices of the crafty. . . . He taketh the wise in their own craftiness" (Job 5:12a, 13a).

Darwin's Tidal Hypothesis (1890)

George Darwin, son of the better-known Charles Darwin, anxious to extend the idea of evolution into the inorganic world, concocted an intriguing story of how the earth and moon evolved from a large mass of hot plastic material some four billion years ago.

Beginning with the fact that the moon is constantly receding from the earth a few inches each year and extrapolating backward in time, he deduced that originally there was zero distance between the two bodies. This is, of course, an example of uniformitarian thinking carried to the logical conclusion that it demands.

From angular momentum considerations Darwin computed that the primeval spheroid had a period of rotation of about five hours. The rapidly rotating body was of necessity quite oblate, and subject to vibrations of enormous amplitude.

One fateful day the sun's gravitational pull raised tides of such colossal proportions that the system was disrupted, giving birth to the earth's one and only "daughter." The hypothesis still enjoys surprising popularity, and many of its adherents affirm with great earnestness that the Pacific Basin is the scar from which the moon was ripped.

This fission type of approach to the origin of the earth-moon binary system was pretty well laid to rest in 1931, when Harold Jeffreys demonstrated that even had the necessary resonance been set up, the earth would have been too viscous for partition to occur.[12]

But the question was re-examined in 1963 by Wise and others.[13] Wise chose to change some of the details in the original scheme, considering the system as a pear-shaped Poincaré figure whose long axis lay in the plane of rotation, and choosing a period about half as long as Darwin's.

Presumably the stem end of the pear would fly off if such a high rotational velocity were invoked. But after the original system has been given enough energy for fission to occur, an insurmountable problem arises. The angular momentum at the beginning would then have been some 3.7 times that of the present earth-moon binary system, and theorists are forced to account for the disappearance of the excess energy.

The energy released in slowing the earth down to a 24-hour day would be sufficient to raise the temperature of the entire earth to 2500° Centigrade and melt it, and the great bulk of this energy would be released soon after the moon was ejected.

Others have tried their hand at making the tidal hypothesis work, but with no real success. Dr. Ralph B. Baldwin, author of *A Fundamental Survey of the Moon*, summarized the situation in 1965 by stating that we are left on the multi-pointed horns of a dilemma— there is still no acceptable explanation for the earth-moon system as we know it.[14]

Planetesimal Hypothesis (1900)

At the turn of the century nothing resembling a solid tenable hypothesis for the origin of the solar system *or* the universe had yet appeared on the scene. Still, vast multitudes of people had already been deceived by the cocksure materialism of the 1800's.

Popularized anti-Christian writings such as Ernst Haeckel's *The Riddle of the Universe* assured the general public that the "all-pervasive Law of Substance" adequately explained everything. Men of the scientific world knew better, however, and were desperately seeking a new synthesis that, unlike the previous attempts, would be in line with the astronomical and geological observations.

In 1900 Chamberlain and Moulton of the University of Chicago offered their Planetesimal Hypothesis as a substitute for the nebular approach.[15] Assuming that the earth had been formed gradually by the accretion of small solid particles similar to meteorites, they set forth the idea that the solar system had formed from a vast swarm of planetesimals or tiny planets, revolving around a central mass in intersecting elliptical orbits.

The pieces were gradually swept up into planets and satellites by gravitational attraction. This neatly solved the problem inherent in all previous hypotheses of the nebular type—namely, the reluctance of the material to coalesce into solid bodies. How simple! To produce a solid, simply begin with a solid! But this is somewhat unsatisfying to the intellect.

One might well ask how this highly rigged picture of ready-made particles revolving around a ready-made sun came into being. Chamberlain and Moulton sought to answer that very question. Their first assumption in this endeavor, unfortunately, proved to be erroneous—that the spiral nebulas observed in the heavens were in fact other solar systems in the making.

Further study disclosed the existence of stars in the arms of these nebulas and revealed that their dimensions were of a far grander scope than any single solar system. But they proceeded to postulate a dynamic encounter between our own sun and another star to produce such a nebula, which in turn would hopefully yield the necessary planetesimals. The other star approached the sun closely in a hyperbolic orbit.

Although the encounter was brief, it resulted in liberating two bolts of material from the sun, on opposite sides, imparting a circular motion to the material such that it soon became a double-armed spiral. Collisions of particles in the spiral coupled with normal attractive forces allegedly produced the desired planetesimals.

Subsequent mathematical analysis indicated, however, that the angular momentum distribution of the solar system could not be accounted for by the action of only two original stars. Accordingly, there was a ludicrous alternative proposal that *three* stars had happened to be passing the same way at the same time!

Finally, in 1939, the Planetesimal Hypothesis received its inevitable death blow when Lyman Spitzer of Yale demonstrated that the bolts of material ripped from the sun could not possibly condense into solid particles. The material taken from near the sun's surface, with a temperature near 10,000° Fahrenheit, would simply keep expanding. It is retained in its normal compact form only by the immense gravitational pull of the sun.

Jeans-Jeffreys Tidal Hypothesis (1917)

This alternative close-encounter explanation of the solar system was the work of Sir James Jeans and Harold Jeffreys in 1917.[16] In their scheme, a star passing near the sun pulled loose a cigar-shaped gaseous filament—thick in the middle but tapering at the ends.

As the gaseous filament became more elongated, parts of it condensed, giving it the very picturesque appearance of a string of pearls. The more massive globules toward the center of the string ultimately formed the heavier planets such as Jupiter and Saturn, while the ends of the string became the innermost and outermost planets of the solar system.

Spitzer's refutation of the Planetesimal Hypothesis in 1939 served equally well to lay this hypothesis to rest. The advent of World War II found the slate wiped clean with regard to explanations of the solar system—every proposed evolutionary mechanism had been decisively refuted.

Von Weizsäcker's Nebular Hypothesis (1944)

The delusions of the planetesimal and tidal type of thinking had reigned for nearly half a century, with nothing more attractive forthcoming to resolve the dilemma. Finally these speculations were abandoned as hopeless and a new trend was initiated.

The year 1944 saw the beginning of a wholesale return to Kant and Laplace, as the first of a series of revised nebular hypotheses appeared on the scene. But very few of the leading cosmogonists seem to trust one another when it comes to the rendering of the specific details, so a number of separate variations and modifications have sprung up. Carl F. von Weizsäcker, who had gained considerable stature in the thirties through his studies of thermonuclear reactions in the sun, led the way with an approach that appeared to overcome some of the difficulties of the older nebular hypotheses. The initial stages of von Weizsäcker's *modus operandi* were similar to Laplace's. A large cloud of gas and dust already in slow rotation gradually contracted and flattened out. Instead of spinning off a ring as Laplace had envisioned, the first important event was the sudden contraction of the central part of the cloud, forming the sun. He was then faced with the problem of how to slow down the rotation of the sun to somewhere near the presently observed rate. Von Weizsäcker's great ingenuity came to the fore at this point as he devised a mechanism for transferring angular momentum from the sun out to the surrounding cloud.

As the sun became hotter through nuclear reactions it induced turbulences in the cloud which ultimately gave rise to a semi-permanent system of eddies. These eddies, which were turned by the sun's rotational motion, functioned as roller bearings, carrying angular momentum from the sun to the periphery of the system. In the regions between the eddies condensation took place to form small solid particles or planetesimals. The planetesimals aggregated into larger bodies called protoplanets, which eventually formed planets and satellites.

One novel feature of this hypothesis is that it purports to account for the spacing of the planets in the solar system according to the pattern known as "Bode's Law."

Another innovation was an explanation of the fact that our solar system contains such a generous measure of heavy elements as compared with the rest of the universe. Von Weizsäcker suggested that a large portion of the lighter elements had been repelled outward by the sun and permanently lost. Most of the postwar hypotheses have been of this general type—of such a nature that planetary systems are held to be an everyday phenomenon throughout the universe, and life is considered to be a common inevitable occurrence. This thought has great appeal to the modern cosmogonists.

One question that has been raised by some of von Weizsäcker's critics concerns his use of five vortices per ring, to yield results in accord with "Bode's Law." Why, they ask, wouldn't this produce *five* planets in each orbit rather than just one? Another crucial question involves the stability of the system of eddies. As Whitcomb has pointed out,[17] it is questionable whether the vortices would last even 10 or 100 years; yet the hypothesis requires millions of years of such action for the planetary accretion to be completed. There are still other difficulties which will be discussed later under Kuiper's Protoplanet Hypothesis.

One can judge something about von Weizsäcker's hypothesis by the number of modifications that have been deemed necessary by various astronomers:

(a) D. Ter Haar of Purdue University saw fit to substitute nuclei of condensation for vortices.

(b) Kuiper made such extensive modifications that he developed an almost independent hypothesis.

(c) Fred Hoyle, who had formerly endorsed a binary star hypothesis, has now largely fallen in line with recent nebular trends. But in place of Weizsäcker's "roller bearing" mechanism Hoyle advocates an idea proposed by the Swedish physicist Alfvén—a "magnetic clock spring" contrivance for transferring angular momentum from the sun to the evolving planets.[18]

(d) Other variations to the basic von Weizsäcker system have been promoted by Urey, Chandrasekhar, and Schmidt.

Whipple's Dust Cloud Hypothesis (1948)

Fred Whipple of Harvard University proposed a new hypothesis in 1948 consisting of three evolutionary stages: (1) aggregation of interstellar material into a discrete cloud, (2) formation of the sun and planets, and (3) development of the detailed structure within the system.

To compress the interstellar material into a compact enough structure for gravitational attraction to be effective, Whipple utilized a proposal of Lyman Spitzer that light pressure from surrounding stars may be capable of forcing the material together. The cloud that is thus formed, although not rotating as a whole, contains local turbulences which give rise to streams of material spiralling inward toward the center of the system.

The streams condense into protoplanets, and the center of the cloud collapses to form the protosun. The protoplanets gradually acquire more circular orbits and grow in size by accretion to become the planets as we know them.[19] Here again we are relegating a discussion of some of the problems involved to the next section, on the Protoplanet Hypothesis.

THEORIES OF THE ORIGIN OF THE UNIVERSE

A little thought will disclose that inherent in the Whipple-Spitzer hypothesis is an intriguing "chicken-versus-egg" type of dilemma:

(a) If stars and planets condense from interstellar dust that is forced together by light pressure, where does the light pressure come from? From other stars.

(b) Where did those stars come from? By condensation of material utilizing the light pressure from still other stars.

(c) But where did the first stars come from? We have succeeded only in pushing the basic problem further back in time, but we have failed completely in explaining the ultimate origin of anything.

As neatly as the Bible answers the "chicken-versus-egg" problem, it yields the *only possible* answer to this dilemma: the universe didn't evolve—it was suddenly created.

Protoplanet Hypothesis (1951)

Gerald P. Kuiper, an American astronomer, extended von Weizsäcker's work and added enough original material to it to warrant its being considered as a separate hypothesis. Kuiper advocated replacing von Weizsäcker's orderly arrangement of eddies by a random distribution, and indicated that the protoplanets would form in the centers of the eddies rather than in the regions of intersection.

A key point of this scheme is that the protoplanets were formed in darkness—the sun at this stage was still too diffuse to emit light. Eventually its contraction permitted a significant increase in temperature. Large quantities of radiant energy became available to disperse the hydrogen-helium envelopes of the protoplanets and bring their chemical composition into line with that of the present planets.

Kuiper believes that the same general mechanism by which a planetary system forms can also give rise to binary or multiple stars. In fact, planetary systems such as our own should only occur about one percent of the time, the other 99 percent presumably forming some type of star system. Assuming that our galaxy contains 100 billion stars, about one billion of them would have planetary systems.

One might legitimately ask what brought enough of the tenuous interstellar material together to bring the density of the cloud up to the point where gravitational contraction could begin. Kuiper treats the problem lightly and places his faith in a "chance eddy" that conveniently delivered all of the necessary raw materials to the proper location. But to say that such a "chance eddy" did its work 100 billion times or even one billion times in our own galaxy is to make a rather strong appeal to the long arm of coincidence!

We are dealing here with a highly rarified material, less dense even than the vacuum of a thermos bottle. If we could push enough of it together from all sides to increase the density appreciably, would it not tend to expand again when left to itself, to occupy the surrounding void? And even if the nebula could be held together forcibly, would the particles really cooperate by aggregating together?

Kuiper, of course, realizes the weaknesses of his system, and unlike many of the cosmogonists, acknowledges that there may be insuperable difficulties. He goes so far as to state, with reference to the general problem of the solar system, that it is not a foregone conclusion that the problem has a scientific solution.[20]

We come now to the formidable riddle of the "anomalous" members of the solar system that are troublesome to all the hypotheses: (1) those whose orbits are inclined to the ecliptic, such as Pluto and many of the asteroids, comets, and meteors; (2) the 11 satellites out of the 32 in the solar system that revolve the "wrong way"; (3) Uranus and Venus with their retrograde rotation, and (4) the "oversize" satellite with which the earth has been endowed.

The best the cosmogonists can do is to declare that these anomalies were not the case originally. By resorting to *catastrophism* of one form or another that worked to upset the original order, they seek to explain their way out of the dilemma *caused by their penchant for uniformity*.

For instance, to explain Pluto's highly inclined orbit, a very popular theory, proposed by Lyttleton, places it originally in an orbit around Neptune. Through some misfortune Neptune lost its "grip" on Pluto, allowing it to assume a bold sweeping orbit around the sun. Did this type of accidental occurrence produce each of the many "irregularities" in the solar system?

What strange tragedy befell Uranus and her retinue of five moons that they are tipped at such a curious angle? Whatever it was must have been a phenomenon of gigantic proportions—Uranus is nearly 30,000 miles in diameter, and is tilted 98 degrees from the plane of its orbit!

And why is our moon so large compared to the other moons in the solar system? There are some who maintain that it is a former planet. If so, by what extraordinary coup was the earth able to "wrest" it from the clutches of the sun?

If "the present is the key to the past," how can we accept such *ad hoc* speculations, when no such "accidents" have actually been observed? It requires a strong faith in the unlikely and a vivid imagination to fill in the missing details.

THE UNIVERSE

Primeval Atom Hypothesis (1927)

According to an idea set forth in 1927 by Georges Lemaitre, a Belgian Jesuit, the present universe is the result of the radioactive disintegration of a gigantic atom. This "superatom" had a radius perhaps as great as the radius of the earth's orbit, consisted only of closely packed neutrons, and had a brief existence corresponding to the neutron's half-life of thirteen minutes.

Following the blast there were three phases in the evolution of the universe: (1) rapid expansion, (2) deceleration caused by gravitation giving rise to an unstable equilibrium situation, and (3) followed by a renewed expansion which we now observe in the red shifts of distant galaxies.[21]

During the first and third stages galaxies and stars were structured by fortuitous aggregations of the ever-expanding materials.[22] Lemaitre even stated that the presently observed cosmic rays are the "fossil rays" which emanated from the original explosion and still "testify to the primeval activity of the cosmos." [23]

This hypothesis has been largely supplanted by the Gamow "Big Bang" hypothesis which is far more sophisticated from a mathematical standpoint. Both hypotheses, however, are philosophically unappealing—they embrace the doctrine of uniformitarianism back to the beginning, at which time they abandon it and resort to catastrophism.

It would seem that the cosmogonist should choose between uniformitarianism or catastrophism, but not greedily demand both. Also, it is a regrettable form of blasphemy to consider the universe—the intricate handiwork of God—to be mere debris left from the destructive action of a nuclear disintegration. One very interesting respect in which Lemaitre's hypothesis differs from all the others is that the primeval atom was created *ex nihilo*; a few minutes prior to the fireworks there had been nothing. Suddenly the "superatom" appeared. Thus, Lemaitre's effort represented a strange marriage of science and Scripture.

"Big Bang" Hypothesis (1947)

While Lemaitre's recent obituary notices held him to be the actual originator of the "Big Bang" hypothesis,[24] George Gamow has without question been its leading proponent since the 1940's. Professor Gamow has done an effective job of promoting the cause. A prolific writer, he has authored many books in the popular vein on a wide variety of subjects. His style is clear and persuasive, and he utilizes ingenious sketches and "homey" analogies that have endeared him to the hearts of science lovers the world over, earning him an awesome following. Because of Gamow, the "Big Bang" hypothesis probably enjoys a more widespread acceptance today than any other cosmogony of the universe, past or present.

Gamow has scaled up Lemaitre's "fireworks" to a far more impressive order of magnitude. While Lemaitre was content to begin with a primeval nucleus that would fit within our solar system, Gamow envisions an *already infinitely big* structure which suddenly exploded some five billion years ago, and ultimately expanded by an additional factor of 10^{44} to its present state!! (One might well ask at this stage how an explosion can be propagated over an infinite distance.)

He has named his primordial material "ylem." This remarkable substance is said to have a density of 10^{14}g/cc, or one hundred trillion times the density of water! How did such an unlikely material ever get there to begin with? As a result of the "Big Squeeze"!

The pre-ylem condition of the universe was simply a contraction phase which apparently had been in progress from eternity past. When it had contracted to its limiting density of 10^{14}g/cc, a violent elastic rebound occurred. During this brief catastrophic episode the atoms as we know them were synthesized from neutrons in the intense heat of the blast in less than an hour.[25]

Since then, "various differentiation processes"[26] have produced stars in a few hundred million years, and man in a period of some five billion years.[27] He appears to believe that the expansion will continue indefinitely.[28]

Hannes Alfvén, professor of plasma physics at the Royal Institute of Technology, Stockholm, also one of the world's leading cosmologists, is vigorously opposed to the idea that the universe could ever have attained such a fantastic density by virtue of a previous contraction. As particles come together in such a contraction there will be little actual contact. Consequently there can be little chance of packing them together.

To illustrate this point Alfvén resorts to an amusing analogy set forth in the style of Gamow.[29] He asks his readers to visualize a housefly that has been condemned to death by a firing squad. The hapless fly is placed in the center of a large circle while an unusually large number of marksmen stand shoulder to shoulder around the circumference of the circle. If each man, firing on signal, can achieve perfect aim and timing, the bullets will aggregate together into one large cannonball. (We can forget about the fly.)

Such might happen, that is, in an idealized mathematical dream-world. But in real life the bullets will for the most part go streaking by one another without colliding. And so it is with particles in the contraction phase of the universe. They would fail to "cooperate" in the formation of the postulated ylem.

Another problem, which has been recognized by Gamow and his co-workers, has to do with the production of the elements during the initial stages of the expansion. This view of atom-building is based on successive neutron-capture reactions to achieve elements of increasing atomic weights in a stepwise manner, starting from a 100-percent-neutron content in the ylem.

At the end of the first 30 minutes slightly more than half of the ylem has been converted into hydrogen, slightly less than half into helium.[30] There is an impasse, however, when we attempt to go past helium. A gap exists at mass 5 among nuclides that can actually be formed, since neither a proton nor a neutron can be attached to a helium nucleus of mass 4. Various ingenious devices have been attempted to patch up the scheme at this point, but to our knowledge nothing truly satisfactory has been forthcoming.

Gamow has also conceded that many of the heavier elements quite possibly weren't produced during the "Big Bang" at all, but were built up at a later date in the hot interiors of stars.[31]

It should be borne in mind that the Gamow hypothesis is predicated upon a Doppler interpretation of the red shifts of distant galaxies. While this is the simplest and most straightforward way to account for the red shifts, several present-day theorists remain unconvinced. Accordingly, several different non-Doppler cosmologies are being investigated, most of them based on some sort of "tired light" or time-depletion phenomenon. One such cosmology is the static universe of Gerald S. Hawkins.[32]

Even if we grant the basic premise of an expanding universe, we are on hazardous ground if we attempt to extrapolate this expansion back to a superdense state. To do so is to risk falling into the trap of uniformitarianism warned against in II Peter 3:3-5. A study of some relevant portions of Scripture indicates the distinct possibility that most, if not all, of the expansion took place at the time of the creation:

> I have made the earth, and created man upon it: I, even my hands, have stretched out the heavens, and all their host have I commanded (Isa. 45:12; also Isa. 48:13a).

> He hath made the earth by his power, he hath established the world by his wisdom, and hath stretched out the heavens by his discretion (Jer. 10:12; cf. also 51:15).

Steady-State Hypothesis (1948)

We come now to the most incredible hypothesis of all—that of continuous creation. First, let us try to imagine an infinitely old, infinitely big universe that is constantly expanding! As infinitely big as it might be already, it keeps increasing its size as galaxies recede from one another.

Rather than having the universe become depleted of matter as it expands, the originators of this scheme have suggested that *new* matter appears *out of nowhere* to replenish what has been lost in any given region of space. If the density of matter in the universe can be maintained thereby at a fairly constant level, we have what is commonly referred to as a steady-state situation.

In 1948 Fred Hoyle, Hermann Bondi, and Thomas Gold set forth their now-famous "steady-state cosmology." (Actually, the idea of continuous creation had been suggested as early as 1925 by Sir Oliver Lodge[33] and 1928 by Sir James Jeans.[34]) The self-creating matter is said to be hydrogen (or neutrons which soon decay into the constituent parts of hydrogen). And this self-creating matter possesses the astonishing ability to condense into galaxies, within which evolve stars, planets, satellites, comets, plants, animals, and people. We ourselves, then, are condensations out of nothingness formed by natural processes—the progeny of a mere vacuum—if the chain of reasoning is to be carried to its logical conclusion.

With regard to the question of just where the newly originated matter comes from, Hoyle has averred that such a query is "meaningless and unprofitable." [35] However, the continuous creation hypothesis has been dignified somewhat by the introduction of a "creation field." This has been done by a bold extension of Einstein's equations of the four-dimensional space-time continuum.[36] The "C-field," as it is called, is said to propagate through space much as an electric or gravitational field, but is effective at greater distances than any of the recognized types of fields.

As in the case of known fields, the C-field results from the presence of matter. If there are several contributions to the strength of the C-field in any given region, their effect is additive and can build up the intensity to the point where "matter happens." A particle forms if the C-field carries at least as much energy as the rest mass of the particle.

Operating in the manner Hoyle envisions, there is energy to spare. Baryons such as neutrons can be created with high initial velocities,[37] in a mode akin to the process of pair-production, in which electrons and positrons are formed from gamma rays. The created matter is capable of generating a C-field of its own which can participate in the formation of more matter, and so on it goes. The succession of events might be likened to a biological lineage, with each generation of matter being created in accordance with some kind of "genetic code" carried by the C-field.

It is most difficult to reconcile this type of thinking with the well-established first and second laws of thermodynamics. The *first law*, known as the law of conservation of energy, would, of course, forbid the condensing of matter "out of nowhere," inasmuch as matter is recognized as being a form of energy. Hoyle's defense to this objection has been that we cannot balance the energy books strictly and completely in any locality because no such region forms an entirely closed system.[38]

Suppose, however, that rather than discussing a particular locality we consider the universe as a whole. The rate of creation in just the observable part of the universe has been estimated by Hoyle to be 10^{32} tons of material each second.[39] In the whole universe, of course, it might be considerably more. Here we have new material continually appearing on the plus side of the ledger with nothing to offset it.

The bookkeeping becomes most strained when viewed in this light, but such, apparently, is the paradoxical nature of infinity. To ease this situation the steady-state cosmologists have expressed the desire to rewrite the first law to read that the amount of mass-energy *per unit volume* remains constant, so that the newly formed matter just exactly compensates for the expansion of the universe. There is *not*, however, one shred of experimental evidence to warrant such a change!

Similarly, this school of thought is at odds with the *second law*. If the universe is truly "running down" as the second law implies, how can it maintain a steady state? And how can anyone with a knowledge of this law declare that the universe is infinitely old? If it actually did date from eternity past it would long since have run down. To make the universe infinitely old is to make of it a gigantic perpetual motion machine. One needn't delve too far into the study of thermodynamics to learn that perpetual motion is impossible, but an ardent pantheist could conceivably have a high enough esteem for "Nature" to believe that it could perform even the impossible.

Most devastating to the steady-state cosmology, however, has been the recent accumulation of observable data. In a lecture delivered September 6, 1965, at a meeting of the British Association for the Advancement of Science, Hoyle admitted that there are several different types of findings that spell trouble for the steady-state cosmologist. The *crucial question* deciding the issue is whether the universe was once more dense than it is now. If so, then obviously there is an "unsteady" state with respect to time, and the cosmology is dealt a cruel blow. Hoyle cited evidence indicating that the universe was indeed more dense at one time, from the following lines of investigation:[40]

1. Radio astronomy counts by Martin Ryle and his associates indicate a density of radio sources too great to be compatible with the steady-state cosmology.

2. Red-shift measurements of fifteen quasi-stellar objects indicate that the universe has expanded from a state of higher density. The number of quasars studied is still rather small to carry any great weight, but a trend is indicated.

3. A radio background at a wavelength of 7 cm has been observed by Penzias and Wilson. There is no known way that this phenomenon can be explained by present astrophysical processes. One might be tempted to conclude, therefore, that the radiation originated at some time in the past when the universe was different from what it is today.

4. Helium-to-hydrogen ratios for stars and gaseous nebulas within our own galaxy indicate such a high helium content that it cannot

be accounted for by thermonuclear production from hydrogen. Here again, something other than present processes must have been acting in the past to bring this state of affairs about.

5. The structure of elliptical galaxies is more satisfactorily explained as a result of expansion from a highly dense state than by any condensation process.

In view of these findings, which taken together seem overwhelmingly to refute the steady-state hypothesis, *Hoyle announced that he no longer chose to believe the cosmology he had championed for so long!*[41] In its place, however, we have something new. In a recent book Hoyle describes his "Radical Departure" hypothesis which retains the concept of continuous creation, but oscillations from a steady-state situation are permitted. Our part of the universe is likened to a gigantic bubble which is undergoing the "bounce" phase of a local oscillation.

This notion is, of course, still very young, and will probably be "developed" more as time goes on. While we cannot yet tell how long it will successfully survive new experimental findings, there is no reason whatsoever for the Christian man of science to "wait and see," or reserve judgment on the matter. We should reject the hypothesis without hesitation or apology because of its clear-cut violation of both science and Scripture.

One wonders why the theologians have failed to speak out more forcefully against continuous creation as an explanation for the world we live in—a system that denies the fact of a beginning or a creation, that reduces man to a chance materialization from the void, and leaves little room for God. Just where *does* God fit into the picture?

The continuous creation cosmologists would have Him abdicate His creatorship; if the universe is infinitely old, then it never needed to be created. It was always there coexisting with God. The next question that arises is how much control He could wield over the universe if it were not, in fact, His own handiwork. They have succeeded, then, in casting doubts upon His omnipotence. In reality, a theistic continuous creation cosmology is virtually untenable; hence, it is rarely attempted. It is far more natural to weld it to an atheistic or pantheistic world view.

One might think that God could be inserted into the picture as the motivating force behind the continuous creation. But He would then be a God of incompleteness and imperfection, never having finished His work of structuring the universe, and whose continuing efforts merely serve to keep an endless treadmill in motion. The following verses state unequivocally that creation is *not* a continuing process:

> Thus the heavens and the earth were finished, and all the host of them (Gen. 2:1).
>
> For in six days the Lord made heaven and earth, the sea, and all that in them is, and rested the seventh day (Ex. 20:11a).

Another conflict centers around the continuous creationist's insistence that the universe extends infinitely far in all directions. This would give an infinite number of galaxies, each containing some 100 billion stars. Scripture reveals that although the number of stars is extremely great, and in fact innumerable as far as man is concerned, there is a definite total number of stars known to God: "He telleth the number of the stars; he calleth them all by their names" (Psa. 147:4).

Still another problem involves the fact that this hypothesis makes no provision for the symmetry between particles and anti-particles. As Alfvén has pointed out,[42] a continuous creation of neutrons without a corresponding creation of antineutrons to offset them is in direct violation of the very basic principle of particle-antiparticle symmetry.

Alfvén's Ambiplasma Hypothesis (1965)

In an attempt to obviate the difficulties of the foregoing systems, O. Klein, former professor of theoretical physics at the University of Stockholm, propounded a new view of the origin of the universe in the mid-1950's. Alfvén's updated version of this conception which appeared in *Review of Modern Physics* in 1965,[43] probably represents the most advanced thinking on the subject to date.

Alfvén begins with an extremely tenuous mixture of koinomatter (regular matter) and anti-matter, occupying an enormous spherical region of space perhaps 10^{12} light years in radius.[44] He calls his primordial material "ambiplasma." Basically it was a mixture of protons, anti-protons, electrons, and positrons.[45]

Over a period of *trillions of years*, gravitational attraction will gradually shrink the sphere and increase its density. As this happens opportunities will increase for particles to come in contact with their antiparticles and undergo annihilation. In the case of proton-antiproton annihilation reactions, neutrons and electromagnetic radiation would result, leaving electrons and positrons. The radiation thus produced has a very significant effect in the overall picture.

After a few trillion years, the radiation intensity will increase to the extent that its outward push will not only hinder the gravitational contraction, but eventually reverse its direction completely. Thus we have arrived at an expanding universe without the need for catastrophism—a philosophical improvement over the "fireworks" type of hypothesis. Meanwhile, localized regions of perhaps a billion light-years across begin clumping together to form galaxies.

Professor Alfvén concedes that there are serious difficulties concerning the mechanism of galaxy formation. He is uncommitted as to whether the process began during the contraction of the metagalaxy (the observable part of the universe), or during the hypothetical 10 billion years since the beginning of the expansion. The detailed development within each galaxy at still later stages, he says, poses an even more formidable problem.[46]

Existing conjectures as to the formation of individual stars within a galaxy are based on the assumption of a condensing mass consisting exclusively of koinomatter. While these methods might be applied equally well to a system of antimatter, they break down disastrously when applied to a mixture of the two—presumably the realistic case. As the protostars contracted, bringing matter and anti-matter particles closer together, annihilation reactions would soon blast them out of existence.

To overcome this Alfvén has invoked an admittedly speculative mechanism by which koinomatter and antimatter become segregated into different regions of space separated by thin buffer zones of ambiplasma. Such, however, is a difficult feat to accomplish, and could well be analogous to the statistical improbability of spontaneously separating lukewarm water into regions of hot water and cold water. The separation of a mixture can be one of the knottiest problems of all, even when work is done on the system from the outside.

Alfvén confesses that there are several problems involved here and that a systematic study of the question has not yet been undertaken.[47] The hypothesis is too new and unexplored yet to think in specific terms of when and where the supposed segregation might take place. Actually, we are in a veritable wilderness of unknowns at this point, because the observational data tell us so little.

We are uninformed, for instance, as to whether every second galaxy in the metagalaxy contains antimatter, or whether every second star in the galaxy contains antimatter, or whether the entire observable part of the universe contains koinomatter, with all of the antimatter placed at great distances in unobservable locations. Until it is known toward what finished product these segregation mechanisms are supposed to be working, it is rather futile to engage in any guesswork concerning the details of their operation.

We would submit that a large part of the trouble in devising an adequate mechanism for galactic evolution centers around the uphill nature of the process. Clearly we are attempting here to do the statistically improbable. Which, we would ask, is a more probable distribution of material—an undifferentiated mass of ambiplasma or an intricately structured galaxy with highly organized parts each performing its specific function? We might ask equally well which is more statistically probable—a pile of stones or a stone house? The undifferentiated ambiplasma and the pile of stones are obviously the more probable structures.

The probability of a structure decreases as its organization increases. The natural direction for spontaneous processes, in keeping with the second law of thermodynamics, is from the *less* to the *more* probable. Therefore we are doing the statistically improbable at each stage of the supposed galactic evolution, and we are expected to believe that such has been happening for untold ages! As Williams has pointed out in his paper on entropy,[48] an occasional process that results in a more ordered, more complex product would be possible. But to postulate that a system would do the statistically improbable repeatedly over millions and billions of years is to betray a complete lack of belief in the second law!

Which Alternative?

If a person is bent on rejecting the facts of the creation as revealed in the Scriptures, we might ask which of the many schemes, specifically, he is going to put in its place. It is a most significant fact that every attempt, thus far, to bypass the book of Genesis sooner or later has run counter to some well-established scientific principle or principles.

However, even if a framework of cosmic evolution could be found that harmonizes with every known law (and this is undoubtedly impossible because of the entropy principle), there would be no guarantee that such was in fact what actually happened. And, more important, there would still be no accounting for the existence of the raw materials or the laws that governed their interactions.

Where *did* the laws of physics come from? *Is* there a naturalistic explanation? This question is probably just as vital as the less sophisticated problem of accounting for the material in the world that is so apparent to our senses. Did the laws of physics evolve from simpler laws? Did the Stefan-Boltzmann Law, which is a fourth power relationship, evolve its way up the evolutionary ladder by gradual stages from a first-power law? Did Coulomb's Law and Newton's Law of Gravitation, reasoning from their remarkable similarity, descend from a common ancestor? Such nonsense points up rather nicely the utter bankruptcy of the evolutionary approach in explaining one of the most important features of the universe—its orderliness.

All of the conflicting "scientific" cosmogonies do appear to agree on one thing—namely, that the Genesis account of origins is wrong. Aside from this one united front which they present, they oppose one another in countless ways. The cosmogonists have chosen to reject the witness of the one authoritative Source of information on the subject at hand. In so doing they have condemned their efforts to failure because of their ignorance of the basic axiom that "the fear of the Lord is the beginning of knowledge" (Prov. 1:7a). And without him there is no explanation of origins because "without him was not anything made that was made" (John 1:3b).

What Is the Universe?

Scientists are thoroughly stymied by the nature of the *present* world. Why should we speculate about where it came from when we don't even know what it is? A little reflection will serve to demonstrate that our ignorance is so great that we find ourselves mired down in the quicksand of conjecture merely attempting to describe our physical environment.

Let us consider the sub-microscopic makeup of things for a moment:

What is matter really made of? Atoms.

What are atoms made of? Subatomic particles.

Of what are these subatomic particles constituted? It is strongly suspected that each of these in turn possesses a complex internal structure. The neutron, for instance, apparently has a dense positive core surrounded by a negative meson cloud.[49]

Of what are these parts constituted? There are those who are satisfied with the explanation that each ultimate particle is a highly concentrated and localized bundle of energy.

But what is energy? Our stock definition that it is the ability to do work tells us nothing of its structure.

We do know, however, that it occurs in quanta. A quantum is a small bundle. Bundle of what? Energy!

Thus we are able to circumnavigate semantically in this realm without ever penetrating the *most vital problem* of all—namely, "What is the basic stuff of which we and the world we live in are made?" Stating the problem in another way, we may use atoms and fundamental particles to explain matter, but then we may not turn around and use matter to explain the atoms and particles. One is led, then, to the inescapable conclusion that there is a spiritual groundwork underlying the material world. ". . . and by him all things consist" (Col. 1:17).

From the macroscopic point of view our ignorance of the universe is still more woeful. We might touch momentarily on the problem of gravitation. With all our fields, tensors, curved space, and other artificialities, we are still at a loss to explain why an object falls to the ground, or why the earth behaves as though it were swinging from the sun on a steel cable, when in fact the intervening space is practically a vacuum.

A hypothetical particle, the graviton, has been invoked to explain gravitation as an exchange force. But there is widespread pessimism concerning the prospects of verifying its existence, at least for the time being. We are not even sure of the things we used to "know." For instance, the constant "G" in Newton's Law of Gravitation is suspected to change in accordance with the density of the universe.[50] If it can be shown that the laws of nature change, the principle of uniformity is apt to lose some of its popularity. A myriad of new question marks will then loom into view as we look back in time.

There are many other perplexing questions. What are the quasi-stellar objects and where are they located? Are the observed red shifts of distant galaxies due to the Doppler effect, some other effect, or both? Are portions of the universe composed only of antimatter? Does the universe, as is so often asserted, appear fundamentally the same to observers located at various points within it? How numerous are planetary systems? How do cosmic rays acquire such fantastic energies? It does not appear unreasonable to this writer to desire answers to these very basic questions concerning the present status of the cosmos, before embarking on a spree of conjecture concerning the remote past.

Limiting God

Were we to insist that one of the existing hypotheses must be the correct one, or even that some yet-to-be-devised scheme will in fact be the true one, we would be limiting God to the use of processes that we ourselves are capable of understanding. How utterly foolish and unrealistic! "For the wisdom of this world is foolishness with God" (I Cor. 3:19a). In fact, "the foolishness of God is wiser than men; and the weakness of God is stronger than men" (I Cor. 1:25). With an unlimited variety of methods and processes at His command, why should He restrict himself to the use of only those few of which we have some awareness?

Having seen the failures of the various imaginations that have been engaged in apart from the Word of God, it is tempting to try to synthesize a picture of the creation of the universe based on the scriptural clues to the methods God used. It is our belief, however, in view of the miraculous nature of the creation, that such an endeavor would be as futile as trying to "explain" the feeding of the multitudes, the healing of the sick, or the raising of the dead. Were we able to explain such events they would, of course, cease to be miracles.

It is through just such great mysteries and wonders as these that God has demonstrated His power to mankind. "Great things doeth he, which we cannot comprehend" (Job 37:5b; also Job 9:10a). "For my thoughts are not your thoughts, neither are my ways your ways, saith the Lord. For as the heavens are higher than the earth, so are my ways higher than your ways, and my thoughts than your thoughts" (Isa. 55:8, 9). "No man can find out the work that God maketh from the beginning to the end" (Eccl. 3:11).

Shifting Sand

If we can project into the future from what we have seen thus far, we may safely state that the present ideas will prove to be quite transitory. And not only is there a continual change within the field of cosmogony itself, but also within the individual cosmogonist. There is the ever-present struggle to bend an existing hypothesis to make it fit the newly discovered facts, or, in other cases, an embarrassed disillusionment, the discarding of former views and the initiation of a hopeful new synthesis. *Clearly, truth cannot be that flexible!*

Professor Bondi makes the surprising admission, however, that such theories are not necessarily *meant* to be true! Their chief purpose, he states, is to be fertile—to provide new ideas for fruitful avenues of research.[51] But how many of the popular writers make the true intent of the theorists clear to the general public?

The *impression* that is almost always left with the reader is that such speculations constitute a "scientific alternative" to Genesis. With a steady diet of such material in the magazines and newspapers, it is small wonder that the man in the street is starting to look to nebulas, cosmic explosions, and creation fields as the source of his being, rather than the creator God.

There was a day when the church had sufficient vitality to speak out forcefully against such blasphemy. Today, what "backbone" exists in the true church is limited to a few isolated pockets of resistance. Most disturbing of all is the manner in which many professing Christians take in these ideas and fondle them with such complete naiveté, totally oblivious to their inherent dangers.

Why, indeed, should we be any more favorably disposed toward cosmic evolution than organic? Yet there are those among us who have compromised to the extent that "without form and void" is taken to mean a "vast undifferentiated nebula or dust cloud," and "let there be light" is interpreted as incipient thermonuclear reactions that have begun in the "baby stars" some several million years later.

When we bend the scriptural account of creation to fit some such artificial notion we are in grave danger of doing violence to its intended meaning. Such compromise can distort our thinking and mask the clear simple truths of Scripture from our consciousness. There is no conceivable reason to be intimidated by a mere hypothesis.

Still, so many would rather take the easy route by retreating from a sound scriptural stand and attempting to accommodate the speculations of the day. How much more intellectually honest is the person who undertakes a critical study of the various hypotheses and learns to recognize them for what they are—guesswork perpetrated in the name of science.

NOTES AND REFERENCES

1. W. C. Dampier, *A Shorter History of Science*, Meridian Books (Cleveland: The World Publishing Company, 1957), p. 59.

2. A. Rupert Hall and Marie Boas Hall, *A Brief History of Science* (New York: Signet Science Library, The New American Library, 1964), p. 152.
3. Isaac Newton, "Four Letters to Richard Bentley," in *Theories of the Universe*, Milton K. Munitz, editor (Glenco, Ill.: The Free Press, 1957), p. 212.
4. Robert E. D. Clark, *The Universe—Plan or Accident?* (Philadelphia: Muhlenberg Press, 1961), p. 80.
5. *Ibid.*, p. 49.
6. George Gamow, *The Creation of the Universe*, Revised Edition (New York: Bantam Books, 1952), p. 1.
7. Theodore A. Ashford, *From Atoms to Stars* (New York: Holt, Rinehart, and Winston, 1960), p. 583.
8. Gamow, *op. cit.*, pp. 109, 110.
9. Robert H. Baker, *Astronomy*, 8th Edition (Princeton, N. J.: D. Van Nostrand Company, 1964), pp. 270-272.
10. Ashford, *op. cit.*, p. 586.
11. John C. Wnitcomb, Jr., *The Origin of the Solar System* (Philadelphia: Presbyterian and Reformed Publishing Company, 1964), pp. 9-18.
12. *Ibid.*, p. 20; see also Ralph B. Baldwin, *A Fundamental Survey of the Moon* (New York: McGraw-Hill, 1965), p. 36.
13. *Ibid.*, p. 37.
14. *Ibid.*, p. 42.
15. John C. Duncan, *Astronomy*, 5th Edition (New York: Harper and Row, 1954), pp. 313-316.
16. S. Rosen, R. Siegfried, and J. M. Dennison, *Concepts in Phyisical Science* (New York: Harper and Row, 1965), p. 524.
17. Whitcomb, *op. cit.*, p. 12.
18. Fred Hoyle, *Astronomy* (New York: Doubleday and Company, 1962), pp. 269, 270; see also by same author, *The Nature of the Universe* (New York: Signet Science Library, The New American Library, 1960), pp. 84-87.
19. Fred L. Whipple, "The Dust Cloud Hypothesis," *Scientific American*, Vol. 78, No. 5, pp. 34-45 (May 1948).
20. David Bergamini, *Life Nature Library: The Universe* (New York: Time Incorporated, 1962), pp. 92, 93, 104, 105.
21. James A. Coleman, *Modern Theories of the Universe* (New York: Signet Science Library, The New American Library, 1963), p. 135.
22. *Ibid.*, pp. 135, 136.
23. Georges Lemaitre, "The Primeval Atom," in *Theories of the Universe*, Milton K. Munitz, editor (Glenco, Ill.: The Free Press, 1957), p. 353.
24. George S. Mumford, "News Notes: Belgian Cosmologist," *Sky and Telescope*, Vol. 32, No. 5, p. 275 (Nov. 1966).
25. Gamow, *op. cit.*, pp. 42-72.
26. *Ibid.*, p. 28.
27. *Ibid.*, p. 137.
28. George Gamow, *Matter Earth and Sky* (Englewood Cliffs, N. J.: Prentice-Hall, 1958), p. 550.

29. Hannes Alfvén, *Worlds-Antiworlds* (San Francisco: W. H. Freeman and Company, 1966), pp. 21, 22.
30. Gamow, *Creation of the Universe*, p. 67; see also by same author, "The Evolutionary Universe," *Scientific American*, Reprint No. 211, W. H. Freeman and Company, San Francisco, pp. 8, 9 (Sept. 1956).
31. Gamow, *Creation of the Universe*, p. 71; see also, William A. Fowler, "The Origin of the Elements," *Scientific American*, Reprint No. 210, W. H. Freeman and Company, San Francisco, pp. 7, 8 (Sept. 1956).
32. Paul W. Hodge, *Galaxies and Cosmology* (New York: McGraw-Hill Book Company, 1966), p. 161.
33. Theodore Graebner, *God and the Cosmos* (Grand Rapids, Mich.: Eerdmans Publishing Company, 1946), p. 37.
34. Coleman, *op. cit.*, pp. 161, 162.
35. Fred Hoyle, *Frontiers of Astronomy* (New York: Harper and Brothers, 1955), p. 342.
36. Fred Hoyle, "The Steady State Universe," *Scientific American*, Reprint No. 218, W. H. Freeman and Company, San Francisco, p. 5 (Sept. 1956).
37. Fred Hoyle, *Galaxies, Nuclei and Quasars* (New York: Harper and Row, 1965), p. 123.
38. Hoyle, "Steady State Universe," p. 5.
39. Hoyle, *Nature of the Universe*, p. 110.
40. Fred Hoyle, "Recent Developments in Cosmology," *Nature*, Vol. 208:111 (Oct. 9, 1965).
41. *Ibid.*, p. 113.
42. Alfvén, *op. cit.*, p. 99.
43. Hannes Alfvén, "Antimatter and the Development of the Metagalaxy," *Review of Modern Physics*, 37:652 (1965).
44. Alfvén, *Worlds-Antiworlds*, p. 68.
45. George S. Mumford, "News Notes: Antimatter May Matter," *Sky and Telescope*, Vol. 31, No. 5, p. 264 (May, 1966).
46. Alfvén, *Worlds-Antiworlds*, p. 78.
47. *Ibid.*, p. 82.
48. Emmett L. Williams, "Entropy and the Solid State," *Creation Research Society Quarterly*, Vol. 3, No. 3, p. 23 (Oct. 1966).
49. Donald J. Hughes, *The Neutron Story*, Anchor Books (New York: Doubleday and Company, 1959), p. 75.
50. George Gamow, *Gravity*, Anchor Books (New York: Doubleday and Company, 1962), pp. 139-141.
51. Hermann Bondi, *The Universe at Large*, Anchor Books (New York: Doubleday and Company, 1960), p. 35.

Chapter 3

Physical Considerations Pertinent to the Problem of Creation vs. Evolution

ENTROPY AND THE SOLID STATE

EMMETT L. WILLIAMS, JR., PH.D.*

Introduction

The thermodynamic quantity of entropy plays a role as important as that of energy in every field of physics, chemistry, and technology but is generally not very well understood. The effect of entropy on solids, particularly metals, has been investigated by many scientists.

To give a better understanding of entropy, this article is a discussion and review of the disordering effect of entropy on the structure of crystalline solids. It is well to keep in mind that this tendency toward disorder and randomness is universal because of the principle of entropy increase.

Entropy can be considered from two standpoints. First, in classical thermodynamics entropy is described in a rather abstract manner as a thermodynamic variable of the system under consideration; secondly, in statistical mechanics it is defined as a measure of the number of ways in which the elementary particles (for instance atoms or molecules) may be arranged in the system under the given circumstances.[1] The latter method applies to the solid state.

Entropy in Classical Thermodynamics

The concept of entropy originated in classical thermodynamics under conditions where heat can be converted into work.[2] The quantity of heat $\int_1^2 dQ$ necessary to bring a system from state 1 to state 2 is not uniquely defined since it depends on the path followed from 1 to 2.

*Department of Physics and Chemistry, Bob Jones University

However, the thermodynamic quantity $\int_1^2 \frac{dQ}{T}$, where T is the absolute temperature, has a value which is independent of the path followed. This is true only if the path is reversible and the integration is carried out so that each quantity of heat is divided by the temperature at which it is introduced.[3] This quantity calculated from a temperature of absolute zero is called the entropy (S) of the system.

$$S = \int_O^T \frac{dQ_{rev}}{T} \tag{1}$$

Some systems, such as solid solutions, have a finite value of entropy even at absolute zero and S in equation 1 must be replaced by $S - S_o$. The measurement of the entropy of a system in classical thermodynamics depends on the measurement of quantities of heat. Entropy is the central concept in classical thermodynamics.[4] Considering the second law of thermodynamics, the entropy of an isolated system tends to a maximum; therefore this quantity is a criterion for the direction in which processes can take place.

This is the principle of the increase in entropy. Although it refers to an isolated system, it is nevertheless of extremely general application because all materials that are in any way affected by a process may be included within an isolated system.[5]

Entropy in Statistical Mechanics

Classical thermodynamics is concerned only with macroscopic systems, and such systems can be described by temperature, pressure, volume, chemical composition, etc. However, classical thermodynamics is not concerned with what happens on an atomic level.

This can be illustrated as follows. If the energy content of a particular system is known, then each of the molecules in the system will not necessarily have the same energy (total energy of system divided by the total number of molecules). Some molecules will have more or less energy than this average energy per molecule, but taken as an entirety all of the molecules will have an energy corresponding to the energy of the system. If the temperature of the system is raised from T_1 to T_2 thermodynamically, this is considered a single event. On the atomic level an immense number of collisions of the molecules occurs, and this change is considered an average value of very many events.[6]

Thermodynamics can be applied to the atomic level if the methods of statistical mechanics are utilized. When dealing with such a large number of molecules the specification of the state of each separate particle is impossible, and it is necessary to resort to statistical methods.

Also it should be realized that a thermodynamic state is comprised of many states on the atomic scale, or a thermodynamic state can be realized in many ways. These possibilities of realization are called micro-states.[7] Let the number of micro-states be denoted by w, then the statistical definition of entropy (S) is

$$S = k \ln w \tag{2}$$

where k is Boltzmann's constant, and

$$k = \frac{R}{N_o} \tag{3}$$

where R is the gas constant per mole, and N_o is Avogadro's number.

Entropy tends to a maximum, and this means according to equation (2) a tendency towards the most probable state. According to this statistical interpretation of entropy the second law does not hold entirely rigidly.[8] It is not absolutely certain, but only highly probable, that the entropy will increase in each process spontaneously taking place in an isolated system.

A logical question to ask is, what is the most probable state? The state which can be described by the largest number of micro-states will be the most probable since it has the greatest possibility of appearance. When considering the internal configuration of a system there are really only two different states, ordered and disordered.

Since entropy is determined a different way in statistical mechanics than in classical thermodynamics (counting micro-states vs. measuring quantities of heat) it would be well to ask the question, how close do the results calculated by each method check? Fast[9] states that "one of the finest achievements of physics and chemistry is that these two paths generally lead to the same result, while divergences which appear can be explained by the theory in a completely satisfactory manner and even serve to endorse it."

The concept of entropy has become as fundamental as the energy concept. Emden writes,

> As a student, I read with advantage a small book by F. Walk entitled *The Mistress of the World and Her Shadow*. These meant energy and entropy. In the course of advancing knowledge the two seem to me to have exchanged places. In the huge manufactory of natural processes, the principle of entropy occupies the position of manager, for it dictates the manner and

method of the whole business, whilst the principle of energy does the bookkeeping, balancing credits and debits.[10]

Entropy and Probability

To illustrate the relationship of entropy and probability a simple example will be discussed.[11] The aim is to deduce the macroscopic properties of a system as statistical resultants of the properties of its particles.

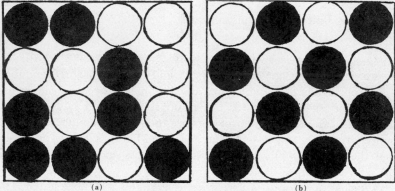

(a)   (b)

Figure 1. Some possible arrangements of balls in a box.

A man is blindfolded and has to pack 16 equal-sized balls in a flat, square box; eight of the balls are white and eight are black. He is able to arrange the balls in a square pattern in the box but will have no control over the distribution of the colors. The kind of arrangement that might result is shown in Figure 1(a) when the distribution is random or disordered. An ordered distribution as shown in Figure 1(b) may turn up, but is very unlikely.

There are approximately 13,000 different ways of arranging the balls in the box. This calculation is shown in Appendix I.

Therefore the chance of the distribution in Figure 1(b) appearing is only about 1 in 13,000. The improbability of this particular arrangement is not due to the ordered distribution of the colors, but to the fact that this is only one of many possible distributions, all with the same probability of appearance. The particular arrangement shown in Figure 1(a) is equally improbable.

The essential difference between 1(a) and 1(b) is that 1(a) is in a large class of distributions all of which are disordered. Almost all of the 13,000 distributions fall into this category so that the chance of some disordered distribution appearing is practically unity. The arrangement in 1(b) is ordered, and it is unique in this respect. Thus the chance of some ordered distribution appearing is very small.

In any rearrangement of the balls in the box the "system" remains the same, only the internal configuration changes. Any natural rearrangement that may occur will normally be to a disordered state, because of the high number of disordered states as compared to the ordered states.

It should be realized from this discussion that many different arrangements of atoms in a system may give the same total system energy content. A given temperature, pressure, volume, etc., does not necessarily mean the same exact atomic arrangement every time this temperature, pressure, volume, etc., are attained. Many different atomic configurations are possible within a system at a constant temperature, pressure, volume, etc. This is particularly true of the solid state when considering the number of different ways the atoms and vacancies can be arranged on the various lattice sites.

Considering again equation (2), if, according to the second law of thermodynamics, S increases in any spontaneous process, then w increases; which means the arrangement of the particles in an isolated system goes toward a more probable distribution. Since the number of micro-states (w) is greater for the disordered arrangements (more possible disordered arrangements), the system goes to a more disordered state. Therefore it can be seen when considering configuration entropy, it is a measure of the disorder in a system, and the system tends to go to a more disordered state since there is an entropy increase.

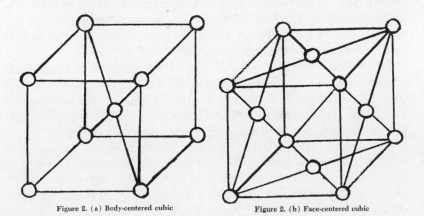

Figure 2. (a) Body-centered cubic   Figure 2. (b) Face-centered cubic

The Effect of Entropy on the Solid State

Considering crystalline solids, their atoms or molecules are arranged in a regular pattern with a definite periodic repeat of a basic unit cell.[12] There are several types of basic unit cells.

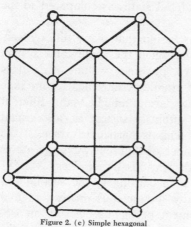

Figure 2. (c) Simple hexagonal

Three types of unit cells are shown in Figure 2: (a) is body-centered cubic, (b) is face-centered cubic, and (c) is simple hexagonal. The white spheres represent atoms and the lines between the spheres simply help to visualize the basic unit structure. Actually the spheres should be glued together for, as in the case of metals, the outer electron clouds of the atoms overlap and the spheres are "touching."

The resultant crystal structure is imagined by stacking in three dimensions these unit cells around and on each other. This symmetrical arrangement is grossly misleading for it implies a perfect static pattern whereas the crystalline state is *neither static nor perfect.*[13]

Disorder in solids results from vibration of the atoms, presence of impurities, and presence of structural defects. For this discussion, only structural defects such as vacant lattice sites and dislocations are considered. Vacant lattice sites are classified as point defects and are illustrated in Figure 3. The atomic distances around the vacant site are distorted because of the missing atom and lattice strain is present for some distance away from the vacancy.[14]

Dislocations are line defects, and a very simple representation of a dislocation is shown in Figure 4. This is an edge dislocation and may be considered in the simplest sense a missing row of atoms in part of the crystal lattice, or as an extra row of atoms in the other part of the crystal lattice that is shown.

The question may be asked: why are these imperfections present in solids? Their presence causes disorder in the crystalline lattice, and disordered states are more probable statistically. Thus the entropy of the solid is increased by having imperfections present, since the solid tends toward the most probable state.

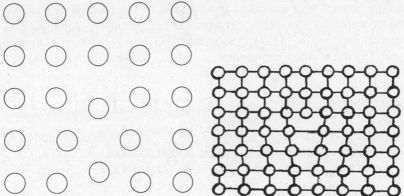

Figure 3. Illustration of a vacant site causing nearest neighbor lattice distortion.

Figure 4. Representation of an edge dislocation.

The same argument as developed with the 16 colored balls can be applied to crystals containing 10^{20} atoms or more, and the only difference is to increase enormously the number of distributions of the disordered kind, but not of the ordered, so that the chance of finding a crystal in a disordered state becomes almost certain.[15] From equation (2) any state that is more probable statistically will cause an increase in entropy, and this is the factor that inclines the system towards disordered states. Therefore the second law of thermodynamics is satisfied.

The stability of crystalline disorder is illustrated as follows:[16] Consider an elemental crystal containing vacancies. There are N atoms arranged on N atom sites in the crystal. The free energy of the perfect crystal is G_p. Remove n atoms from the crystal and place them on the surface forming n vacant sites. Each of these vacancies has an entropy of formation $\triangle H_v$ (heat gained or lost by the solid by removing an atom from a filled site, creating a vacancy) and a vibrational entropy of $\triangle S_v$ resulting from the disturbance of the nearest neighbor atoms in the lattice.

There is a configurational entropy change associated with the formation of n vacancies given by

$$\triangle S_c = S_n - S_p = k \ln w - k \ln w' = k \ln \left(\frac{w}{w'} \right)$$

where S_n is the entropy of the crystal with n vacancies, S_p is the entropy of the perfect crystal. The number of possible micro-states for the crystal with vacancies is w, and w′ is the number of possible micro-states for the perfect crystal. Using the above equation and introducing $\triangle G = \triangle H - T\triangle S$, where $\triangle G$ is the Gibbs free energy and T is the absolute temperature it can be shown (see Appendix II) that

$$\triangle G = G_n - G_p = n(\triangle - T\triangle S_v) + kT \left[N\ln\left(\frac{N}{N+n}\right) + n\ln\left(\frac{n}{N+n}\right)\right] \quad (5)$$

Figure 5 is a plot of $n(\triangle H_v - T\triangle S_v)$, $\triangle S_c$ and G as a function of n. The entropy contribution, $\triangle S_c$, is always negative. As can be seen, G is a function of n. From Figure 5, $G = f(n)$ is simply the algebraic

addition of $n(\triangle H_v - T\triangle S)$ and $kT \left[N\ln\left(\frac{N}{N+n}\right) + n\ln\left(\frac{n}{N+n}\right)\right]$.

As an example, using equation 4 (Appendix II) in a somewhat simpler form, the equilibrium amount of vacancies at a given temperature can be calculated. Considering copper at 1000°K for a cubic centimeter of crystal (5×10^{22} lattice sites) there should be about 10^{16} vacancies.[17]

Dislocations are thermodynamically unstable. A simple calculation[18] shows that the entropy term for a dislocation is small. There-

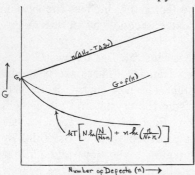

fore the free energy is minimized only if all of the dislocations are removed from the crystal. However the presence of other lattice defects and their action in crystals can cause the generation of dislocations.

Also, an imperfect solid crystal can grow by a dislocation mechanism easily from the liquid state, whereas the growth of a perfect crystal from the liquid is

Figure 5. Free energy of a crystal as a function of defect concentration.

extremely difficult, if not impossible. Even if dislocations are considered thermodynamically unstable they always have been found in solid crystals,[19] and the mechanisms of dislocation generation depend on other existing lattice defects.

Solids, particularly those that are crystalline, are often looked upon as having a regular structure. This is *not true*, since imperfections in the lattice of the solid cause disordering of the structure. This causes an entropy increase in the solid, making it more stable thermodynamically. This is also the reason it is impossible to obtain materials that are absolutely pure.

The same line of reasoning could be used when introducing foreign atoms into a perfect crystal as when introducing vacancies. Besides increasing the entropy of the crystal by the number of possible ways the foreign atoms can be statistically arranged, the size difference of the foreign atom causes lattice strain within the crystal which also disorders the parent lattice.

If a perfectly pure crystal could be made, the first time it touched a foreign substance, it would tend to absorb and dissolve impurity atoms. The only way a perfectly pure substance could be produced and maintained would be in a perfect vacuum, touching nothing.

It should be realized that imperfections in solids are of more than minor importance, since they actually control many of the properties of the solids. Such phenomena in metals as elastic and plastic deformation, diffusion, precipitation hardening, radiation damage, etc., can be explained by the presence of various lattice imperfections. Then, to explain many observed effects in solids, it is necessary to assume lattice disorder rather than lattice perfection.

Again, it needs to be stressed that *crystalline solids are disordered,* since many people—including some scientists—have an idea that crystals have highly ordered, regularly arranged atomic structures, thus violating the second law of thermodynamics. Such a concept is far from the truth. Crystalline solids are more ordered than gases and liquids, but they are interlaced with structural defects that destroy lattice regularity.

The Entropy Principle as a Universal Law

This very simplified discussion of the effect of entropy on the solid state can be applied to other natural systems to illustrate the stability of disorder and randomness.

Dr. H. M. Morris[20] has suggested that the principle entropy increase is a direct result of the curse God placed on the creation as a result of Adam's sin (Gen. 3:17-19). The creation process would be of course directly opposite to the entropy principle of present scientific processes. In looking over His newly finished creation the Lord saw that it was very good (Gen. 1:31).

If the perfect holy God created, then the creation would be perfect. Here would be perfection in nature, perfection in the universe, and as for the solid state, perfect crystals. However, today we find very little, if any, perfection in nature, and this change from order to disorder must have occurred by divine edict later than Genesis 1:31. He spoke all nature into being, and then cursed His perfect creation because of man's sin.

Thus the perfectly ordered crystalline materials that God created have degenerated into atomically disordered materials because of the operation of the second law of thermodynamics. The crystalline lattices in solids no longer exhibit order but are filled with defects that interrupt order and cause disorder.

Evolution is statistically highly improbable if not impossible. From the statistical approach of considering entropy increase, an occasional process that results in a more ordered, more complex product would be possible. However, millions and billions of years of constant violations of the second law of thermodynamics are impossible if this law is valid. Every time a simpler organism becomes more ordered and more complex, the statistically improbable event occurs. And such events are *highly* improbable. The second law of thermodynamics has not been proven wrong in any experiments conducted to verify it.

Creation requires a Creator, and the Creator controls His creation and the principles that govern it. Evolution does not require a creator, and depends only on chance and natural selection (both are statistical processes). Also all laws of science now operating would have always been operating, and evolution is supposed to operate under present scientific processes.

However present processes do not favor any type of evolutionary development. The question of logic may enter the argument: what is more logical, a Creator as revealed in His Word doing what He said He did, or a process of statistical chance always occurring in such a way so as to favor the statistically improbable and violate a basic scientific law? Romans 1:19-22 has the answer to those who choose to believe the latter.

The Ruin-Reconstruction Theory

The ruin-reconstruction theory in the Scofield Reference Bible (page 3, footnote 3; page 4, footnote 3) brings up an interesting point concerning entropy. The "first" creation had undergone divine judgment and the earth and all of the remains would then have a high entropy content because of the supposed disorder and death. Then God places another creation on this one, and this new creation would have a low entropy content because it was perfect at the end of this "new" creation period. The two systems could not stay in equilibrium with each other without the "latter" creation increasing in entropy.

Here is a paradox, an old disordered system in intimate contact with an ordered system. What happened when the newly created animals and man breathed in dust or ate anything from the disordered system? The intake in any way of any disordered material would destroy the ordered perfection of the newly created creatures.

Therefore, God would not have had to curse His new creation; it was already becoming disordered immediately after creation. Did God then lie to us about the necessity of the curse? The disordered system in contact with the new creation would have eventually disordered it.

Would the seeds possibly left over from the previous judgment, being disordered (higher entropy content), yield disordered or perfect plants? If the ground was already cursed from the previous judgment, why did God have to curse it again? Was He deceiving us? One could ask many questions like this.

Possible explanations could be given, such as God perfecting the earth before the "second" creation" by ordering the rocks, dirt, fossils, etc., before placing the "new" creation on this. However, the Scriptures give no indication of this. Any time Christians deviate from the Word of God to try to justify the Word in the light of modern science, their theories demand explanation after explanation and never solve the problem.

Why not believe what God said? The Scriptures plainly state the heavens and earth were created in six days, and because of Adam's sin this creation was cursed, and the principle of entropy increase became operative.

APPENDIX I

Calculation of Different Ways of Arranging White and Black Balls in a Box

If only the white balls are numbered, then each of the total number of *different* arrangements of white balls would be realizeable in

8! different ways, because eight unnumbered white balls can be distributed over eight positions in only one way, while eight numbered balls can be distributed in 8! different ways. This is true since the white balls are assumed to be exactly alike if unnumbered. Therefore, if one is exchanged with another the arrangement is identical. If only white balls are moved (leaving the black ones in place) all of the resulting arrangements are the same. Only when white and black positions are exchanged is there any change in arrangement. The same reasoning applies to the black balls.

Considering the 16 possible positions for the balls

$$N = \frac{16!}{8!\,8!} \approx 13,000$$

where N = total number of *different* arrangements.

16! is total number of arrangements if all balls were numbered.

8! is to account for the white balls being alike.

8! is to account for the black balls being alike.

(Note: 8! is read "the factorial of 8" and means the product of 8 and all the lower integers, including 1; i.e., 8 x 7 x 6 x 5 x 4 x 3 x 2 x 1.)

Appendix II

Calculation of Free Energy Change by Adding Vacancies to a Crystal

Since $w' = 1$ for the perfect crystal, and there are n vacancies and N atoms arranged among $(N + n)$ sites, then

$$\triangle S_c = k \ln w = k \ln \left[\frac{(N+n)!}{N!\,n!}\right].$$

Using Stirling's approximation

$$\triangle S_c = -k \left[N \ln\left(\frac{N}{N+n}\right) + n \ln\left(\frac{n}{N+n}\right)\right]$$

and

$$\triangle G = G_n - G_p = n \triangle H - T(\triangle S_c + n \triangle S_v)$$

where G_n is the free energy of the crystal with n vacancies, G_p is the free energy of the perfect crystal, and $\triangle G = \triangle H - T \triangle S$.

Substituting

$$G - G_p = n\triangle H_v + kT\left[N\ln\left(\frac{N}{N+n}\right) + n\ln\left(\frac{n}{N+n}\right)\right] - nT\triangle S_v \qquad (4)$$

Separating equation (4)

$$G - G_p = n(\triangle H_v - T\triangle S_v) + kT\left[N\ln\left(\frac{N}{N+n}\right) + n\ln\left(\frac{n}{N+n}\right)\right] \qquad (5)$$

NOTES AND REFERENCES

1. J. D. Fast, *Entropy.* Phillips Technical Library, Endhoven, 1962.
2. *Ibid.*
3. *Ibid.*
4. *Ibid.*
5. G. N. Hatsopoulos and J. H. Keenan, *Principles of General Thermodynamics* (New York: John Wiley and Sons, 1965).
6. O. Bluh and J. D. Elder, *Principles and Applications of Physics* (New York: Interscience, 1955).
7. Fast, *op. cit.*
8. *Ibid.*
9. *Ibid.*
10. R. Emden, *Nature, 141*:908, 1938.
11. A. H. Cottrell, *Theoretical Structural Metallurgy* (London: Edward Arnold, 1955).
12. K. Lonsdale, *Chemistry,* 38:14, 1965.
13. *Ibid.*
14. H. G. Van Buren, *Imperfections in Crystals* (Amsterdam: North-Holland, 1960).
15. Cottrell, *op. cit.*
16. R. A. Swalin, *Thermodynamics of Solids* (New York: John Wiley and Sons, 1962).
17. *Ibid.*
18. J. Weertman and J. R. Weertman, *Elementary Dislocation Theory* (New York: Macmillan, 1964).
19. *Ibid.*
20. H. M. Morris, *The Twilight of Evolution* (Grand Rapids: Baker Book House, 1963).

Chapter 4

Radioactivity Dating Indicates A Young Earth

1

RADIOCARBON DATING†

R. H. BROWN, PH.D.*

Introduction

It is common knowledge that radiocarbon laboratories have determined ages for organic material which in a vast number of cases appear to to be in conflict with the specifications concerning the earth's history given by the book of Genesis and endorsed by the Gospel writers and the apostle Paul in the New Testament. There is an evident need for intensive and careful study in the broad field of radiocarbon dating in order to find the agreement that we have been assured exists between the book of nature and the written Word.

In approaching any body of scientific literature it is well to keep in mind the unavoidable tendency of an investigator to harmonize the information available to him with his general world view. The human mind is designed to integrate and summarize its observations into generalized principles and viewpoints. This characteristic is necessary for the development of understanding and capability. As a consequence of their cultural and educational background, most of the radiocarbon specialists have a world view that is based on uniformitarianism and progressive evolutionary development of life.

In using some of the information provided by Carbon-14 analysis, the seeker for truth who begins with the commonly accepted uniformitarian viewpoint may experience a more difficult and devious

†Portions of this article appear in chapter form in the forthcoming book, *Creation—Accident or Design?* by Harold G. Coffin, Research Professor at the Geoscience Research Institute, Andrews University, Andrews Mich. 49104.

*Professor of Physics, Walla Walla College, Walla Walla, Washington

path toward a fuller understanding than would have been the case if his initial viewpoints had conformed with the guidelines set forth in the Bible. Where scientific observation relates to the divinely inspired testimony, we have been assured that an honest search for truth will result in both increased understanding and in confirmation of the inspired testimony.

Individuals who are leaders in the development and application of Carbon-14 dating techniques are men and women of high ideals, who are intensely devoted to finding truth in their areas of investigation and are meticulous in maintaining a distinction between speculation and firmly substantiated evidence. However, with Carbon-14 dating, as in many other areas of human thought, the dogmatism with which speculative conclusions are advocated commonly increases with the distance one goes from prime sources of information.

Survey of Physical Phenomena

Before considering some recent developments on radiocarbon dating, many readers may appreciate a brief survey of the physical phenomena involved. Stars eject into space some of the matter of which they are composed. This ejected matter represents the chemical composition of its parent star and, consequently, is made up of hydrogen, small amounts of helium, and traces of more complex atoms.

Some of the atoms in this ejected matter are affected by forces which strip away the outer negative electric charge (electrons) and accelerate the positively charged nucleus to extremely high speeds. These high speed atomic nuclei which drift around through interstellar space are called primary cosmic rays.

The earth is constantly bombarded from all directions with primary cosmic ray particles. These particles have sufficient energy to break up atoms which they encounter on reaching the upper levels of the earth's atmosphere. The break-up of nitrogen and oxygen atoms by primary cosmic rays produces neutrons and atoms of carbon, boron, beryllium, helium, hydrogen, and possibly lithium.

Neutrons are uniquely effective agents for producing atomic transmutation. The most frequent reaction produced by neutrons in air transmutes nitrogen into carbon which has 14 units of mass as compared with the 12 units characteristic of ordinary carbon (16½ percent heavier than an ordinary carbon atom), and is radioactive (that is, unstable). In the order of 22 pounds of radioactive carbon are produced per year in the earth's upper atmosphere as a result of reactions produced by primary cosmic rays. This radioactive carbon is oxidized to carbon dioxide, which in turn is mixed throughout the atmosphere by air currents and utilized by plants along with nonradioactive carbon dioxide to form carbohydrates. The high solubility of carbon dioxide in water transfers a large portion of the earth's radioactive carbon to the oceans. Radioactive carbon is distributed through all living material as a result of the dependence of animal life upon plant food.

Death Stops Intake of Carbon-14

Death of a plant or an animal terminates the processes by which its tissue structure receives Carbon-14 from the environment. Since Carbon-14 is unstable and spontaneously converts to nitrogen, the remains of once-living material will contain progressively smaller amounts of Carbon-14 with the passage of time. Laboratory measurements on known amounts of radioactive carbon have established, within an uncertainty of less than 100 years, that in 5,730 years, half of an initial amount of Carbon-14 will "disappear" as a result of radioactive decay into nitrogen. On the basis of this information, 5,730-year-old remains of plants and animals may be expected to contain half as much radioactive carbon as they did at death.

For convenience, data on the radioactive carbon content of a sample is reported by specifying a "radiocarbon age." The radiocarbon age describes the relative amount of radioactive carbon in the sample in terms of the relative amount of radioactive carbon in an oxalic acid standard supplied by the U. S. National Bureau of Standards. The NBS oxalic acid standard of Carbon-14 activity is adjusted to provide a reference based on the average Carbon-14 activity of wood which was growing in A.D. 1850.

The strength in which the NBS standardized oxalic acid is supplied is such that 95 percent of its specific radiocarbon activity is equivalent to the specific radiocarbon activity to be expected from wood growing in A.D. 1950 under conditions that prevailed in A.D. 1850. The radiocarbon age of a sample is the number of years that would be required for the specific radiocarbon activity level defined by the NBS oxalic acid standard to decay to the specific activity level measured in the sample.

Radiocarbon "Time" Is Relative

Radiocarbon ages are based on a 5,568-year half-life for Carbon-

14 decay (the average of early less-precise measurements), rather than on the more accurate value of 5,730 years, in order to avoid confusion in comparing recent determinations with the large number of radiocarbon ages that appeared in the literature during the time when 5,568 years was the best available value for Carbon-14 half-life. Since the radiocarbon time scale is arbitrary and does not directly measure real time, there is no need for basing it on an absolutely accurate determination of half-life.

Those who are unhappy with the 5,568-year half-life convention can convert radiocarbon ages to a 5,730-year-based scale with a simple multiplication by 1.03. A sample with a specific radiocarbon activity equal to one half 95 percent of the specific radiocarbon activity of the NBS oxalic acid standard is assigned a radiocarbon age of 5,568. The radiocarbon date for the time when this sample ceased to exchange carbon with its environment would be 5,568 B.P., or 3618 B.C. (5,568—A.D. 1950).

In summary it may be said that radiocarbon ages are based on a 5,568-year half-life and are standardized against preindustrial-revolution conditions (A.D. 1850), and that A.D. 1950 is used for the zero point on the radiocarbon time scale.[1]

Reasons for basing radiocarbon ages on conditions in A.D. 1850 are of interest. Since A.D. 1850, man has introduced into the earth's atmosphere large amounts of carbon dioxide produced by the use of fossil fuels—coal, oil, and natural gas. These fossil fuels contain a negligible amount of Carbon-14 and are described as "infinite age" on the radiocarbon time scale. During the 100-year period between A.D. 1850 and A.D. 1950, use of fossil fuels released infinite age carbon equivalent to approximately 11 percent of the total carbon presently contained in the atmosphere. Had this contribution of nonradioactive carbon been confined to the atmosphere it would have reduced the radiocarbon activity of the atmosphere by approximately 10 percent.

The actual decrease experienced (Suess effect) was only one to three percent and probably averaged a strong one percent, indicating that a large portion of the carbon released to the atmosphere by man's use of fossil fuels has been absorbed in the ocean (95 percent of the carbon in the earth's carbon dioxide exchange system is contained in the ocean).

Another factor related to human activity that influences the radiocarbon concentration in the atmosphere is the release of neutrons by atomic reactors and nuclear weapons.

By using as a "contemporary" reference the most recent radio-carbon activity level that has not been significantly affected by human activity, radiocarbon ages can more readily be used in studies of the past. The most accurate value for the "contemporary" activity level is considered to be 13.6 disintegrations per minute per gram of plant or animal carbon.

Radiocarbon and Historical Ages

Measurements made in radiocarbon dating laboratories throughout the world do *not* determine dates or historical ages of samples. The laboratory procedures only determine the amount of radioactive carbon which a sample contains at present. The historical time lapse since a given specimen was a part of a living organism which ex-changed carbon with its environment is an *interpretation* based in part on its radiocarbon age. The postulation of a date or age associ-ated with the sample requires an *assumption* concerning the relative amount of radioactive carbon in the environment which supported the life of the organism from which the sample has been derived.

Major research effort is being directed toward developing reliable correlations between radiocarbon age and historical age. If the relative amount of radioactive carbon in the atmosphere had been at the A.D. 1850 level throughout the time life has existed on the earth, radiocarbon ages, when adjusted to the 5,730-year half-life, would be identical with historical age. Tree-ring dating has established a pre-cise and reliable chronology extending back to 59 B.C. By measure-ing the radiocarbon activity in precisely dated wood fiber, a chart can be prepared for converting radiocarbon age into historical age over the past 2,000 years. Such a chart shows fluctuations in the relative amount of Carbon-14 in the atmosphere during this period, but these fluctuations appear to have been limited within a range of less than five percent of the A.D. 1850 level.

Because of the fluctuations in the atmosphere, Carbon-14 activity and the difficulties in standardizing one radiocarbon laboratory against another, the minimum uncertainty in any radiocarbon age is commonly considered to be plus or minus 100 years.[2] Accordingly, if there are no contamination problems, the historical age of a sample which has a radiocarbon age no greater than about 2,000 years may confidently be considered to lie within a range of uncertainty equal to plus or minus twice the uncertainty specified for the radiocarbon age, providing this range is no less than plus or minus 200 years.[3]

Attempts to derive historical age from radiocarbon age yield increasingly uncertain conjectures for samples older than 2,000 years. Tree-ring chronology has been extended from 59 B.C. to approximately 2400 B.C. using the Bristlecone Pine. The growth characteristics of this tree make it unsatisfactory for the establishment of a precise long-term growth-ring sequence. Attempts to correlate Bristlecone Pine growth-rings with radiocarbon ages indicate that either ring counting has over-estimated the age of the oldest Bristlecone Pine material by 500 to 1,000 years, or the relative amount of Carbon-14 in the atmosphere around 2000 B.C. was in the order of ten percent greater than in A.D. 1850.

Radiocarbon Dating and Genesis

Aside from the information supplied in the Book of Genesis, there is at present no firm basis for inferring historical age for any sample with a radiocarbon age greater than 3,500 to 4,000.

Those who accept the Genesis account as inspired and historically valid interpret the radioactive age for ancient material, such as Tertiary oyster shells, anthracite coal, mineral oil, natural gas, et cetera, to indicate that the atmosphere of the earth before the Genesis Flood had a relative Carbon-14 activity no greater than 1/100, and possibly less than 1/1000 of the level that became established by 1500 B.C. (A relative Carbon-14 activity of 1/128 the contemporary level corresponds to decay over seven half-lives, or a radiocarbon age of 39,976. $2^7 = 128$; $7 \times 5,568 = 39,976$.)

Although up to the present no basis has been found for precise and reliable conversion between historical age and radiocarbon ages greater than 3,500, radiocarbon age determinations in the 4,000 to 30,000 range do, nevertheless, give important support to the Book of Genesis. With a particularly appropriate figure of speech, radiocarbon dating has been described by a leading archaeologist as having an effect on previously held archaeological viewpoints equivalent to the devastation produced by an atom bomb.

Radiocarbon dating of spruce trees buried by glacial advance in Wisconsin has forced geologists to *reduce* the presumed time which has elapsed since major glacial advance from 25,000 solar years to 11,400 radiocarbon years. Assuming a one-to-one correspondence between radiocarbon years and solar years results in a drastic compression of the time which previously had been considered available for the development of Western civilization.

Remarkable scarcity of objects which are clearly associated with human activity, and which have radiocarbon ages in excess of 12,000, suggests that the human population has grown from a small beginning in a short period of time. It is highly significant that the greatest radiocarbon ages firmly related to human activity are provided by material from the Middle East, the Ukraine, and the Mediterranean Basin.

Radiocarbon ages for the oldest evidences of man indicate that the earth was populated as a result of migration which spread out in all directions from the Middle East area, reaching the Western Hemisphere by way of Alaska. Radiocarbon dating has established that the recent glacial periods in northern Europe and and northern North America were coincident, that the earliest appearance of man in North America coincided closely with the latest advance of glacial ice across Wisconsin, and that both North America and northern Europe were settled rapidly after the first appearance of man in these regions.

Radiocarbon Age and Farming

By the time corresponding to a radiocarbon age of 7,200, farming had been established throughout a strip of approximately ten degrees latitude in width extending from Greece across southern Asia Minor to Iran. During the succeeding period of time represented by a span of 1,200 "years" on the radiocarbon time scale, farming extended over the Nile delta, northern Egypt, Babylonia, and central Europe.

By the time corresponding to a radiocarbon age of 5,000, farming had become established in northwestern Europe, northwestern Africa, and the Ukraine. Data are lacking concerning the spread of agriculture eastward from Babylonia, but there are remains in India from the highly developed Harappa culture which have radiocarbon ages as great as approximately 4,300. This culture developed elaborate irrigation facilities and had a written language which appears to be unrelated to the writing of subsequent Asian cultures and which modern man has been unable to decipher.

The limited time suggested by radiocarbon dating for the spread of human population over the earth, and for the development of ancient civilization, has led many individuals whose world view is *not* based on the information given in the Bible to seek support for the postulate that in the ancient past the earth's atmosphere contained a *greater* relative amount of Carbon-14 than it has over the

3,000-year period up to A.D. 1850. (Every doubling of the initial relative amount of Carbon-14 in a specimen over the relative amount which characterizes material living in A.D. 1850 would add 5,730 solar years to the difference between the historical age and the radiocarbon age of the specimen, if the historical age is greater than a radiocarbon age based on assumed initial conditions equivalent to those which existed in A.D. 1850.) Search for firm evidence to support a higher Carbon-14 level in the ancient atmosphere has not been fruitful.

Since primary cosmic ray particles are deflected away from the earth by its magnetic field, the role of this field in the Carbon-14 production rate has been investigated. Detailed calculation indicates that a complete disappearance of the earth's magnetic field would no more than double the present Carbon-14 production rate, with consequent extension of the time indicated by the oldest radiocarbon dates by no more than 6,000 years.

A higher level of Carbon-14 activity would be brought about by an increase in the primary cosmic ray activity. Since studies of the cosmic ray effects in meteorites indicate that the cosmic ray flux in the solar system has remained close to its present level over a period of time many orders of magnitude greater than that with which radiocarbon dating is concerned, the only possibility for a large increase in the relative amount of Carbon-14 appears to be through a reduction in the amount of nonradioactive carbon in the atmosphere.

An addition of 17,190 solar years to the historical age of ancient material in this manner would require a reduction of the atmospheric carbon dioxide to one eighth its present concentration ($17,190 = 3 \times 5,730$; $\frac{1}{2} \times \frac{1}{2} \times \frac{1}{2} = \frac{1}{8}$). Since only 0.053 percent by weight of the earth's atmosphere is carbon dioxide at present, and since the fossil record indicates much more extensive and more luxurious vegetation than now covers the earth, a significant reduction of atmospheric carbon dioxide below the present level does not appear to be a reasonable postulate.

It seems much more suitable to think of the earth's ancient atmosphere as characterized by a higher, rather than a below-modern, carbon dioxide composition. Coal, oil, and gas reserves, limestone beds, shales, and vast amounts of organic materials scattered in gravel beds throughout the planet indicate that before the Flood the biosphere was many times richer in carbon than it is today. A plant or animal that might have lived at a time when the biosphere contained the same amount of Carbon-14 but eight times the amount of non-radioactive carbon characteristic of contemporary conditions would at its death have a radiocarbon age of 17,190 "years" in comparison with contemporary materials.

We have already noted that the testimony of radiocarbon dating and the testimony of the Book of Genesis taken together support the view that prior to the Flood the relative amount of radioactive carbon in the atmosphere and in living things was at most 1/100 or possibly less 1/1000 of its present value. The reader must be cautioned that harmony between the historical requirements of the Book of Genesis and radiocarbon ages cannot be obtained by postulating a hundred-fold greater concentration of carbon dioxide in the pre-Flood atmosphere, since carbon dioxide becomes highly toxic when it reaches unit percent levels. It is the amount of carbon in the entire carbon dioxide exchange system, not the relatively small amount contained in the atmosphere, that determines the Carbon-14/Carbon-12 ratio with which we are concerned.

While there are at present no scientific data to indicate that any of the following changes have taken place, it is worth noting that each one is within the range of possibility and would *increase* the relative amount of radioactive carbon in the atmosphere over its pre-Flood level:

(1)   reduction of the earth's magnetic field from a pre-Flood intensity which kept most of the primary cosmic ray particles from interacting with the atmosphere;

(2)   loss of an outer region of water vapor which absorbed primary cosmic rays and cosmic-ray-produced neutrons before they had opportunity to react with nitrogen in the atmosphere;

(3)   removal by rains during and after the Flood of a large portion of the carbon dioxide characteristic of the pre-Flood atmosphere and conversion of this carbon dioxide to precipitated carbonates and carbonates carried in solution by the post-Flood oceans. (It has been reliably estimated that the carbon in the earth that is not presently contained in minerals or fossils is distributed: 86.2 percent in solution in the oceans in a chemical form not directly associated with organic material, 8.7 percent in organic material contained in the oceans, 3.5 percent associated with organic life on land, and 1.6 percent in the atmosphere.)

Thus it seems that continuing developments in the investigation of radioactive dating are certain to bring yet broader and more firm support for the information God has given to us through the written Word.

NOTES AND REFERENCES

1. Stuiver and Suess, Editorial Statements, *Radiocarbon*, Vol. 8, 1966; Half-Life Statement, *Proceedings of the Sixth International Conference on Radiocarbon and Tritium Dating.*
2. *Ibid.*, pp. 27, 213, 340, 453.
3. *Ibid.*, p. 256.

RADIOCARBON CONFIRMS BIBLICAL CREATION (AND SO DOES POTASSIUM-ARGON)

Robert L. Whitelaw, M.S.*

Introduction

Despite the undisguised evolutionary presuppositions that pervade the teaching of earth sciences today, particularly in the many attempts to "fit" the dating of rocks, fossils, and artifacts into approved geological time-tables, when one looks carefully at the various "time-clocks" proposed, the biblical creationist finds himself on surer ground than ever before.

All these time-clocks fall into two classes—the *quantitative* and the *qualitative*. The quantitative clocks are those means by which an actual age in years might be determined. The qualitative are those phenomena that indicate greater or lesser age without determination of actual years.

Of the *quantitative* clocks, only two remain in scientific favor today: the Radiocarbon Method and the Potassium-Argon Method. All others involve shaky assumptions, each assumption often contingent on the previous.

Turning to the *qualitative* time-clocks, two facts are found common to all: (1) Many positively point to, or require, a relatively recent origin of matter. (2) Not a single one can be found to *establish* the evolutionary scale of time, or the order of the geologic ages, or even refute the Bible!

Evolutionist Faces Dilemma

Faced with this dilemma, the evolutionist today clings desperately to the faith that Radiocarbon and Potassium-Argon—or some new clock undiscovered—can be made to support his theories.

But when we look carefully at the basic constants and assumptions

---

*Nuclear Consultant and Professor of Mechanical Engineering, Virginia Polytechnic Institute, Blacksburg, Virginia

in the Radiocarbon Method, we find that it not only confirms biblical history, but also points unmistakably to biblical creation. And when we look with equal care at the highly regarded K-Argon clock for dating rocks we find that it is meaningless *unless* one assumes a creation date; and one creation date turns out to be just as good as another!

In short, neither one of these much-quoted time-clocks is found to *establish* the date of any rock, fossil, or artifact beyond the date of biblical creation, namely about 5000 B.C.

A word here is in order on biblical creation. Does the Bible establish a date, as well as a method? In a specific sense it does not; but in a general sense it most assuredly does. The general *method* is fiat creation—a perfect, natural order brought out of nothing by the word of a sovereign God. The general *time* is clearly at the creation of the first man and woman; a time delineated with sufficient clarity (Gen. 5 and 11 are not just casual genealogies!) that we can establish it about 5000 B.C., yet also with sufficient obscurity that it is not merely an adding-machine problem, as Ussher seemed to think. (See Chart 1)

CHART 1

RECONSTRUCTION OF APPROXIMATE CHRONOLOGY TO BIBLICAL CREATION

Eras	Time	Reference
ERA I: Antediluvian Age (Creation to Flood) (Sources: comparison & evaluation of LXX, Hebrew, Samaritan Pentateuch, et al.)	2000 yrs.	Gen. 5
ERA II: Flood to Crucifixion of Christ	3000 yrs.	
Flood to Abram's departure (1070 years)		Gen. 11
Abram to Exodus (430 years)		Ex. 12:41; Gal. 3:17
Exodus to Temple (580 years)		I Kings 6:1; Acts 13
Temple to Babylonian captivity (363 years)		Kings and Chronicles
Babylonian captivity (70 years)		Jeremiah and Daniel
Cyrus' edict to the Cross (487 yrs.)		Ezra 1 and Daniel 9
ERA III: Present Age (since the Cross)	1938 yrs.	

6918

The Carbon-14 Time-clock

This ingenious method by W. F. Libby,[1] put in simple terms goes as follows: High energy cosmic rays from outer space are absorbed in the earth's upper atmosphere by knocking free neutrons out of the nuclei of oxygen, nitrogen, argon, etc. These free neutrons, emerging at high energy, are slowed down by collision with air molecules, after which most of them are captured in the nuclei of nitrogen atoms, which, of course, are everywhere abundant. This capture in turn releases two isotopes, Carbon-14 and monatomic hydrogen, H-1. The C-14 soon combines with the oxygen of the air to form radioactive carbon dioxide, which diffuses uniformly throughout the lower atmosphere along with natural carbon dioxide.

(NOTE: There is *no* reliable secular means of dating any historical event prior to Christ *apart* from the Bible. Few historians know this, and fewer still are those who admit it. Almost all the elaborate charts and dates of ancient empires published today have been built up from Ptolemy's Canon, or supposed synchronisms with solar eclipses, or Greek archons, or olympiads, all of which methods can be shown worthless.)

The radiocarbon in the carbon dioxide of the atmosphere thus enters into the "carbon exchange cycle" by which all life is sustained. On land, by the action of photosynthesis (in sunlight), all vegetation removes CO_2 from the air, converting it into new growth, flower, and fruit. Herbivorous animals eat the vegetation, and carnivorous animals eat other animals, thus diffusing the CO_2 from the air throughout both vegetable and animal kingdoms. Meanwhile, all air-breathing animals take the oxygen of the air and exhale carbon dioxide from their bodies, thus completing the cycle.

In the sea, a similar cycle prevails. Phytoplankton remove the dissolved carbon dioxide and are then eaten, and shellfish exchange carbon dioxide for carbonate and bicarbonate ions in forming their shells.

The "turnaround time" for this cycle has been estimated as 500 to 1,000 years; so that after several thousand years from creation, all *living things* in the carbon exchange reservoir should be uniformly radioactive with each other and with the earth's atmosphere, *provided the intensity of the cosmic rays striking the earth varied little over a thousand years.*

This was Libby's first assumption, which was reasonably substantiated by samples of flora and fauna from many parts of the earth, and the atmosphere itself, all showing specific activities between 14.5 and 16.3 disintegrations per minute per gram.

Death Starts Radiocarbon Clock

Now consider what happens when a living organism dies, whether plant or animal, for it is here that the C-14 clock begins to measure time.

At the instant of death, exchange of carbon with the world reservoir ceases, while the fraction of radiocarbon which was present at death continues to decay at the uniform rate (exponential) by which 50 percent changes back to nitrogen every 5,568 years (this being known as its "half-life"). Thus, if a dead organism—whether it be a piece of wood out of Pharaoh's tomb, or a fossil leaf or bone—is analyzed for radioactivity centuries later, its intensity will be 50 percent after 5,568 years, 25 percent after 11,136 years, and so on.

(Editor's Note: Half-life for carbon is an estimate, and 5,568 has been preferred. More precise values might be 5,730 or 5,760 years.)

With such knowledge, it would appear to be a simple matter to calculate the elapsed time since death of such a specimen, provided that (a) no seepage of water or other factor had added C-14 to the specimen since death, and (b) *the fraction of radiocarbon it possessed at death is known.*

The first proviso can be met by selecting specimens with great care. The second is much more difficult. Libby and his colleagues tackled it as follows: They reasoned that if the *present rate of production* of radiocarbon in the atmosphere can be shown equal to the *present rate of disintegration*, then we could safely assume that cosmic radiation has remained constant at its value throughout the history of living matter. (This assumption is not strictly valid for several reasons, but let us examine what they found.)

The *average* rate of production of free neutrons by cosmic rays in the outer atmosphere was computed by measurement to be 2.6 neuts/cm^2 per second.

The production rate of radiocarbon was assumed equal to the neutron production rate, since each neutron soon finds a nitrogen nucleus and produces an atom of C-14, except for about one percent which produce tritium.

The total amount of carbon in the world exchange reservoir was next estimated by careful analysis, and found to be:

	gm/sq. cm. earth's surface
In ocean "carbonate"	7.25
In ocean dissolved organic	0.59
In biosphere and atmosphere	0.45
Total	8.29

Dividing the neutron production rate of 2.6 by the 8.29 grams of carbon in the exchange reservoir (for 1 sq. cm. of earth's surface) gives a *specific* production rate of radiocarbon today equal to .314 atoms/gm-sec, or 18.8 atoms/gm-minute.

Production, Disintegration Differ

When Libby compared this production rate of 18.8 with the specific activities between 14.5 and 16.3 which he had found, he reconciled them by the statement: "The agreement seems to be sufficiently within the experimental errors involved so that we have reason for confidence in the theoretical picture. . . ."[2]

That is to say, even though the present production rate of radiocarbon *differs* from the present disintegration rate (with the best of valid corrections applied) by almost 20 percent, *they were assumed to be the same.* For one reason this made reading the timeclock easy. But even more, if the discrepancy were allowed, a recent origin of cosmic radiation would also have to be allowed, which was unthinkable. Quoting Libby directly:

> If one were to imagine that the cosmic radiation had been turned off until a short while ago, the enormous amount of radiocarbon necessary to the equilibrium state would not have been manufactured, and the specific radioactivity of living matter would be much less than the rate of production calculated from the neutron intensity. . . .[3]

Thus, despite the discrepancy of almost twenty percent shown above, the investigators proceeded to reason that no such "turning on" of cosmic radiation could have occurred, and that "there exists at the present time a complete balance between the rate of disintegration of radiocarbon atoms and the rate of assimilation of new radiocarbon atoms for all material in the life-cycle."[4]

Still later, the dating method was applied to ancient matter. Yet no date older than about 30,000 years was found, a matter of no small consternation among uniformitarian scientists, to whom 30,000 years is just yesterday.

Potential Means of Adjustment

What, then, is the truly objective approach to the radiocarbon production and disintegration rates reported? Clearly, it should be compared with the *total* scientific data before us, of which the biblical record itself is a most important part, not lightly to be ignored. And in doing so, the creationist quickly notes that the observed deficiency between disintegration rate and production rate is *exactly* what one would expect if biblical creation be true. To explain the relative magnitudes of the two rates a number of possible explanations lie before us:

(1) Intensity of cosmic radiation has been constant since creation, giving the production rate of 18.8 C-14 atoms/gm.-minute calculated by Libby. The *present* average specific activity in the carbon-exchange reservoir of 16.1 dis/gm.-m. then leads us back to a creation date of 15,000 years ago. (See Figure 1)

(2) The cosmic radiation today is producing neutrons (and therefore C-14 atoms) at a rate more like 3.5 per second per sq. cm. of earths surface, i.e., 35 percent higher than Libby estimated. The higher value is adequately supported by the 4½ to 1 variation with latitude, and the 5:1 variation with altitude reported in Libby, 1955.

A similar re-evaluation of carbon in the exchange reservoir, in the light of data by Rubey[5] warrants reducing the amount from 8.29 to about 7.8 gm./sq. cm. The new and better value of specific production rate of C-14 atoms would then be 3.5/7.8, giving .45 atoms/gm.-sec. or 27 atoms/gm.-minute.

If 27 atoms/gm.-min. have been produced on the average since creation, and the present disintegration rate is only 16.1, this indicates creation about 7,000 years ago in accord with Scripture. (See Figure 2)

Thus it is that the Carbon-14 timeclock discovered by modern science not only points clearly to an early "turning on" of cosmic radiation, i.e., a universe that appeared quite recently, but even better, the closer one examines the hands of this clock the more one confirms the very chronology of Scripture—as every true scientist should expect.

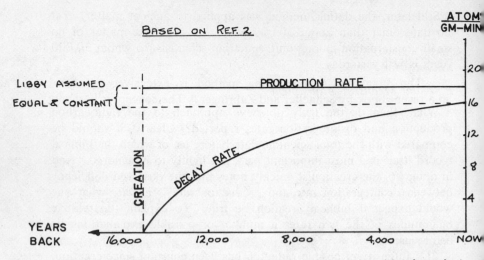

Figure 1. Possibly the intensity of cosmic radiation has been constant since creation, giving the production r of 18.8 C-14 atoms/gm.-minute calculated by Libby. The present average specific activity in the carb reservoir of 16.1 disintegrations/gm.-minute then leads back to the creation date of 15,000 years ago.

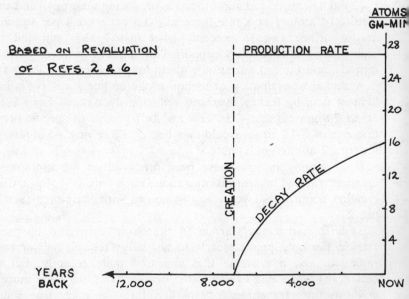

Figure 2. Cosmic radiation today is producing neutrons and therefore C-14 atoms at the rate of 27 atoms/g minute. If 27 C-14 atoms/gm.-minute have been produced on the average since creation, and the pres disintegration rate is only 16.1, this indicates creation about 7,000 years ago in accord with Scriptures.

The Potassium-Argon Timeclock

Let us look now at the second timeclock to which scientists today have turned, finding scant support for their geologic ages in the radiocarbon clock.

The Potassium-Argon dating method is extensively analyzed in a recent book by Schaeffer and Zahringer.[6] The concept is basically simple except that it involves a thoroughly unscientific assumption which nullifies the whole method, as will readily be seen.

First, it was discovered (in 1905) that all natural potassium is radioactive, and second, that its beta activity is due to the tiny fraction of K-40 which it contains (12 parts in 100,000). It was then found that K-40 decays simultaneously in two ways, 92 percent of the decay being beta emission, to yield Ca-40 and 8 percent by isomeric transition and gamma emission to yield Argon 40.

This latter emission has a half-life of 1.31 billion years and converts an atom of metallic K-40 into an atom of gaseous Argon-40. That is to say, every 1,310,000,000 years half of the original K-40 (which was less than 1/10,000 of the original potassium) would appear as Argon-40 gas.

Now since potassium-bearing rocks are plentiful in the earth's crust, this timeclock seemed made to order to verify the multibillions of years postulated by evolutionary geology. Only two problems needed to be solved: (1) how to measure the fantastically small quantities of argon trapped in the rock specimen, and (2) how to determine what portion of this argon, in all those billions of years, came from potassium decay, and what portion came in from the earth's atmosphere, where, unfortunately, it is very plentiful (almost 1 percent by volume).

About 190 pages of Schaeffer and Zahringer's report are devoted to explaining the brilliant techniques by which the first problem has been solved, and to citing the many ancient dates thereby affixed to sediments, rocks, and meteorites of all kinds. Only two pages (7-8) are given to solving the second problem—how much of the argon came from potassimum decay—a solution which is absolutely vital to any age determination.

It is this problem, and its solution, which demands careful scientific examination.

Potassium to Argon Decay Studied

Since argon accounts for almost one percent of the earth's atmosphere, over a period of many years some atmospheric argon will be absorbed into any sample being taken. However, and this is of vital importance, the atmospheric argon trapped in a tiny sample of internal potassium that has supposedly been decaying for billions of years *would have the isotopic distribution of billions of years ago,* which would by no means be that of today.

Now isotopic distribution in atmospheric argon today is 99.6 percent Argon-40, 0.337 percent Argon-36, and 0.063 percent Argon-38, all the isotopes being stable. Armed with this information, the Potassium-Argon Method was then constructed on a brilliant deduction based on a colossal oversight!

It was deduced that, if the tiny sample of argon taken in a rock specimen contained an infusion of atmospheric argon, it would show up by the presence of Ar-36, since the argon that decayed from potassium in the specimen would be pure Ar-40. (The trace of Ar-38 was dismissed as too small to be detected.) This being so, it becomes a simple matter to measure the quantity of Ar-36 in the specimen, multiply it by 295.6 (i.e., the Ar-40/Ar-36 ratio in the air) to determine the amount of Ar-40 that came in from the atmosphere, and finally subtract this amount from the total Ar-40 found. Thus, the remainder would be the Argon-40 formed over billions of years from potassium alone. The equation for this operation is given[7] as:

$$\text{Radioargon-40} = \text{Total Argon-40} - 295.6 \times \text{Argon-36} \quad (1)$$

And the colossal assumption behind this equation, without a shred of data or logic to support it, is that over the eons of time the radioargon was being formed, the ratio of Ar-36 to Ar-40 in the atmosphere *has remained exactly the same as it was the day the rock was formed.* One could scarcely find a more glaring example of the blinding power of the uniformitarian faith!!

Facts Nullify K/Ar Timeclock

What, then, are the scientific facts and probabilities that nullify the above assumption, and even turn the hands of this timeclock toward creation?

First, it can be shown that Ar-36 is a probable product of cosmic radiation bombarding the earth's outer atmosphere, just as is radiocarbon. Several nuclear reaction sequences leading to Ar-36 in the presence of free energetic neutrons and photons can be shown.

Second, it follows that over a billion-year span (assuming such a span really occurred!) the Ar-36 in the atmosphere would have slowly increased compared to the Ar-40, barring some process of Ar-36 destruction not yet found.

Third, it follows that if cosmic radiation began with creation only a few thousands of years back, the present Ar-36 fraction may easily have built up from zero even in that short time.

Finally, then, it follows that the constant "295.6" in equation (1) must increase rapidly with specimen age, and for a specimen which trapped a piece of atmosphere at the instant of creation it would be highest of all, and completely unknown.

The conclusion is that equation (1)—but with a totally unknown constant—is just as valid for rocks formed at a creation 7,000 years ago as for rock formed at a creation 7,000,000,000 years ago. It tells absolutely nothing about the date of the rock until one first assumes a date of creation *and* a rate of buildup of Ar-36 in the air thereafter. Only then can the constant even be estimated, much less be determined exactly.

In closing it should be noted that the basic equation (1), even as it stands, is used to determine quantities of radioargon (left side of equation) in *trillionths* of a cubic centimeter, as the *difference* between two quantities on the right side each a thousand to ten thousand times greater. Every scientific investigator knows how untrustworthy is such a procedure. In this particular case the probable error in the result is well over 50 percent.

The errors of ± 10 percent cited for many samples in the latter pages of Schaeffer and Zahringer are estimated gravimetric errors only. The authors apparently ignore the dominating influence of uncertainty and variations in the constant of 295.6, which, of course, swamps out all others.

This then is the timeclock without hands—without even a face— upon which evolutionary faith now depends to prop up its desperate belief in a world that never began, a creation that never occurred, and a Creator who never created and no longer exists!

And the record of Scripture was never so sure!

NOTES AND REFERENCES

1. W. F. Libby, *Radiocarbon Dating* (Chicago: University of Chicago Press, 1952; second edition, 1955).
2. *Ibid.*, 2nd ed., p. 7.
3. *Ibid.*

4. *Ibid.*, p. 8.
5. W. W. Rubey, "Geological Evidence Regarding the Source of the Earth's Hydrosphere and Atmosphere," *Science*, 112:20 (1950).
6. O. A. Schaeffer and J. Zahringer, *Potassium Argon Dating* (New York: Springer Verlag, 1966).
7. *Ibid.*, p. 8.

RADIOCARBON AND POTASSIUM-ARGON DATING
IN THE LIGHT OF NEW DISCOVERIES IN COSMIC RAYS

ROBERT L. WHITELAW

Introduction

Of the various "clocks" proposed for dating events in geological history, the two in principal favor today are radiocarbon, for events in the biosphere, and potassium-argon, for events in the lithosphere.

The C-14 or radiocarbon clock presumes to date the death of any biological specimen, animal or vegetable, with reasonable accuracy up to six or eight half-lives of Carbon-14 (about 45,000 years). It has been in extensive use since 1950 by leading universities of the world, as witness the exhaustive listings of almost 10,000 dates in the annual journal, Radiocarbon.

(It should be noted here, in passing, that these dates, available for any layman to read, have profoundly disturbing implications for the famous geological time scale and for the eons of time demanded by the evolutionist. Almost every uncovered biological specimen is found to be datable; every fossil, bone, cultural deposit, buried log, vegetation, gyttja, peat, and even much coal and petroleum; all appear to lie within the measureable 45,000 year figure!)

The potassium-argon clock presumes to date entrapment of any tiny sample of potassium-bearing rock, based upon assumptions and methods described earlier,[1] and generally yields dates between 1 and 10 billion.[2]

Both Clocks Based on Assumption

Both clocks are *absolutely* dependent upon accurate knowledge of a tiny constituent of the earth's atmosphere at the time of the event being dated. The radiocarbon clock (as proposed by Libby[3] and faithfully adhered to by the scientific community since) *assumes* that the C-14 concentration throughout the living world was the same at the death of the specimen as it is today.

This assumption is based on two prior assumptions: (a) that the production rate of C-14 in the outer atmosphere had long before approached equilibrium with its decay rate, i.e., that "creation," if it occurred at all, was long before living matter; and (b) that no cosmic events occurred in the last 45,000 years that could possibly change the C-14 production rate or decay rate.

A relatively recent creation date was, of course, too preposterous for any "respectable" scientist to contemplate, although other events far more preposterous, so long as they do not demand the hand of a Creator, are "scientifically" quite believable, as Wald[4] and others openly testify.

Assumptions of Potassium-Argon Clock

Turning to the potassium-argon clock, we find it hanging upon a thread of assumption even more tenuous than that of the radiocarbon clock.

The fraction of total argon in the atmosphere today is about 9/10 of one percent, and about 0.337 percent of this (1 part in 300) is *now* known to be the isotope Argon-36, the balance being Argon-40. Furthermore, the very existence of A-36 in the atmosphere has been known and measurable only within the last 25 years, so that we cannot even say for sure what its concentration was a mere 100 years ago!

Nonetheless, in order to read the potassium-argon clock, its advocates blandly *assume* that when the tiny rock specimen was trapped in the molten state, no matter how many billion years ago, the fraction of A-36 in the total argon trapped with it *was the same as it is today!* And they further *assume* that whatever atmosphere infused next to the sample throughout geologic time always had this same fraction of A-36.

In looking at these two sets of assumptions—those for the radiocarbon vs. those for the potassium-argon clock—we find an interesting disparity. From the very first, Libby made his case for the radiocarbon clock on the fact that the earth is *not* an isolated system; that its outer atmosphere is in fact constantly bombarded by high-energy cosmic rays (of energy and even substance unknown!); and that these rays produce free neutrons, which in turn react with nitrogen nuclei to produce Carbon-14.

Potassium-argon clock-readers, on the other hand, build their case essentially upon an opposite assumption. They demand an earth whose atmosphere maintains its ratio of A-36/A-40 unaltered over time spans that dwarf the imagination. Billions of years of solar radiation, magnetic flares, interstellar dust—not to speak of notable eruptions and cataclysms upon the earth's surface—are swept aside as of no consequence.

Show us, we are told in effect, what could possibly change the atmospheric inventory of Argon-36; and until you do we will take our scieintific stand upon the ratio A-40/A-36 being 295.6 yesterday, today, and forever!

Which View of Atmosphere Correct?

Which of these two views of the earth's atmosphere is correct? To answer we need only let the scientific facts speak for themselves, and the later the facts the better the case, as we shall see.

With respect to radiocarbon being constantly produced in the outer reaches of the atmosphere by cosmic rays, clearly Libby was correct, even though the actual nature of cosmic rays was not fully known. He was even correct in discovering that the production rate is apparently still some 20 percent greater than the decay rate, a fact which points directly toward a recent creation as detailed in a previous paper.[5] His only significant error was in dismissing this 20 percent difference as "experimental error" on the grounds that a recent creation was unthinkable.

Next, let us look at the idea that the A-40/A-36 ratio has been fixed at 295.6 throughout geological time. This is certainly no fundamental, inviolate physical relationship like the gravitational constant, or e = mc²! Rather, this ratio involves a temporary state of only one region of the geosphere, irradiated and bombarded from without, infused with dust and vapor from within, constantly being stripped of nitrogen, carbon dioxide, and oxygen in one place and replenished elsewhere, and all these elementary processes well known since only yesterday, so to speak!

Yet we are being asked to believe that two of the constituents of this atmosphere, the most active and unstable region of earth, have maintained the same ratio for billions of years. Surely by every canon of scientific method, the burden of proof is upon those who put forward such a theory.

Case Against Constant Argon Ratio

But the case against a constant argon ratio in the atmosphere— the main "prop" of the potassium-argon method—rests upon still better evidence.

First, it is not difficult to postulate a number of reasonably probable A-36 production processes: (a) If cosmic rays are rich in high-energy photons, as in the Van Allen belt, one sequence of gamma-n reactions leads from Argon-40 to Argon-36. (Argon-40 bombarded by an energetic photon loses a neutron and becomes Argon-39, and so on down to Argon-36.) (b) Another sequence may well employ the high-energy neutrons both in and from cosmic rays. An n-alpha reaction converts Argon-40 to Sulphur-37, which promptly decays to Chlorine-37 with a half-life of 5.04 minutes. A further n-2n or gamma-n reaction produces Chlorine-36, which slowly decays to Argon-36 (half-life 3×10^5 years). (c) Still another source of Argon-36, by similar proceses, can be the chlorine in sea-spray carried to high altitudes by great storms, or potassium-bearing volcanic dust from the many eruptions that have shaken the earth.

The *second* and even more potent argument in favor of Argon-36 build-up in the atmosphere is the astounding new knowledge of the nature and energy of cosmic rays themselves—information so new and unexpected that it is rocking the foundations of *any* notion of atmospheric equilibrium.

New Knowledge of Cosmic Rays

An excellent survey of this new knowledge of cosmic rays, still growing in its total implications, is given by Stephen Rosen in *Science and Technology*.[6] The entire article is pertinent, but it suffices to quote a few passages for one to begin to realize how much "science" must now be unlearned and how much has yet to be learned:

> Since the advent of instrumented satellites and space probes, many new questions have arisen, and consequently there are now additional problems to solve. For instance, we are still not certain where cosmic rays come from, nor precisely how they travel here. We do not know how or why they are able to reach the energies they do—energies that far exceed those we can produce in our biggest accelerations. . . .
>
> For instance, we have not always known that cosmic rays are energetic, extraterrestrial protons and nuclei of heavier elements. Until the 1930's they were thought to be electrons. . . .
>
> The curve in Fig. 1 . . . suggests that something is happening on a galactic scale—the sources of the cosmic rays may be chang-

ing, or perhaps they are coming from different "storage regions."
. . .

The highest energy of a cosmic ray observed—10^{20} eV— is *more than a billion times* the energy obtainable at present in the most powerful accelerators on earth. . . .

It seems likely, but is by no means a certainty, that all of these *high-energy* particles are protons. There is no doubt, however, that the great majority of *all* cosmic-ray particles are protons, exceeding nuclei heavier than helium by about 13 times. Particles representing helium nuclei amount to perhaps 8 percent of the total, and the remaining heavier nuclei less than 1 percent. . . .[7]

Additional confirmation of these startling findings is given in a brief survey of work by P. H. Fowler, which is reported in *Scientific Research*.[8]

Conclusions

Further references and quotations would only enhance implications of these new discoveries, the key words being "energy," "changing," and "do not know"! Suffice it to say, in closing, that the nucleus of Argon-36 is only *nine* times heavier than helium, so that even if no mechanism whatsoever were found for conversion of other isotopes into Argon-36, *a certain fraction of cosmic rays themselves* are now known to be the nuclei of argon. And since we are talking about a buildup of Argon-36 to only 1/30,000 part of the atmosphere, the number of years of cosmic rays necessary may be well within the 7,000 years since biblical creation!

NOTES AND REFERENCES

1. R. L. Whitelaw, "Radiocarbon Confirms Biblical Creation," *Creation Research Society Quarterly*, 5:78-83 (1968).
2. O. A. Schaeffer and J. Zahringer, *Potassium-Argon Dating* (New York: Springer Verlag, 1966).
3. W. F. Libby, *Radiocarbon Dating* (Chicago: University of Chicago Press, 1955).
4. George Wald, *The Origin of Life, the Physics and Chemistry of Life* (New York: Simon & Schuster, 1955), p. 3.
5. Whitelaw, *op. cit.*
6. Stephen Rosen, *Science and Technology*, November 1968, pp. 22-30.
8. *Scientific Research*, October 28, 1968, p. 25.

4

COSMOLOGICAL IMPLICATIONS OF EXTINCT RADIOACTIVITY FROM PLEOCHROIC HALOS

ROBERT V. GENTRY, M.S.*

Pleochroic halos, which are minute discolorations formed in such substances as biotite (mica)[1] and cordierite[2] by alpha particle emission from small radioactive inclusions in the host material, have in some cases been investigated with reference to the stability of the decay constant over geological time.[3]

It has been reported in this connection that autoradiographic studies on Pre-Cambrian mica show slightly radioactive inclusions for type D halos.[4] These D halos were previously thought to be due to Ra-226 ($T_{1/2} = 1620$ years) by Henderson, and have heretofore been considered completely devoid of radioactivity.[5] In addition the D halos were previously described as possessing no ring structure.

However, in my own research a light outer ring surrounding the inner aureole has been observed in some very dense D halos[6] in the Ballyellen mica. Further research on D halos reflects alpha activity, possibly from U-236 or Np-237 with an admixture of U-238 and U-235, whereas the U-238 contribution seems to predominate in the later stages.

A largely overlooked aspect of pleochroic halo phenomena involves the restrictions which certain types of halos place on the time period of formation of the basic crustal material of the earth from raw matter, irrespective of the theory that is used to account for the primary existence of the matter. It is to be expected that nuclides with long half-lives, such as U-238 ($T_{1/2} = 4.5 \times 10^9$ years) and Th-232 ($T_{1/2} = 1.4 \times 10^{10}$ years), would produce halos, and such is the case.[7]

It is not generally recognized that halos due to certain short half-life polonium isotopes (sometimes erroneously identified as "emanation halos"[8]) also exist in far greater abundance than uranium and

---

Associated with the Institute of Planetary Science, Columbia Union College, Takoma Park, Maryland

thorium halos in some mica samples. All previous attempts to account for the existence of the polonium halos have been from the standpoint of a hydrothermal mode of formation.[9]

In the hydrothermal mode it is envisaged that radioactive solutions containing U-238 and daughter products flowed through a small conduit in the mica, thus causing coloration along the conduit and in some cases coloration about small inclusions due to preferential precipitation of certain elements. There is little question that some halos have formed by this process as in many instances uniform coloration may be observed surrounding minute veins in the mica. However, some halos appear to have developed around very small nuclei in the conduits with no trace of radioactive staining along the vein, thus implying that the radioactive nuclides responsible for halo formation were primary constituents of the nucleus.

Two Hypotheses Possible

More significantly, personal observations of a large number of halos indicate that in many cases the polonium, uranium, and thorium halos have formed around very small inclusions with no visible conduit or crack in the mica connecting the halo nuclei. In this case where halos have formed about point nuclei there are only two possibilities: either (1) the small radioactive inclusions crystallized first with the mica subsequently forming around them, or (2) the inclusions were introduced somehow after the mica was formed.

Although the latter case has been considered a possibility[10] there are serious questions about this hypothesis, especially for the polonium halos. Halo nuclei of 1-2 microns in radius are not uncommon for the polonium halos and it is difficult to conceive of a mechanism that would introduce inclusions of this size into large thick mica crystals without leaving a damage trail of some sort which would be optically visible. The relatively short half-life of the Po isotopes raises still another objection to this hypothesis by severely restricting the allowable time period for secondary deposition.

Furthermore, when cleaving the mica to obtain surfaces on which the halo nuclei are exposed, the mica definitely shows evidence of having completely enclosed the inclusion, thus indicating that it had crystalized around the inclusion. It is also significant that polonium halos have been found in cordierite,[11] so that the secondary depositional mode is especially ruled out for this mineral.

Thus by process of elimination, the most clearly evident mode of

108

halo formation for the polonium halos (which arise from point nuclei) is that halo nuclei contained either polonium isotopes or short half-life beta decaying isotopes of bismuth or lead at the time of mica crystallization. For example, since beta emitters do not produce coloration in mica, the formation of the disc-like Po-210 halo may have resulted from either Po-210 ($T_{1/2} = 138$ days) directly, or from Bi-210 ($T_{1/2} = 5$ days) or Pb-210 ($T_{1/2} = 22$ years) by beta decay into Po-210.

The two-ring Po-214 halo could have formed directly from Po-214 ($T_{1/2} = 164$ u sec.) or from the beta emitters Bi-214 ($T_{1/2} = 19.7$ min.) or Pb-214 ($T_{1/2} = 26.8$ min.). The three ring Po-218 halo differs from the above halos in that it was either formed directly from Po-218 ($T_{1/2} = 3$ min.) or possibly from the nuclides Bi-218 or Pb-218 which beta decay into Po-218.

The significant point here is that, while the properties of Bi-218 and Pb-218 are as yet unknown,[12] they are probably beta emitters with half-lives much shorter than that of Po-218. (The same conclusions are obtained even if progenitors with atomic number less than 82 are considered as the initial parent nuclides of these halos, since they, too, would be short half-life beta emitters.)

Since Po-214 and Po-210 are alpha emitters which are successive decay products of Po-218, a three-ring halo, such as one shown in Figure 1 will result from the initial presence of about 10^9 atoms of either Po-218, Bi-218, or Pb-218 in the central inclusion. The inner ring in Figure 1 is due to alpha emission from Po-210 (radius = 18.8 microns); the second ring corresponds to Po-218 (radius = 22.5

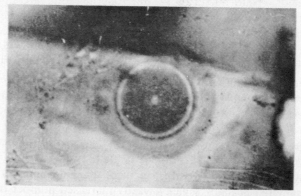

Fig. 1 Po-218 Halo (Enlarged 470X)

microns); while the outer ring corresponds to Po-214 (radius = 34 microns).

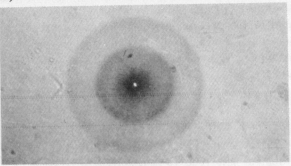

Fig. 2 Po-214 Halo (Enlarged 540X)

The halo in Figure 2 shows an inner ring due to Po-210, an outer ring due to Po-214, and can be accounted for by the initial presence

Fig. 3 Po-210 Halo (Enlarged 470X)

of either Po-214, Bi-214, or Pb-214 in the central inclusion. Figure 3 shows overlapping Po-210 halos due to the presence of either Po-210, Bi-210, or Pb-210 in the inclusions.

It can be demonstrated that the radon isotopes were not progenitors of these polonium halos, since other rings would be visible due to alpha particle emission from these isotopes if this were the case. Using the fission track etching process,[13] numerous background fission tracks may be observed to emanate from the central inclusion of U-238 halos, while no background fission tracks have been observed to emanate from the central inclusion of the polonium halos.

In addition, several mica samples containing U-238 and polonium halos have been irradiated with a neutron flux of about 10^{17} n/cm². These irradiated U halos reveal a vastly increased number of induced fission tracks, while the irradiated polonium halos still exhibit a complete absense of tracks. These experimental results indicate the absence of U in polonium halos and contradict the hypothesis that the polonium isotopes in these halos were initially derived from uranium.

Autoradiographic experiments carried out over a period of several months sometimes reveal alpha particle tracks from the U and Th halos, but none have ever been observed from the polonium halos. It is also possible to rule out preferential deposition of short-life nuclides due to laminar flow of radioactive solutions as a possible source of the radioactivity of these halo nuclei, since gross discoloration over wide areas is evident where laminar flow occurs.

New Halo Type

In addition, a new type of pleochroic halo (type Y) has been found in a Canadian mica. The Y halos bear no relation to the well-known U-238 and Th-232 halos, since both the magnitude of the halo radii and the ring structure are anomalous. The Y halos have an outer radius of about 26 microns, corresponding to an alpha particle energy of about 6.6 MeV.

Although it is not possible to unequivocally identify the isotope responsible for the Y halos, Bi-211 ($T_{1/2} = 2$ m) has correct decay energy and is tentatively identified as the parent nuclide. As was the case for the polonium halos, a fission track analysis revealed the absence of uranium in the central inclusion of this halo.

Figure 4 is a micrograph of the two Y halos referred to above. The light inner ring in one of the halos corresponds closely to the size of the Po-210 halo, thus implying the central inclusion may have initially contained a combination of the alpha emitters Bi-211 and Po-210. An alternate explanation would be that the inclusion initially contained Pb-211 and Pb-210, with beta decay respectively into Bi-211 and Po-210.

Recent acquisition of Wiman's[14] remaining halo collection revealed the presence of a halo of about 55-60 micron radius as measured from the edge of a large inclusion, thus tending to establish the existence of halo radii far in excess of any expected from U or Th halos. It was pointed out previously that only fairly short half-life alpha emitters could be responsible for these giant halos.[15]

Conclusion

It thus appears that short half-life nuclides of either polonium, bismuth, or lead were incorporated into halo nuclei at the time of mica crystallization and significantly enough existed without the

Fig. 4 Y Halos (Enlarged 470X)

parent nuclides of the uranium series. For the Po-218 halo only a matter of minutes could elapse between the formation of the Po-218 and subsequent crystallization of the mica; otherwise the Po-218 would have decayed, and no ring would be visible. The occurrence of these halo types is quite widespread, one or more types having been personally observed in the micas from Canada (Pre-Cambrian), Sweden, and Japan.

The point in question, and one which has not been heretofore considered seriously, is whether any of these variant halos represent *prima facie* evidence of extinct natural radioactivity due to primordial short half-life alpha emitters. It is believed that the accumulated evidence from the polonium halos, the Y halos, and the giant halos provides an affirmative answer to this question.

It is difficult to reconcile these results with current cosmological theories which envision long time-periods between nucleosynthesis and crustal formation. It is suggested that these halos are more nearly in accord with a cosmological model which would envision an instantaneous fiat creation of the earth. The words of Scripture relative to this event are, "By the word of the Lord were the heavens made; and all the host of them by the breath of his mouth. For he spake, and it was *done;* he commanded, and it stood fast" (Psa. 33:6, 9).

Acknowledgments

I wish to express my sincere appreciation to Drs. H. B. S. Cooke, C. G. I. Friedlaender, G. C. Milligan, and E. W. Guptill of the Geology and Physics Departments, Dalhousie University, Halifax, for the loan of Dr. Henderson's fine pleochroic halo collection. Dr. Joly's halo specimens, which were very kindly loaned to me by Dr. J. H. J. Poole of Trinity College, have been of exceptional value, and Dr. D. E. Kerr-Lawson, Swastika Labs, Swastika, Ontario, generously made a gift of his remaining halo specimens.

Valuable mica specimens were also received from Dr. J. A. Mandarino, Royal Ontario Museum, Dr. B. Loberg, Stockholm University, Dr. I. Hayase, Kyoto University, Dr. F. Mendes, Lisbon University, Dr. M. Matthias, University of Cape Town, and Dr. R. Gorbatschev, University of Uppsala. Certain facilities of the Oak Ridge National Laboratory were kindly made available through the courtesy of Dr. A. E. Cameron and Mr. Rodger Neidigh of ORNL.

Finally, I wish to express my gratitude to Drs. C. L. Thrash, A. M. Thrash, L. B. Hewitt, Charles Graves, and Mr. R. E. Crawford for support of this research through a grant from the Archaeological Research Foundation of New York City.

NOTES AND REFERENCES

1. J. Joly, "The Genesis of Pleochroic Halos," *Phil. Trans. Roy. Soc.,* London, A 217:51 (1917); see also D. E. Kerr-Lawson, *Pleochroic Haloes in Biotite from Near Murray Bay.* University of Toronto Studies, Geological Series, No. 24:54-71 (1927).
2. C. Mahadevan, "Pleochroic Halos in Cordierite," *Ind. J. Physics,* 1:445 (1927).
3. J. Joly, "The Age of the Earth," *Nature,* 109:480 (1922).
4. R. V. Gentry, "Pleochroic Halos and the Age of the Earth," *Am. J. Phys.,* 33:878A (1965).
5. G. H. Henderson, *Proc. Roy. Soc.,* A 173:250 (1939).
6. Robert V. Gentry, "Variant Pleochroic Halos and Extinct Radioactivity," *Trans. Am. Geophysical Union,* 47:421 (1966).
7. G. H. Henderson and L. G. Turnbull, *Proc. Roy. Soc.,* A 145:582 (1934).
8. G. H. Henderson and F. W. Sparks, *Proc. Roy. Soc.,* A 173:238 (1939).
9. G. H. Henderson, *Proc. Roy. Soc.,* A 173:250 (1939).
10. Kerr-Lawson, *op. cit.*
11. Mahadevan, *op. cit.*
12. *General Electric Chart of the Nuclides,* Knolls Atomic Power Laboratory 1964 Edition.

13. P. B. Price and R. M. Walker, "Fossil Tracks of Charged Particles in Mica and the Age of Minerals," *J. Geophys. Res.*, 68:4847 (1936).

14. E. Wiman, "Studies of Some Archaean Rocks in the Neighbourhood of Uppsala, Sweden, and their Geological Position," *Bull. Geol. Inst. Univ. Uppsala*, 23:1 (1930).

15. Robert V. Gentry, "Abnormally Long Alpha Particle Tracks in Biotite (Mica)," *Applied Physics Letters*, 8:65 (1966).

Chapter 5

Geological Evidence Clearly Indicates
A Catastrophic Origin
Of Sedimentary Strata

1

SEDIMENTATION AND THE FOSSIL RECORD:
A STUDY IN HYDRAULIC ENGINEERING[1]

HENRY M. MORRIS, PH.D.*

Introduction

The relationship of the field of hydraulic engineering to the evolution-creation question at first may seem somewhat tenuous. There is, nevertheless, a very real and significant connection.

Hydraulic engineering is that profession which seeks to devise and build systems and structures for the most effective control and utilization of the earth's water resources. It is necessarily based on a thorough understanding of the sciences of hydrology and hydraulics.

Hydrology is the science dealing with the earth's natural waters and their distribution, especially in the forms of precipitation, stream flow, and ground water. Hydraulics deals with the forces, velocities, and frictional resistances associated with flowing fluids.

One of the most important functions of the earth's natural waters is that of erosion, transportation, and deposition of sediments. Mechanics of sedimentation phenomena control formation and development of river systems. Rivers not only carry the waters back to the ocean from whence they came, but also they serve to carry off large quantities of sediment eroded from their drainage basins, depositing them finally along their flood plains or in deltas near their mouths. Deltaic sediments are gradually re-worked by wave action

---

*Professor of Hydraulic Engineering and Head of the Department of Civil Engineering at Virginia Polytechnic Institute, Blacksburg, Virginia

and by littoral currents until finally deposited more or less permanently along the continental shelves and slopes. Thus land surfaces are gradually being cut down and ocean basins filled.

These sedimentation processes are highly important to both the geologist and the hydraulic engineer. Most geologic processes involve water in one way or another, but the processes of sedimentation are by far the most important, since most of the earth's land surface consists of sediments, either still loose and unconsolidated or else compacted and hardened into sedimentary rocks. In order to understand and explain geologic formations and phenomena, therefore, the geologist should have a thorough understanding of the processes of sedimentation.

The hydraulic engineer has a more immediate and practical need for such knowledge. He is concerned with the silting-up of canals, reservoirs, and harbors, with the stability of structures built along river channels, with erosion of valuable lands, with bank-caving and channel-shifting in alluvial rivers, and with numerous other practical and costly problems associated with the hydraulics of sedimentation as connected with the design of hydraulic structures and systems.[2]

Hydraulic engineers, therefore, have been engaged for the past four decades, especially, in intensive laboratory and analytical studies dealing with the processes of sedimentation. These phenomena are extremely complex, but much has been learned and will continue to be learned concerning them.

Geologists, on the other hand, with a few noteworthy exceptions, have continued to favor a qualitative and descriptive, rather than quantitative and mathematical, approach to sedimentation. It should be obvious, however, that the degree of confidence that can be placed in their interpretations of sedimentary deposits of the past is directly dependent upon their understanding of sedimentary processes in the present. The present state of knowledge of sedimentation mechanics, even of those hydraulic engineers who are most actively involved in such studies, is certainly not such as to warrant placing overmuch confidence in interpretations of the sedimentary deposits of the past by anyone, and especially by anyone not thoroughly conversant with modern studies in sediment hydraulics.

Now the bearing of this discussion on the subject of evolution is simply that the sedimentary rocks laid down in the past constitute the repository for the fossilized remains of former living plants and animals. And this fossil record of life during earth's past history is really the *only* non-circumstantial, historical evidence presumably supporting the theory of organic evolution.

The question, therefore, of *how* the fossil-bearing sediments were originally laid down is of extreme significance to the evolution-creation controversy. Can the sedimentary processes of the earth as now constituted adequately explain them? Were they deposited very slowly, over long ages, or rapidly and violently? Under what circumstances, and in what kinds of environments, were they originally eroded, transported, and deposited?

Such questions can never be fully resolved scientifically, for the simple reason that events of the past are not reproducible. However, the goal of obtaining the most reasonable and probable answer clearly requires, as a minimum prerequisite, a thorough understanding of all sedimentation phenomena, environments, and processes as they exist at present. And until paleontologists and historical geologists have acquired such knowledge and have demonstrated its consistency with their uniformitarian and evolutionary interpretation of the fossil record, we are fully warranted in rejecting the entire concept of organic evolution.

The various contentions in the foregoing general discussion will now be discussed and documented in somewhat more detail.

Role of Water in Geologic Interpretation[3]

Of all physical factors involved in the study of geology, one of the most obvious and certain facts is that water has been the primary geologic agent in shaping the earth's surface. The planet earth, uniquely among all bodies in the universe in so far as any real knowledge goes, has been equipped with an abundant supply of water, and this fact is profoundly important in the understanding of earth history.

This water supply is intricately associated with almost all the physical processes and structures of the earth. Approximately 71 percent of the earth's surface is, in fact, covered with water. Plant and animal life is composed mainly of water; the human body, for example, is more than two-thirds water! Most chemical processes of importance involve water, as do biologic processes. No wonder the Apostle Peter said: ". . . heavens came into existence long ago by the word of God, and an earth also, which was formed out of water and by means of water" (II Pet. 3:5b, Amplified Bible).

It is also obvious that even the 29 percent of the earth's surface which is dry land has in the past been covered with water, and that most of the rocks on the surface were originally laid down by moving water. Rock formations are usually classified as igneous, metamorphic, or sedimentary, with the latter formed primarily by deposition of sediments out of water after transportation from some source area. It is significant that most surface rocks are sedimentary rocks.

> By volume, sedimentary rocks are about one-tenth as abundant as igneous rocks in the earth's crust; but when it comes to the rocks exposed at the earth's surface, sedimentary rocks or sediments, as they are sometimes called, cover nearly three-fourths of the land surface.[4]

Furthermore, many of the igneous rocks at the earth's surface are underlaid by sedimentaries, upon which they flowed after eruption through volcanic vents or fissures. Similarly, many of the metamorphic rocks at the surface represent rocks which were sedimentary rocks (e.g., marble, transformed from limestone by processes of metamorphism).

Thus it is evident that probably all of the earth's surface either now is, or has been at some time or times, completely submerged by water, and that these waters have been profoundly effective in the very formation of the rocks themselves, as well as the surface features of the earth's physiography.

Of course, this is not surprising to the student of Scripture. According to biblical revelation, there have been two periods in earth history when the surface of the earth was completely submerged by water. The first was immediately after the creation of heaven and earth, when the earth is said to have been covered with water (Gen. 1:2, 3). Second, the earth was again fully inundated at the time of the Great Flood, in the days of Noah (Gen. 6-9). In both cases, it is certain that much geological work must have been accomplished on the earth's crust by the waters (as affirmed in II Peter 3:5, 6).

But modern geologists have been unwilling to accept so simple an explanation for the earth's sedimentary rocks, especially since it involves a world-wide catastrophe with supernatural overtones. Instead, it has, for more than a hundred years, been assumed more "scientific" to explain the great masses of sedimentary rocks, sometimes several miles in thickness, in terms of the ordinary processes of sedimentation which are in operation in the present world.

Biblical and other ancient literature of the Middle East is dominated by a tradition of universal deluge. Characteristic of this
view is an extremely short time scale for the duration of our
planet—measured in thousands rather than in billions of years.
One flood during this period sufficed to explain all evidences of
former seas on land. . . . Little by little, the excrescences of
the Middle Ages were shaken off by the developing science of
geology. . . . By the end of the nineteenth century, only religious fundamentalists . . . refused to accept the overwhelming
evidence that not once but many times the seas have crossed
where land lies now.[5]

Uniformitarian versus Catastrophic Sedimentation

There thus seem to be two possible types of explanations for the
fact that essentially all of the earth's surface has been, at some time
or times in the past, beneath the sea. One is that of catastrophism,
the other that of uniformitarianism.

In the one, a tremendous cataclysm of water, pouring down from
the skies and up from the subterranean deeps, produced a year-long
debacle of erosion and deposition of sediments that could have accounted for at least most of the sedimentary deposits in the earth's
crust.

In the other, the very slow processes of weathering, denudation,
river flow, delta deposition, land subsidence and emergence, and
similar geomorphologic processes, acting over many hundreds of
millions of years, have combined to produce these formations.

In both cases, the amount of geologic work accomplished is the
same, but the power required—the time-rate of work accomplished—
is vastly different. It is a question of whether great forces and energies were at work during a short period of time, or small energies
operating over great expanses of time.

In either case, the bulk of the work was accomplished prior to
recorded human history, and therefore the process is not subject to
scientific examination. It is completely impossible to *prove* scientifically, whether catastrophism or uniformitarianism provides the
true explanation.

The best that can be done is to examine the ancient sediments
and compare them with modern processes of sedimentation, to see
whether the latter are producing deposits which are comparable in
character to those of the geologic column, and also, on the basis of
what we know about hydraulics, to try to estimate the possible type
and extent of sedimentation that could occur in a world flood, in

order to evaluate the sedimentary rocks in terms of this possibility.
The decision between the two alternatives will very likely be, to some extent, subjective. This kind of study is necessarily bound up with probabilities and presuppositions. The very same deposit will seem to one student to give overwhelming evidence of rapid deposition and to another it will seem to have been laid down very slowly and gradually. The true explanation is not necessarily determined by majority vote!

It is salutary to keep constantly before us, in deciphering geologic history, the fact that we are outside the domain of true *science*. The viewpoint favored here, of course, is that of catastrophism. The deposits can be understood quite adequately in this context, but this is not the same as saying that catastrophism can be proved scientifically (which means experimentally). By the same token, it should be clearly recognized that neither can uniformitarianism be proved scientifically.

Our purpose here, therefore, is simply to show that aqueous catastrophism provides a possible and reasonable explanation for the sedimentary rocks, and that uniformitarianism is beset with serious difficulties. The conclusions one may draw from this fact will depend largely upon his own philosophic preferences, or perhaps prejudices.

Sedimentation, Paleontology, and Evolution

The importance of the study of the processes of sedimentation as related to the geological record lies mainly in its contribution to the theory of evolution. The fossil record, as preserved in the sedimentary rocks of the earth's crust, is by all odds the most important of the so-called evidences for evolution. As Kerkut has said:

> The most important evidence for the theory of Evolution is that obtained from the study of paleontology. Though the study of other branches of zoology, such as Comparative Anatomy or Embryology, might lead one to suspect that animals are all inter-related, it was the discovery of various fossils and their correct placing in the relative strata and age that provided the main factual basis for the modern view of evolution.[6]

That is, the earth's vast areas and thickness of sedimentary rocks, comprising as they do about three fourths of the earth's land surface, are supposed to have been laid down over aeons of geologic time, each layer in turn containing fossils typical of the life of the period of its own deposition. Older rocks contain only primitive forms of life, and the fossils become increasingly complex and modern in more and more recent deposits. Thus, although other evidences of evolution are circumstantial in nature, and may be explained either in terms of evolutionary kinship or in terms of direct creation, the fossil record purports to provide an actual documentary history of organic evolution.

But at the same time, the rock layers themselves are dated as to their relative antiquity by the fossils they contain!

> Vertebrate paleontologists have relied upon "stage-of-evolution" as the criterion for determining the chronologic relationships of faunas. Before the establishment of physical dates, evolutionary progression was the best method for dating fossiliferous strata.[7]

Rocks containing simple fossils are thus assumed to be old, and those with complex fossils are young. The physical dates referred to are not by any means as yet considered determinative in establishing geologic age, since any radioactive dating which appeared to contradict the previously determined geologic age would be discarded immediately as erroneous.

> The standard time scale is derived directly from the standard column and from no other source, except for late Pleistocene details. The fossils of the units in the standard column and of other units in other columns are still our principal guides in stratigraphic correlation, although we cordially welcome the statistical calibration of the standard column, in years, from radiometric data.[8]

There is thus clearly a very subtle circle of reasoning involved in the stratigraphic interpretation of the sedimentary rocks of the earth's crust. The basis for their relative dating is entirely paleontological, on the assumption of evolutionary progression over the geologic ages.

But then, the only real evidence for this evolutionary progression is the fossil record. And, as a matter of fact, even this is only true in small part. Dating is accomplished not by the fossil assemblages as a whole, but only by certain "index fossils," which are supposed to be sure criteria of the various specific stages in evolutionary history.

> The best example of how *qualitative* and *non-statistical* paleontological correlation is, is provided by the already-mentioned fact

that only a minority of fossils of most faunas (and this often amounts to the minority of one fossil species or genus only!) are reliable time indices or index fossils. The great majority of fossils are, conversely, either inferior (parachronological) time indices or have little or no practical biochronological value (ecostratigraphical indices). Any single, readily identifiable specimen or fragment of a known diagnostic ammonite, belemnite, planktonic foraminifer, graptolite, trilobite, etc., is, therefore, often more significant for the dating and correlation of the rock units concerned than all the rest of their faunas taken together.[9]

The most trustworthy indicators of evolution and geologic age, therefore, seem to be a relatively restricted number of simple marine organisms. These were presumably of world-wide provenance, so that they can be used for correlation on a world-wide basis, and are found in rather clearly distinguishable vertical series with the simpler and less specialized forms in the lower layers, and the more complex and differentiated forms in the upper layers.

And these marine indicators, of course, are all found in stratified rocks, which originally were deposited as sediments by moving water, most probably in fairly shallow marine environments. This latter is confirmed by Krumbein and Sloss:

> Taken as whole, the sublittoral environment is perhaps the most important from the viewpoint of stratigraphic analysis. Twenhofel (1950) estimated that about 80 per cent of the sediments in the geologic column were deposited in water less than 600 feet deep.[10]

Dr. Walter E. Lammerts, in a personal communication, has called attention to an important example of a specific index fossil and how its occurrence might well be better interpreted in terms of sedimentary sorting during deposition rather than in terms of its unique occurrence during a particular geologic age. He says:

> The foraminifera group called fusulinids are considered excellent index fossils indicating the middle Pennsylvanian in distinction from the schwagerinids which are indicative of the Permian. But these schwagerinids, such as the genus *Schwagerina, Pseudoschwagerina* and *Parafusulina;* are quite different in both wall structure and shape. Accordingly one would expect them to be segregated into different strata strictly on this basis alone! Furthermore they may well have occupied ecologically distinctive niches and thus been buried in different places.

> Many of the foraminifera are arenaceous and so would not in general be found mixed with the calcareous forms. Though

unfortunately the fusulinids and schwagerinids seem to be extinct, it would be most interesting if tests could be run on the comparative rapidity with which these various genera sink in water. It is very likely, if not certain, that they would show different rates of settling, which is thus an obvious reason why they should now be found segregated into distinctive strata.

The reasonableness of this suggestion is pointed up by the fact that decanting is, right today, used as an effective method of sorting out different foraminiferal specimens. Joseph Cushman, probably the greatest authority on "forams," says:

> Another method by which rough sorting can be done is by decanting. If the material is shaken up in a tall vessel of some sort, the lighter specimens will stay in suspension for a short period and can be poured off, leaving the heavier ones on the bottom. Successive stages will separate most of the calcareous tests from the sand and heavier foraminifera.[11]

The effectiveness and significance of hydrodynamic sorting, as a mechanism for producing particular assemblages which seem superficially to be chronological markers or index fossils will be discussed further in a later section. Here we merely note that even those relatively few organisms which have served as index fossils may themselves really have a hydraulic basis, rather than genuine evolutionary or chronologic significance.

In summary, the real basis for the theory of evolution seems to consist mainly of the series of marine index fossils found in the geologic column. These are found in hardened, stratified sediments deposited originally in shallow epicontinental seas, supposedly over hundreds of millions of years of geologic time, and then uplifted in more recent times to form in many cases our present mountainous regions. The processes of sedimentation by which these great fossiliferous beds were originally formed thus become of great interest and significance.

Inadequacy of Uniformitarianism

For over a hundred years, the dogma of uniformity has been the pride and backbone of geologic interpretation. Geologic processes in operation in the present era—*especially those of sedimentation,* which are obviously the most important of all geologic processes since they have produced the rocks whose fossils form the basis of geologic analysis—are supposedly capable of accounting for all these sediments in the geologic column. In the familiar catch phrase of James Hutton, "the present is the key to the past."

However, the principle of uniformity turns out to be entirely inadequate right at this most important aspect of geologic interpretation. Modern processes of sedimentation are in general quite incapable of accounting for the sedimentary rocks of the geologic column. This is true whether the environment of deposition is thought to be geosynclinal, deltaic, lagoonal, or some other.

As a matter of fact, it is increasingly being recognized by modern geologists that uniformitarianism has failed. It is, of course, still tenaciously held in opposition to any form of biblical catastrophism or creationism, but it is widely acknowledged that it is not at all adequate when it comes to correlating the geologic formations with modern processes and their rates. In a recent article, a California geologist has said, for example:

> The doctrine of uniformitarianism has been vigorously disputed in recent years. A number of writers, although approaching the subject from different directions, have agreed that this doctrine is composed partly of meaningless and erroneous components and some have suggested that it be discarded as a formal assumption of geologic science.[12]

Similarly, David Kitts, of the University of Oklahoma, has noted this problem:

> There is widespread agreement among geologists that some special principle of uniformity is a fundamental ingredient of all geologic inference.. . . . Despite this general agreement about the importance of the principle, geologists hold widely divergent views as to its meaning. So divergent are these views, in fact, that one is led to conclude that there has been little or no resolution of the problems which gave rise to the famous controversies between the "uniformitarians" and the "catastrophists" in the nineteenth century. Though the problems have not been solved, the controversy has subsided.[13]

It is thus admitted that, although uniformitarianism has not proved adequate to account for the strata, and that catastrophism has not been proved false, yet nevertheless "the controversy has subsided." Of course, this is because the forces of naturalism and evolutionism have attained essentially universal dominance in science and any form of supernatural catastrophism is excluded from further discussion. As Valentine says:

Frequently the doctrine of uniformitarianism is used fruitfully to explain the anticatastrophist viewpoint of history, and to illuminate the practical working method of consulting nature for clues to natural history.[14]

Or, as George Gaylord Simpson has put it:

It is a necessary condition and indeed part of the definition of science in the modern sense that only natural explanations of material phenomena are to be sought or can be considered scientifically tenable. It is interesting and significant that general acceptance of this principle (or limitation, if you like) came much later in the historical than in the non-historical sciences. In historical geology it was the most important outcome of the uniformitarian-catastrophist controversy. In historical biology it was the still later outcome of the Darwinian controversy and was hardly settled until our own day. (It is still far from settled among non-scientists.)[15]

One might note, in passing, the self-preserving assumption by Professor Simpson that all who might disagree with his naturalistic presuppositions are "non-scientists," especially since it is certainly true that neither catastrophism nor creationism can possibly be disproved "scientifically." One can invent his own definition of "science," of course, and frame it so as to exclude any possibility of teleological explanation, and this is what Simpson and others have done. It still remains true that uniformitarianism has proved sterile as far as much of historical geology is concerned:

It seems unfortunate that uniformitarianism, a doctrine which has so important a place in the history of geology, should continue to be misrepresented in contemporary texts and courses by "the present is the key to the past," a maxim without much credit.[16]

The biblical creationist, of course, has no objection whatever to the concept of the uniformity of *natural law*, as prevalent in the present cosmos. It is the assumption that present *processes* (which operate within the framework of uniform natural law) must always operate at the same rates as at present with which he takes issue. This latter assumption is even bold enough to claim that the processes, and even the laws, produced themselves, by means of themselves!

The basic distinction between the laws of nature and the processes which operate within the framework of those laws, and between a valid and a fallacious uniformitarianism, have been discussed in the previous chapter, "Science versus Scientism in Historical Geology.[17] In general it can be argued quite persuasively that the very existence of natural laws presupposes a Creator by whom such laws were brought into existence. Since this is so, the permanence and inviolability of such laws is dependent upon the will of the Creator, and our knowledge of these characteristics is contingent upon His revelation to us concerning them.

Even within the framework of the semi-permanence of natural law and basic cosmic processes which has been established and revealed by God (Gen. 8:22), it is still true that process *rates* may and do vary tremendously. Each process, and the rate at which it operates, is found to depend upon many different parameters, and a change in conditions for even one of these may materially change the process rate.

For example (and this is obviously the example most pertinent to our present discussion), sediment erosion, transportation, and deposition is a process that may take place very slowly or exceedingly rapidly. A very large number of variables go into the determination of sedimentation rates. An incomplete list would include:

(a) *hydraulic factors,* such as channel slope, shape, and size; quantity of water available; roughness of channel bed and sides; variability of water flow; and water temperature;

(b) *topographic factors,* such as shape and size of watershed, slope and aspect of the terrain, nature of the soil and its vegetal cover, tributary network, and ground water conditions;

(c) *meteorological factors,* such as frequency and intensity of storm rainfall, direction of air mass movements, and duration of rainfall;

(d) *sedimentary factors,* such as size, shape, variability, specific gravity, and chemical character of the sediment being transported.

Other influences could be added, but even this list will indicate how futile it would be to try to establish any kind of *average rate* of sedimentation, and then to extrapolate such a rate for hundreds of millions of years into the past to try to explain the immense sedimentary formations of the earth's crust! There is no *a priori* reason whatever why rapid (or catastrophic) formation of these beds would not provide as satisfactory an explanation—and as fully in accord with the assumption of uniform natural law—as would slow deposition over millions of years.

Mechanics of Sedimentation

In principle, it should be possible by induction to examine the

character of a given sedimentary deposit; and, therefrom, to determine (1) the nature of the source area from which the sediment had
been eroded initially, (2) the magnitude and nature of the water
flow which had transported it, and (3) the character and extent of
the basin into which it had finally been dropped. In actuality, however, owing to the excessive number of variables which may have
contributed to the phenomenon, as above enumerated, it is normally
quite impossible to make such extrapolations with any degree of
assurance.

It is customary to consider sedimentation under the three stages
of erosion, transportation, and deposition. Since the first and last
of these necessarily involve non-uniform conditions (either degrada-
tion or aggradation), it is easiest to consider the transportation phase
first, as an equilibrium, or quasi-equilibrium, state. That is, it is
assumed that the sediment transported by the flow is constant with
time and distance, with any localized erosion being offset by localized
deposition. Non-equilibrium conditions are then characterized either
by a net erosion or a net deposition of sediment.

A great many studies have been made in laboratory flumes, and a
smaller number in actual streams, of rates of sediment transport.
Numerous empirical formulas have been derived and some have
been employed with fair success in engineering problems. Typical
of these formulas is the following,[18] attributed to M. L. Albertson and
R. L. Garde, of Colorado State University:

$$G_s = \frac{1.36 \ W \ V^4 \ n^3}{k^3 \ d^{1.5} D \ (10^{15})}$$

In this formula, G_s represents the total number of pounds of
sediment being transported each second past any given point in the
stream. W is the stream width, V is the velocity of flow in feet per
second, and n is a channel "roughness coefficient," which measures
the hydraulic resistance to flow. The depth of flow, in feet, is D,
and the diameter of sediment particles is d, also in feet. The effect
of temperature is measured by the "kinematic viscosity" of the water,
k. Typical values of k and n might be, respectively, about 0.00001
square feet per second, and 0.035, although they can vary over a
wide range.

The formula applies only to a uniform channel, with flow at constant velocity, for sediment composed predominantly of sand grains
of only one size. Even with these limitations it is able to give only

very approximate answers. Many formulas attempt to distinguish between the suspended sediment load, the saltional (rolling and bouncing) load, and the bed load. Also, depending on the velocity and other factors, the forms of dunes on the bed may change materially, thus changing the hydraulic roughness and modifying the flow.

The problem of course is compounded if any of the factors become non-uniform. If there is a change in the channel cross-section, velocity, or roughness, or if the sediment is of varying sizes, then it becomes almost impossible to make calculations of sediment transport which are quantitatively accurate, although it may be possible to determine whether there will be scour or deposition.

And calculations become necssarily still more complex if non-equilibrium conditions exist—that is, if material is being eroded or deposited, instead of simply transported. It is thus quite clear that any truly quantitive understanding of the processes and rates of sediment deposition, even in the environments of the present, is still far from being attained. Consequently, the idea that the sedimentary rocks of the earth's crust, with their fossil contents, can be explained in terms of present processes of sedimentation on the application of uniformitarian principles is nothing but wishful thinking.

The Necessity of Catastrophism

Since we have no scientific basis for quantitative evaluation of ancient sedimentary processes, it is obvious that the question of catastrophism versus uniformitarianism in sedimentary interpretation is still very much an open question. If it then begins to appear that many of the present geologic formations could not have been formed at all by modern, slow rates of deposition, the presumptive evidence for catastrophism as the most likely explanation is rendered all the stronger.

As a matter of fact, even most modern sedimentary phenomena must be attributed to brief, intense periods of sedimentation, rather than normal, slow, uniform periods. More than half of all sediments transported and deposited by modern rivers are carried during flood periods, when the river is overflowing its banks.

There are a number of remarkable phenomena characterizing the sedimentary rocks of the earth's crust that seem to be clear evidences of catastrophic deposition and which thus belie the evolutionist's assumption of uniformitarianism. These include among them the following:

(1) *Fossil Graveyards.* It is well known that when a living organism dies, especially one of the larger animals, its remains soon disappear, because of the efficiency of scavenger organisms and the decay processes which immediately go to work on it. Yet, in the earth's sedimentary rocks, there are buried vast numbers of plants and animals of all kinds, often in great fossil "cemeteries," where thousands, even millions, of organisms may be found crushed together and buried by the sediments. Even after centuries of collecting great quantities of fossils all over the world, new "graveyards" continue to be found.[19]

It is a matter of the most elementary scientific logic to recognize that phenomena such as these must be attributed to very rapid burial, or otherwise they could never have been preserved. And since most such fossil graveyards have been buried in water-laid sediments, they clearly give witness to the fact of aqueous catastrophism.

(2) *Polystrate Fossils.* Stratification (or layered sequence) is a universal characteristic of sedimentary rocks. A stratum of sediment is formed by deposition under essentially continuous and uniform hydraulic conditions. When the sedimentation stops for a while before another period of deposition, the new stratum will be visibly distinguishable from the earlier by a stratification line (actually a surface). Distinct strata also result when there is a change in the velocity of flow or other hydraulic characteristics. Sedimentary beds as now found are typicaly composed of many "strata," and it is in such beds that most fossils are found.

Not infrequently, large fossils[20] of animals and plants—especially tree trunks—are found which extend through several strata, often 20 feet or more in thickness. A young Dutch geologist, N. A. Rupke, has suggested that these be called "polystrate fossils" and has documented[21] numerous remarkable examples of this phenomenon. (See Figure 1.)

It is beyond question that this type of fossil must have been buried quickly or it would not have been preserved intact while the strata gradually accumulated around it. And since the strata entombing these polystrate fossils are no different in appearance or composition from other strata, it is probable that neither was there any significant difference in the rapidity of deposition.

Figure 1. Polystrate tree-trunk near Essen-Kupferdreh (Germany). (Photo by Klusemann).

(3) *Ephemeral Markings*. Another evidence of very rapid deposition is the preservation of what Rupke[22] calls "ephemeral markings." These constitute a special type of fossil originally formed as a transient marking on the surface of a recently deposited layer of sediment. These include such phenomena as: (a) ripple marks; (b) rain prints; (c) worm trails, and (d) bird and reptile tracks.

It is a matter of common observation that such fragile structures, once formed, are very quickly obliterated by subsequent wind or air currents or by later erosion and sedimentation. The only way they could be preserved is by means of abnormally rapid burial (without concurrent erosion), plus abnormally rapid lithification.

It would indeed be difficult, if not impossible, to point to examples of such fossils in the process of formation at present. Sudden burial by turbidity currents is frequently suggested. For example, Adolf Seilacher, Geologisches Institut University of Frankfurt, Germany, says:

> The post-depositional sole trails of Flysch psammites occur only in thinner beds up to a thickness particular to each species. This proves instantaneous deposition of the individual beds, as postulated by the turbidity-current theory. The majority of the sole trails are predepositional mud burrows washed out and cast by turbidity currents. Thus erosion of an unusual type must have preceded every turbidite sedimentation.[23]

But the remarkable fact is that "ephemeral markings" of this type are found in great abundance in the ancient sedimentary rocks of practically all geologic "ages," including the most ancient. Furthermore, they appear equally fresh, when exposed in the present time, regardless of what the particular geologic age is supposed to be, whether Proterozoic or Tertiary or anywhere in between. It seems quite clear that only some kind of overwhelming catastrophic sedimentary phenomenon can really account for these markings and their preservation.

(4) *Preservation of Soft Parts.* Numerous instances are known where the fossil remains do not consist of petrifications or molds or the like, but where the actual soft tissues of the organism have been preserved. This is true even in very "ancient" strata, and often such fossils are found massed together in large numbers.[24] Not only do these deposits speak very plainly of very rapid burial by the sediments, but they also make the contention that they have remained unaffected by decay, erosion, etc., for many millions of years exceedingly difficult to believe.

(5) *Phenomena of Stratification.* Not only do the fossils contained in the sedimentary strata demonstrate the necessity of catastrophic deposition, but the very strata themselves indicate this. As already noted, most of the earth's surface is covered with sediments or sedimentary rocks, originally deposited under moving water. This in itself is *prima facie* evidence that powerful waters once covered the earth. Furthermore, as already mentioned, even under modern conditions most sedimentary deposits are the result of brief, intense periods of flood run-off, rather than slow, uniform silting.

Laboratory evidence that a typical sedimentary deposit may form quite rapidly is found in the work of Alan Jopling at Harvard, who made a long series of studies on delta-type deposition in a laboratory flume and then applied the results to the analysis of a small delta outwash deposit, supposedly formed about 13,000 years ago. His conclusion was as follows:

> It may be concluded therefore that the time required for the deposition of the entire delta deposit amounted to several days. . . . Based on the computed rate of delta advance and the thickness of individual laminae, the average time for the deposition of a lamina must have been several minutes.[25]

The fact that many sedimentary formations in the stratigraphic column consist of gravels or conglomerates, or even boulders, is further testimony to hydraulic activity of high intensity, as is the frequent occurrence of "cross-bedding" phenomena, indicating rapidly changing current directions.

(6) *Alluvial Valleys.* Practically all modern rivers course through

valleys that once carried far greater volumes of water than they do now. This is indicated not only by the universal presence of old river terraces high on the valley walls but even more by the vast amounts of sands and gravels lying beneath the present flood plains, which now fill what were formerly the stream channels.

> Subsurface explorations of meandering valleys in the Driftless Area of Wisconsin, by means of a refraction seismograph, reveal large filled channels similar to those previously determined in English rivers where the augering technique was used. The channels are asymmetrical in cross profile and attain their greatest depths at valley bends. In cross-sectional area at probable bankfull they are some 25 times as large as the present stream channels.[26]

This sort of thing is practically universal. The Mississippi Valley, for example, consists of alluvial deposits extending to depths of 600 feet! All of this indicates that the rivers of the world, in very recent times (probably during and after the continental uplifts terminating the year of the Great Flood) carried tremendous volumes of water and sediment.

(7) *Incised Meanders.* Another universal characteristic of alluvial streams is the phenomenon of meandering. Many analytical and experimental studies have been made to determine the cause and mechanics of meandering, but these have been only partially successful. It is well accepted, however, that stream meandering requires relatively mild stream gradients and easily eroded banks. If the slopes are steep and the sides resistant, then erosion will occur primarily at the beds, and the stream will cut down essentially vertically, forming a canyon section.

Most remarkable, therefore, are the intricate meandering patterns found frequently incised in deep gorges in high plateau and mountainous areas. These would seem to defy any explanation in terms of the ordinary hydraulics of rivers, and geologists' suggestions (superposed meanders, for example!) seem to be oblivious of such hydraulics.

Clearly some kind of catastropic origin is indicated. Great regions of horizontal sedimentary beds, still relatively soft and erosible when uplifted following the Deluge, riven by great fissures during the uplift process, possibly provide a realistic model of conditions suitable for formation of these structures. The initial cracks could have been rapidly widened and deepened into the present meandering gorges as great volumes of water were being rapidly drained off the rising plateaus.

Evidence of a Single Depositional Epoch

The above is not, of course, a complete, but only a representative, list of evidence of aqueous catastrophism. Neither does the scope of this paper allow for discussion of various types of formations which superficially may seem to require very slow process rates. This has already been done to some extent elsewhere.[27]

It can be said that in general catastrophism provides a very adequate framework of interpretation for most, and probably all, the features of the known geologic column. Uniformitarianism, on the other hand, while satisfactory as a framework for some parts of the data, seems utterly inadequate to account for most of them.

There is one question, however. Even though admitting the validity of the concept of aqueous catastrophism to explain many of the geologic phenomena, as many geologists readily are doing today, there is still almost universal resistance to the idea of one, single, catastropic epoch such as described in the Bible. Historical geologists still prefer a general framework of uniformitarianism and great ages, even though they are willing to recognize any number of intense and widespread floods and other local catastrophes occurring within that framework.

Thus the question is whether the numerous evidences of catastrophic sedimentation, including those discussed in the preceding pages, were caused by one great cataclysm or by a great number of lesser catastrophes.

If it were not for the religious implications, and were it only a matter of seeking a logical explanation of the actual physical data, the application of the principle of Occam's Razor (which cautions against the unnecessary multiplication of hypotheses) would lead quickly to a decision in favor of the one great cataclysm.

To insist that there have been great numbers of violent geologic catastrophes (in all parts of the world and through all the aeons of geologic time) sufficient to explain the many evidences of catastrophism; and further knowing (a) that many of these catastrophes must have been far greater than anything ever observed in the modern world, and (b) that uniformitarianism is utterly inadequate to incorporate them within any kind of experimentally quantitative framework, would surely seem to suggest a strong religious bias against the concept of the biblical record of the great Deluge and favoring an evolutionary interpretation of history.

The various evidences for catastrophism cited previously—the fossil graveyards, polystrate fossils, ephemeral markings, and others —are generally found more or less indiscriminately among strata throughout the entire geologic column. There are no evidences of progressive changes in the characteristics of catastrophism throughout the supposed geologic ages, such as should be expected in response to changing climatic and geophysical regimes as postulated throughout the earth's evolution. Sedimentary deposits of the Proterozoic Era have essentially the same physical characteristics as those of the Tertiary, or any others, the only significant difference being the fossil assemblages, especially the index fossils, contained in them.

And of course the fossil assemblages themselves are better explained in terms of aqueous cataclysm than of evolutionary uniformitarianism. They are supposed to show increasing complexity, and therefore evolution, with the passage of geologic time, but this interpretation is belied by the fact of the great gaps which exist between all the major kinds of creatures in the fossil record, which gaps are essentially the same as the gaps between the same kinds of plants and animals in the modern world.

The fact that, in general, the fossils are found segregated into assemblages of similar sizes and shapes is exactly what would be expected as a result of diluvial processes, since turbulent water is a highly effective "sorting" agent. In his flume studies at Harvard, Jopling found, for example, that even when the flows were steady and uniform, and when the sediments transported were randomly mixed to begin with, the flow would sort them out.

> Segregation invariably occurs even when uniform conditions of sediment transport prevail, and where the various size grades of the sediment have been thoroughly mixed to begin with. This segregation occurs on either a plane, rippled, or duned bed, and it is evident in both the transverse and longitudinal directions.[28]

This sorting action is basically produced because the amount of hydrodynamic "lift and drag" forces on immersed objects are directly related to the size and shape of the objects. The same applies, of course, to objects falling vertically through water, so that objects which are similar in shape (and thus, supposedly, more "primitive") would tend to settle out of a decelerating flow more rapidly and thus be buried more deeply than would objects of complex geometry. This tendency would be further augmented by the fact that these simpler organisms (shells, for example) normally are of somewhat greater specific gravity than "higher" organisms.

It would be reasonable to expect, therefore, that the hydraulic activity of a world-wide Flood would tend to deposit organisms of similar sizes and shapes together and that the depth of burial would be in order of increasing complexity from the bottom up. Furthermore, this is directly parallel to the elevation of the normal habitat of organisms.

Other things being equal, since the simpler organisms dwell at lower elevations, it would be expected that they would be buried at lower elevations. And still further, the mobility of animals is rather closely related to their complexity, so that higher animals would escape burial for longer periods.

All of these factors would contribute toward the preservation of fossils in the Flood sediments in just the order in which they are now usually found, whereas the usual evolutionary interpretation is obviously inadequate.

These three factors—hydraulic, ecologic, and physiologic—would of course tend to act only statistically, rather than absolutely, so that the very numerous exceptions to the usual order which have been found are not particularly surprising. They *are* an embarrassment to the evolutionist, however, since fossils in the wrong stratigraphic order would indicate a reversal of evolution and thus completely upset the assignment of geologic ages.

It is typical of evolutionary reasoning that such anomalies and contradictions can never be allowed to bring into question the basic assumption of evolution. Consequently, a further multiplication of hypotheses is employed, invoking the possibility of great earth movements as a means of explaining how the fossiliferous strata have been rearranged into the "wrong" order. Vast horizontal "thrust faults" by which great thicknesses of sedimentary strata have been uplifted and then translated horizontally over the adjacent regions, have typically been offered as mechanisms explaining the many areas where "ancient" fossil-bearing formations have been found on top of "recent" formations.

It is interesting that another hydraulic principle has been employed to explain how such movements are possible, since it is well known that ordinary mechanical sliding, even if the sliding planes were lubricated, would be physically impossible on such a large scale without completely destroying the structural integrity of the sliding formations. The presently accepted explanation is that the thrust block was "floated" into place by abnormally high internal fluid pressures along the thrust plane.

These pressures, in order to be effective, would have to be far higher than in ordinary ground water and are supposedly caused by compression of water trapped in the sedimentary interstices when the sediments were originally deposited. That is, as the original sediments were gradually compressed and lithified, the "connate water" contained in the soil pores was somehow sealed off from any possible escape channels and was eventually so compressed as to develop elastic pressures capable of actually lifting and "floating" the huge rock overburden above it.

This is indeed a remarkable hypothesis. The "seal" around the sides of the thrust blocks (not infrequently hundreds or thousands of square miles in extent) must have been quite elastic itself, permitting great vertical and horizontal motions of the block and yet preventing any escape of the highly compressed water in the process. In a cogent analysis of this hypothesis, Platt has pointed out:

> Obviously an important factor is the quality of the seal that forms in the clay or shale. No matter how small the permeability in the relatively impermeable layer that effectively seals the connate water beneath the thick sequence, some leakage does occur. . . . Hence, if fluid support is to be available to "float" the rocks, the thrust movement must occur soon (geologically) after the deposition of the final weight of the thick sediments. If the delay is sufficient, the seal of shale becomes very good, but there is no fluid left to seal off.[29]

This requirement for early flotation of the block, suggested by Platt, of course is at cross purposes with the long period of time supposedly required for compression and lithification of the sediments before the fluid could develop the required pressures. The even more important problem of how the necessary seal could be maintained during the period of thrust action is not mentioned at all.

It is concluded, therefore, that the concept of one great hydraulic cataclysm, accompanied by great volcanic and tectonic activities, on a world-wide scope, provides a much more realistic model to explain the sedimentary strata and the fossil record, than does the philosophy of evolutionary uniformitarianism, with its utterly un-scientific multiplication of hypotheses and manipulation of data.

NOTES AND REFERENCES

1. This paper was originally presented at the Christian Schools Conference, held at the St. Thomas Episcopal School, Houston, Texas, April 15-17, 1967.

2. Committee on Sedimentation, "Sediment Transportation Mechanics: Nature of Sedimentation Problems," *Journal of the Hydraulics Division, American Society of Civil Engineers*, Vol. 91, No. HY2, March 1965, pp. 251-266.

3. Portions of the following discussion have been taken from an article by the author entitled "Hydraulics, Sedimentation and Catastrophism," *Creation Research Society Quarterly*, Vol. 3, May 1966, pp. 51, 52.

4. James H. Zumberge, *Elements of Geology*, Second Edition (New York: John Wiley and Sons, 1963), p. 44.

5. Malcolm C. McKenna, "The Undersea History of America," *Science Digest*, Vol. 57, April 1965, pp. 90-91.

6. G. A. Kerkut, *Implications of Evolution* (Oxford: Pergamon Press, 1960), p. 134.

7. J. F. Evernden, D. E. Savage, G. H. Curtis, and G. T. James, "K/A Dates and the Cenozoic Mammalian Chronology of North America," *American Journal of Science*, Vol. 262, February 1964, p. 166.

8. A. O. Woodford, "Correlation by Fossils," in *The Fabric of Geology*, ed. C. C. Albritton, Jr. (Reading, Mass.: Addison-Wesley, 1963), p. 109.

9. J. A. Jeletzky, "Is It Possible to Qualify Biochronological Correlation?" *Journal of Paleontology*, Vol. 39, January 1965, p. 138.

10. W. C. Krumbein and L. L. Sloss, *Stratigraphy and Sedimentation*, Second Edition (San Francisco: W. H. Freeman Co., 1963), p. 261.

11. Joseph A. Cushman, *Foraminifera, Their Classification and Economic Use*, Fourth Edition (Cambridge: Harvard University Press, 1950), p. 27.

12. James W. Valentine, "The Present Is the Key to the Present," *Journal of Geological Education*, Vol. XIV, April 1966, p. 59.

13. David B. Kitts, "The Theory of Geology," in *The Fabric of Geology* (1963), p. 62.

14. James W. Valentine, *op. cit.*, p. 60.

15. George G. Simpson, "Historical Science," in *The Fabric of Geology* (1963), p. 32.

16. James W. Valentine, *op. cit.*, p. 60.

17. Henry M. Morris, "Science Versus Scientism in Historical Geology," *Creation Research Society Quarterly*, Vol. 2, July 1965, pp. 19-28.

18. For a discussion of the background of this equation, as well as other methods used in sediment calculations, see *Applied Hydraulics in Engineering* by Henry M. Morris (New York: Ronald Press, 1963), pp. 321-336. This is a standard textbook for senior and graduate courses in hydraulic engineering, currently used at about 75 colleges and universities.

19. A typical recent example is described by W. W. Dalquest and S. H. Mamay, "The remains of 400 or more Permian amphibians were found in a series of siltstone channels confined to an area of 50 square feet. . . . The fossils are mostly or entirely of heavy-bodied, weak-limbed forms that probably could not walk about on land." In "A Remarkable Concentration of Permian Amphibian Remains in Haskell County, Texas," *Journal of Geology*, Vol. 71, September 1963, p. 641.

20. N. A. Rupke, "Prolegomena to a Study of Cataclysmal Sedimentation," *Creation Research Society Annual*, Vol. 3, May 1966, No. 1, pp. 16-37. Another instance, not described by Rupke, is mentioned by F. M. Broadhurst in an article entitled, "Some Aspects of the Paleoecology of Non-Marine Faunas and Rates of Sedimentation in the Lancashire Coal Measures," *American Journal of Science*, Vol. 262, Summer 1964, pp. 865-866. He says:

> In 1959 Broadhurst and Magraw described a fossilized tree, in position of growth, from Coal Measures of Blackrod near Wigan in Lancashire. This tree was preserved as a cast, and the evidence available suggested that the cast was at least 38 feet in height. The original tree must have been surrounded and buried by sediment which was compacted before the bulk of the tree decomposed, so that the cavity vacated by the trunk could be occupied by new sediment which formed the cast. This implies a rapid rate of sedimentation around the original tree. . . . It is clear that trees in position of growth are far from being rare in Lancashire (Teichmuller, 1956, reaches the same conclusion for similar trees in the Rhein-Westfalen Coal Measures), and presumably in all cases there must have been a rapid rate of sedimentation.

21. Rupke, *op cit.*, pp. 21-25.

22. *Ibid.*, pp. 25-29.

23. A. Seilacher, "Paleontological Studies on Turbidite Sedimentation and Erosion," *Journal of Geology*, Vol. 70, March 1962, p. 227.

24. See *The Genesis Flood*, by John C. Whitcomb, Jr., and Henry M. Morris (Nutley, N. J.: Presbyterian and Reformed Publishing Co., 1961), pp. 159, 160, for a discussion of various examples of this phenomenon.

25. Alan V. Jopling, "Some Principles and Techniques Used in Reconstructing the Hydraulic Parameters of a Paleo-Flow Regime," *Journal of Sedimentary Petrology*, Vol. 36, March 1960, p. 34.

26. G. H. Drury, "Results of Seismic Explorations of Meandering Valleys," *American Journal of Science*, Vol. 260, November 1962, p. 691.

27. See *The Genesis Flood*, pp. 405-421.

28. Alan V. Jopling, "Laboratory Study of Sorting Processes Related to Flow Separation," *Journal of Geophysical Research*, Vol. 69, August 15, 1964, p. 3413.

29. Lucien B. Platt, "Fluid Pressure in Thrust Faulting, A Corollary," *American Journal of Science*, Vol. 260, February 1962, p. 107.

2

REVIEW OF *SURTSEY: THE NEW ISLAND IN THE NORTH ATLANTIC*

Wilbert H. Rusch, Sr., M.S.*

Surtsey: The New Island in the North Atlantic by Sigurdur Thorarinsson. Publisher: Almenna Bokafélagio, Reykjavik, Iceland, 1964.

This little volume consists of 31 pages of text, written in Icelandic by the Icelandic geologist Thorarinsson. It is followed by 24 pages of English translation by Sölvi Eysteinsson.

The remainder of the work, consisting of some 50 pages, contains the photographic record of the birth and development of Surtsey. Most of the photographs are in color, and are most beautiful. This new island lies approximately 70 km. south of Iceland proper.

Iceland is believed, according to present theory, to be an emergent part of the Mid-Atlantic Ridge. This is the most tremendous mountain system on earth, running the length of the Atlantic Ocean. The center part of the Ridge is undergoing tension, indicated by the rift valley that extends for most of its length. The rift is indicated on Iceland by the numerous gaping fissures that are found through the middle belt of the island. Surtsey Island is considered to lie on the under-water extension of the ridge.

The story of the birth and development of the island is very fascinating, documented as it is by the series of photographs that are part of the book. Probably the most fascinating aspect of the whole record is the rapidity with which the island developed, as well as the series of changes it underwent in the process. In view of the usual approach to geomorphology, the paragraphs included below make fascinating reading. The summary, as it were, begins on page 52 of the English translation, where we read the following:

> And when they now wander about the island which was being born then, they find it hard to believe that this is an island whose age is still measured in months, not years. An Icelander, who has studied geology and geomorphology at foreign universities is later

---

*Concordia Junior College, Ann Arbor, Michigan

taught by experience in his homeland that the time scale he had been trained to attach *to geological developments is misleading* when assessments are made of the forces—constructive and destructive—which have moulded and are still moulding the face of Iceland. What elsewhere may take thousands of years [is this necessarily so in the light of what follows?—W.H.R.] may be accomplished here in one century. All the same, he is amazed whenever he comes to Surtsey, because the same development may take a few weeks or even a few days here.

On Surtsey, only a *few months* have sufficed for a *landscape to be created* which is *so varied and mature that it is almost beyond belief.* Here we not only have a lava dome with a glowing lava lake in a summit crater and red-hot lava-flows rushing down the slopes, increasing the height of the dome and transforming the configuration of the island from one day to another. Here we can also see wide sandy beaches and precipitous crags lashed by breakers of the sea. There are gravel banks and lagoons, impressive tephra (basaltic ash) cliffs, greyish-white from the brine and silicium which oozes out of the tephra, giving them a resemblance to the White Cliffs on the English Channel (the White Cliffs or Chalk Cliffs of Dover). There are hollows, glens and soft undulating land. There are fractures and faultscarps, channels and screes. There are often furious gales and sandstorms, which reduce visibility to zero, and Aegir, the Northern counterpart of Neptune, deals blows of no less violence. You may come to a beach covered with flowing lava on its way to the sea with white balls of smoke rising high up in the air. Three weeks later you may come back to the same place and be literally confounded by what meets your eye. Now there are precipitous lava cliffs of considerable height, and below them you will see boulders worn by the surf, some of which are almost round, on an abrasion platform cut into the cliff, and further out there is a sandy beach where you can walk at low tide without getting wet. The next time you are there, glowing lava-falls rush over the sea-cliff. One day, the surf may cut a large section out of a tephra wall. The next, the lava may spread across the sandy beach, protecting the cliff from further inroads by the sea (emphasis added).

At another page, reference is made to the work of the Canadian geologist, W. M. Mathews, who has explained the formation of some mountains in British Columbia, referred to as *tuyas*, in the same fashion as the structures that are basic to Surtsey. It is also postulated that diving explorations would reveal that the base of Surtsey would show the presence of pillow lavas.

Could one raise the question as to the validity of the assumptions underlying time scales of geomorphology at this point? On this point alone, this book makes extremely fascinating reading. And a further plus is the superb photography which copiously illustrates the action. I suggest it is well worth reading.

PROLEGOMENA TO A STUDY
OF CATACLYSMAL SEDIMENTATION

N. A. RUPKE*

"when we see the thing done, it is vain to dispute
against it from the unlikelihood of the doing it."
—John Ray
(Letter to Tancred Robinson/22 Okt./1684)

Sedimentation as it takes place today is a calm and slow process
acting on a small scale—Holocene sediment is accumulating little
by little in various sedimentary environments. If the greater part
of the earth's sedimentary rock was deposited at this modern rate
it would have required vast periods of time.

However, an abundance of phenomena which appear in the pre-
Quaternary rock testify to a completely uncommon mode of sedimentation which might be called "cataclysmal"; i.e., sequences of
considerable thicknesses were rapidly formed during a large-scale
deposition. Likely, this cataclysmal event, as evidenced by the Work
of God (Nature), fell together with the Noachian Deluge, as narrated
by the Word of God (Scripture).

In the present article the historical development of the concept of
cataclysmal deposition is traced ever since the birth of geology as a
science. Further, the lines of evidence in regard to this concept are
partly viewed. Finally, some results of field work are presented.

Referential procedures are changed according to the nature of
subject-matters. In regard to terminology the Geological Nomenclature (English, Dutch, French, German) of the Royal Geological
and Mining Society of the Netherlands is followed.

Ph.H. Kuenen, Professor and Head of the Geological Institute at
the State University of Groningen, is not responsible for any view
expressed in the present article.

---

*State University of Groningen, The Netherlands

Short History of Relevant Ideas

   1. *Nicolaus Steno* (1631-1687). In the 17th century the true method of interpreting nature was proposed by Francis Bacon (1561-1626) in his *Novum Organum Scientiarum* (1620). He defended

the value of methodically executed experiments against Aristotle (384-322 B.C.) and his mediaeval votaries. Generally speaking, Bacon raised up the shield of empiricism as the means by which the physical world could be disclosed.[1]

   The first investigator who applied the empirical method to geological questions was Nicolaus Steno (Figure 1). His "Prodrome" on a dissertation marked the birth of geology as a science, and especially of stratigraphy.

   In this "Prodrome," to which the proper dissertation was never added, Steno expressed the then

Figure 1. Nicolaus Steno. (After a portrait in the Pitti Palace).

uncommon view that the strata of the earth are due to the deposits of a fluid.[2] Furthermore, he conceived the principle of superposition in writing: "At the time when any given stratum was being formed, all the matter resting upon it was fluid, and, therefore, at the time when the lowest stratum was being formed, none of the upper strata existed." [3]

   Steno also grasped some causes of stratification. Strata lacking heterogeneous bodies, he argued, were of primeval origin, whereas fossiliferous strata were formed during the antediluvian period and during or since the Noachin Deluge by inundations caused by violent winds or downpours. Among other things he wrote: "Different kinds of layers in the same place can be caused either by a difference of the particles which withdraw from the fluid one after the other, as this same fluid is gradually disintegrated more and more, or from different fluids carried thither at different times." [4]

   Besides, Steno made a stand against Aristotle and his disciples, who upheld the view that fossil remains of buried organisms were produced *in situ* by a certain "Vis Formativa," "Vis Plastica," or

"Quid Vis." He maintained the real organic character of fossils, and gave it as his view "that the formation of many mollusks which we find today must be referred to times coincident with the universal deluge." [5]

The main effect of this universal and recent catastrophe Steno confined to the earth's geomorphogenical characteristics. In this context it is noteworthy that he concluded his "Prodrome" by showing that the biblical data of primeval creation and subsequent devastation constitute a framework wherein all results of geological observations could successfully be contained, arranged, and distinctly conceived.[6] Consequently, the "Prodrome" was not only a landmark in the development of geology in general; it also made its author the founding father of deluge geology. Curiously this historical truth has not been stressed up till now as far as I know.

By reason of his scientific ability, uniformitarian geologists have tried to claim Steno—making him, in subscribing to the Noachian Flood, a victim of church dogma and theological authority.[7] But on the contrary, a careful reading of Steno's "Prodrome" leads to the inference that his knowledge of biblical history stimulated his discovery that the earth's crust contains the record of a sequence of historical events, and made it a matter of course that fossils were the remains of mainly marine creatures thrown out on the continents by the running flood waters.[8]

2. *John Ray* (1627-1705). Though Steno's "Prodrome" became widely known among his contemporaries, John Ray took the lead up to a point in geology. The latter's ideas in this case were couched in the celebrated *Three Physico-Theological Discourses*.[9]

The "Discourses" went through several editions until well into the 18th century. In those Ray brought up much of novelty and importance, e.g., his observations on the hydrological cycle. However, as regards stratigraphy his "Discourses" did not represent an improvement upon Steno's "Prodrome," because Ray also attributed the earth's layers to local though tempestuous inundations, mainly occurring during antediluvian times.

He held the view that at first the earth was covered with water; that the land was raised up by subterranean fires; and that as a result the waters were driven back. He continued in writing: "Afterwards when the greatest part of the earth was raised, the skirts were alternated by the sediments of rivers and floods, whence and from the several inundations of the sea came the several beds or layers of earth." [10]

Yet Ray did not go beyond the framework of biblical history, and in consequence he in fact was a deluge geologist. The outcome of the Noachian Flood he mainly restricted to tectonical catastrophes. Amidst these he supposed the tearing apart of the continents where he guessed that the Old and the New World formerly were linked together.[11] This primitive pangea concept, also conceived by Adriaan Buurt (1711-1781) and other 18th century scientists, foreshadowed Alfred Wegener's continental drift theory.

Further, Ray adopted Steno's idea of fossils as organic remains, and disputed the opposite view of many of his contemporaries. He himself viewed the scattered fossil remains as a result of the universal deluge waters. To Edward Lhwyd (1660-1709) he expressed relating to his "Discourses": "I have inserted something concerning formed stones as an effect of the deluge, I mean their dispersion all over the earth. Therefore you will find all I have to say in opposition to their opinion who hold them to be primitive productions of nature in imitation of shells." [12]

In the presence of these data it is somewhat surprising to read in Byron C. Nelson's The Deluge Story in Stone: "Of those in England who opposed the Flood theory because they did not believe that fossils were the remains of former living things, the most prominent was John Ray"; [13] by mischance this incorrect information entered into the otherwise excellent The Genesis Flood of John C. Whitcomb and Henry M. Morris.[14] As Nelson does cite the "Discourses," he seems to have read them; but unfortunately he did not read them well, ascribing to Ray opinions which, indeed, he expounded, but only in order to argue against these.

3. John Woodward (1667-1727). Up to now a clear notion of the formation of stratified rock of considerable thickness was not presented. The first to take the right road in this case was John Woodward of Gresham College. This keen-witted scientist, being intimately acquainted with most of England's stratified formations, wrote in elucidation of these "An Essay" in which he proposed his theory of a Universal Solvent.

Woodward launched into speculations concerning the Noachian Flood, assuming that the upper part of the earth's crust was wholly dissolved in the all covering waters, constituting a muddled mass. From this the solid constituents would have settled down according to specific gravities, thus bringing about stratum super stratum, in which the organic bodies and parts thereof would have sealed up after gravity sorting.

It is noteworthy that the main argument for the rapid formation of subsequent strata consisted in the phenomenon of stratification itself. The same phenomenon is taken up by modern catastrophists to make out a good case for their convictions. Specifically, Woodward stated in his "Essay" with regard to the mentioned muddle:

> That at length all the Mass that was borne up in the Water, was again precipitated, and subsided towards the bottom. That this Subsidence happened generally, and as near as possibly could be expected in so great a Confusion, according to the Laws of Gravity; that Matter, Body or Bodies, which had the greatest quantity or degree of Gravity, subsiding first in order, and falling lowest; that which had the next, or a still lesser degree of Gravity, subsiding next after, and settling upon the precedent; and so on, in their several courses; that which had the least Gravity sinking not down till last of all, settling at the Surface of the Sediment, and covering all the rest. That the Matter, subsiding thus, formed the Strata of Stone, of Marble, of Cole, of Earth, and the rest; of which Strata, lying one upon another, the terrestrial Globe, or at least as much of it as is ever displayed to view, doth mainly consist.

Woodward continued with treating of gravity sorting and he went on to say:

> That for this reason the Shells of those Cockles, Escalops, Perewinckles, and the rest, which have a greater degree of Gravity, were enclosed and lodged in the Strata of Stone, Marble, and the heavier kinds of Terrestrial Matter; the lighter Shells not sinking down till afterwards, and so falling among the lighter Matter, such as Chalk, and the like, in all such parts of the Mass where there happened to be any considerable quantity of Chalk, or other Matter lighter than Stone; but where there was none, the said Shells fell upon, or near unto, the Surface.[15]

It stands beyond all argument that Woodward's theory of a Universal Solvent was an inadequate theory. Nevertheless it contained some constructive notions; e.g., that of gravity sorting which foreshadowed Henry M. Morris' concept of hydrodynamical selectivity.[16] Such, in some measure modern, ideas went beyond the grasp of several of Woodward's contemporaries, who cried down his "Essay." Even Ray turned against him, though they basically took the same position, as Karl A. von Zittel rightly stated.[17]

Aside from stratigraphy, Woodward's writings were of lasting value for paleontology. He took pains to demonstrate that the fossils were organic remains laid down in the deluge. Consequently he scorned the ideas of Edward Lhwyd on the one hand and Martin Lister (1638-1712) and Robert Plot (1640-1696) on the other that fossils were but "Lapides sui generis," or resulted from an "Aura seminalis." Woodward wrote in this case

> that they are so far from being formed in the Earth, or in the Places where they are now found, that even the Belemnites, Selenites, Marchasits, Flints, and other natural Minerals, which are lodged in the Earth, together with the Shells were not formed there, but had Being before ever they came thither: and were fully formed and finished before they were reposed in that manner.[18]

Thus Woodward swept away forever the wrong opinion concerning fossils; and he showed together with his adherent Johann Jacob Scheuchzer (1671-1733), [who translated the "Essay" into Latin 1704) and also wrote the *Herbarium Diluvianum* (1709) and other excellent writings], the way for a better understanding of the fossiliferous strata.[19]

In this context it is worth noting that Johann Jacob's brother Johann Scheuchzer (1684-1738) used a half water filled bowl in showing that the Noachin Flood could have been caused by a sudden stopping of the earth's rotation and a consequent gushing forth of violent tidal waves. An account of this experiment was given in a dissertation on *Lapides Figurati* read in the year 1710 before l'Academie Royale des Sciences. Irrespective of the adequacy of this elucidation to the historical events two conclusions are at hand: viz. that, to my knowledge, it was Johann Scheuchzer who was the first to execute a geological experiment and not Horace-Bénédict de Saussure (1740-1799), as claimed by Ph. H. Kuenen;[20] and that with this experiment the cataclysmic character of the Genesis Flood was distinctly conceived.[21]

4. *George-Louis Leclerc, Comte de Buffon* (1707-1788). During the second half of the 18th century, geology was retarded in its auspicious development by the impact of the writings of George-Louis Leclerc, Comte de Buffon.[22]

In this matter Buffon was preceded actually by his compatriot Benoit de Maillet (1656-1738), who drew up a cosmic system after

Cartesian fashion, published posthumously in 1748 under the title of *Telliamed*.[23]

De Maillet maintained that the strata of the earth and even the mountains were built up beneath the level of the sea by the ocean currents and by the flux and reflux of the tides. Consequently the earth's stratified rock could not have been deposited in a short space of time but only gradually during several millennia. De Maillet wrote about certain strata: "Undoubtedly they were formed in that place by a current coming from north-west, and from the sea-side, which manufactured them there successively one after another in a period of many thousands of years" (translated from the French).[24]

Buffon lined up with de Maillet's assertions in this case.[25] Moreover, on the subject of time he did not mere guess-work, but introduced a time-dimension, based on an alleged refrigeration of the globe, which he had brought into being as a glowing mass torn from the sun by a striking comet.[26]

Thus a dating method was introduced within the framework of evolutionary cosmogony. Yet Buffon's maximum estimate of the earth's age remained in the order of 75,000 years.[27] None the less, it was plain that his system was contradicted by the biblical cosmogony. As a result, Buffon tried to explain away all physical implications of the Noachian Deluge, substituting for the cataclysm concept, his tranquil theory, in which any geological effect of the deluge was denied. The passage in question in Buffon's *Preuves de la Théorie de la Terre* ran as follows:

> After all, it is easy to convince oneself that it is neither in one and the same time, nor by the effect of the deluge, that the sea left uncovered the continents which we inhabit; because it is certain, by the testimony of the sacred books, that the earthly paradise was in Asia, and that Asia was a continent inhabited before the deluge; in consequence, it is not in that time that the seas covered that considerable part of the globe. So the earth was, before the deluge, broadly the same as she is today; and that enormous quantity of water, which the divine justice brought down on the earth to punish the culpable men, caused in fact the death to all creatures; but it produced not a single alteration on the surface of the earth; it destroyed not even the plants, because the pigeon brought back an olive-branch (translated from the French).[28]

So Buffon introduced the concept of an earth history passed off quietly in the course of periods of long duration; and although Buffon took a lot of geological data from Woodward's "Essay," he frequently made a stand against him and thus Woodward's influence was eclipsed by Buffon on account of the latter's eloquent diction.[29]

5. *Jean-André Deluc* (1727-1817). Still a new champion of biblical catastrophism appeared on the scene in the person of Jean-André Deluc (de Luc) who became an adversary of the Buffonian cosmogony. This Swiss naturalist made himself a name by his meteorological observations and experiments and by his travels through many parts of the European continent. His name was attended by authority for most of his contemporaries, and he wielded great influence in his day.

In one of his early writings, viz. *Lettres Physiques et Morales, sur l'Histoire de la Terre et de l'Homme. Adressées a la Reine de la Grande Bretagne* (1778-1780), Deluc introduced the term "geology" instead of the then usual designation "cosmology." [30]

Deluc set himself to bear out Moses' account of cosmogony by natural history. Unfortunately, he took his stratigraphical data from Horace-Bénédict de Saussure, being the contemporary leading mineralogist, who held the view that granitic rock took shape as a layered deposit, being precipitated by a process of crystallization in a primordial fluid.[31] In consequence this chemical process must have been a gradual one and would have taken up much space of time.

In order to fall in with Saussure's view in this case, Deluc conceived of the days of creation as of periods of indeterminate length.[32] In elucidation of the Noachian Flood he conjectured that the mainland of before, hanging over huge cavities, collapsed, by which an enormous basin came into being, taking in all ocean waters. As a result the ocean floor of old became the mainland which we inhabit today.[33] Thus he rendered an account of fossils and of a lot of other geological data.

Deluc's ideas were enunciated by one of his intimates, namely the Dutch poet William Bilderdijk (1756-1831), in a treatise which constituted the first original Dutch dissertation on geology. Bilderdijk turned against the Buffonian doctrine of a geomorphogenical history of long duration. He wrote:

> It was, since Buffon, a cherished idea, that awe-inspiring space of time in which he led us about. The hugeness thereof startled and interested. But, actually, he who accounts for an effect by a force which must have acted infinitely to produce the effect to be accounted for does not make clear anything. Everything in

the corporeal world takes place in a time-dimension (translated from the Dutch).[34]

Bilderdijk referred to the physical chronology drawn up by Deluc, for the period since the universal flood.

In doing this Deluc had made use of some dating methods based on natural processes; e.g., the formation of vegetable mold; the reduction of tongues by marine abrasion; or stream erosion.[35] He proved to be aware of the fact that the last mentioned process could not have worked uniformly. He wrote: "at first the rivers carried away to the ocean a quantity of materials incomparably larger than that which they carry away today" (translated from the French).[36] From these Deluc inferred "that our continents are not old; and that not any other phenomenon contradicts that inference" (translated from the French).[37]

Unfortunately, Deluc's influence was largely eclipsed by George Cuvier (1769-1832), who got the theory accepted that the present-day condition of the earth's crust resulted from a sequence of cataclysms in the course of lengthened periods.[38]

6. *James Hutton* (1726-1797). The philosophy of uniformitarianism in the earth's science, advanced in the "Telliamed" and advocated by Buffon, was brought into vogue by the writings of James Hutton and his countryman Sir Charles Lyell (1797-1875). Hutton made his doctrine public before the Royal Society of Edinburgh in a paper entitled "Theory of the Earth; or an Investigation of the Laws observable in the Composition, Dissolution, and Restoration of Land upon the Globe" (read 1785), which paper was afterwards developed into his renowned *Theory of the Earth, with Proofs and Illustrations* (1795).

In these works Hutton upheld the view that the laws of nature had acted uniformly throughout history. Thus the phenomena of the earth's crust were to be made clear by means of changes still in progress today. In consequence these changes would have taken up vast periods of time in order to account for the earth's characteristics. As a result Hutton scorned the idea of catastrophism, and he wrote in his paper of 1785:

> But though, in generalizing the operations of nature, we have arrived at those great events, which, at first sight, may fill the mind with wonder and with doubt, we are not to suppose, that there is any violent exertion of power, such as is required in order to produce a great event in little time; in nature, we find

no deficiency in respect of time, nor any limitation with regard to power.[39]

In pursuance to this time-philosophy Hutton maintained that the strata now exposed on our continents were deposited little by little in the course of geological time; treating of limestone he stated:

> We are led, in this manner, to conclude, that all the strata of the earth, not only those consisting of such calcareous masses, but others superincumbent upon these, have had their origin at the bottom of the sea, by the collection of sand and gravel, of shells, of corralline and crustaceous bodies, and of earths and clays, variously mixed, or separated and accumulated.[40]

These assertions led to a vigorous controversy in which Deluc took action as an adversary of stature against the uniformitarian doctrine.

Nevertheless, the Huttonian modernism gained grounds—mainly because John Playfair (1748-1819) interfered in the controversy in support of Hutton's "Theory of the Earth." How important a place was awarded to time in uniformitarianism was put into words by Playfair as follows: alluding at a vast progression of daily operations, he wrote: "TIME performs the office of *integrating* the infinitesimal parts of which this progression is made up; it collects them into one sum and produces from them an amount greater than any that can be assigned." [41]

Yet the Huttonian "Theory" did not win a wide acceptance among geologists until it was championed by Sir Charles Lyell. He stated that his method "endeavours to estimate the aggregate result of ordinary operations multiplied by time"; and further on he wrote: "For this reason all theories are rejected which involve the assumption of sudden and violent catastrophes and revolutions of the whole earth, and its inhabitants." [42] Lyell frequently challenged the catastrophic school of geologists, primarily in the person of Woodward, and as a result he completely expelled all deluge geology from the professorial chair.[43]

7. *George Fairholme* (dates unknown). Up to now hardly any examination of the earth's strata was carried out in order to decide in the time-energy dilemma. In his *Geologie* Bilderdijk wrote in view of the uniformitarian systems: "Fortuitous observations, suggested by mining, and partly ill-noticed or -imagined, being always insufficient, defective, and only local, produced false and rash conclusions, upon which the imaginations, which passed for demonstrations or

real inferences, were built" (translated from the Dutch).[44] Even Lyell in his celebrated *Principles of Geology* did nothing but lining out the probability of slow deposition of sedimentary rock, and by no means did he establish the actuality of it.

The search for the testimony of stratified rock itself with regard to the rate of its formation was initiated by some 19th century deluge geologists. Among these the sharp-witted George Fairholme took the lead in writing the *New and Conclusive Physical Demonstrations*,[45] which constituted a landmark in the development of deluge geology. In it Fairholme exposed sedimentary structures, bespeaking a rapid deposition of successive strata to a very great thickness, and he conjectured that the earth's stratified rock was built up by an abnormal tidal action—afterwards called the tidal theory.

Fairholme's work was elaborated by some 19th century votaries. Yet a deluge geologist of stature did not appear on the scene until the 20th century, when George McCready Price (1870-1963) published his epoch-making *The New Geology* (1923). The main merit of Price has been his having taken hold of the crystallized time-table of geological ages. Price's arguments in this case are for the most part couched in his *Evolutionary Geology and the New Catastrophism* (1926). Unfortunately, in dealing with the order of the earth's strata little attention was given to the rate of formation of stratified rock.

Now then, even after one got well-posted as to the earth's crust, Huttonian geology was not scorned—primarily in consequence of its being connected with a non-biblical philosophy of life. Francis C. Haber observes: "Hutton's thought was a development of natural theology and the timeless world-machine view." [46] Today this philosophical heritage is playing a trick with the greater number of the world's geologists.

Though it is attempted to justify uniformitarianism on account of the great number of adherents of this philosophy, it should be borne in mind that the "majority" cannot be an argument in science and its problems; for, as noted by German poet and scientist Johann Wolfgang von Goethe (1749-1832): "Nothing is more repulsive than the majority: for it consists of not many forceful leaders, of scapegraces who accommodate themselves, of weaklings who assimilate themselves, and the crowd who trundles behind, without any acquaintance of its own mind" (translated from the German).[47]

Next following I have dealt with some conclusive data on the rapid formation of much of the earth's stratified rock.

Main Arguments to Rapid Deposition

1. *Polystrate Fossils.* In spite of the prevailing hypotheses of graduality and, along with this extreme length of the earth's history, the conditions in which most fossils all over the world are unearthed bear testimony to an extraordinary, rapid, and often cataclysmal process of sedimentation. One of these conditions is displayed by a group of fossils in what I propose to call a "polystrate position." By this concept is meant the fossil remains of huge animals and petrified tree-trunks, extending through a thick bed or, properly speaking, through two or more strata of sedimentary rock.

Such—so to be termed—"polystrate fossils" are found in many parts of the world; their height may be tens of meters and, despite this, their *topmost parts are as well preserved as the basal ones.* These facts indicate that the petrified remains were sealed up before decay and, in consequence, were buried in their polystrate position by rapidly deposited layers of sediment shortly after or even when they died or were torn up by the roots.

It is not as common to come across polystrate animal remains as those of upright tree-trunks; yet they are found. Van der Vlerk and Kuenen report: "In the United States a thick, apparently uninterrupted deposition of sands and clays is found, in which the entire bodies with the skin-impression of huge pre-historic reptiles are met with." [48] In case the sedimentation had been uniform the giant carrions would not be covered within 5,000 years; therefore, van der Vlerk and Kuenen conclude: "The only possibility is that immediately after the death the dead body was covered and as it were ensiled by a thick bed of sediment." [49]

Other polystrate fossils are mainly restricted to truncated tree trunks. These are found chiefly in the Carboniferous series; though they are found as well in exposures of Mesozoic and Cenozoic formations.[50] Geikie writes: "It is not uncommon in certain Carboniferous sandstones to find huge sigillaroid and coniferous trunks imbedded in up-right or inclined positions." [51]

Further he states: "It occasionally happens that an erect trunk has kept its position even during the accumulation of a series of strata around it." [52] Geikie concludes: "We can hardly believe that in such cases any considerable number of years could have elapsed

Figure 2. Polystrate tree-trunk near Essen-Kupferdreh (Germany). (Photo by Klusemann).

between the death of the tree and its final entombment." [53]

This inference is the more conclusive when the tree trunks are six to nine meters high. It is noteworthy that such dimensions are not exceptional. About a decenniad ago in the neighborhood of Essen-Kupferdreh in Germany over the seam Angelika, a series of *Lepidophyta* was unearthed at interspaces of 3 to 5 meters. Klusemann and Teichmüller report: "These stumps are are 7.5 m. in height and must have been still higher before they were cut down by the Ruhr in the Riss glacial epoch." [54] (See Figure 2.)

Afterwards, when in the same area the deposits over the seam Sonnenschein were exposed, again upright tree trunks standing over seven meters came to light, which likewise must have been still higher before the glacial age. The mentioned authors remark: "Because the *Sigillaria* properly speaking constituted only bark-tubes when their insignificant wood-body had become putrefied they may have been more transitory than, for instance, the solid oak or Sequoia trunks of today." [55] As a result the enclosure of the truncated tree trunks cannot have taken up much space of time. Klusemann and Teichmüller conclude: "Perhaps it were some months, perhaps some years, but certainly not much longer";[56] and this estimate is even the maximum one.

These polystrate trunks were found over a wide area. It also occurs that such fossils display a remarkable vertical dispersion; e.g., at The Joggins on Nova Scotia. Dunbar writes: "Here erect trunks are recorded at 20 horizons distributed at intervals through about 2,500

Figure 3. Polystrate tree-trunk near Edinburgh (England). (After Witham).

feet of beds." [57] Only a wholly uncommon process of sedimentation can account for conditions like these.

The fossilized tree stems are not only found erect. They also occur in positions, forming an angle with the lie of the strata, varying from nothing up to 90°. A striking example of this was reported by Tayler,[58] and by Nelson,[59] who made reference to a lofty trunk, exposed in a sandstone quarry near Edinburgh, which measured no less than 25 meters and, intersecting 10 or 12 different strata, leaned at an angle of about 40° (compare with Figure 3).

Similar examples are mentioned by Geikie.[60] In addition he states that the internal microscopic structure of the relevant trees was well preserved. Further, Geikie conjectures: "In such examples, the drifted trees seem to have sunk with their heavier or root end touching the bottom and their upper end pointing upward in the direction of the current." [61] Moreover, as stated by Arber,[62] in some districts the prone stems far exceed those still upright.

Now then, as already noted by Fairholme,[63] an inclined stem constitutes a stronger testimony to rapidity in deposition than even an upright one:

> for while the latter might be supposed to have been capable of retaining an upright position, in a semi-fluid mass, for a long time, by the mere laws of gravity, the other must, by the very same laws, have fallen, from its inclined to a horizontal position, had it not been *retained* in its inclined position by *the rapid accumulation* of its present stony matrix (emphasis added).[64]

A special class of polystrate stems is constituted by stumps which extend up through a coal seam, together with some layers of sandstone and sandy slate, or even through two or more of these coal seams and all interbedded strata. Curiously few references are made to this and, if any, for the most part by earlier authors.[65] Even so, examples are unusually abundant; consequently, the coal beds were rapidly deposited just as well as the above-mentioned inorganic sequences.

Somtimes the upright position of the erect stumps is claimed to prove their having grown where they now stand—*in situ*.[66] However, there are several facts which invalidate the hypothesis that they were of an autochthonous origin. More often than not they were devoid of both branches and roots, and, as a result, they cannot have grown where they now stand. They also are found at various heights. Whereas, had they grown *in situ* their basal parts must be rooted in one particular stratum.

In view of these facts Arber writes: "It is not certain that these trunks, despite their upright position, are *in situ*. They are much more probably drifted material, like the sandstones which enclose them." [67] And, what's more, examples are found which appeared to be *upside down*, or, in other words, which have their root end uppermost. On account of these facts, there is no question but that the relevant stems were of an allochthonous origin (compare with Figure 4).

Besides, it must be remembered that a drifted tree stem will often float upright, for its center of gravity is situated at the lower end of that stem, which constitutes the heavier one. In this context, Fair-

Figure 4. Polystrate tree-trunks near Saint-Etienne (France). (After Brongniart).

holm wrote: "the stem of a tree, especially if it be long, and have consequently a great disproportion between the weight of its two extremities, would naturally sink in a fluid, and perhaps still more in a semi-fluid, with its root end downwards."[68] This actually is observed along the banks of the great rivers; Arber writes: "in the deltas of large rivers to-day, the bases of trees of large size, sometimes with fragments of roots still attached, may be deposited in a more or less upright position, though they have been transported for a considerable distance." [69]

Moreover, as pointed out by Grand'Eury,[70] the petrified tree stems more often than not display a thickened trunk base. Now Hörbiger[71] conjectured that the relevant trunks functioned like the spindle of a natural hydrometer (Senkwaage) by which the massive rhizome constituted the bulb (Senkgewicht); as a result they tended to float upright and were deposited in that position as soon as the current quieted. Accordingly Nilsson states: "The anatomical structure of a plant part determines its position in a measure." [72]

Curiously, the upright stems usually are cut off according to a shear plane which coincides with a bedding plane. They are not fractured obliquely, as often occurs today when a tree has broken off above the roots. It is asserted by Potonié that the shear planes were brought about by a water level of old.[73] However, this contention cannot be supported by any modern analogy whatsoever.

On the contrary, a comparison between the mentioned features and recent analogs brings to light an unequivocal discrepancy. An examination of Stump Lake in North Dakota by Aronow showed considerable level fluctuations within a few centennia: "The lake levels seem to respond in a very sensitive manner to slight climatic changes." [74] Among the many stumps once rooting *in situ* only one specimen was left. It was found in an advanced state of decomposition and all similarity with fossil examples was lacking.

In addition, something else excludes that a water level came into play here; viz., that there are fossil tree stems which are sheared off at various heights.[75] In order to elucidate this enigma, Hörbiger[76] conjectured that the relevant trunks were embedded by a huge tidal wave, bringing about stratum super stratum, during a furious cold. As a result the upper parts of the soaked trunks, standing above the frozen level of the last bed, became hard as nails and were sheared off on a level with the bedding plane by the next tidal wave; to this Nilsson adds that on account of certain causes some tree stems were not snapped off until a fresh bed was deposited and their parts, still standing out, were struck by a next impetus.[77]

Personally, I am of the opinion that the polystrate fossils constitute a crucial phenomenon both to the actuality and the mechanism of cataclysmal deposition. Curiously, a paper on polystrate fossils appears to be a "black swan" in geological literature. Antecedent to this synopsis a systematic discussion of the relevant phenomena was never published. However, geologists must have been informed about these fossils. In view of this it seems unintelligible that uniformitarianism has kept its dominant position.

In order to make this clear, as best I can, I present a historical analogue: the anatomist Vesalius (1514-1564) pictured the human liver with five lobes;[78] three of these he could never have observed. Nevertheless, Vesalius pictured them—apparently in imitation of Galenus (131-200), whose conceptions were true dogmas until well into the 16th century. Nowadays, most geologists uphold a uniform process of sedimentation during the earth's history; but their views are contradicted by plain facts. Nevertheless, uniformitarianists insist on their point—obviously they line up with Huttonian philosophy. A case like this is no more a matter of geological argument; I can but present it as a curious example of those who intend to trace the psychology of scientific dogmas.

2. *Ephemeral Markings.* A classification of sedimentary structures may be executed on the basis of several criteria; e.g., according to the time and site of formation.[79] In that manner the structures are divided into non-organic and organic types, the latter being produced by all sorts of organisms. The former are divided into "syndepositional structures" (produced by the mode and site of deposition of the settling material) and "non-syndepositional structures" (produced by the disturbance of the deposited particles).

If the disturbance of the boundary plane between sediment and water, i.e., of the depositional interface, is produced from above, then the structures are called "metadepositional," and if from below, "postdepositional." The meta- and postdepositional structures are not distinguished in regard to time. Among the non-organic, as well as the organic structures, a profusion of specimens are very transient— primarily those located on surfaces. When the depositional interface moves upwards as sedimentation continues, they easily are obliterated.

Sedimentary structures, characterized by pronounced transiency, I propose to classify as "ephemeral markings." As a rule they are not preserved in the sedimentary complexes of the Quaternary—in which system also bedding is scarce. On the other hand, the ephemeral markings are frequently recorded in all earlier systems. Their preservation more often than not requires quite a rapid deposition of covering sediment; and their astounding abundance suggests that the sedimentation was cataclysmal both to rapidity and extent. Dozens or even—when subdivided—hundreds of types of ephemeral markings are known at present and their number is still swelling. In this paper only certain types can be treated; e.g., ripple marks, rain prints, trails, and tracks.

(a) *Ripple Marks.* As early as the middle of the previous century two basic types of ripple marks were clearly discerned; viz., the symmetrical or oscillation ripple marks, and the asymmetrical or water current ones. The former are produced by wave action in stagnant water, the latter by water currents not exceeding certain critical current velocities. Gradually an amplified division was proposed.[80] However, it only applies to recent ripple marks. Concerning fossilized structures obviously identical with ripple marks, the binary division may be still useful.

The conditions producing the structures at issue have been thoroughly studied for a long time; int. al. by Darwin[81] or recently by Kirchmayer[82] and Tanner.[83] Curiously, the factors which favor or prevent the preservation of ripple marks are barely given attention. An attempted systematic discussion is contained in Bucher's paper of 1919. In this context it is worthy of mention that ripple marks are extremely transitory. As a rule they are wiped out soon after they are produced. Geikie states: "On an ordinary beach, each tide usually effaces the ripple-marks made by its predecessor, and leaves a new series to be obliterated by the next tide." [84]

However, ripple marks—chiefly mud ripples—become preserved in recent deposits—as reported by Trusheim[85] or by van Straaten.[86] Nevertheless, examples are extremely exceptional—especially with regard to sand ripples. Accordingly, Kemper[87] remarks that only endogenous structures stand a good chance of becoming preserved. As a rule, surface markings are destroyed by the currents and the sustained reworking of the sea-bottom material ("ständige Materialumlagerung am Meeresboden").

For all that, Kemper came across well-preserved current ripples in the Bentheimer Sandstein. He writes: "The more startling is a slab with current ripple marks. . . ." [88] The preserved ripple marks constitute a serious problem—especially in regard to the symmetrical type. Kindle and Bucher write:

> The preservation of typical oscillation ripples under a thick layer of coarse sand, as is frequently seen in many sandstone formations, offers a more difficult problem than the preservation of current ripples, as the very existence of oscillation ripples excludes the possibility of any current erosion in the vicinity of the sedimentary surface.[98]

However, fossilized ripple marks constitute one of the most common sedimentary structures in pre-Quaternary sequences. They are found in most exposures of any group all over the world; and, as a rule, they are markedly well preserved. Relating to sand ripples, Inman states: "they are one of the sedimentary structures frequently preserved in the geologic record." [90] For obvious reasons the ripple marks must have been rapidly covered with sediment shortly after they were formed. Bucher's words are: "They must all, soon after their formation, be sufficiently covered with sediment settling on them from above." [91]

As a rule the ripple marks occur only at the bedding planes of the layers—curiously not within these. This absence of ripples within the layers itself suggests that the latter were formed by an uninterrupted sedimentation. Often the ripple marks are seen from bedding plane to bedding plane in a series of layers of which each more often than not stands several feet. Practically invariably the layers succeed each other with an astounding regularity. These conditions suggest a periodical deposition, as of ebb and flow, though it must have been of an uncommon rapidity and on a large scale, i.e., cataclysmal.

Presumably the sediment conveyors were huge tidal waves as assumed in the tidal theory[92]—which waves must have been generated abundantly during the Noachian Deluge.[93] However, it cannot be clear at first sight why the sediment conveyors did not obliterate the ripple marks. Some possibilities are proposed here—though it does not concern the actuality but only the mechanism of cataclysmal sedimentation.

Perhaps some ripples were of the firm type not seldom found on sandy beaches. Kindle and Bucher write: "Such ripple marks would survive the passage of sand-bearing currents, and speedy burial might result without damage to their form." [94] Perhaps the sediment conveyors were inter- or overflows in a large body of water and did not scrape along the bottom. Perhaps the ripple marks were frozen during deposition intervals—as supposed by Nilsson.[95] As a matter of fact, fossil ice crystal marks are found on sandstone surfaces.[96]

(b) *Rain Prints*. From the metadepositional structures the rain prints are found. A raindrop falling on a surface of soft sand or wet mud produces a pit margined by a ragged rim. When the wind drives aslant the raindrop, the imprint is ridged up to one side. The raised margin indicates the direction toward which the wind blew.

Obviously these structures are extremely ephemeral. As a rule they are washed out within a few hours. Despite this, rain prints are often found in the fossil record. Geikie writes: "The familiar effects of a heavy shower upon a surface of moist sand or mud may be witnessed among rocks even as old as the Cambrian period." [97] However, as remarked by Twenhofel,[98] it is doubtful if they really have so frequent an occurrence as suggested in the literature.

Perhaps the supposed rain prints were produced by agents similar to raindrops though not identical with them. The imprints may be hail-, drip-, or spray, and splash-prints. The tendency for these imprints is to have a greater width and depth than the rain prints. Nevertheless there cannot have been a difference in regard to transiency worth the name. Consequently, all mentioned types require a rapid deposition of the layers covering them. Add to this the fact that the imprints are often found at successive bedding planes. As a result a large-scale deposition seems to have built up the relevant sequences in a short space of time.

(c) *Trace Fossils*. The occurrence of some types of trace fossils leads to identical conclusions. A variety of animal trails and tracks is produced in unconsolidated sand and mud. Generally—by reason of the softness of the sediment—the markings are quickly wiped out by wind or water action. Especially this holds good in regard to sand; for, as stated by Shrock, "the nature of this material is such that markings made on its surface have relatively little chance of being preserved." [99] Lately the same is stressed by Whitcomb and Morris.[100] For all that, trails and tracks may become fossil.[101] However, this does not alter the fact that examples of preserved trails and tracks in recent deposits are singular to a high degree.

Now then, despite this, they are found in the fossil record in countless numbers and sometimes over vast areas. Moreover, they may be classified among the phenomena to be observed in all systems and even in all series. The types are diverse. Twenhofel writes:

They consist of worm trails from the rocks of all ages since the Proterozoic; tracks of crustaceans, as perhaps *Climatichnites* from the Cambrian of Wisconsin, which resembles the trail of a small automobile and may be an algal impression, and double rows of pits, as in the Richmond of Anticosti, where they have been followed over a 6-inch bed of limestone for 75 miles; tracks of amphibians from the Kansas Coal Measures; and the famed reptile tracks of the Newark sandstone.[102]

Frequently the interpretation of trails and tracks is still doubtful. A relevant structure consists of parallel, concentric furrows, about two mm. in width, which is classified as "Helminthoida" and, usually, is described as "guided meander" or "spiral track."[103] It is known through thousands of examples from the Cambrian system till the Tertiary. Schäfer[104] connects it with analogues produced on a recent mud flat. About the recent traces, he states they cannot become fossils—even with favorable sedimentation circumstances. Thus from the outset the preserved specimens must have been much more deepened. However, even then their preservation can be brought about only by the covering with sediment soon after they were producd.

(d) *Bird Tracks.* Also bird tracks are reported; e.g., by de Raaf, Betts and Kortenbout van der Sluijs[105] in the Lower Oligocene of Navarra and Zaragoza in northern Spain. The basal part of the formation is made up by calcareous shales intercalated with siltstones. Upwards the sequence grades into a much more arenaceous succession with scores of beds with bird tracks. de Raaf *et al.* write: "Bird-tracks, both on sandstones or siltstones (occasionally on ripple marked surfaces or associated with salt pseudo-morphs) and on shales (evidenced as natural casts on the sole of overlying arenaceous beds), occur in the entire arenaceous succession, although more frequently in its lower parts." These numerous and well-preserved bird tracks require a rapid deposition of the capping layers.

In the conclusion of their report de Raaf *et al.* remark:

> It finally remains to consider the extraordinary, and often beautiful, preservation of a truly amazing abundance of bird-tracks in an area of the order indicated. It is hard to see how tracks abounding in all directions so repeatedly could be preserved at all with such regularity without invoking eolian action. Only thus can we envisage the much-repeated mechanism of quick burial and most successful preservation of the tracks after their imprint in exposed wet arenaceous to clayey sediments, first

with wind-blown silt and sand derived from drying flats and only later by more sediment transported by water.[106]

The mechanism of preservation here postulated may have played a part—but the mentioned conditions imply a wholly uncommon process of sediment-conveying and -settling.

More often than not various ephemeral markings are found on one and the same bedding plane, i.e., ripple marks, rain prints, mud cracks, and trails or tracks occurring together and mutually strengthening the testimony of each to cataclysmal sedimentation. It should be noted that together with the mentioned bird tracks observed by de Raaf *et al.*, ripple marks, rain prints, and mud cracks were also perceived.

The rapidness by which these marking must have been covered is emphasized by the very recent observations on flysch and graded graywackes. The term "flysch" refers to sedimentary complexes made up of shaly-marly sediments and medium-thick sandstones. The hard, dark rock, denominated as "graywacke," often occurs in flysch-like sequences and it resembles the flysch sandstones. Whenever cropping out, the lutite layers easily crumble away, exposing the undersides or "soles" of the sandstones. Mostly the soles are sharply defined and show a variety of surface markings, which as a rule were designated as "hieroglyphs"—a term applied to any markings found on bedding planes. Today the term "sole markings" is generally accepted.

These markings are the casts of structures in the underlying shales or marls produced there by organisms, currents, or other agents. The diverse types are described by Kuenen,[107] Pettijohn and Potter,[108] Dzulinsky and Walton,[109] *et al.* There are tracks, burrows, rill marks, flute casts, etc. Now then, the typical features of flysch and graded graywackes are interpreted by Kuenen and Migliorini[110] in terms of a certain type of density current, viz., the "turbidity current" ("troebelingsstroom").

The relevant deposits are considered according to the turbidity current hypothesis, as "resedimented rock" or, usually, as "turbidites." Kuenen summarizes the now widely accepted hypothesis:

> Briefly, the hypothesis of resedimentation assumes that the detrital sediment is first deposited near the coast, e.g., on a delta. At intervals a mass of this material starts to slide down the slope and changes to a turbulent current, propelled by its excess weight over that of the clear surrounding water. On reaching a decrease

in slope, the current is retarded, becomes overloaded, and starts to lose sediment.[111]

So the pre-existing structures on the superface were preserved and casts of these formed upon the bases of the capping layers. Concerning the preservation of these structures it is stated by Kuenen: "The fact that such delicate markings as grazing tracks and trails, if that is what they are, have been imprinted on the graywackes of resedimented series apparently demonstrates that some turbidity current caused no erosion but started deposition at once and thus conserved pre-existing bottom markings." [112] This deposition came about "very suddenly and swiftly." [113]

More often than not the material involved must have been really immense and the velocity of the currents may have come to some 100 km per hour.[114] Besides, the amazing rhythmic bedding of flysch deposits, which is without modern analogue, suggests that the entire sequences were built up by a periodical and—as it were—pulsating succession of turbidity currents. If the turbidity current hypothesis is right, then the turbidites were, strictly speaking, deposited in a cataclysmal way.

None the less, Kuenen claims that the lutites were formed slowly by pelagic sedimentation and, as a result, the intervals between the deposition of successive sandy beds tended to be long.[115] However, evidence is growing that the lutite layers were rapidly formed. Dzulinsky and Walton write: "Although emphasis has been laid on the operation of turbidity currents in the formation of sands, the hypothesis may also be applied to fine-grained beds. There is little doubt that the lower parts of most shaly layers associated with flysch sandstones commonly belong to the same sedimentary episode as the underlying arenite." [116]

And further they remark: "Even in seemingly homogeneous shales, close examination frequently reveals a number of graded units. True pelagic deposits are probably very insignificant in flysch sediments and this contention finds some support in the evidence that thick shaly-flysch units have accumulated in short-time intervals." [117]

However, if the original material was "first deposited near the coast, e.g., on a delta," [118] accumulating there gradually, then a succession of turbidity currents, rapidly generated after each other, cannot be accounted for. A succession of turbidity currents can be accounted for if the sediments of entire coastal regions and marine slopes were loosely packed and easy to disturb; and if agents, generating the turbidity currents, were abundant and intensive.

Typically, these conditions are existing within the framework of deluge geology. As regards the period when the deluge waters fell, Whitcomb and Morris write:

> The newly deposited sediments were still relatively soft and unconsolidated, and the imposition of new gradients and currents over them when the land began to rise would have immediately induced scouring action on a large scale. The mixture of water and mud thus formed would, in flowing downslope, itself cause tremendous submarine erosion and ultimate redeposition.[119]

During this period, eustatic movements, earthquakes, and volcanic activity, competent to generate turbidity currents, must have been very numerous.

Lack of space prevents continued enunciation of the arguments for cataclysmal deposition—though a profusion of arguments might be brought to the front, e.g., (1) the thanatocoenoces or "fossil graveyards," (2) the excellent preservation of even soft parts of single or packed up organisms, or (3) the phenomenon of stratification as an indication of some recurrent tidal wave phenomena of abnormal character.[120] These lines of evidence are commonplace since Buckland[121] and Miller.[122]

On the other hand, the facts classified here as "polystrate fossils" and "ephemeral markings" are barely referred to in the literature on catastrophic geology—though the former phenomena are most conclusive and the latter are much more common in sedimentary complexts than any of the other facts. Without question they constitute strong arguments in favor of cataclysmal deposition, and, generally, support catastrophism as a scientific principle to interpret the earth's history. It would be gratifying if competent scientists were alive to collect and publish examples of the mentioned fossils and markings. In conclusion of this article I present some results of field work in The Netherlands (Winterswijk) and in Belgium (The Ardennes).

Some Results of Field Work

1. *Winterswijk.* In The Netherlands the Mesozoic is covered practically everywhere with complexes of Tertiary and Quaternary sediments. Only in some areas they crop out; e.g., in the Geldersche Achterhoek where int. al. Triassic limestones are covered only with

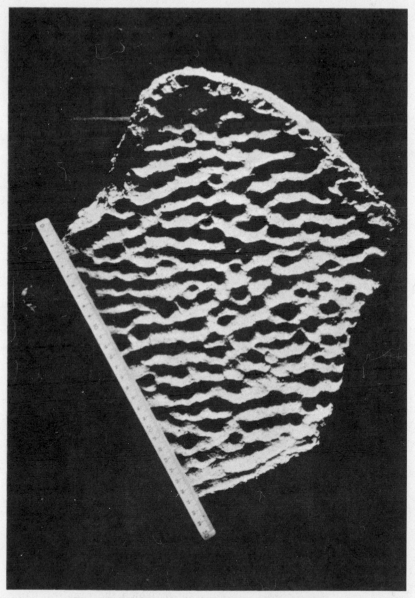

Figure 5. Ripple marks in the Winterswijk Muschelkalk (The Netherlands). (Specimen from the author's collection).

thin beds of Pleistocene till or niveo-eolian cover sands. The lime-stones contain *Myophoria* species and consequently are classified as Muschelkalk; generally, it is assumed that the deposits belong to the Lower Muschelkalk. In the vicinity of Winterswijk on the Vossenveld the limestone is being exploited by the N. V. Winterswijkse Steen- en Kalkgroeve. In that area the Muschelkalk has a formation thickness of 40 to 50 meters and is excavated in two quarries; viz., the Old Quarry and about one kilometer eastward, the New Quarry. Both I have visited several times.

In the Old Quarry the limestone displays a layered structure; it is built up of thin beds or even of laminae. On the surfaces of most beds ripple marks occur. They are of various sizes and types— though for the most part they consist of interference wave ripple marks. On an average the wave length is 1.5 cm. and ranges from 1 to about 2.5 cm. As a rule the crests are sharply defined and the specimens show no indication of levelling of the ripple ridges (Fig-ure 5). The Old Quarry abounds with ripple marks; they are found at various horizons and I traced them over an area of some 20,000 to 30,000 square meters. It is a riddle to me how Faber can say that ripple marks are rarely seen in this exposure.[123]

Figure 6. Rain print in the Winterswijk Muschelkalk (The Netherlands). (Specimen from the author's collection).

In this same quarry many pits occur which look like imprints made by raindrops; they do not extend in the limestone under-neath and consequently are not crossed burrows. The average diameter is 4.5 mm., whereas imprints of 2 and 7 mm. are also found. For the most part the imprints are but few or not rimmed—though I recorded also rain prints with extremely well-preserved rims. Now and then the impressions are elliptical and margined but to one side; the elevated side indicates the direc-tion in which the raindrop came down (Figure 6). In places, the prints abound and they are found at *various horizons*. Frequently

Figure 7. Rill marks (?) in the Winterswijk Muschel-kalk (The Netherlands). (Specimen from the author's collection).

they are found on slabs with fossilized mud cracks; the cracks are restricted to thin beds or laminae being only some few mm. thick. For instance, on a surface enclosed by superficial mud cracks and being about 10 cm.^{2}, some 10 to 15 rain prints occurred.

In the New Quarry also thin beds and laminae are extant; in addition, thick layering is observable. On the relevant surfaces ripple marks are relatively infrequent—whereas rain prints are very abundant and often occur on laminae criss-crossed by mud cracks.

Frequently surface markings of puzzling character appear which were not described or determined until now; Faber seems to make reference to it when he writes that he came across some patterns which he could not place.[124]

In Figure 7 a specimen is pictured. Kuenen suggests by personal communication that the structure was produced during consolidation—though he does not vouch for the truth of his guess. Personally, I incline to the opinion that the structure was produced by streamlets of flowing water which eroded minute channels—called rill marks. I observed a recent ephemeral structure identical to Figure 7 on the beach of the Dutch isle of Schiermonnikoog.

On beaches the back-washing wave is followed by a film of water which finally divides into streamlets. Sometimes the streamlets flow back in zigzag line and produce tiny channels round about rhomboid patches which are not eroded away; the extremities of some diamonds may run out into tongues of sediment. The same was observed by Twenhofel, who states:

On beaches composed of fine sands, the returning waters of waves

> may be succeeded by a net-work of anastomosing rills or small currents whose minute erosion produces a sculpturing of the beach surface resembling ·the surface of a *Lepidodendron* tree, the uneroded surface or polygons between the minute currents being diamond-shaped, with the long axes of the diamonds normal to the water's edge.[125]

Now then, the mentioned features are displayed by the pictured surface; viz., the uneroded diamonds and the tongues of sediment (e.g., middle left)—though on a small scale as compared with rill marks on sandy beaches. Little joints which are of secondary character confuse the original structure as does the clearly visible trail.

Trails and tracks are not abundant though they are found (compare with Figure 7); a trackway is recorded of *Chirotherium* [sic!] *peabodyi*.[126]

Evidently both the Old and the New Quarry hold a profusion of ephemeral markings; viz., ripple marks, rain prints, mud cracks, rill marks, and, incidentally, trails and tracks. Without question the delicate structures here determined as rill marks are very transient. Consequently, all recorded markings must have been rapidly covered with sediment.

Within the framework of Huttonian geology, it is assumed that the limestone sequences were deposited by the settling of calcareous skeletons of marine micro- and macro-organisms. On account of rain prints, mud cracks, etc., it is assumed that the Winterswijk Muschelkalk originated in shallow water, e.g., a lagoon. Van Straaten[127] supposes that in the north half of the Adriatic some 20 grams of lime per square meter per annum, i.e., 0.00008 cm. per annum, is deposited.

In regard to the Winterswijk limestone, the rate of lime deposit could not have been much more—for the distinct bedding and lamination and other phenomena are thought to prove that conditions of life were unfavorable. It is beyond dispute that in sedimentary environments like this no ephemeral markings could have been rapidly covered and preserved; in other words, uniformitarianism cannot account for the Winterswijk Muschelkalk.

In order to account for the excellent preserved conditions of countless ephemeral markings which occur through the entire deposit it is necessary to assume that lime beds were rapidly deposited after each other. This implies that the calcareous materials were not auto- but allochthonous, and were transported from elsewhere. Moreover, the regular bedding suggests that the sediment transport was governed by rhythmic and—as it were—pulsation depositional patterns.

2. *The Ardennes.* The relief of eastern Belgium is dominated by an orogen called the Ardennes; in the folding process only Paleozoic sequences were implicated; they are intersected by the Meuse and her tributaries—e.g., the Ambléve or the Bocq. In their valleys, often Devonian and Carboniferous sand- and limestones are exposed. The Famennien—a stage of the Upper Devonian—consists for the most part of psammites. They are excavated on a large scale for the purpose of paving and building; as a result the Famennien is largely exposed and most data are obtained from the relevant quarries.

On entering a psammite exposure the regular bedding is striking; beds of psammites succeed each other with astounding regularity—more often than not *thin beds of shale* constitute the partings of the arenaceous units.

Almost invariably on the bedding planes, ripple marks occur which are of various types. Both symmetrical and asymmetrical ripple marks are found—though the former more frequently than the latter. Often it is possible to trace these marks over the entire surface of an exposed bed. When ripple marks are first exposed they appear to be—for the most part—extremely well preserved. In this connection, I offer two examples:

In Figure 8A, symmetrical wave ripple marks are pictured which occurred in a quarry near Aywaille sur Ambléve; on an average the

Figure 8A. Ripple marks in the Aywaille psammite (Belgium). (Photo by Rupke).

Figure 8B. Ripple marks on the beach of Schiermonnikoog (The Netherlands). (Photo by Rupke).

Figure 9A. Ripple marks in the Yvoir psammite (Belgium). (Photo by Rupke).   Figure 9B. Ripple marks on the beach of Schiermonnikoog (The Netherlands). (Photo by Rupke).

wave length is 4 to 6 cm; the crests are still sharp.

In Figure 9A, asymmetrical current ripple marks are pictured—though the pattern was altered by wave action. This specimen occurred in a quarry near Yvoir in the valley of the Bocq. The wave length is about 3.5 cm.; there is no sign of levelling of the ripple ridges. In this context it is worthy of mention that these ripple marks occurred on sandy slabs.

Rain prints are not abundant in the psammites: van Straaten[128] even reports that "he did not find one single unambiguous example." However, they in fact are found, since I came across an example in the quarry near Aywaille sur Ambléve (Figure 10). The surface shows two imprints being slightly rimmed on the right, toward which the water drops must have been directed. Otherwise, the imprints may—properly speaking—present spray- or splash prints. The imprints occur isolated, being about 1.5 cm. in width while one is clearly elliptic. In the splash zone of a beach I observed two nearby splash prints of identical feature; both the fossil and the recent imprints were without great depth.

In regard to trails there is no shortage; on the contrary, they are typical of the Famennien. In Figure 11, is depicted a trail which I found in the quarry near Yvoir in the valley of the Bocq. It occurred on a rippled surface, and lengthwise to a trough; the surface marking is rimmed on both sides and the little ridges are amazingly well preserved. Perhaps the trail was produced by a worm, though it is difficult to determine the true nature of the agent.

It is believed by van Straaten that the Psammites du Condroz—

Figure 10. Splash (?) prints in the Aywaille psammite
(Belgium). (Specimen from the author's collection).

Figure 11. Worm (?) trail in the Yvoir psammite (Belgium). (Specimen from the author's collection).

the arenaceous faces of the Upper Famennien in the Ardennes—
were formed in "a tidal lagoon, bordered by tidal flats and receiving
a more or less periodical supply of fluvial material"; [129] the supply
must have been limited by a minimum of 0.03 mm. per annum and
a maximum of 0.6 mm per annum.[130]

However, these uniformitarian suppositions cannot be brought
into agreement with the mentioned phenomena. It is true that an
alternation of sandy and shaly laminae may be brought about in recent deposits; viz., as tidal- or storm-surge lamination on tidal-flats
or marshes.[131] However, such laminae are only some few mm. or, at
most, some cm. thick. But the sandstone- and limestone beds,
parted by shaly units, as observed in exposures of the Famennien
and—just as well—of various other sequences in the Ardennes, more
often than not measure several decimeters in thickness and occasion-
aly even much more. In fact, the distinct alteration of sandstone or
limestone beds with shales suggests a tidal action and a consequent
periodical deposition. But from the outset these tides must have
acted much more intensively and extensively than the known tides of
today in order to bring about beds of the mentioned thickness. Perhaps a periodical succession of tidal waves of great sedimentary
competency came into play here.

In Holocene deposits ripple marks are preserved, but it applies
mainly—maybe exclusively—to ripple marks in mud. Ripple marks
in sands are extremely transient. In Figures 8B and 9B, ripple marks
are depicted as observed on the sandy beach of Schiermonnikoog.
Figure 8B represents symmetrical wave ripple marks which are
somewhat modified by erosion. Figure 9B shows asymmetrical
current ripple marks—downstream slope on the left, so current from
the right—and crosswise symmetrical wave ripple marks which likewise are modified by erosion.

These patterns were photographed shortly after they were laid
bare; nevertheless, the ripples became already blurred on account
of sun- and wind action (Figure 8B on the right and Figure 9B on
the left). For that in the mentioned Ardennes exposures, many
specimens are extant of amazingly well-preserved ripple marks occurring on sandy bedding planes covered by shale- or sandstone beds.
These conditions, bespeaking rapid deposition of successive beds, are
absolutely unequalled in Holocene sediment. This statement is even
more valid in regard to splash marks and worm(?) trails—being
extraordinarily ephemeral, but nevertheless preserved in the Famen-

nien. As a result uniformitarianism is deficient in accounting for the sedimentary phenomena of the Famennien, and of analogous sequences in the Ardennes.

Undoubtedly the actuality of cataclysmal deposition is apparent from a profusion of sedimentary phenomena. Yet the mechanism of rapid formation of sedimentary complexes is somewhat difficult to conceive—though enlightening elucidations are already given,[132]

Perhaps—as to limestone—ooze from antediluvian deep-seas was stirred up and transported by tidal waves, generated during the Noachian Deluge. Then because of current-sorting, the finer materials (e.g., lime- and clay particles) were deposited in one locality, and the coarser (sands, etc.) in another—though frequently not perfectly sorted. Indeed, the Winterswijk Muschelkalk is composed of limestone, and also of marl, shaly marl, marly shale, and even of some calcareous sandstones.

However, and most importantly, the reader should bear in mind that the conceivability of cataclysmal sedimentation cannot constitute a criterion as to the actuality of it. It is unsound to argue: "Non est, nam non potest," as is frequently done by Huttonian geologists. In this connection, the words of John Ray, cited at the beginning of the present article, are worth laying to heart, and accordingly I claim with all the authority of empiricism: "Potest, nam est."

December 1965
Verl. Stationsweg 48,
Zuidlaren, Nederland.

NOTES AND REFERENCES

1. Francis Bacon, *Novum Organum Scientiarum*, Lib. I Cap. LXXXII, Lib. II, Cap. X et passim.
2. Nicolaus Steno, *De Solido intra Solidum naturaliter Contento*, pp. 26-32; Facsimile-Edition, ed. W. Junk, no. 5, 1904. An English translation entitled *The Prodromus of Nicolaus Steno's Dissertation concerning a Solid Body enclosed by Process of Nature within a Solid* with an introduction and explanatory notes by John G. Winter appeared in 1916, University of Michigan Studies, Humanistic Series, Vol. XI, Part II.
3. John G. Winter, in *ibid.*, p. 230.
4. *Ibid.*, p. 227.
5. *Ibid.*, p. 258.
6. Cf. pp. 66-76; original edition.
7. Sir Andrew Geikie, *The Founders of Geology*, 1897; Dover Republication 1962, p. 60.

8. G. W. von Leibnitz wrote concerning Steno: "saepe ipsum nobis narran-
   tem audire memini, ac gratulantem sibi, quod sacrae historiae and gen-
   eralis diluuii fidem naturalibus argumentis, non sine pietatis fructu,
   astrueret"; Protogea, Par. 6; *Sumni Polyhistoris Godefridi Gvilielmi
   Leibnitii Protogea*, pp. 12-13; 1749.
9. John Ray, *De Wereld van haar Begin tot haar Einde. In drie Natuur-
   kundige Godgeleerde Redeneringen*, II: *Den algemeenen Zuudvloed,
   desselfs Oorzaken en Uitwerkingen*, pp. 62-98; 1765 (being the Dutch
   translation of his "Discourses").
10. Charles E. Raven, *John Ray, Naturalist, His Life and Works*, 1950, p. 438.
11. John Ray, *op. cit.*, p. 148.
12. Charles E. Raven, *op. cit.*, p. 431.
13. Byron C. Nelson, *The Deluge Story in Stone*, 1931, p. 37.
14. John C. Whitcomb and Henry M. Morris, *The Genesis Flood* (Philadel-
    phia: Presbyterian and Reformed Publishing Co., 1961), p. 90.
15. John Woodward, *An Essay toward a History of the Earth*, pp. 73-76; 1702.
    Extracts are given by Melvin E. Jahn and Daniel J. Woolf (See "The
    lying stones of Dr. Johann Bartholomew Adam Beringer being his Litho-
    graphiae Wirceburgensis," Notes, pp. 176-178; 1963).
16. Whitcomb and Morris, *op. cit.*, pp. 273-274.
17. Karl Alfred von Zittel, "Geschichte der Geologie und Paleontologie,"
    p. 41; *Geschichte der Wissenschaften in Deutschland, Neuere Zeit*, Band
    23, 1899.
18. Woodward, *op. cit.*, p. 19.
19. In almost every publication dealing with Woodward, he is put on a level
    with Thomas Burnet (Compare *Telluris Theoria Sacra: orbis nostri origi-
    nem and mutationes generales, quas aut jam subiit, aut olim subituru est,
    complectens* 1681) and with William Whiston (Compare *A New Theory
    of the Earth, From its Original, to the Consummation of all Things,
    Wherein The Creation of the World in Six Days, The Universal Deluge,
    And the General Conflagration, As laid down in the Holy Scriptures, Are
    Shewn to be perfectly Agreeable to Reason and Philosophy* [1696]).
    This trio is taken as representative as regards early deluge geology;
    however, wholly unjustly. Burnet and Whiston did not leave intact the
    biblical framework of early history and undermined at will the inspired
    authority of scriptural passages or even of whole books; consequently, they
    were no more deluge geologists than theistic evolutionists are real crea-
    tionists.
    A recent evaluation of Woodward's work is given by V. A. Eyles, "John
    Woodward, F.R.S. (1665-1728)," *Nature*, Vol. 206, No. 4987, May 29,
    1965, pp. 868-870.
20. Ph.H. Kuenen, "Experiments in Geology," *The Transactions of the Geo-
    logical Society of Glasgow*, Vol. XXIII, 1958, p. 1.
21. See *Histoire de l' Academie Royales des Sciences*, Année 1710. *Avec les
    Memoires de Mathematique et de Physique, pour la meme Année*, pp.
    19-21, 1712. Cf. *Journal des Scavans*, Octobre 1713, p. 459, 1713.
22. Louis Leclerc, Comte de Buffon, *Théorie de la Terre* (1749) and *Des*

Epoques de la Nature (1778), constituting his voluminous *Historie Naturelle* (1749-1782).

23. Benoit de Maillet (1656-1738), *Telliamed ou Entretiens d'un philosophe indien avec un missionaire francois sur la diminution de la mer, la formation de la terre, l'origine de l'homme, etc.*, published posthumously in 1748; "Telliamed" represented the anagram of "de Maillet."

24. *Ibid.*, Tome II, pp. 19-20; cf. p. 58; Nouvelle edition 1755.

25. See "Preuves de la Théorie de la Terre," Art. VII, *Oeuvres Completes de Buffon et de ses Continuateurs*, Tome I, pp. 150-162; 1828.

26. *Ibid.*, Art. I, pp. 110-123.

27. Buffon, "Des Epoques de la Nature," passim.

28. *Loc cit.*, Art. V; *ubi sup.*, p. 135. Cf. Gen. 8:11; this biblical passage constitutes a classical argument against biblical catastrophism; it was dealt with by Samuel Bochart, *Hierozoicon*, Lib. I, Chap. 6; Bocharti Opera, Tom. III, pp. 27-30; 1712; by Mattheus Polus and Simon Patrick, *Verklaring van Mozes eerste Boek, genoemd Genesis, uit de Engelsche Verklaringen van de heeren Patrik, Polus Wels, en andere voorname Engelsche Godgeleerden*, H.1., pp. 98-99; 1741—being the Dutch translation of their exegetical studies; by Theodorus Christophorus Lilienthal, *Die gute Sache der in der hl. Schrift Alten und Neuen testaments enthaltenen gottlichen Offenbarungen*, Chap. XV, Par. 8; 1760-1780; and a recent discussion of the question is given by Whitcomb and Morris in *The Genesis Flood*, pp. 104-106.

29. George Cuvier, *Historie des Progrés des Sciences Naturelles, depuis 1789 jusqu'a ce jour*, p. 184; présenté 1808; 1826.

30. Jean-André Deluc, *Lettres Physiques et Morales, sur l'Histoire de Terre et de l'Homme*, Tome, 1779, p. 7; cf. his *Lettres sur l'Histoire Physiques de la Terre, adressées au Professeur Blumenback* (1798) and his *Abrégé de Principes et de Faits concernant la Cosmologie et la Géologie* (1802).

31. Horace-Bénédict de Saussure, *Voyages dans les Alpes, precédés d'un Essai sur l'Histoire naturelle des Environs de Geneve*, Tome I, pp. 145-149, Tome II, pp. 376-386; 1803.

32. Jean-André Deluc, *op. cit.*, Tome V, Partie II, p. 836.

33. *Ibid.*, pp. 649-650.

34. Willem Bilderdijk, *Geologie*, p. 109; 1813—published anonymously.

35. Jean-André Deluc, *op. cit.*, pp. 490-505; cf. Willem Bilderdijk, *op. cit.*, Chap. 6.

36. Jean-André Deluc, *op. cit.*, p. 498.

37. *Ibid.*, p. 505.

38. George Cuvier, "Discours surles Révolutions de la Surface du Globe," pp. 6-8 et passim.

39. *Transactions of the Royal Society of Edinburgh*, Vol. I, Part II, 1788, pp. 293-294.

40. *Ibid.*, p. 221.

41. John Playfair, *Illustrations of the Huttonian Theory of the Earth*, facsimile reprint, Dover Republications 1956, p. 117.

42. Sir Charles Lyell, *Principles of Geology* (or the modern changes of the

the earth and its inhabitants considered as illustrative of geology), Vol. I, Bk. I, Ch. XIV, 1867, p. 325.

43. The controversy between catastrophism and uniformitarianism is discussed as a whole by R. Hooykaas, *Natural Law and Divine Miracle*, 1960, 2nd impr. 1963; the view of many geologists of today in this case is expressed by M. G. Rutten, *The Geological Aspects of the Origin of Life on Earth*, 1962; Dutch edit., 2, 1965, pp. 23-39.

44. Bilderdijk, *op. cit.*, p. 104.

45. George Fairholme, *New and conclusive Demonstrations*, 1837, pp. 392-404.

46. Francis C. Haber, "Fossils and the Idea of a Process of Time in Natural History" in *Forerunners of Darwin: 1745-1859*, ed. Bentley Glass, Owsei Temkin, William L. Straus, Jr., 1959, p. 244.

47. Johann Wolfgang von Goethe, *Ueber Naturwissenschaft*, IV; Goethe's *sammtliche Kerke in vierzig Banden*, Dritter Band, 1840, p. 300.

48. I. M. van der Vlerk and Ph.H. Kuenen, *Geheimschrift der aarde*, Zeist, de Haan, Arnhem, van Loghum Slaterus, 1962, 7th impr., trans. from the Dutch.

49. *Ibid.*, p. 64.

50. Fairholme, *op. cit.*, p. 392; cf. R. R. Schrock, *Sequence in Layered Rocks* (New York: McGraw-Hill 1948), p. 293, and H. Nilsson, *Synthetische Artbildung. Grundlinien einer exakten Biologie* (Lund: Gleerups, 1953), p. 718.

51. A. Geikie, *Text-book of Geology* (London: MacMillan, 1903), 4th edition, p. 654.

52. *Ibid.*

53. *Ibid.*

54. H. Klusemann and R. Teichmüller, "Begrabene Wälder im Ruhrkohlenbecken," *Natur u. Volk*, 84:374-375, translated from the German.

55. *Ibid.*, p. 379.

56. *Ibid.*

57. C. O. Dunbar, *Geology* (New York: Wiley, 1960), 2nd ed., p. 227.

58. W. E. Tayler, *Voices from the Rocks* (or proofs of the existence of man during the paleozoic or most ancient period of the earth: a reply to the late Hugh Miller's *Testimony of the Rocks* [London: 1857]).

59. Nelson, *op. cit.*, p. 111.

60. Geike, *op. cit.*, p. 655.

61. *Ibid.*

62. E. A. Newell Arber, *The Natural History of Coal* (Cambridge University Press, 1912), p. 114.

63. Fairholme, *op. cit.*, pp. 393-394.

64. *Ibid.*, p. 394.

65. W. Bölsche, *Im Steinkohlenwald* (Stuttgart: Franckh'sche Verlagshandlung, 1918),16th impr., p. 34; cf. G. McCready Price, *The New Geology* (Mountain View: Pacific Press, 1923), p. 462.

66. A. Brongniart, *Prodrome d'une histoire des végétaux fossiles* (Paris: F. G. Levrault, 1828), pp. 183-184; cf. Ch. Schuchert, *A Text-book of Geology*,

Part II, *Historical Geology* (New York: Wiley, 1924), 2nd ed., p. 401, and Dunbar, *op. cit.*, p. 227.
67. Arber, *op. cit.*, p. 101.
68. Fairholme, *op. cit.*, p. 393.
69. Arber, *op. cit.*, p. 106.
70. M. C. Grand'Eury, *Géologie et paléontologie du bassin houiller du Gard* with atlas (Saint-Etienne: Théolier, 1890), p. 244 (compare with Plate XIII, Figure 7).
71. Ph. Fauth, *Horbigers Glacial-Kosmogenie. Eine Neue Entwickelungsgeschichte des Weltalls und des Sonnensystems* (Kaiserslautern: Kayser, 1913), p. 443.
72. H. Nilsson, *Synthetische Artbildung. Grundlinien einer exakten Biologie* (Lund: Gleerups, 1953), p. 716, translated from the German.
73. H. Potonié, *Die Entstehung der Steinkohle und der Kaustobiolithe überhaupt* (Berlin: Borntraeger, 1910), 5th ed., p. 120.
74. S. Aronow, "On the postglacial history of the Devils Lake region, North Dakota," *J. Geol.* (1957), 65:410.
75. Cf. Grand'Eury, *op. cit.*
76. Fauth, *op. cit.*, p. 445.
77. Nilsson, *op. cit.*, p. 718.
78. Vesalius, *Tabulae Anatom Sex* (1538).
79. P. J. C. Nagtegaal, "An approximation to the genetic classification of non-organic sedimentary structures," *Geol. Mijnbouw* (1965), 44:347-352.
80. W. H. Bucher, "Ripples and related sedimentary surface forms and their paleogeographic interpretation," *Am. J. Sci.* (1919), 47:208; E. M. Kindle and Bucher, "Ripple mark and its interpretation" (1932), in W. H. Twenhofel, *Treatise on Sedimentation* (New York: Dover, 1961), 2nd ed., p. 654; L. M. J. U. van Straaten, "Megaripples in the Dutch Wadden Sea and in the Basin of Arcachon (France)," *Geol. Mijnbouw* (1953), 15:1-2.
81. G. H. Darwin, "On the formation of ripple mark in sand," *Proc. Roy. Soc. London* (1883), 36:18-43.
82. M. Kirchmayer, "Beobachtungen an rezenten Wellenfurchen (=Wasser-Rippeln)," *N. Jb. Geol. Palaont.*, (1960), 10:446-452.
83. W. F. Tanner, "Origin and maintenance of ripple marks," *Sedimentology* (1963), 2:307-311.
84. Geikie, *op. cit.*, p. 643.
85. F. Trusheim, "Rippeln im Schlick," *Natur u. Museum* (1929), 59:76, Abb. 6.
86. L. M. J. U. van Straaten, "Longitudinal ripple marks in mud and sand," *J. Sediment. Petrol.* (1951), 21:54.
87. E. M. Kemper, "Uber einige Spurenfossilien des Bentheimer Sandsteins," *Grondboor en Hamer* (1965), No. 3, juni, p. 79.
88. *Ibid.*, translated from the German.
89. Kindle and Bucher, *op. cit.*, pp. 652-653.
90. D. L. Inman, "Environmental significance of oscillatory ripple marks," *Eclogae Geol. Helv.* (1958), 51:522.
91. Bucher, *op. cit.*, p. 242.

92. Nilsson, *op. cit.*, passim.
93. Whitcomb and Morris, *op. cit.*, passim.
94. Bucher, *op. cit.*, p. 653.
95. Nilsson, *op. cit.*, p. 689.
96. W. H. Twenhofel, *Treatise on Sedimentation* (New York: Dover, 1932), 2nd ed., 1961, p. 644.
97. Geikie, *op. cit.*, p. 644.
98. Twenhofel, *op. cit.*, pp. 677-680.
100. Whitcomb and Morris, *op. cit.*, pp. 166-168.
101. Cf. Shrock, *op. cit.*
102. Twenhofel, *op. cit.*, p. 675.
103. A. Seilacher, "Die geologische Bedeutung fossiler Lepensspuren," *Z. deutch. geol. Ges* (1954), 105 (II): passim; R. C. Moore (ed.) *Treatise on Invertebrate Paleontology*, Part W (University of Kansas Press, 1962), p. 200; W. Schäfer, *Aktuo-Palaontologie nach Studien in der Nordsee*, Frankfurt am Main, Waldermar Kramer (1962).
104. W. Schäfer, "Aktuopaläontologische Beobachtungen; 4: Spiralfährten und 'geführte Mäander,' " *Natur u. Museum* (1965), 95:83-90.
105. J. F. M. de Raaf, C. Betts, and G. Kortenbout van der Sluijs, "Lower Oligocene bird-tracks from Northern Spain," *Nature* (1965), 207: 146-148.
106. *Ibid.*, p. 147.
107. Ph.H. Kuenen, "Sole markings of graded graywacke beds," *J. Geol.* (1957), 65:231-258.
108. F. J. Pettijohn and P. E. Potter, *Atlas and Glossary of Primary Sedimentary Structures* (Berlin: Springer, 1964).
109. S. Dzulinsky and E. K. Walton, *Sedimentary Features of Flysch and Graywackes* (Amsterdam: Elsevier, 1965).
110. Ph.H. Kuenen and C. I. Migliorini, "Turbidity currents as a cause of graded bedding," *J. Geol.* (1950), 58:91-127.
111. Kuenen, *loc. cit.* (1957), p. 232.
112. *Ibid.*, p. 233.
113. *Ibid.*, p. 232.
114. Cf. Kuenen, "Experiments in geology," *Trans. Geol. Soc. Glasgow* (1958), 23:3.
115. Ph. Kuenen, "Graded bedding, with observations on Lower Paleozoic rocks of Britain," *Verhandel. Koninkl. Ned. Akad. Wetenschap., Afdel. Natuurk.* (1953), Sect. I, 20 (3):7; by the same author, "Sole markings of graded graywacke beds," *J. Geol.* (1957), 65:232, and "The shell pavement below oceanic turbidites," *Marine Geol.* (1964), 2: passim.
116. Dzulinsky and Walton, *op. cit.*, p. 11.
117. *Ibid.*
118. Kuenen, *loc. cit.*, note 111 above.
119. Whitcomb and Morris, *op. cit.*, p. 269.
120. Cf. J. M. MacFarlane, *Fishes, the Source of Petroleum* (New York: Macmillan, 1923); G. McCready Price, *The New Geology* (Mountain View: Pacific Press, 1923); Nilsson, *op. cit.*; I. Velikovsky, *Earth in Upheaval*

(London: Gollancz and Sidgwick and Jackson, 1956); and Whitcomb and Morris, *op. cit; et al.*

121. W. Buckland, *Geology and Minerology, Considered with Reference to Natural Theology* (Bridgewater treaties; London: Pickering, 1836-1837).

122. H. Miller, *The Old Red Sandstone* (or new walks in an old field; Edinburgh: Hamilton, 1840, 2nd ed. 1858).

123. F. J. Faber, "De Winterswijkse Muschelkalk," *Geol. Mijnbouw* (1959), 21:25.

124. *Ibid.*, p. 31.

125. Twenhofel, *op. cit.*, p. 671.

126. F. J. Faber, "Fossiele voetstappen in de Muschelkalk van Winterswijk," *Geol. Mijnbouw* (1958), 20:317-321, 448; C. O. van Regteren Altena, "Kritische opmerkingen over *Chirotherium peabodyi* Faber," *Geol. Mijnbouw* (1958), 20:447-448.

127. L. M. J. U. van Straaten, *De shelf* (Groningen: Wolters, 1963), pp. 12-13.

128. L. M. J. U. van Straaten, "Sedimentology of recent tidal flat deposits and the Psammites du Condroz (Devonian)," *Geol. Mijnbouw* (1954), 16:36.

129. *Ibid.*, p. 25.

130. Cf. *ibid.*, p. 45.

131. R. Richter, "Eine geologische Exkursion in das Wattenmeer," *Natur u. Museum* (1926), 56:306; "Gründung und Aufgaben der Forschungstelle für Meeresgeologie 'Senckenberg' in Wilhelmshaven," *Natur u. Museum* (1929), 59:25-26.

132. G. McCready Price, *The New Geology* (Mountain View: Pacific Press, 1923), pp. 679-692; cf. J. F. Twisden, "On possible displacements of the earth's axis of figure produced by elevations and depressions of her surface," *Quart. J. Geolo. Soc. London* (1877), 34:35-48, and Nilsson, *op. cit.*, passim.

4

THE REVELATION OF PALYNOLOGY

Wilbert Rusch, Sr.

Introduction

It has frequently been admitted that the only real compulsive evidence for evolution (amoeba to man form) must lie in the geological record. And yet that record often contains evidence that apparently mitigates against a history of phylogenetic developments, i.e., forms developing from simple to complex, which typifies the developmental schemes so prevalent in biology and geology texts in the past.

In recent years a new branch of plant science has developed which is called palynology. This is the study of microspores and pollen grains of plants. Palynology as an organized science is possible because of the ornamentation and sculpture of the surface of the pollen grains, a feature of great value for classification purposes.

Pollen grains have outer walls known as the exine. This is composed of an amazingly durable substance called sporopollenin. Since the outer walls of the spores are rather durable, they seldom undergo replacement or chemical alteration, and are also resistant to most forms of chemical and biological decay. Fossil pollen usually consists solely of this exine.

Among other features, these grains may have thin areas in their outer walls in the form of germinal pores or furrows, or both. The furrow is called the colpus. Pollen grains may then be classified as one of two possible types. The monocolpate, with one germinal furrow, occurs in monocotyledons, cycads, cycadeoids, and seed ferns, as well as some woody dicotyledons. The tricolpate type, with three germinal furrows, is found in most dicotyledons.

Preparation and Interpretation

Preparation of microspores for paleontological study is a rather lengthy process. Microfossils must be liberated from the sedimentary matrices and then concentrated by methods such as centrifugation and density gradients. Rigorous cleanliness is essential at all steps to guard against contamination by drifting present day samples. Once extraction is completed, the polleniferous material is mounted on a microscope slide. Good photomicrographs of the resulting samples require exposure at different focal planes so that all the detail of structure and sculpture may be observed.

After these features of pollen grains were recognized, attention was given to the Pleistocene peat and lacustrine (lake-bed) sediments in an attempt to reconstruct the flora of that time on the basis of the pollen grains present. This procedure was later extended for the same purpose to the Tertiary formations of western Nebraska to similarly determine the grasses present at the time of deposition of these sediments.

Palynologists have been able to assign microspores that have been found in Cenozoic and Mesozoic rocks to modern families, modern genera, and sometimes to modern species of the plant world. Statistical comparisons of "pollen rains" of the present to fossil pollen distribution and counts have been the basis of attempts to estimate the abundance of fossil parent plants at the time of deposition of sediments. As the techniques of palynology were refined, it has been possible to extend the search for and study of fossil microspores into Paleozoic formations.

Palynology Extended to Paleozoic

Results of this extension have been rather startling. One can usually find statements in texts implying that the Cambrian plants are the simplest possible—namely, all algae, or that the whole life record of the Cambrian is marine.[1] Museum displays give the same message in their beautiful but imaginative reconstructions of Cambrian life.

But within the last 15 years, spores of vascular plants have been discovered in the Lower Cambrian of Kunda in Estonia; the Pre-Baltique of the U.S.S.R.; the Upper Cambrian of Kashmir, and the Salt Range of India.[2] Such reports were usually met with skepticism and suspicions of contamination.

However, in 1953 Krychtofowitch reported the discovery of lycopodiaceous shoots in the Cambrian of East-Siberia. In addition, various workers report the findings of small fragments of tracheids which show simple and bordered pits.

Agreement in Research Reports

Leclerq of the Department of Paleobotany at the University of Liege, Belgium, discusses these finds and others in an article, "Evidence of Vascular Plants in the Cambrian." [3] Although holding to the concept of evolution, he believes that the presence of vascular (woody) plants in the Cambrian seems established. Axelrod, of the University of California,[4] agrees, pointing out that approximately 60 Cambrian spore genera are now on record.

Leclerq feels that these results definitely raise the question of the *polyphyletic* origin of the vascular plants. He also feels that the Psilophytales would seem to be eliminated from their usual position as the first land plants. The evidence for this rests not only on the Cambrian discoveries, but also the Silurian strata from Victoria, Australia, which have yielded vascular plant compression associated with *Monograptus*, a graptolite.[5] Axelrod concurs, as is evident, when he says that the plants of the continental interiors were more highly evolved than the contemporaneous psilophytes which lived near the shore of seas.

Leclerq also discusses the remarkable difference in the vegetation of the Lower Devonian compared to the Middle and Upper Devonian. The Upper Devonian shows preserved structures of pteridophytes such as Filicales and Calamitales (ferns and related forms) and gynmosperms such as Coniferales and Cordaitales (conifers and related forms) including some tree forms. The Middle Devonian also shows the same groups represented, but not in the tree-form. The Lower Devonian shows essentially herbaceous and semi-aquatic psilophyte-like as well as lepidodendroid forms. What Leclerq finds so astonishing is the marked discrepancy in the latter two flora so close together in time. He considers that the Lower Devonian were also present during Middle Devonian while Middle Devonian forms were present during Lower Devonian.

Relevance to Creation versus Evolution

What has all this to do with creation versus evolution? The Lower and Middle Devonian situations would seem to indicate that, due to the shortness of time sufficient to allow Lower Devonian flora to "evolve" into Middle Devonian, we have instead the following situation:

(a) A Lower Devonian flora, which may have existed also in the

Middle Devonian, but this particular flora has not yet been found as fossils.

(b) Conversely, the Middle Devonian flora also existed in the Lower Devonian, but no fossils have been discovered.

The distinctness of the two flora may be due to a shift in environment, bringing into the area a new flora, already in existence in other, like environments, but not previously found as fossils, rather than an evolution from one flora to another. This explanation may well be validly applied to other fossil sequences.

Austin Clark[6] once wrote that on the basis of the fossil record, the creationist has all the better of the argument, since there is not the slightest evidence that any of the major groups arose from any other. He also has pointed out that this record does not support a tree of life, but rather presents the evolutionist with the necessity of explaining the development of a whole forest of trees (polyphyletic evolution).

This difficulty is not being eliminated, but rather amplified, hence the increasing appearance of the concept of polyphyletic evolution; and this concept is difficult to separate from creation with variation. It is to be noted that Leclerq in his article refers to the fact that the question of polyphyletic evolution is again raised by this new evidence. This would seem to support the persistence of type, as well as the sudden appearance of new types referred to at length by the German paleontologist, O. Kühn.[7]

Furthermore, it is now legitimate to consider the existence of land animal forms, associated with these land plants, that might also have existed in the early Paleozoic, contrary to the present picture presented. Just as only fragmentary microfossils of land plants remain, so the animal remains would also either be absent or so small as to be unrecognizable as such.

Most of the early Paleozoic sedimentary rocks are marine, not continental, and so we should expect very few records of land life to be preserved in them. While such records might once have been present in the non-marine deposits, most of these might have been eroded, and the record thus lost. But certainly it should be clear that the reconstruction of biofacies presented in so many texts and museum displays as a complete representation of life at a given time may not really be completely representative at all, and thus be quite biased.

184   WHY NOT CREATION?

Conclusion

In conclusion, some of the new finds in the field of paleontology, rather than driving the last nail in the coffin of creation, would seem to continue to keep it alive as a viable alternate theory to that of evolution.

NOTES AND REFERENCES

1. Raymond C. Moore, *Introduction to Historical Geology* (New York: Mc-Graw-Hill, 1958), pp. 126, 157. See also Edgar Spencer, *Basic Concepts of Historical Geology* (New York: Crowell, 1962), p. 237; and A. O. Woodford, *Historical Geology* (San Francisco: Freeman, 1965), p. 271 (however, note contradiction on p. 327).
2. A. K. Ghosh and A. Bose, "Spores and Tracheids from the Upper Cambrian of Kashmir," *Nature* (1952), 169:1056-1057; K. Jacob, Mrs. Ch. Jacob, and R. N. Shrivastava, "Evidence for the Existence of Vascular Land Plants in the Cambrian," *Current Science* (1953), 22:34-36; and K. Jacob, Mrs. Ch. Jacob, and R. N. Shrivastava, "Spores and Tracheids of Vascular Plants from the Vindhyan System, India," *Nature* (1953), 72:166-167.
3. S. Leclerq, "Evidence of Vascular Plants in the Cambrian," *Evolution* (1956), 10:109:113.
4. Daniel Axelrod, "Evolution of the Psilophyte Paleoflora, *Evolution* (1959), 13:264-275.
5. W. H. Lang and I. C. Cookson, "On a Flora Including Vascular Land Plants Associated with *Monograptus* in Rocks of Silurian Age from Victoria, Australia," *Philosophical Transactions of Royal Society of London* (1935), Series B, 224:421-449.
6. A. H. Clark, "Animal Evolution," *Quarterly Review of Biology* (1928):523.
7. O. Kühn, "Typologische Betrachtungweise und Paläontologie," *Acta Biotheoretica* (1942), VI:55-96.

Chapter 6

Paleontological Evidence

1

WILLIAM J. MEISTER DISCOVERY OF HUMAN FOOTPRINT WITH TRILOBITES IN A CAMBRIAN FORMATION OF WESTERN UTAH

Melvin A. Cook, Ph.D.*

Early in June, 1968, I was introduced to Mr. Meister by Burton Tew, Research Scientist, Baccus Works, Hercules Incorporated. Mr. Meister had with him a most remarkable fossil specimen of a human footprint embedded in which were two very distinct and easily recognizable trilobites and several smaller, less distinct ones.

The specimen comprised two approximately inch-thick slabs displayed in a plaster-of-paris cast. One slab contained the footprint and its associated trilobites and the other its mold. The footprint was that of the right foot of a human wearing a sandal. The rock in which the print was impressed was obviously natural, genuine, and characteristic rock.

Since Mr. Meister's interesting discovery, other persons have found similar but less spectacular specimens in the same area, two of which have been shown to me.

In late August, Dean Bitter, educator in the public schools of Salt Lake City, showed me a specimen of rock with two sandal-shod footprints he claimed to have found in diggings in a hill at Antelope Springs near that where the Meister fossil was discovered. Later, Mr. Meister showed me a specimen he said was discovered by George Silver, a friend, in the same location as the original discovery.

While neither of these specimens revealed tribolites in the footprints themselves, one of them showed a small trilobite in the same

---

*Professor of Metallurgy, University of Utah, and President, IRECO Chemicals, West Jordan, Utah

rock. The sandals appeared to be of the same vintage in the five prints that have been exhibited to me.

In a telephone conversation with Dr. Clifford Burdick and Mr. Meister, I learned that Dr. Burdick had discovered the footprint of a barefoot child when he went with Mr. Maurice Carlisle to the site of the Meister discovery to check the authenticity of it.

While I am by no means an authority on fossils and footprints, the Meister specimen seems to me clearly to speak for itself. Even aside from any doubt as to the identity of the formation in which the discovery was made, it is a serious contradiction of conventional geology. That is, the feature of this specimen is the *intimate, simultaneous* occurrence of modern (sandal-shod) men with trilobites. Furthermore, no intellectually honest individual examining this specimen can reasonably deny its genuine appearance. Finally, in my judgment, Mr. Meister is a fine gentleman of complete honesty and integrity.

DISCOVERY OF TRILOBITE FOSSILS IN SHOD FOOTPRINT OF HUMAN IN "TRILOBITE BEDS"—A CAMBRIAN FORMATION—ANTELOPE SPRINGS, UTAH

WILLIAM J. MEISTER, SR.*

As a trilobite collector and "rockhound," I have often enjoyed searching the "trilobite beds" of Antelope Springs, about 43 miles northwest of Delta, Utah, for my favorite fossil. Although I had previously found many excellent trilobite specimens in this so-called Cambrian formation, none can compare with my astonishing discovery of June 1, 1968.

I arrived at Antelope Springs on Decoration Day in company with my wife and two daughters and Mr. and Mrs. Francis Shape and their two daughters. We all remained at this location four days. Upon arrival we immediately began chiseling at the rock in search of trilobites.

Trilobite Within Footprint

On the third day while the Shapes were relaxing in camp (the four girls were with us), I broke off a large, approximately two-inch-thick slab of rock. Upon hitting it on the edge with my hammer, it fell open like a book. To my great astonishment I saw on one side the

---

*Drafting Supervisor, Baccus Works, Utah, Hercules Incorporated

footprint † of a human with trilobites *right in the footprint itself.* The other half of the rock slab showed an almost perfect mold of the footprint and fossils. Amazingly the human was wearing a sandal!

The footprint measured 10¼ inches in length, 3½ inches in width at the sole, and 3 inches in width at the heel. The heel print was indented in the rock about an eighth of an inch more than the sole. The footprint was clearly that of the right foot because the sandal was well worn on the right side of the heel in characteristic fashion. A photograph of the footprint and its mold are shown in Figure 1.

The most remarkable feature of the footprint was that it had in it several easily visible trilobites. One of the most distinct trilobite fossils occurred on the right side of the heel of the footprint. An enlargement of this fossil is shown in Figure 2. Another of comparable size was found toward the front of the footprint, an enlargement of which is shown in Figure 3. Some of the smaller trilobites may be seen in the enlargement from the sole shown in Figure 4. These enlargements were kindly made for me by Enno N. Drown, photographer at Hercules Incorporated.

Shortly after discovering the human footprint with its associated trilobites, I mounted my specimen in plaster-of-paris to make sure it would not become mutilated, and, in company with Burton Tew, an associate at Hercules Incorporated, I showed it to Professor Melvin A. Cook of the University of Utah. He recommended that we show it to some of the geologists at the University of Utah, but I was not able to find one who would take time to examine it. However, I was able to obtain considerable favorable publicity from the Deseret *News* (Figure 5 was taken by a Deseret *News* photographer), and an article was carried by UPI nationally as well as internationally.

Further Corroborating Finds

On July 4, I accompanied Dr. Clarence Coombs, Columbia Union College, Tacoma, Maryland, and Maurice Carlisle, graduate geolo-

---

† Editor's Note: In telephone conversation, Dr. Melvin Cook has reported that, according to William J. Meister, the trilobite beds are located about halfway up a 2,000-foot, fairly high, mountain face. (See Figure 6.) The strata are horizontal. Meister was forced to stop many times as he climbed up the face of the mountain. He had to make footholds in order to climb and to work in the area which was about halfway up the side. There was a ledge-like protrusion from the face below the working area. Quite obviously this footprint could not be the result of any carving, since, until found by Meister, it was covered by the strata above.

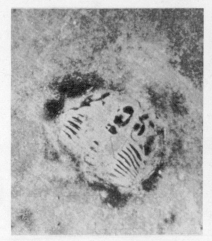

Figure 2. Enlargement of fossil Trilobite from heel part of Figure 1. Photo by Enno Drown.

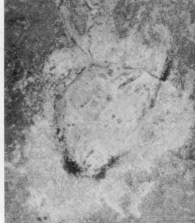

Figure 3. Enlargement of fossil Trilobite from front portion of footprint of Figure 1. Photo by Enno

Figure 4. Enlargement of instep portion of footprint of Figure 1, showing several small fossil Trilobites. Photo by Enno Drown.

Figure 5. William J. Meister with "opened" two-inch thick slab of rock in which he found footprint containing fossil Trilobites. *Deseret News* photograph.

gist University of Colorado at Boulder, to the site of the discovery. After a couple of hours of digging, Mr. Carlisle found a mudslab which he said convinced him that the discovery of fossil tracks in the location was a distinct possibility, since this discovery showed that the formation had at one time been at the surface.

The first week in August, Dr. Clifford Burdick, well-traveled consulting geologist of Tucson, Arizona, visited the site of the discovery at Antelope Springs with Mr. Carlisle. On this visit Dr. Burdick found a footprint of a barefoot child in the same location as my discovery. He showed me this footprint August 18. The day before, my family and I had met Dr. Burdick at Antelope Springs. While there we found another sandal print. Dr. Burdick continued, and on Monday, August 19, he informed me by letter that he had found a second child's footprint.

In addition to my discovery and that of Dr. Burdick, a friend of mine, George Silver, digging alone in this location, discovered more footprints of a human or human beings also shod in sandals. His specimen, which he showed to me (I also showed this specimen to Dr. Melvin Cook), had two footprints, one about a half inch above and on top of the other. Finally, Dean Bitter, teacher in the public schools of Salt Lake City, discovered other footprints of human beings wearing sandals much like those found by George Silver and me. Both Dr. Cook and I have seen his specimens found at Antelope Springs, some distance from the site of my discovery.

Figure 6. Field view of mountain face where footprint containing fossil Trilobites was found by William J. Meister.

While I had previously been little concerned with the different

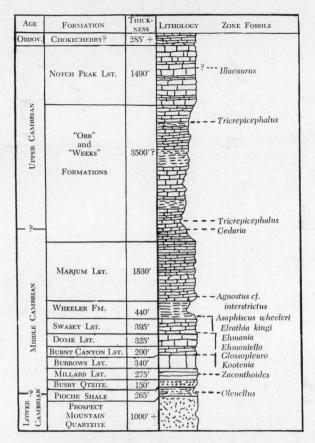

Age	Formation	Thickness	Lithology	Zone Fossils
Ordov.	Chokecherry?	285' +		
Upper Cambrian	Notch Peak Lst.	1490'		? --- Illaenurus
	"Orr" and "Weeks" Formations	3500'?		Tricrepicephalus
?				Tricrepicephalus / Cedaria
Middle Cambrian	Marjum Lst.	1530'		
	Wheeler Fm.	440'		Agnostus cf. interstrictus / Asaphiscus wheeleri / Elrathia kingi
	Swasey Lst.	395'		
	Dome Lst.	325'		Ehmania / Ehmoniello
	Burnt Canyon Lst.	200'		Glossopleuro / Kootenia
	Burrows Lst.	340'		
	Millard Lst.	275'		Zaconthoides
	Busby Qtzite.	150'		
Lower ? Cambrian	Pioche Shale	265'		Olenellus
	Prospect Mountain Quartzite	1000' +		

Chart 1. House Range Cambrian Columnar Section.

explanations of the fossil record, my discovery of a shod, and therefore obviously modern, human footprint associated intimately with trilobites has converted me completely to the story of the Bible. That is, the Bible alone provides a possible explanation of this remarkable occurrence of trilobites and humans obviously alive and together at the same time. To me it seems clear that this particular fossil is in some way related to Noah's Flood, but just how I do not know.

Leland J. Davis, Consulting Geologist of Salt Lake City, kindly agreed to outline for me the geology and stratigraphy of the formations where the discoveries described above were made. Following is the letter he wrote to me on August 30, 1968:

DAVIS AND DAVIS
CONSULTING GEOLOGISTS
2060 Ribbon Lane
Salt Lake City 17, Utah
CR 7-0106
August 30, 1968

Mr. W. J. Meister
4341 West 5015 South
Salt Lake City, Utah
Dear Sir:

At your request the following is a geologic and stratigraphic report on the Cambrian sequence of the Trilobite fossil collecting area near Antelope Springs in West Central Utah. The area is located approximately 50 miles west of Delta, Utah.

General Geology

The Antelope Springs area is located in the Basin and Range Province. The House Range is the major structural feature in the area and is a typical northerly trending basin—range "block" consisting almost entirely of Cambrian strata. The dip of the strata is generally easterly. The steep west slopes of the House Range are traditionally conceived as a dissected fault scarp, together with its more gentle dipping eastern slope. In many places this eastern flank is characterized by dip slopes, and has led to a general belief that the range has been elevated and tilted along a normal fault at its western base.

Increased evidence of Tertiary thrusting in the Great Basin should also be considered a possibility in this area.

Stratigraphy

(a) *Correlation.* Chart 1 is a columnar section of the Cambrian strata. Widespread continuity of strata units in the miogeosynclinal cordilleran region is a well-known correlation of Cambrian strata that involve rock units (formations only). Wheeler (1948) has shown that biostratigraphic and lithologic correlations are rather closely parallel in the more calcareous (non-detrital) portions of the succession; while divergence between these two types of correlation (temporal transgression) is usually evident in the detrital units, especially those nearest the Cambrian base.

For example, the Burnt Canyon limestone is probably closely contemporaneous in both the House Range and at Pioche, Nevada; whereas the Pioche shale appears to have begun its accumulation considerably earlier at Pioche than in the House Range area mentioned. This indicates a near shore environment existed in the Antelope Springs area during the deposition of the Cambrian strata.

(b) *Wheeler Formation.* The Wheeler is exposed in the Wheeler Amphitheatre east of Antelope Springs on the east slope of the House Range. This area is famous for its fossil trilobites (especially *Elrathia* and *Agnostis*) and phosphatic brachiopods. The Wheeler consists of dull sooty-gray, fine-grained, thin, fissile, shaly limestones and calcareous shales. This formation is a valley and slope-maker with platy shale ledges wherever found in the House Range.

Very truly yours,
LELAND J. DAVIS
Consulting Geologist

LJD/b

NOTES AND REFERENCES

Walcott, C. D., Cambrian sections of the Cordilleran area, Smithsonian Miscl. Coll. (1908), vol. 53, no. 5, pp. 167-230.

Wheeler, H. E., Late pre-Cambrian stratigraphic cross section through southern Nevada, Univ. Nev. Bull. (1948), vol. 42, no. 3; Geol. and Mining Ser., no. 47, 61pp.

Guidebook to the Geology of Utah, No. 6, Geology of the Canyon, House and Confusion Ranges, Millard County, Utah, Intermountain Association of Petroleum Geologists, 1951.

2

FOSSIL MAN IN THE LIGHT OF THE RECORD IN GENESIS

ARTHUR C. CUSTANCE, PH.D.*

The Evolutionary Faith

> *Man is a primate and within the order of Primates is most closely related to the living African anthropoid apes.*

So wrote F. Clark Howell[1] recently, thus providing us with a good example of the kind of confident pronouncement with which evolutionary literature abounds. As it stands, it is purely assumptive. Just because members of a family are apt to look alike, it is not at all safe to assume that all "look-alikes" are related.

Howell's first statement, "Man is a primate," is true enough; but his second statement, which is presented as though it were equally factual, is simply supposition without any positive proof whatever. Within the order of Primates man may most closely *resemble* the living African anthropoid apes from an anatomical point of view, but it is quite another thing to state categorically that he is closely *related* to them.

Resemblance and relationship are by no means the same thing. Howell does admit in the next sentence that he is not sure how far removed the relationship is, but the basic assumption still remains that the blood relationship exists. Very few readers except those expert in the subject would discern the presumption in Howell's statement. All that the facts indicate is similarity.

Relationship is totally unprovable by an appeal to morphology. If Howell had said, "Man is anatomically most *like* the African anthropoid apes," his statement would have been quite correct. As it stands, his statement is completely hypothetical. He is confusing hypothesis with fact.

The extent to which the anthropologists today exercise faith, holding to be true and firmly established what in fact is only hopefully

---

*Research scientist and group head of the Human Engineering Laboratory, Defence Research Board, Shirley Bay Site, near Ottawa, Ontario, Canada

believed, is borne out by several of the following quotations, all of which are from top flight experts in the field. Raymond Pearl, for instance, presents a beautiful example of hopeful possibilities stated as high probabilities by circumlocution when he said:

> While everyone agrees that man's closest living relatives are to be found in the four man-like apes, gorilla, chimpanzee, orangutan, and gibbon, there is no such agreement about the precise structure of his ancestral pedigree. The evidence that he had a perfectly natural and normal one . . . is overwhelming in magnitude and cogency. But exactly what the individual steps were, or how they came about, is still to be learned. There are nearly as many theories on the point as there are serious students of the problem. All of them at present, however, lack that kind of clear and simple proof which brings the sort of universal acceptance that is accorded to the law of gravitation, for example.
>
> Only on one point, and that one a little vague, can there be said to be general agreement. It is that, on the weight of the evidence, it is probable that at some remote period in the past for which no clear paleontological record has yet been uncovered, man and the other primates branched off from what had theretofore been a common ancestral stem.[2]

In this quotation the phrase "a perfectly natural and normal pedigree" means, of course, an evolutionary one. Pearl assures us that the evidence for this is overwhelming in magnitude and cogency, but in the next breath he speaks only of possibilities and adds that even for these there is no clear paleontological evidence. Many anthropologists today, twenty years after the above was written, would argue that the paleontological evidence is now at hand in the form of a wide range of cattarrhine anthropoidea loosely cataloged together as *pithecines*. These creatures include such types as *Dryopithecus, Ramapithecus, Kenyapithecus*, and of course the more popularly known *Australopithecines*.

Disagreements on Relationships.—But a study of the literature in which these fossils are examined indicates first of all that there is considerable disagreement as to their precise status and relationship with one another, and secondly, that there is considerable debate whether they really stand in the line leading to *Homo sapiens*, though hopefully people like Robinson try to slide them across in the family tree so that they at least fall under the heading of hominoidea, whence man is supposed to have evolved. At the present moment it appears to me that there has not been enough time yet to achieve a clear picture, and even granting that evolution *were* true it still seems unlikely that *Homo sapiens* arrived via a *pithecine* route.

The trouble is that the *Australopithecines* had very small brains indeed, a mean cranial capacity of 575 cc.[3] compared with the normal for modern man of 1450 cc., and yet appear to have been tool users. Since by definition man is a cultured animal and tools are an essential part of his cultural activity, some investigators have credited these primitive apes with culture, and for this reason elevated them to manhood, though at a very low level of course. But there are many who hold that a creature cannot be said to be a "cultured" animal merely because it *uses* tools. Birds use tools, for example, but this could hardly be considered as cultural activity.[4]

I do not know of any unequivocal evidence that the *Australopithecines* deliberately manufactured tools, which is a very different thing. There *is* evidence of what *look* like manufactured tools, but it is highly debatable whether they were actually the work of the *Australopithecines* themselves. It has been argued that the *Australopithecines* were hunted by early man and that these tools were left by the hunters.

In the second place, it used to be held that cranial capacity and intelligence were closely related. This is seriously questioned today, although there is general agreement that a human being cannot be normal with a cranial capacity below 800 cc., the so-called "cerebral Rubicon." [5] If there is no real relationship between these two indices, then the very small *Australopithecine* brain might still qualify as "human." But there is certainly no general agreement on the matter. In any case, modern man with his far larger brain is represented by fossils which were contemporary with the latest in the *Australopithecine* line, so it still seems unlikely that that *Homo sapiens* arrived by this route.

Leakey, writing in 1966 with reference to *Homo habilis,* a supposed *maker* of tools, for a number of reasons rejects any such linear series as *Australopithecus africanus-Homo habilis-Homo erectus* (the latter being essentially man as we now know him). "It seems to me," he says,[6] "more likely that *Homo habilis* and *Homo erectus* as well as some of the *australopithicines,* were all evolving along their own distinct lines by Lower Pleistocene times." And again, "I submit that morphologically it is almost impossible to regard *H. habilis* as representing a stage between *Australopithecus africanus* and *Homo erectus.*" Leakey adds,

I have never been able to accept the view that *Australopithecus* represented a direct ancestral stage leading to *H. erectus,* and I disagree even more strongly with the present suggestion of placing *H. habilis* between them. . . . It is possible that *H. habilis* may prove to be the direct ancestor of *H. sapiens* but this can be no more than a theory at present. . . .

All that can be said at present is that there was a time at Olduvai when *H. habilis, Australopithecus (Zinjanthropus) boisei* and what seems to be a primitive ancestor of *H. erectus* were *broadly contemporary and developing along distinct and separate lines* (emphasis added).[7]

The debate continues, and though specialists do not question man's evolutionary origin, the conclusive links are still missing.

The problem is that although there *are* a substantial number of fossil candidates which can be manipulated into the proper kind of sequence, the chain seems to lead rather to modern apes—or to extinction—than to man. For certain periods of geological history there are promising successions of fossil forms which look as though they ought to lead to man, but they do not. Very recently, Elwyn L. Simons observed:

Within the past fifteen years a number of significant new finds have been made. . . . The early primates are now represented by many complete or nearly complete skulls, some nearly complete skeletons, a number of limb bones, and even the bones of hands and feet. In age these specimens extend across almost the entire Cenozoic era, from its beginning in Paleocene epoch some sixty-three million years ago up to the Pliocene which ended roughly two million years ago. . . . But they do not lie in the exact line of man's ancestry.[8]

Imaginative Thinking All-Important.—When the significance of the data is a subject of so much debate, it is clear that a great deal depends upon imaginative thinking, each authority being persuaded that he is merely reading the evidence, but the disagreement which exists between authorities demonstrates clearly that the evidence can be "merely read" in several different ways. For this reason, Melville Herskovits[9] observed that "no branch of Anthropology requires more of inference for the weighing of imponderables, in short, of the exercise of scientific imagination, than pre-history."

Many years ago, Professor Wilson D. Wallis[10] pointed out that there is a kind of law in the matter of anthropological thinking about fossil remains which goes something like this: the less information we

Zinjanthropus, drawn for the Sunday Times of April 5, 1964.

Zinjanthropus, drawn by Neave Parker for Dr. L. S. B. Leakey, and published by the Illustrated London News and Sketch, Jan. 1, 1960.

Zinjanthropus, drawn by Maurice Wilson for Dr. Kenneth P. Oakley.

Figure 1. Three different reconstructions of the same fossil *Zinjanthropus* into "flesh and blood" head and face.

have by reason of the scarcity of the remains, the more sweeping can our generalizations be about them. If you find the bones of a man who has died recently, you have to be rather careful what you say about him, because somebody might be able to check up on your conclusions. The further back you go, the more confidently you can discuss such reconstructions, because there is less possibility of anyone being able to challenge you. Consequently, when only a few fossil remains of early man were known, very broad generalizations could be made about them, and all kinds of genealogical trees were drafted with aplomb.

A few wiser anthropologists today decry the temptation to draft genealogical trees which, as I. Manton said, are more like "bundles of twigs" rather than trees in any case.[11] And when it comes to the reconstruction of a fossil find into a "flesh-and-blood" head and face, the degree of divergence can be even more extraordinary as is shown, for example, in those concocted to represent *Zinjanthropus* for the London *Sunday Times,* the *Illustrated London News,* and for Dr. Kenneth Oakley by Maurice Wilson, respectively (Figure 1).[12] The reconstruction of man's evolutionary history is still much more of an art than a science. The original fossil skull is shown in Figure 2.

Moreover, as has been recognized for many years and emphasized very recently by J. T. Robinson,[13] habits of life, climate, and diet can tremendously influence the anatomical features of the skull, indeed, to such an extent that two series of fossil forms which may very well be in fact a single species are by some authorities put into different genera. I have in mind the *Australopithecins* and *Paranthropus*. How can one take seriously family trees in which the lines of connection are drawn solely on the basis of similarity or dissimilarity in appearance when these similarities or dissimilarities could be nothing more than evidence of a difference in diet? Such cultural or environmental factors can cause not only two members of a single species to diverge sufficiently to be put into two different genera, but two different genera can for the same reason *converge* until they have the appearance of belonging to the same species. There are some extraordinary examples of convergence.[14]

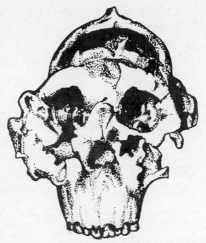

Figure 2. Original fossil skull of *Zinjanthropus* upon which reconstructions shown in Figure 1 were based.

Morphology No Guide to Relationships.—It is evident, therefore, that morphology in itself is not really any kind of guide at all to lineal relationships. Indeed, even the finding of the skeletons of a mother and a child buried together, although it might be presumptive evidence of a mother-child relationship, could never be taken as absolute *proof*. Almost all fossil remains are "proved" to be related in this way or that, only in the sense that if you agree to the theory of evolution to start with, the relationship might be reasonably assumed. But in itself similarity of form does not prove relationship.

Those who see in their own finds, or who wish to see in them, more of man than the ape tend to classify them by tacking the suffix—*anthropus* on to their name. Those who are reemphasizing rather the *antiquity* of their finds may tend to classify them as—*pithecus*. Thus one has two alternative temptations, one being to stress *antiquity* of man's supposed ancestors, and the other the *humanness* of them.

One other factor clearly enters into these naming games and that is the prestige of having made a find which initiates a new genus or sub-family or category of some kind. Thus von Koenigswald calls his Javanese find *Meganthropus*, whereas others see it as merely representative of one branch of the *Australopithecines*. Similarly, Leakey labels his Olduvai finds as *Zinjanthropus*, whereas others would rob his specimens of their unique status by reducing them also to a mere *Australopithecine*.[15]

The unfortunate thing is that the very naming of these finds can give to them a weight of importance which can be quite unjustified. The name creates the significance, not the find itself. One thing is certain: not one of these specialists is ever *tempted* to make any pronouncement regarding their particular finds which puts the slightest question mark against their evolutionary origin. Evolution is unchallengeable!

LeGros Clark has pointed out that "practically none of the genera and species of fossil hominoids [and this includes all the *Australopithecines* according to Robinson—A.C.C.] which have from time to time been created have any validity at all in zoological nomenclature." [16] And again,

> Probably the one single factor which above all others has unduly, and quite unnecessarily, complicated the whole picture of human phylogeny is the tendency for the taxonomic individualization of each fossil skull or fragment of a skull by assuming it to be a new type which is specifically, or even generically, distinct from all others.[17]

In the popular mind, the *Australopithecines* are constantly being presented as though they were little by little filling the gap between man and his animal ancestors, and the temptation has been for "fossil-finders" to contribute to this confusion by attaching names to their finds which are intended to reinforce this impression.[18] In point of fact, not only are these names unjustified in many cases, but the line itself appears to have continued its imagined evolutionary development right up into Pleistocene times when modern man was already in existence. This has the unfortunate consequence of making man as old as his supposed ancestors, which seems nonsense to me, but in the evolutionist's credo this is his faith—"the substance of things hoped for, the evidence of things not seen. . . ."

Faith Without Sufficient Reason.—There is no question that the theory of evolution is useful as a teaching aid to assist in the orderly arrangement of the data that are available. And there is no doubt also that when the theory is presented for popular consumption, i.e., omitting any mention of problems which remain to be solved before it can unequivocally be considered factually established, it has a certain compulsiveness about it, for it appears to explain everything.

This, as a matter of fact, is one reason why there are a few authorities of stature within the camp who nevertheless feel somewhat uneasy about it all in its current theoretical formulation. For a theory which can be made to explain everything by manipulating the threads of the argument to suit the occasion is really unsound for the basic reason that it could never be disproved. As Medawar[19] observes, if a theory is so flexible that the same explanation can be used to account for two entirely contrary tendencies, than the theory is meaningless.

Once it was held that man's enlarging brain caused his emergence as *Homo sapiens*, the great tool-users, so that smaller-brained creatures were lower in the scale. Now that the small-brained creatures have turned up as tool-users, it is being argued that the very use of tools is what enlarged the brain to man size! Evolutionary theory is highly "adjustable." Medawar says, "When we speak, as Spencer was the first to do, of the survival of the fittest, we are being wise after the event: what is fit or not fit is so described on the basis of a retrospective judgment. It is silly to profess to be thunderstruck by the evolution of organism A if we should have been just as thunderstruck by a turn of events which would have led to the evolution of B or C instead."

A few years ago, Professor T. H. Leith[20] underscored the fact, which I believe is of fundamental importance, that in order to be useful a theory must be so structured that some critical experiment is conceivable which if it is actually false could prove it to be so. As Medawar[21] has pointed out, since absolute proof is beyond our power (for there may always turn up one more piece of evidence which is irreconcilable), the best we can do in any area of research is to seek constantly for error in the hypothesis.

The result of each experiment which does not demonstrate a flaw serves either to confirm the present hypothesis or to purify it by forcing its modification. But the theory of evolution is so flexible that it is simply not possible to conceive of a critical experiment which *could* disprove it. All research seems to be ultimately devoted to proving the theory, not to challenging it. How could one challenge it?

In the meantime, it may be useful enough, heuristically, or even as a philosophy which ministers to our materialism, but it is nevertheless held as an act of faith—indeed Huxley would define it as a kind of religion.[22] As such, there is a large element of emotion involved in

its defense. In a recent book, This View of Life, Simpson reveals this
quite remarkably. There are some sections in which he reiterates
ad nauseam the basic tenet of his faith: "Evolution is a fact." [23]

Circular Reasoning Very Common.—Circular reasoning plays a
large part in current evolutionary anthropology, perhaps as large a
part as it does in modern geology, although it is not as readily admitted. The circularity of the reasoning goes something like this:
we know that human evolution is true and therefore there must be a
succession of forms from some proto-human being up to man spread
over the appropriate time scale of millions of years.

Since one can, by disregarding geographical location and taking
some liberties with an expansive time scale, line up a set of candidates in fossil form which make what is euphemously termed a "nice
sequence," this proves that human evolution is a fact. The possibility
that there might be any other explanation for similarity of form is
not even considered.

The point is that the mere arbitrary lining up of man-like fossils,
even when the temporal ording is correct, does not prove descent.
The assumption is made that descent is the explanation, and the line-
up is then used to prove the assumption.[24] This is characteristically
circular, as much geological reasoning is.

This kind of evolutionary sequence was once very popular in
cultural anthropology: artifacts developed progressively from simple
to complex by known stages; religion evolved continuously from
animism to monotheism; art passed from a very low stage of crude
representation to its modern sophisticated(?) level of abstraction; in
short, everything evolved. Little by little most of these classically
familiar evolutionary schemes have been discarded as being either
purely arbitrary mental creations or positively contrary to fact. Christian readers sometimes see references to the abandonment of these
cultural evolutionary constructs and unfortunately gather the impression that all evolutionary ideas are being abandoned—which is
not so at all.

Doubts Africa as Cradle of Man.—Unfailingly, human and prehuman fossils are still being set forth in such a way as to create the
impression that linear relationships actually have been demonstrated
between them. As Howell puts it, "Man . . . is most closely related to
the living African anthropoid ape," and that's a fact!

It is too soon for us to be able to see the true significance of the many new fossils from Africa and elsewhere, each of which tends, by its discoverer, to be hailed as *the* missing link, until it is challenged as to its significance by the man who is lucky enough to find an even more primitive (or human-like!) fossil. Because most of these fossils have been turning up in Africa, at the present time it is popular to hail Africa rather than the Middle East as the true home of man in spite of the fact that the *Australopithecine* line leads to modern apes and not to man at all, according to many experts.

But there are ways in which the Middle East can still be shown to be the most reasonable cradle of man and that group of fossils widely scattered over the world (in Asia, Africa. and Europe) which by general consensus of opinion *do* represent early man, such as the *Homo erectus* series, can be accounted for without making them man's *ancestors*. After all, there is no need to assume automatically that everything that looks like an ancestor *is* an ancestor . . . it could be a *descendant*. If one believes in evolution, the former is a reasonable enough assumption on account of the fact that these fossil skulls are so very primitive in appearance. If one believes that man was created, the logic of the argument is not nearly so compelling—for degeneration is as likely as improvement.

On the other hand, provided that one can, for the sake of gaining a new perspective, ignore for the present the time element involved (and there are many uncertainties here), there is a way in which all those fossil remains which are generally agreed to belong within the family of man, *Homo sapiens*, can be accounted for without appealing to evolutionary processes of any kind. And this way is not only reasonable in itself, but has substantial support from what we know of man's early history on the basis of archaeology, the records of antiquity, and modern research into the effects of food, climate, and habit of life on human physique.

An Alternative Faith

Whether we believe that the Flood in Noah's day was geographically local or universal, most of those who read this Annual will certainly agree that from the point of view of the world's human population the Flood was an overwhelming catastrophe which left this earth with eight sole human survivors. The same basic agreement would, I believe, be found with respect to the period of time which has elapsed since these eight souls began to re-people the

204 WHY NOT CREATION?

world, a period which cannot be much more than four or five thousand years at the most.

It seems unlikely, even making all conceivable allowances for gaps in genealogies which some are persuaded must exist,[25] that one could push back the date of the Flood beyond a few thousand years B.C. In this case, we are forced to conclude that, except for those who lived between Adam and Noah and were overwhelmed by the Flood and whose remains, I believe, are not very likely to be found, all fossil men, all prehistoric cultures, all primitive communities of the past or the present, and all civilizations since, must be encompassed within this span of a few thousand years. On the face of it the proposal seems utterly absurd.

However, I think there are lines of evidence of considerable substance in support of it. In setting this forth all kinds of "buts" will arise in the reader's mind if he has any broad knowledge of current physical anthropology. An attempt is made to deal specifically with a number of these "buts" in other papers by the author,[26] yet some problems remain unsolved, particularly the question of the time element. However, one does not have to solve every problem before presenting a hypothetical reconstruction. After all, the orthodox view is shot full of them, and yet it is still held to be a respectable one!

Main Contention Presented.—It is our contention that Noah and his family were real people, sole survivors of a major catastrophe, the chief effect of which was to obliterate the previous civilization which had developed from Adam to that time. When the Ark grounded, there were eight people alive in the world . . . and no more.

Landing somewhere in the highlands north of Mesopotamia, they began to spread as they multiplied, though retaining for some time a homogeneous cultural tradition. The initial family pattern, set by the existence in the party of three sons and their wives, gave rise in the course of time to three distinct families of man. According to their patriarchal lineage, these families have been termed appropriately—Japhethites, Hamites, and Shemites, but in modern terminology would be represented by the Indo-Europeans (Caucasoids), the Mongoloid and Negroid peoples, and the Semites (Hebrews, Arabs, and some more ancient branches of the family such as the Assyrians, etc.) respectively.

At first they kept together, but within a century or so they began to break up and subsequently some of the family of Shem, some of the family of Ham, and perhaps a few of the family of Japheth arrived from the East in the southern section of the Mesopotamian Plain.[27] Here it would appear from the evidence discussed elsewhere by the author[28] the family of Ham became politically dominant, initiated a movement to prevent any further dispersal by the erection of a monument high enough to be a visible rallying point on the flat plain, and brought upon themselves a judgment which led to their being forcibly and rapidly scattered to the four corners of the earth. Part of this we know only from the Bible; but part of it we know also from archaeological evidence.

The fact is that in every area of the world where Japhethites have subsequently settled, they have always been preceded by Hamites. This pattern applies in every continent. In prehistoric times the circumstance seems always to be true, the earliest fossil remains of man being Mongoloid or Negroid in character and in head shape, while those that came last belonging to the family of Japheth, i.e., Caucasoid. Indeed, in pre- and early historic times, the pattern of events is repeated again and again, whatever cultural advances the pioneering Hamites had achieved tended to be swallowed up by the succeeding Japhethites.

The record of Japheth's more leisurely spread (i.e., "enlargement," Gen. 9:27) over the earth has been marred consistently by his destruction of the cultures which were already in existence wherever he arrived in sufficient force to achieve dominion. It happened in the Indus Valley, it happened in Central America, it happened to the Indian tribes of North America, it happened in Australia, and only numerical superiority of the native population has hitherto preserved parts of Africa from the same fate.

Now in spite of the claims made for the implications based upon the South African discoveries of recent years, it still remains true that whether we are speaking of fossil *Man*, ancient civilizations, contemporary or extinct native peoples, or the present nations of the world, all lines of migration which are in any way traceable or deducible seem to radiate from the Middle East like the spokes of a wheel.

Nature of Evidence to Be Presented.—Before presenting some of the evidence, it will be well to summarize briefly the nature of the evidence. Along any migratory route there will be settlements each of which differs slightly from the one which preceded it and the one which stems from it. As a general rule, the direction of movement tends to be reflected in the gradual loss of cultural artifacts which continue in use back along the line, but either disappear entirely forwards along the line or are less effectively copied or merely represented in pictures or in folklore.

When several lines radiate from a single center, the picture presented is more or less a series of ever-increasing circles of settlements, each sharing fewer and fewer of the original cultural artifacts which continue at the center, while each witnesses the appearance of completely new items developed to satisfy new needs which were not found at the center. The further from the center one moves along any such routes of migration the more new and uniquely specific items one is likely to find which are not shared by the other lines, while there will yet be preserved a few particularly useful or important links with the original home base. Entering such a settlement without previous knowledge of the direction from which the settlers came, one cannot be certain which way relationships are to be traced without some knowledge of the culture content of settlements up and down the line in each direction.

There is usually, however, some quite specific type of evidence which allows one to separate the artifacts which have been brought *with* the newcomers from those which have been developed on the site. This is particularly the case whenever complex items turn up, the materials for the making of which would not be available locally. Sometimes the evidence is, as it were, secondhand, existing in the form of an article which is clearly a copy and has that about its construction which proves it to be so.

For example, certain Minoan pottery vessels are clearly copies of metal prototypes, both in the shape they take and in their ornamentation. Where the pottery handles of these vessels join the vessel itself little knobs of clay are indicated which serve no functional purpose, but which are clearly an attempt to copy the rivets which once secured the metal handle to the metal bodies of the prototype.[29] These prototypes are found in Asia Minor, and it is therefore clear which way the line of migration is to be traced, for it is inconceivable that the pottery vessel with its little knobs of clay provided the metalworker with the clues as to where he should place the rivets.

Tendency for Loss of Culture.—In the earliest migrations, which, if we are guided by the chronology of Scripture, must have been quite rapid, it was inevitable that the tendency would be markedly towards a loss of cultural items common to the center as one moves out, rather than a gain of new items.[30] Thus the general level of culture would decline at first in certain respects, although oral traditions and things like rituals and religious beliefs tend to be surrendered or changed much more slowly. In due time, when a large enough body of people survived in any one place which was hospitable enough to favor permanent settlement, a new culture center would arise with many of the old traditions preserved, but some new ones established of sufficient importance that waves of influence would move out both forward and backward along the lines whence the settlers had come.

Accompanying such cultural losses in the initial spread of the Hamitic peoples would often be a certain coarsening of physique. Not only would people tend to be in many cases unsuited for the rigors of such a pioneering life and be culturally degraded as a consequence, but food itself would often prove grossly insufficient or unsuitable to their unaccustomed tastes. Not infrequently the food would at first be inadequate for the maintenance of full bodily vigor and the development of entirely normal growth of the young, for dietary disturbances have their effects upon growth patterns.

Indeed, as Dawson[31] long ago observed, the more highly cultured an immigrant is when he arrives at a frontier, the more severely is he handicapped and likely to suffer when robbed of the familiar accouterments of his previous life. This has been noted by those who have studied the effects of food deficiencies upon the form of the human skull for example, a subject dealt with in some detail by the author elsewhere.[32]

The effect upon the technological achievement of the newcomers is obvious enough, for a highly educated lady who had never made bread, or mended her own clothes, or cultivated a garden would be far worse off on the frontier when she first arrived than would a London charwoman. Thus the most likely cause of a particularly degraded society at the beginning would not be a *low* cultural background but a high one! And this is certainly the situation that Genesis presents us with immediately after the Flood.

Cradle of Mankind in Middle East.—Meanwhile, the occasional establishment, along the various routes of migration, of what might be called "provincial" cultural centers whose influences spread in all directions would greatly complicate the patterns of cultural relationship in the earliest times. By and large, the evidence which does exist strongly supports a "Cradle of Mankind" in the Middle East, from which there went out just such successive waves of pioneers who were almost certainly not Indo-Europeans (i.e., Japhethites).

These pioneers were Hamitic, either Mongoloid or Negroid in type for the most part, but with some admixture; and they blazed trails and opened up territories in every habitable part of the earth. They did so, often, at great cost to their own cultural heritage, and to the detriment of the refined physique still to be found in their relatives who continued to reside at their point of origin. In each locality they ultimately either established a way of life which made maximum use of the resources available . . . , or circumstances overwhelmed them and they died out leaving a few scattered remnants behind whose lot must have been appallingly difficult in their isolation and whose physical remains bear witness to that effect.

The Japhethites followed them in due course, often taking advantage of the established technology as the Puritans were to do in North America thousands of years later, sometimes displacing them entirely, sometimes absorbing them so that the two stocks were fused into one, and sometimes educating them in new ways and then retiring. India has seen all three patterns. The Indus Valley people were overwhelmed and entirely displaced or absorbed, and this admixture thousands of years later was once more educated in new ways by a further influx of Japhethitic settlers who have since surrendered their dominant status.

One further factor bears upon the degenerative form which so many of the earliest fossils of man seem to show. Although the life span of man declined quite rapidly after the Flood, for several hundred years many people survived to what would today be considered an incredible old age. If we add to the isolation and deprivation of some of these more scattered early pioneers the possibility of their living well past the century mark or perhaps even much longer, the ultimate effect upon their physique would be tremendously accentuated. It has been noted, in fact, that the skull sutures are almost obliterated in some specimens, a circumstance which might reasonably be interpreted as evidence of very extreme old age.[33] Extreme old age would often tend to modify the skull towards the conventional man-ape form.

More Detailed Examination of Evidence.—So much, then, for the broad picture. We shall now turn to a more detailed examination of the evidence: (1) that the dispersal of man took place from a center somewhere in the Middle East and that this dispersal accounts for fossil man, and (2) that those who formed the vanguard were of Hamitic stock, using the term "Hamitic" to mean all the descendants of Noah who were not in the line of Japheth or Shem.

Before man's evolutionary origin was proposed, it was generally agreed that the Cradle of Mankind was in Asia Minor or at least in the Middle East area. Any evidence of primitive types elsewhere in the world, whether living or fossil, were considered proof that man had degenerated as he departed from the site of Paradise. When evolution captured the imagination of anthropologists, then primitive fossil remains were once again hailed as proof that the first men were constitutionally not much removed from apes.

One problem presented itself, however, almost from the beginning, and this was that these supposed ancestors of modern man always seemed to turn up in the wrong places! The basic assumption was still being made that the Middle East was the home of man, and therefore these primitive fossil types, which were turning up anywhere but in this area, seemed entirely misplaced. Osborn, in his *Men of the Old Stone Age*, accounted for this anomaly by arguing that they were migrants. He asserted his conviction that both the human and animal inhabitant of Europe, for example, had migrated there in great waves from Asia and from Africa. In the latter case, he wrote that it was probable that the source of the migratory waves was also Asia, northern Africa being merely the route of passage.

This was his position in 1915, and when the third edition of his famous book appeared in 1936, he had modified his original views only slightly. Thus Osborn has a map of the Old World with this subscription, "Throughout this long epoch Western Europe is to be viewed as a peninsula, surrounded on all sides by the sea and stretching westwards from the great land mass of eastern Europe and Asia— which was the chief theatre of evolution, both of animal and human life." [34]

However, in 1930, and contrary to expectations, Professor H. J. Fleure had to admit: "No clear traces of the men and cultures of the later part of the Old Stone Age (known in Europe as the Aurignacian, Solutrean, and Magdalenian phases) have been discovered in the central highland of Asia." [35]

The situation remained essentially the same when, twenty years later, Wilhelm Koppers observed:

> It is a remarkable fact that so far all the fossil men have been found in Europe, the Far East, and Africa, that is, in the marginal

regions of Asia that are most unlikely to have formed the cradle of the human race. No remains are known to us from central Asia where most scholars who have occupied themselves with the origin of men would place the earliest races.[36]

It is true that some fossil men have now been found in the Middle East, but far from speaking against this area as being central to subsequent migration, they seem to me to speak indirectly—and therefore with more force—in favor of it. We shall return to this subsequently.

Migratory Movements Considered.—Professor Griffith Taylor of the University of Toronto, in speaking of migratory movements in general whether in prehistoric or historic times, wrote:

> A series of zones is shown to exist in the East Indies and in Australasia which is so arranged that the most primitive are found farthest from Asia, and the most advanced nearest to Asia. This distribution about Asia is shown to be true in other "peninsulas" [i.e., Africa and Europe—A.C.C.], and is of fundamental importance in discussing the evolution and ethnological status of the peoples concerned. . . .
>
> Which ever region we consider, Africa, Europe, Australia, or America, we find that the major migrations have always been from Asia.[37]

After dealing with some of the indices which Taylor employs for establishing possible relationships between groups in different geographical area, he remarks: "How can one explain the close resemblance between such far-distant types as here set forth? Only the spreading of racial zones from a *common* cradleland can possibly explain these biological affinities" [38] (emphasis in original).

Then subsequently, in dealing with African ethnology, he observes,

> The first point of interest in studying the distribution of the African peoples is that the same rule holds good which we have observed in the Australasian peoples. The most primitive groups are found in the regions most distant from Asia, or what comes to the same thing,—in the most inaccessible regions. . . . Given these conditions it seems logical to assume that the racial zones can only have resulted from similar peoples spreading out like waves from a common origin. This cradleland should be approximately between the two "peninsulas," and all indications (including the racial distribution of India) point to a region of maximum evolution not far from Turkestan. It is not unlikely that the time factor was similar in the spread of all these peoples.[39]

In a similar vein, Dorothy Garrod wrote:

> It is becoming more and more clear that it is not in Europe that
> we must seek the origins of the various paleolithic peoples who
> successfully overran the West. . . . The classification of de Mor-
> tillet therefore only records the *order of arrival* in the West of a
> series of cultures, each of which has originated and probably
> passed through the greater part of its existence elsewhere (em-
> phasis added).[40]

So also wrote V. G. Childe:

> Our knowledge of the Archaeology of Europe and of the Ancient
> East has enormously strengthened the Orientalist's position. In-
> deed we can now survey continuously interconnected provinces
> throughout which cultures are seen to be zoned in regularly
> descending grades round the centres of urban civilization in the
> Ancient East. Such zoning is the best possible proof of the
> Orientalist's postulate of diffusion.[41]

Henry Field, in writing about the possible cradle of *Homo sapiens,*
gives a very cursory review of the chief finds of fossil man (to that
date, 1932), including finds from Java, Kenya, Rhodesia, and
Heidelberg, and then gives a map locating them; and he remarks:

> It does not seem probable to me that any of these localities
> could have been the original point from which the earliest men
> migrated. The distances, combined with many geographical
> barriers, would tend to make a theory of this nature untenable.
> I suggest that an area more or less equidistant from the outer
> edges of Europe, Asia, and Africa may indeed be the centre in
> which development took place.[42]

It is true that these statements were written before the recent
discoveries in South Africa, or in the Far East at Choukoutien, or in
the New World. Of the South African finds we have already spoken—
—and they do not concern us here since there is no general agreement that they are truly fossils of *man* or even, in the opinions of
some, ancestral to him. The finds at Choukoutien, as we shall attempt to show, support the present thesis in an interesting way. As
for the New World, nobody has ever yet proposed that it was the
Cradle of Mankind in any case, nor do they antedate the supposedly
earliest fossil men in the Old World.

Thus the Middle East could still retain priority as the home of
man, although in the matter of dating it must be admitted that no
authority with a reputation for orthodoxy at stake would ever pro-

pose it was a homeland *so recently*—by our reckoning only 4,500 to 5,000 years ago. The problem of time remains with us and at the moment we have no answer to it, but we can continue to explore further lines of evidence which in most other respects assuredly do support the thesis set forth in this paper.

Physical Types and Culture.—Part of this evidence, curiously enough, is the fact of diversity of physical types found within what appear to have been single families (since the fossils are found all together and seem to be contemporary), which has been a source of some surprise though readily enough accounted for on the basis of central dispersion. Some years ago, W. D. Matthew made the following observation: "Whatever agencies may be assigned as the cause of evolution in a race, it should be at first most progressive at its point of original dispersal. . . ." [43]

Some comment is in order on this observation because there are important implications in it. Lebzelter pointed out that "where man lives in large conglomerations, physical form tends to be stable while culture becomes specialized: where he lives in small isolated groups, culture is stable but specialized races evolve." [44] According to Lebzelter, this is why racial differentiation was more marked in the earlier stages of man's history. The explanation of this fact is clear enough.

In a very small, closely inbreeding population, genes for odd characters have a much better chance of being homozygously expressed so that such characters appear in the population with greater frequency, and tend to be perpetuated. On the other hand, such a small population may have so precarious an existence that the margin of survival is too narrow to encourage or permit cultural diversities to find expression. Thus physical type is variant, but is accompanied by cultural conformity. Whereas in a large and well-established community, a physical norm begins to appear as characteristic of that population, while the security resulting from numbers allows for a greater range of cultural divergence.

At the very beginning, we might therefore expect to find in the central area a measure of physical diversity and cultural uniformity: and at each secondary or provincial center in its initial stages, the same situation would re-appear. The physical diversity to be expected on the foregoing grounds would, it is now known, be exaggerated even further by the fact (only comparatively recently recognized) that when any established species enters a new environment it at once gives expression to a new and greater power of diversification in physical form. As LeGros Clark put it, "High variability (in type) may be correlated with the fact that (at that time) the rate of hominid evolution was proceeding rather rapidly with the development of relatively small and contiguous populations into widely dispersed areas with contrasting and changing environments."[45]

Many years ago, Sir William Dawson remarked upon this in both plant and animal biology. From a study of post-Pliocene molluscs and other fossils, he concluded that "new species tend rapidly to vary to the utmost extent of their possible limits and then to remain stationary for an indefinite time."[46] The circumstance has been remarked upon in connection with insect populations by Charles Brues, who adds that "the variability of forms is slight once the population is large, but at first is rapid and extensive in the case of many insects for which we have the requisite data."[47] Adolph Schultz[48] has confirmed this generalization for primate populations, and Ralph Linton[49] remarks upon it in connection with man.

Thus we have in reality three factors, all of which are found to be still in operation in living populations, which must have contributed to the marked variability of early fossil human remains, particularly where several specimens are found in a single site as at Choukoutien, for example, or at Obercassel, or Mount Carmel.

Three Factors of Variability.—These factors may be summarized, then, as follows: (a) a new species is more variable when it first appears; (b) a small population is more variable than a large one; (c) when a species shifts (or a few members of it) into a new environment, wide varieties again appear which become stable with time. To these should be added a fourth, namely, (d) that small populations are likely to be highly conservative in their culture, thus maintaining many links with the parent body though widely extended geographically.

Fossil remains constantly bear witness to the reality of these factors, but the witness has meaning only, and the facts are best accounted for only, if we assume that a small population began at the center and, as it became firmly established there, sent out successive waves of migrants usually numbering very few persons in any one group, who thereafter established a further succession of centers— the process being repeated again and again until early man had spread into every habitable part of the world. Each new center at the first showed great diversity of physical type, but as the population multiplied locally a greater physical uniformity was achieved in the course of time.

Where such a subsidiary center was wiped out before this uniformity had been achieved and where chance preserved their remains, the diversity was, as it were, captured and frozen for our examination. At the same time in marginal areas where individuals or families were pushed out even further by those who followed them, circumstances often combined to degrade them so grossly that fossil man naturally tends towards a bestial form—but for quite secondary reasons.

That the idea is not altogether unreasonable is borne out by the fact that Le Gros Clark, for example, in discussing Heidelberg Man, asks whether he represents a separate species of man or may not be "merely a deviant peripheral isolate." [50] Clark virtually admits the same possibility for Neanderthal Man. For after referring to him as "an aberrant side line . . . a sort of evolutionary retrogression," he goes on to say, "If the remains of Neanderthal Man are placed in their chronological sequence, it appears that some of the *earlier* fossils, dating from the earlier part of the Mousterian period, are less 'Neanderthaloid' in their skeletal characters (and thus approach more closely to *Homo sapiens*) than the extreme Neanderthal type of *later* date" (emphasis added).[51]

On the other hand, in the earliest stages of these migrations cultural uniformity would not only be the rule in each group, but necessarily also between the groups themselves. And this, too, has been found to be so to a quite extraordinary degree. Indeed, following the rule enunciated above, the most primitive fragments which had been pushed furthest to the rim might logically be expected to have the greatest proportion of shared culture elements, so that links would not be surprising if found between such peripheral areas as the New World, Europe, Australia, South Africa, and so forth— which is exactly what has been observed.

Such lines of evidence force upon us the conclusion that we should not look to these marginal areas for a picture of the initial stages of man's cultural development nor for a picture of his original appearance. It is exactly in these marginal areas that we shall *not* find these things. The logic of this was both evident to and flatly rejected by E. A. Hooten, who remarked:

> The adoption of such a principle would necessitate the conclusion that the places where one finds existing primitive forms

of any order of animal are exactly the places where these animals could not have originated. . . .

But this is the principle of "lucus a non lucendo," i.e., finding light just where one ought not to do so, which pushed to its logical extreme would lead us to seek for the birthplace of man in that area where there are no traces of ancient man and *none of any of his primate precursors* (emphasis added).[52]

Nevertheless, the principle may be true—even if it does contradict evolutionary reconstructions.

William Howells has written at some length on the fact that, as he puts it, "all the visible footsteps lead away from Asia." He then examines the picture with respect to the lines of migration taken by the "Whites" (Caucasoids) and considers that at the beginning they were entrenched in southwest Asia "apparently with the Neanderthals to the north and west of them." He then proposes that while most of them made their way into both Europe and North Africa, some of them may very well have travelled east through central Asia into China, which would explain, possibly, the Ainus and the Polynesians.

Howells thinks that the situation with respect to the Mongoloids is pretty straightforward, their origin having been somewhere in the same area as the Whites, whence they peopled the East. The dark-skinned peoples are, as he put it, "a far more formidable puzzle." He considers that the Australian aborigines can be traced back as far as India with some evidence of them perhaps in southern Arabia. Presumably, the African Negroes are to be also from the Middle East, possibly reaching Africa by the Horn and therefore also via Arabia.

However, there are a number of black-skinned peoples who seem scattered here and there in a way which he terms "the crowning enigma"—a major feature of which is the peculiar relationship between the Negroes and the Negritos. Of these latter, he has this to say:

They are spotted among the Negroes in the Congo Forest, and they turn up on the eastern fringe of Asia (the Andaman Islands, the Malay Peninsula, probably India, and possibly formerly in southern China), in the Philippines, and in New Guinea, and perhaps Australia, with probable traces in Borneo, Celebes, and various Melanesian Islands.

All of these are "refuge" areas, the undesirable backwoods which the Pigmies have obviously occupied as later more powerful people arrived in the same regions. . . .

Several things stand out from these facts. The Negritos must have had a migration from a common point. . . . And it is hopeless to assume that their point of origin was at either end of their range. . . . It is much more likely that they came from some point midway which is Asia.[53]

Agreement on Lines of Migration.—There is, then, a very wide measure of agreement that the lines of migration radiate not from a point somewhere in Africa, or Europe, or the Far East, but from a geographical area which is to be closely associated with that part of the world in which Scripture seems to say that man not only began physically the peopling of the world after the Flood, but also where man began culturally. Looking at the spread of civilization as we have looked at the spread of people, it is clear that the lines follow the same course.

The essential difference, if we are taking note of current chronological sequences, is that whereas the spread of people is held to have occurred hundreds of thousands of years ago, the spread of civilization is an event which has taken place very recently. I think that man was making his long trek to the uttermost corners of the world while at the very same time civilization was blossoming at the center. I think they were contemporary events: human evolutionists do not.

Interpretations of Fossil Data.—It used to be argued that although civilized man is a single species, the far-flung fossil remains of man formed separate species in their own right and were therefore not related to modern man in any simple way. Some authorities have proposed, tentatively, for example, a concept such as this by looking upon Neanderthal Man as an earlier species or sub-species who was eliminated with the appearance of so-called "modern man."[54] The association of Neanderthals with moderns in the Mount Carmel finds seems to stand against this conception.[35] And indeed, there is a very widespread agreement today that, with the exception, of course, of the most recent South African finds, all men—fossil, prehistoric, and modern—are one species, *Homo sapiens.*[56]

Ralph Linton viewed the varieties of men revealed by fossil finds as being due to factors which we have already outlined. As he put it:

If we are correct in our belief that all existing men belong to a single species, early man must have been a generalized form with potentialities for evolving into all the varieties which we know at present. It further seems probable that this generalized form spread widely and rapidly and that within a few years of its appearance small bands of individuals were scattered over most of the Old World.

These bands would find themselves in many different environments, and the physical peculiarities which were advantageous in one of these might be of no importance or actually deleterious in another. Moreover, due to the relative isolation of these bands and their habit of inbreeding, any mutation which was favourable or at least not injurious under the particular circumstances would have the best possible chance of spreading to all members of the group.

It seems quite possible to account for all the known variations in our species on this basis, without invoking the theory of a small number of distinct varieties.[57]

Viewed in this light, degraded fossil specimens found in marginal regions should be treated neither as "unsuccessful" evolutionary experiments towards the making of true *Homo sapiens* types, nor as "successful but only partially complete" phases or links between apes and men. Indeed, as Griffith Taylor was willing to admit, "the location of such 'missing' links as *Pithecanthropus* in Java, etc., seems to have little bearing on the question of the human cradleland." [58] And he might in fact also have said, "on the question of human origins." As he concludes, "They are almost certainly examples of a type which has been pushed out to the margins."

Thus the way in which one studies or views these fossil remains is very largely colored by whether one's thinking is in terms of biological or historical processes. Professor A. Portmann of Vienna remarks:

One and the same piece of evidence will assume totally different aspects according to the angle—palaeontological or historical— from which we look at it. We shall see it either as a link in one of the many evolutionary series that the palaeontologist seeks to establish, or as something connected with remote historical actions and developments that we can hardly hope to reconstruct. Let me state clearly that for my part I have not the slightest doubt that the remains of early man known to us should all be judged historically.[59]

Fossil Man and Modern Man.—This general approach towards the interpretation of the meaning of fossil man has been explored in some detail by Wilhelm Koppers, who considers that "primitiveness in the sense of man being closer to the beast" can upon occasion be the "result of a secondary development." [60] He believes that it would be far more logical to "evolve" Neanderthal Man out

This Neanderthal Skull from La Chapelle-aux-Saints was in due course.....

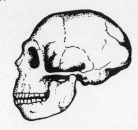

reconstructed thus, for the Field Museum of Natural History, to show how our primitive ancestor looked.

And it was reconstructed thus by J. H. McGregor, to show how 'modern' he really might have been in appearance!

Figure 3. The fossil Neanderthal skull and reconstructions showing how "modern" in many respects Neanderthal Man might have looked.

of modern man than modern man out of Neanderthal Man (Figure 3). He holds, in fact, that they were a specialized and more primitive type—but *later* than modern man, at least in so far as they occur in Europe.

Surprisingly enough, such a great authority as Franz Weidenreich was prepared to admit unequivocally, "no fossil type of man has been discovered so far whose characteristic features may not easily be traced *back* to modern man" (emphasis added)![61] Agreement with this opinion by Griffith Taylor was borne out when he observed, "evidence is indeed accumulating that the paleolithic folk of Europe were much more closely akin to races now living on the periphery of the Euro-African regions than was formerly admitted." [62] Many years ago, in fact, Sir William Dawson pursued this theme and explored it at some length in his beautifully written but almost completely ignored work entitled *Fossil Men and Their Modern Representatives.*[63]

At the Cold Spring Harbor Symposium on "Quantitative Biology" held in 1950, T. D. Stewart, in a paper entitled "Earliest Representative of *Homo Sapiens,*" stated his conclusions in the following words, "Like Dobzhansky, therefore, I can see no reason at present to suppose that more than a single hominid species has existed on any time level in the Pleistocene." [64]

The most primitive types being at the margins and only essentially modern types so far found where civilization had its source, it is to be expected that combinations and intermediate forms would be found in the geographic areas in between. As Alfred Romer observed[65] in commenting on the collection of fossil finds from Palestine (Mugharet-et-Tabun, and Mugharet-es-Skuhl), "while certain of the skulls are clearly Neanderthal, others show to a variable degree numerous neanthropic, i.e., 'modern man,' features," while subsequently he identifies such neanthropic skulls as being of the general Cromagnon type in Europe—a type of man who appears to have been a magnificent physical specimen. He proposes later that the Mount Carmel people "may be considered as due to interbreeding of the dominant race (Cromagnon Man) with its lowly predecessors (Neanderthal Man)."

The assumption is still being made that the lower Neanderthal form *preceded* the higher Cromagnon Man. William Howells says of the Skuhl fossil group, "It is an extraordinary variation. There seems to have been a single tribe ranging in type from almost *Neanderthal* to almost *sapiens*." [66] Le Gros Clark is even prepared to omit the "almost." [67]

Example of Variability.—As an extraordinary example of the tremendous variability which an early small isolated population at the periphery can show, one cannot do better than refer to the finds at Choukoutien in China from the same locality in which the famous Pekin Man was found. These fossil remains came from what is known as the Upper Cave, and consist of a group of seven people who appear to be members of one family: an old man judged to be over 60, a younger man, two relatively young women, an adolescent, a child of five, and a new-born baby. With them were found implements, ornaments, and thousands of fragments of animals.

A study of these remains has produced some remarkably interesting facts, the most important of which in the present context is that, judged by cranial form, we have in this one family a representative Neanderthal Man, a "Melanesian" woman who reminds us of the Ainu, a Mongoloid type, and another who is rather similar to the modern Eskimo woman. In commenting on these finds, Weidenreich expressed his amazement at the range of variation. Thus he wrote:

> The surprising fact is not the occurrence of paleolithic types of modern man which resemble racial types of today, but their assemblage in one place and even in a single family considering

that these types are found today settled in far remote regions.

Forms similar to that of the "Old Man," as he has been named, have been found in Upper Paleolithic, western Europe and northern Africa: those closely resembling the Melanesian type, in the neolithic of Indo-China, among the ancient skulls from the Cave of Lagoa Santa in Brazil, and in the Melanesian populations of today; those closely resembling the Eskimo type occur among the pre-Columbian Amerindians of Mexico and other places in North America and among the Eskimos of western Greenland of today.[68]

He then proceeds to point out the upper Paleolithic melting-pot of Choukoutien "does not stand alone." In Obercassel in the Rhine Valley two skeletons, an old male and a younger female, were found in a tomb of about the same period as the burial in Choukoutien. He says, "The skulls are so different in appearance that one would not hesitate to assign them to two races if they came from separate localities." So confused is the picture now presented that he observes:

> Physical anthropologists have gotten into a blind alley so far as the definition and the range of individual human races and their history is concerned. . . .

> But one cannot push aside a whole problem because the methods applied and accepted as historically sacred have gone awry.[69]

This extraordinary variability nevertheless still permits establishment of lines of relationship which appear to crisscross in every direction as a dense network of evidence that these fossil remains for the most part belong to a single family, the descendants of Ham.

Griffith Taylor links together Melanesians, Negroes, and American Indians.[70] The same authority proposes a relationship between Java Man and Rhodesian Man.[71] He relates certain tribes which seem to be a pocket of an older racial stock with the people of northern China, the Sudanese, the Bushmen of South Africa, and the Aeta of the Philippines.[72] He would also link the Predmost Skull to Arignacian folk and to the Australoids.[73]

Mackowan[74] and Montagu[75] are convinced that the aboriginal populations of Central and South America contain an element of Negroid as well as Australoid people. Grimaldi Man is almost universally admitted to have been Negroid even though his remains lie in Europe,[76] and indeed so widespread is the Negroid type that even *Pithecanthropus erectus* was identified as Negroid by Buyssens.[77]

T. H. Huxley maintained that the Neanderthal race must be closely linked with the Australian aborigines particularly from the Province of Victoria;[78] and other authorities hold that the same Australian people are to be related to the famous Canstadt Race.[79] Alfred Romer relates Solo Man from Java with Rhodesian Man from Africa.[80] Hrdlicka likewise relates the Oldoway Skull with LaQuina Woman; Lachapelle and others to the basic African stock;[81] and holds that they must be related also to Indian, Eskimo, and Australian races. Even the Mauer Jaw is held to be Eskimo in type.[82]

We cannot do better than sum up this general picture in the words of Sir William Dawson, who, far in advance of his time, wrote of fossil man in Europe, in 1874:

> What precise relationship do these primitive Europeans bear to one another? We can only say that all seem to indicate one basic stock, and this is allied to the Hamitic stock of northern Asia which has its outlying branches to this day both in America and in Europe.[83]

While it is perfectly true that the thesis we are presenting has against it in the matter of chronology the whole weight of scientific opinion, it is nevertheless equally true that the interpretation of the data in this fashion makes wonderful sense out of the present evidence and, indeed, would have allowed one to predict both the existence of widespread physical relationships as well as an exceptional variableness within the members of any one family. In addition to these anatomical "linkages" there are, of course, a very great many cultural linkages.

One such linkage, as a single example of what I mean, is the painting of the bones of the deceased with red ochre—a custom which not so very long ago was still being practiced by the American Indians and which has been observed in prehistoric burials in almost every part of the world.[84] Surely such a custom could hardly arise everywhere indigenously on some such supposition as that "men's minds work everywhere pretty much in the same way. . . ." It seems much more reasonable to assume it was spread by people who carried it with them as they radiated from some central cradle.

Cradle of Man Reconsidered.—And this brings us once more to the question of the geographical position of this cradle. Evidence accumulates daily that, culturally speaking, the place of man's origin was somewhere in the Middle East. No other region in the world is as likely to have been the home of man if by man we mean something more than merely an intelligent ape. Vavilov[45] and others[86] have repeatedly pointed out that the great majority of the cultivated plants of the world, especially the cereals, have been traced there as to their origin. Henry Field remarks:

> Iran may prove to have been one of the nurseries of *Homo sapiens*. During the middle or upper Paleolithic periods the climate, flora, and fauna of the Iranian Plateau provided an environment suitable for human occupation. Indeed, Ellsworth Huntington has postulated that during late Pleistocene times southern Iran was the *only* region in which temperature and humidity were ideal, not only for human conception and fertility but also for chances of survival.[87]

Many speculations exist as to the routes taken by Caucasoids, Negroids, and Mongoloids, as the world was peopled by the successive ebb and flow of migrations, and while not one of these speculations really establishes with certainty *how* man originated as *man*, almost all of them make the basic assumption that western Asia is his home as a creature of culture.

From this center one can trace the movements of an early migration of Negroid people followed by Caucasoid people in Europe. From this same area undoubtedly there passed out into the East and the New World successive waves of Mongoloid people, and the time taken need not have been so great. Kenneth Macgowan[88] says it has been estimated that men might have covered the 4,000 miles from Harbin, Manchuria, to Vancouver Island in as little as twenty years, while Alfred Kidder says,

> A hunting pattern based primarily on big game could have carried man to southern South America without the necessity at that time of great localized adaptation. It could have been effected with relative rapidity, so long as camel, horse, sloth, and elephant were available. All the indications point to the fact that they were.[89]

According to de Quatrefages,[90] 600,000 people made a trip from a point in Mongolia to China during winter and under constant attack in just five months, covering a distance of 700 leagues or 2,100 miles, and though this seems to be a staggering trip in so short a time, it actually works out to an average of 14 miles per day.

In Africa, Wendell Phillips,[91] after studying the relationships of various African tribes, concluded that evidence already existing makes it possible to derive many of the tribes from a single racial stock (particularly the Pygmies of the Ituri Forest and the Bushmen of the Kalahari Desert), which at a certain time must have populated a larger part of the African continent only to retreat to less hospitable regions as later Negroid tribes arrived in the country.

Professor H. J. Fleure[92] held that evidence of similar nature towards the north and northeast of Asia and on into the New World was to be discerned by a study in the change of head forms in fossil remains, and it has been suggested that the finds at Choukoutien mean we have encountered some of the first pioneers on their way to the Americas! Moreover, wherever tradition sheds light on the subject, it invariably points in the same direction and tells the same story, many primitive people having recollections of a former higher cultural standing, a circumstance explored elsewhere by the writer at considerable length.

Conclusion.—And thus we conclude that from the family of Noah have sprung *all* the peoples of the world—prehistoric and historic. The events described in connection with Genesis 6 to 10 and particularly the prophetic statements of Noah himself in Genesis 9:25-28 with respect to the future of his three sons, Shem, Ham, and Japheth, together combine to provide us with the most reasonable and best possible account of the early history of mankind. This is a history which, rightly understood, does not at all require us to believe that modern man began with the stature of an ape and reached a civilized state only after a long, long evolutionary history. Rather, we may believe that modern man made a fresh start as a single family who carried with them into an unpeopled earth the accumulated heritage of the pre-Flood world.

Summary

In summary, then, what we have endeavored to show in this paper may be set forth briefly as follows:

a) that the geographical distribution of human fossil remains is such that they are most logically explained by treating them as marginal representatives of a widespread and, in part, forced dispersion of people from a single multiplying population established at a point more or less central to them all, which sent forth successive waves of migrants, each wave driving the previous one further towards the periphery;

b) that the most degraded specimens are representatives of this general movement who were driven into the least hospitable areas where they suffered physical degeneration as a consequence of the circumstances in which they were forced to live;

c) that the extraordinary physical variability of their remains stems from the fact that they were members of small, isolated, strongly inbred bands; whereas the cultural similarities which link together even the most widely dispersed of them indicate a common origin for them all;

d) that what is true of fossil man is equally true of vanished and of living primitive societies;

e) that all of these initially dispersed populations are of one basic stock—the Hamitic family of Genesis 10;

f) that they were subsequently displaced or overwhelmed by the Indo-Europeans, i.e., Japhethites, who nevertheless inherited, or adopted and extensively built upon, Hamitic technology and so gained the upper hand in each geographical area where they spread;

g) that throughout this movement, both in prehistoric and historic times, there were never any human beings who did not belong within the family of Noah and his descendants;

h) and finally, that this thesis is strengthened by the evidence of history which shows that migration has always tended to follow this pattern, has frequently been accompanied by instances of degeneration both of individuals or whole tribes, and usually results in the establishment of a general pattern of cultural relationships which are parallel to those that archaeology has since revealed from antiquity.

NOTES AND REFERENCES

1. F. Clark Howell, "The Hominization Process," *Human Evolution: Readings in Physical Anthropology.* Edited by Noel Korn (New York: Holt, Rinehart and Winston, 1967), p. 85.
2. Raymond Pearl, *Man the Animal* (Bloomington, Indiana: Principia Press, 1946), p. 3.
3. Wilfred Le Gros Clark, "Bones of Contention," (Huxley Memorial Lecture), *Journal of the Royal Anthropological Institute* (1958), 88 (2)136-138.
4. Tool Using: see Kenneth P. Oakley, "Skill as a Human Possession," *A History of Technology*, edited by Charles Singer *et al.* (Oxford, 1954), Vol. 1, pp. 1-37; cf. Mickey Chiang, "Use of Tools by Wild Macaque Monkeys in Singapore," *Nature* (1967), 214:1258-1259. Cf. also K. R. L. Hall, "Tool-using Performances as Indicators of Behavioral Adaptability," *Human Evolution* (ref. no. 1), pp. 173-210; especially p. 195 for a remark by R. Cihak: "The author states that not tool-*using* but tool-*making*

signalizes the critical stage in the transition from ape to human; but it ought to be pointed out that tool-making, as 'shaping an object for an imaginary future eventuality,' is the real boundary between ape and man."

5. Franz Weidenreich, "The Human Brain in the Light of Its Phylogenetic development," *Scientific Monthly* (1948), 67:103-109.

6. L. S. B. Leakey, "*Homo habilis, Homo erectus,* and the AUSTRALO-PITHECINES, *Nature* (1966), 209:1280-1281.

7. *Ibid.*

8. Elwyn L. Simons, "The Early Relatives of Man, *Scientific American* (July 1964), p. 50. Simons' recent discovery in the Fayum of *Aegyptopithecus* reported in his article, "The Earliest Apes," *Scientific American* (December 1967), pp. 28-35, and which he describes as "the skull of a monkey equipped with the teeth of an ape," does not shed light on the nature of the missing link between ape and man—only between monkey and ape.

9. Melville Herskovits, *Man and His Works* (New York: Knopf, 1950), p. 97.

10. Wilson D. Wallis, "Pre-suppositions in Anthropological Interpretations," *American Anthropologist* (July-Sept. 1948), p. 560.

11. I. Manton, *Problems of Cytology and Evolution in the Pteridophyta* (Cambridge, 1950), quoted by Irving W. Knobloch, *Journal of American Scientific Affiliation* (Sept. 1953), 5(3):14.

12. *Sunday Times*, April 5, 1964; and *Illustrated London News and Sketch,* Jan. 1, 1960; see also, *The Fallacy of Anthropological Reconstructions* by the author, Doorway Paper No. 33, Ottawa, 1966.

13. J. T. Robinson, "The Origins and Adaptive Radiation of the Australopithecines," *Human Evolution* (note no. 1), pp. 227, 279, 294.

14. Convergence: Leo S. Berg, *Nomogenesis: or Evolution Determined by Law*, English trans. (Edinburgh: Constable, 1926); David Lack, *Evolutionary Theory and Christian Belief* (London: Methuen, 1967), p. 65; Evan Shute, *Flaws in the Theory of Evolution* (London, Can.: Temside Press, 1961), p. 138ff.

15. G. H. R. von Koenigswald, re, *Meganthropus*, see *Human Evolution*, p. 280 ref. no. 1); and re. *Zinjanthropus*, see "The Fossil Skull from Olduvai," editorial comment in *British Medical Journal* (Sept. 19, 1959), p. 487.

16. Le Gros Clark, *op. cit.*, p. 302.

17. *Ibid.*, p. 299.

18. Thus Sir Solly Zuckerman, "Correlation of Change in the Evolution of Higher Primates," *Evolution as a Process*, edited by J. Huxley *et al.* (London: Allen and Unwin, 1954), p. 301: "The fundamental difficulty has been that in the great majority of cases the descriptions of the specimens that have been provided by the discoverers have been so turned as to indicate that the fossils in question have some special place or significance in the line of direct human ascent as opposed to that of the family of apes."

19. Sir Peter B. Medawar, *The Art of the Soluble* (London: Methuen, 1965), p. 55.

20. T. H. Leith, "Some Logical Problems with the Thesis of Apparent Age," *Journal of American Scientific Affiliation* (1965), 17:119.

21. Sir P. B. Medawar, *The Uniqueness of the Individual* (New York: Basic Books, 1957), p. 76. Similarly, Rudolf Flesch remarked, "The most important thing about Science is this: that it isn't a search for truth but a search for error. . . ." "The Art of Clear Thinking," *Scientific Monthly* (1952), 74:240. See also editorial comment under "The Discipline of the Scientific Method" in *Nature* (Aug. 1, 1959), p. 295: "Since, according to the code of science, no positive assertions are final and all propositions approximations, and indeed provisional, science is seen to advance more by denying what is wrong than by asserting what is right—by reducing, and eventually eradicating, errors rather than by heading straight toward some preconceived final truth."

22. Julian Huxley, "New Bottles for New Wine: Ideology and Scientific Knowledge," *Journal of the Royal Anthropological Institute* (1950), 80: 7-23, especially p. 15b; and his introduction to Teilhard de Chardin, *The Phenomenon of Man* (London: Collins, 1959), where he hails him as the new prophet of the new faith!

23. Gaylord G. Simpson, *This View of Life* (New York: Harcourt, Brace and World, 1964):
    p. vii one of the basic facts . . .
    p. 10 Fact—not theory . . .
    p. 12 no one doubts . . .
    p. 40 all the facts support it . . .
    p. 51 only dishonest biologists disagree . . .
    p. 62 unassailable now . . .
    p. 63 all problems being solved "triumphantly" . . .
    p. 151 Evolution a fact . . creation a dogma . . .
    p. 193 Evolution a fact . . . the truth of evolution . . . proofs . . . all agree . . . proofs of evolution . . . *ad nauseam!*
    In his article, "The Biological Nature of Man," *Science* (1966), 152:475, he wrote, "We are no longer concerned with *whether* man evolved, because we know that he did" (emphasis in original)!

24. R. H. Rastall of Cambridge wrote, "It cannot be denied that from a strictly philosophical standpoint geologists are here arguing in a circle. The succession of organisms has been determined by a study of their remains buried in the rocks, and the relative ages of the rocks are determined by the remains of organisms that they contain." (*Encyclopedia Britannica,* 1956, article on Geology, Vol. 10, p. 168). W. R. Thompson says of Simpson, "Simpson states that homology is *determined* by ancestry and concludes that homology is *evidence* of ancestry" ("Evolution and Taxonomy, *Studia Entomologica,* 1962, 5:567)!

25. On the question of gaps in the biblical genealogies see: *The Genealogies of the Bible*, Doorway Paper No. 24, by the author, 1967.

26. A. C. Custance, *The Supposed Evolution of the Human Skull,* Doorway Paper No. 9, 1957; *Primitive Cultures*: a second look at the problem of their historical origins, Doorway Paper No. 32, 1960; *The Fallacy of Anthropological Reconstructions*, Doorway Paper No. 33, 1966.

27. The existence of the three "families" at this time is noted twice by Vere G. Childe, *New Light on the Most Ancient East* (London: Kegan Paul,

1935), p. 18; *What Happened in History* (Baltimore, Md.: Penguin Books, 1946), p. 81.
28. A. C. Custance, *The Part Played by Shem, Ham and Japheth in Subsequent World History*, Doorway Paper No. 28, 1958. *The Technology of Hamitic People*, Doorway Paper No. 43, 1960. *The Confusion of Tongues*, Doorway Paper No. 8, 1961.
29. On this see J. D. S. Pendlebury, *The Archaeology of Crete* (London: Methuen, 1939), p. 68; and V. G. Childe, *The Dawn of European Civilization*, 5th edition (London: Kegan Paul, 1950), p. 19.
30. W. J. Perry, *The Growth of Civilization* (Baltimore, Md.: Penguin Books, 1937), p. 123.
31. Sir Wm. Dawson, *The Story of the Earth and Man* (London: Hodder and Stoughton, 1903), p. 390.
32. See Note 26 *supra*.
33. Obliteration of skull sutures were noted by Sir Wm. Dawson, *Meeting Place of Geology and History* (New York: Revell, 1904), p. 63.
34. H. F. Osborn, *Men of the Old Stone Age* (New York: 1936), p. 19ff.
35. H. J. Fleure, *The Races of Mankind* (London: Benn, 1930), p. 45.
36. W. Koppers, *Primitive Man and His World Picture* (New York: Sheed and Ward, 1952), p. 239.
37. Griffith Taylor, *Environment, Race and Migration* (Toronto: University of Toronto, 1945), p. 9.
38. *Ibid.*, p. 67.
39. *Ibid.*, pp. 120, 121.
40. Dorothy Garrod, "Nova et Vetera: a plea for a new method in paleolithic archaeology," *Proceedings of the Prehistoric Society of East Anglia*, Vol. 5, p. 261.
41. V. G. Childe, *Dawn of European Civilization*, 3rd ed. (London: Kegan Paul, 1939). In the 1957 edition, Childe in his introduction invites his readers to observe that he has modified his "dogmatic" orientation a little, but he still concludes at the end of the volume: "the primacy of the Orient remains unchallenged," p. 342.
42. Henry Field, "The Cradle of *Homo sapiens*," *American Journal of Archaeology* (Oct.-Dec. 1932), p. 427.
43. W. D. Matthew, "Climate and Evolution," *Annals of the New York Academy of Science* (1914), Vol. 24, p. 180.
44. Lebzelter, quoted by W. Koppers, *op. cit.* (note no. 34), p. 220. His view was sustained by Le Gros Clark, *Journal of the Royal Anthropological Institute* (1958), 88(2):133.
45. Clark, "Bones of Contention," in *Human Evolution* (note 1 above), p. 301.
46. Dawson, *op. cit.*, p. 360.
47. Charles Brues, "Contribution of Entomology to Theoretical Biology," *Scientific Monthly* (Feb. 1947), p. 123ff, quote at p. 130.
48. Adolph Schultz, "The Origin and Evolution of Man," *Cold Springs Harbor Symposium on Quantitative Biology* (1950), 15:50.
49. Ralph Linton, *The Study of Man* (New York: Appleton-Century, 1936), p. 26f.
50. Clark, "Bones of Contention," in *Human Evolution* (note no. 1), p. 239.

51. W. Le Gros Clark, *History of the Primates* (Chicago: University of Chicago, Phoenix Books, 1957), pp. 163, 164.
52. A. E. Hooten, "Where Did Man Originate?" *Antiquity* (June 1927), p. 149.
53. William Howells, *Mankind So Far* (New York: Doubleday Doran, 1945), pp. 295, 298-299.
54. Franz Weidenreich, *Palaeontologia Sinica*, Whole Series No. 127 (1943), p. 276.
55. Alfred Romer, *Man and the Vertebrates* (Chicago: University of Chicago Press, 1948), pp. 219, 221.
56. Fossils of man as a whole: see F. Gaynor Evans in a note. "The Names of Fossil Men," *Science* (1945), 101:16, 17.
57. Linton, *op. cit.*, p. 26.
58. Taylor, *op. cit.*, p. 282.
59. A. Portmann, 1947, *Das Ursprungsproblem*, Eranos-Yahrbuck, p. 11.
60. Koppers, *op. cit.*, pp. 220, 224.
61. Franz Weidenreich, *Apes, Giants and Man* (Chicago: Chicago University Press, 1948), p. 2.
62. Taylor, *op. cit.*, pp. 46, 47.
63. Sir William Dawson, *Fossil Men and Their Modern Representatives* (London: Hodder and Stoughton, 1883), 362 pp.
64. T. D. Stewart, "Origin and Evolution of Man," *Cold Spring Harbor Symposium on Quantitative Biology*, Vol. 15, p. 105.
65. Romer, *op. cit.*, pp. 219, 221.
66. Howells, *op. cit.*, p. 202.
67. Clark, in *Human Evolution* (note 1 above), p. 302.
68. Franz Weidenreich, "*Homo sapiens* at Choukoutien," News and Notes, *Antiquity* (June 1939), p. 87.
69. *Ibid.*, p. 88.
70. Taylor, *op. cit.*, p. 11.
71. *Ibid.*, p. 60. His argument here is based on head form, which he considers conclusive.
72. *Ibid.*, p. 67. He feels only a "common cradleland" can possibly explain the situation.
73. *Ibid.*, p. 134.
74. Kenneth Macgowan, *Early Man in the New World* (New York: Macmillan, 1950), p. 26.
75. Ashley Montagu, *Introduction to Physical Anthropology* (Springfield, Ill.: Thomas, 1947), p. 113.
76. Weidenreich, *op. cit.*, p. 88.
77. Paul Buyssens, *Les trois races de l'Europe et du Monde* (Brussles, 1936). See G. Grant MacCurdy, *American Journal of Archaeology* (Jan.-Mar. 1937), p. 154.
78. Thomas Huxley, quoted by D. Garth Whitney, "Primeval Man in Belgium," *Transactions of Victoria Institute* (London, 1908), Vol. 40, p. 38.
79. According to Whitney, *ibid.*
80. Romer, *op. cit.*, p. 223.

81. Ales Hrdlicka, "Skeletal Remains of Early Man, *Smithsonian Institute, Miscellaneous Collections* (1930), Vol. 83, p. 342ff.
82. *Ibid.*, p. 98. See also William S. Laughlin, "Eskimos and Aleuts: Their Origins and Evolution," *Science* (1963), 142:639, 642.
83. Sir William Dawson, "Primitive Man," *Transactions of Victoria Institute* (London, 1874), Vol. 8, pp. 60, 61.
84. Red Ochre: The custom is common to burials in Paleolithic Europe (Vere Childe, *op. cit.*, pp. 6, 168, 209, 254, 259); in North America (Wm. Dawson, *Fossil Men and Their Modern Representatives* [London: Hodder and Stoughton, 1883]), and in Australia (C. S. Coon, *A Reader in General Anthropology* [New York: Holt, 1948], p. 225), sometimes being applied to the body of the dead, sometimes to infants, and sometimes warriors.
85. N. I. Vavilov, "Asia, the Source of Species," *Asia* (Feb. 1937), p. 113.
86. J. R. Harlan, "New World Crop Plants in Asia Minor," *Scientific Monthly* (Feb. 1951), p. 87.
87. Henry Field, "The Iranian Plateau Race," *Asia* (Apr. 1940), p. 217.
88. Macgowan, *op. cit.*, p. 3 and map on p. 4.
89. Alfred Kidder, "Problems of the Historical Approach: results (in) *Appraisal of Anthropology Today*, ed. by Sol, Tax *et al.*, p. 46.
90. A. de Quatrefages, *L'espéce Humaine* (Paris: Balliere et Cie, 14th edition, 1905), pp. 135, 136.
91. Wendell Phillips, "Further African Studies," *Scientific Monthly* (Mar. 1950), p. 175.
92. Fleure, *op. cit.*, pp. 43, 44.

PALEOBOTANICAL EVIDENCES FOR A PHILOSOPHY OF CREATIONISM

George F. Howe, Ph.D.*

The topic of origins is usually treated as if it lay exclusively in the domain of science. Such classification is unfortunate and erroneous when the limitations of the scientific method are evaluated. Science is properly equipped to cope with problems of "how" here and now. For example, such matters as: "how chromosomes migrate in dividing cells," "how water ascends in the trunks of trees," and "how sugars move in phloem tissue" fall clearly in the sphere of science. Yet none of these sample problems has been thoroughly and absolutely settled. If scientific methods as yet cannot completely solve contemporary problems, how can these same methods be expected to yield absolute answers about origins? This does not belittle the amazing achievements of experimental science, but throws the limitations of the method into full focus. To move from present to primeval past moves from experimental science to speculative and philosophical science. As the late Harry Rimmer has said:

> We may as well state at the very onset that it is crass nonsense to talk about a *science* of origin. In science we deal not with origin. That is rather the sphere of philosophy.[1]

Thus the study of origins is not entirely science, but is rather a philosophical system built upon scientific data.

The most direct line of scientific evidence involved is the fossil record. At least six puzzling propositions become apparent from a study of fossil plants. It is presently maintained that these six premises are readily explained by the "group" or "kind" creation proposal of Genesis, but cannot be adequately interpreted by any evolutionary theory—be it theistic, deistic, or naturalistic evolution.

*Assistant Professor of Biology, Westmont College, Santa Barbara, California; Publications Editor, Creation Research Society, 24635 Apple Street, Newhall, California 91321

Evolutionary explanations of these six theses have of course been devised, but only with considerable embarrassment and rationalization.

1. *Complex forms frequently appear before the simpler ones with no hint of an evolutionary ancestry.*

Most evolutionary schemes postulate the flagellate organisms as working models of a primitive ancestor for all subsequently appearing life. (Flagellates are one-celled green or non-green organisms with a whip-like organ of motility.) Theodore Delevoryas states that there is little hint of *Chlamydomonas* spp. or any supposed flagellate ancestors in early fossil layers.[2] It is maintained by some evolutionists that one would not expect to find fossils of delicate cells such as the flagellates. However, equally delicate structures are recorded in other instances. *Phacotus* (a flagellate-like form) is found in Tertiary remains.[3] Delicate fungal hyphae have been found in Meso-Cenozoic sedimentary rocks,[4] and on leaves from Eocene fossils.[5] Fossils of soft-bodied creatures such as jelly-fish are also known.[6] Wesley reported that rhizoids, fungal hyphae, and blue-green algae are well preserved in chert.[7] Thus the absence of supposed flagellate organisms in early layers cannot be easily rationalized. Likewise, the various groups of algae enter the fossil record with no hint of an evolutionary ancestry.[8] In addition, the fungus groups manifest themselves without any previous phylogeny.[9]

The mosses and liverworts are discrete entities in whatever layer their fossils are found.[10]

The "telome theory" is a popular theoretical plan for deriving the vascular plants (plants with food and water conducting systems) from simple ancestors. This theory suggests that branched leafless Silurian and Devonian plants such as *Rhynia Gwynne-Vaughani* serve as working models of vascular plant ancestors. Accordingly, the branches or "telomes" of the generalized leafless ancestor supposedly condensed and joined, yielding the various plant organs (e.g., leaves) of later vascular plants.

Two distinct and perhaps insurmountable problems face the telome theory. First, although leafless and much-branched, *Rhynia* sp. (and other early psilophytes) are by no means "simple." When they appear in the fossil strata they are already complex in their tissue structure since they have been found to possess conducting cells, stomata, guard cells, spores, etc.[11] These complex land plants manifest them-

selves in the fossil rocks with no previous lineage. Although evolutionists believe these plants have come from the green algae, there
is no known ancestry for them. Secondly, leaves are supposed to have
formed as branch systems (like those of *Rhynia* sp.) condensed and
fused by evolution. In rocks of the same fossil layer (Devonian)
plants with large ginkgo-like (fan-shaped) leaves are also present
(*Platyphyllum, Cyclopteris, Ginkgophyllum, Psygmophyllum, Ger-
manophyton,* and *Enigmophyton*).[12] *Aldanophyton antiguissimum*
is a fossil plant specimen having shoots covered with small leaves
about 9 mm. long. This leafy plant occurs in Siberian Middle Cambrian rock and is thus supposedly older than *Rhynia* sp.[13] Thus
the supposed telome ancestral prototype shows up at the same time
as or even later than the supposed leaf-bearing descendants.

The groups of land plants in general are independent entities as
far back as they are discovered in fossil rock. It is for this reason
that some evolutionists feel obliged to accept a polyphyletic view
of land plant origin. Although cast in a different philosophical framework, a polyphyletic ancestry is exactly what biblical creationism
proposes. Creationism solves the vexing problems encountered by
evolutionists in evaluating the fossil series. Certain creationists believe that the entire fossil record is best interpreted as a layering of
ecological zones during the progressive inundation of the earth at
the time of the great flood. This flood-geological orientation has been
ably defended by Clark[14] and by Morris and Whitcomb.[15]

There is no indication of an evolutionary history for the lycopsids
of today, which are usually small, low-growing, evergreen perennials.
Earliest lycopsids from Silurian (*Baraguwanathia*) and Devonian
(*Drephanophycus*) rocks are complex and specialized plants. Although they have been used as typical ancestors for other plants in
certain evolutionary schemes, it appears that the Lycopsid group
produced no other plant groups.[16]

In the study of Arthrophyta another puzzle presents itself. The
modern arthrophytes are short plants with longitudinally ridged stems
having whorls of branches at various regular intervals. A modern
example is the "horsetail" or "scouring rush." Fossil spore-bearing
structures of an arthrophyte *Cheirostrobus pettycurensis* have been
found. These are complex twelve-membered whorls of two-parted
sporangial-bearing appendages.[17] Delevoryas calculates a total of
144 sporangia (spore sacs) at only one such node! A spore is a

microscopic one-celled reproductive unit. The point is that this extremely complicated and advanced spore-bearing organ appears in the fossil record in the Lower Carboniferous strata—which means according to stratigraphic theory that it existed before most of the simpler arthrophyte spore-bearing structures. The going evolutionary idea is therefore that sporangiate organs evolved from complex to simple. But even if the advanced and simpler types did evolve from complex forms such as *Cheirostrobus pettycurensis*, where did the early intricate forms come from?

A stratigraphic study of fern fossils poses a series of similar enigmas. In the first place, the simpler coenopterids appear mostly in the Carboniferous, after the more complex protopteridales, which show up back in the Devonian.[18] Some evolutionary theorists propose the coenopterids as ancestral to the modern ferns. Delevoryas rejects this idea,[19] since some of the supposedly descendant forms of ferns lived contemporaneously with the coenopterids. Secondly, some ferns were homosporous (bore only one size of spores), while other fossil ferns were heterosporous—bearing two different types of spores, one usually larger than the other. Evolutionary theories generally suggest that the heterosporous plants were derived from the supposedly simpler homosporous forms. In the fossils of the *Stauropteris*, the heterosporous species *S. burntislandica* appears in the Lower Carboniferous, earlier than the simpler homosporous *S. oldhamia* of the Upper Carboniferous![20] Thirdly, Delevoryas has stated on the basis of leaf form and arrangement that some of the most complex of the coenopterid petioles (Zygopteridaceae) appear early in the record—Devonian.[21] (The petiole is the stalk-like basal portion of a leaf.) Fourthly, some fossil ferns produce additional woody tissue (secondary xylem) each year by a growth of cambial tissue as do our trees today. Other fossil ferns produced no new woody tissue once the stem had expanded— like our modern herbs. Some of the earliest ferns or fern-like plants (*Aneurophyton germanicum*) were huge plants that produced secondary xylem. The later and more modern ferns were herbaceous (produced no secondary wood). Once again in the study of fossil ferns a complex arrangement shows up before the simpler counterpart.[22] Fifthly, another fern family (Marattiaceae) manifests itself in well-established fashion in Upper Carboniferous strata with little indication of its previous history.[23] Sixthly, the ferns of the family Gleicheniaceae appear suddenly in about the same stratum.[24] These six examples illustrate that the fossil history of ferns is the sudden appearance of discrete forms rather than the gradual evolution of groups from groups.

In the Arthrophyta, where complex forms appeared first, evolutionary theory suggests that plants changed from complex to simple. However, in a study of ferns and fern-like plants where successively higher strata show simple "pre-ferns" first and complex forms later, evolution is supposed to have gone from simple to complex. It looks as if evolutionary theory is of very little predictive value, but is simply a rationalization or "afterthought" of whatever paleobotanical data appear!

In fossil botany the term "seed" designates a sac (megasporangium), usually containing only one large spore (megaspore) and with a tissue or tissue system (integuments) covering the entire sac. In modern seed plants the seed frequently becomes detached from the main plant and an embryo producer within the seed can yield a new plant. Seeds or seed-like reproductive bodies are found attached to several different kinds of fossil plants. Although hypothetical schemes have been devised, no one knows how the seed came into existence in any of the seed-bearing plants.[25]

Seeds were borne on some fossil plants with fern-like leaves (Pteridospermales or "seed ferns"). Some evolutionists believe that seed ferns arose from the true ferns (fern-like plants without seeds). Some of the seed ferns (*Calatrospermum* spp.) are present earlier in the record than are the true ferns from which they supposedly evolved! For this reason some evolutionists believe ferns and seed ferns have had an entirely independent or "polyphyletic" origin.[26] There is no evidence that the pteridosperms originated from the true ferns. They simply appear in the Lower Carboniferous, leaving no clues of any ancestral history.[27] Once again a miraculous creation by non-evolutionary mechanisms finds ample supporting evidence from the fossil series.

Seed ferns varied in the way seeds were attached to the plant. Some bore their seeds on a truss with many branches (*Eurystoma angulare*). Others such as *Stamnostoma huttonense* had a pair of more symmetrical trusses on each stalk.[28] Others had many seeds borne on stalks within one cupule (*Calathospermum* spp.). Some like *Gnetopsis elliptica* had only a few seeds within a cupule. Still others had only one seed in a much-reduced cupule (*Lagenospermum* spp., *Neuropteris tenufolia,* and *Pecopteris pluckeneti*).[29] In a fascinating paper, Mary Hubbard and the late Wendell Camp have proposed a theoretical plan of seed fern cupule evolution. Andrews[30] likewise presents a plan of cupule evolution on the basis of such finds. The seed-bearing branches of a truss (as in *E. angulare*) supposedly fused to form a many-seeded cupule (as in *Calathospermum* spp.). Subsequent evolution supposedly reduced the number of seeds within the cupule to a stage like *Gnetopsis elliptica*, and finally to one seed in the cupule as in *Lagenospermum* spp. and others.[31] Considering the supposed stratigraphic dates, it is most interesting that the truss-like ancestor appears at about the same time (Lower Carboniferous) as do the supposedly descendant many-seeded cupule and the few-seeded cupule![32] For a known fossil to be the prototype of a supposed ancestor or link in an evolutionary series, it should appear at the appropriate geologic time level. It may be an interesting academic exercise to build evolutionary series from three fossils which first appear at about the same time, but such an endeavor can hardly be taken with any certainty. Forms which show up contemporaneously probably have not given rise to each other. When these fossil finds are viewed objectively—either in a catastrophic or uniformitarian framework of geology—there is no evidence for evolutionary descent since all these forms were contemporaries. Thus Andrews' and Camp and Hubbard's interesting scheme for cupule evolution is particularly speculative. Even if their theory were valid, the complex truss and cupule bearing seeds (ovules) with intricate pollen-trapping appendages (*Gnetopsi* spp.) or pollenation droplets in others make their appearance in the record without clear ancestral information. In fact, Camp and Hubbard state that the ovules on these early fossil forms are more advanced than the ovules or seeds of our modern flowering plants.[33] Andrews[34] presents a series of different fossil seeds as evidence for the evolution of the integument (a cylindrical covering of the seed) from an integument divided into a series of distinct filaments. However, both the "primitive" and "advanced" integument types appear in the same layer—Lower Carboniferous—with no evidence of a common ancestry.

Some fossil plants bore their seeds with no fruity covering and hence were naked-seeded or "gymnosperm" plants. Several distinct groups of gymnosperms make their appearance in the strata. Since some of the gymnosperm plants are found in the same levels as the seed ferns, evolutionists are not sure if the gymnosperms are directly related to the seed ferns.[35] In fact, the cycadophytes (plants like the modern cycads) were already a well-defined set of groups when they first appeared at the Permian and Triassic layers.[36] There is no hint of an evolutionary descent. Henry Andrews believes that they had an origin independent of the seed ferns. He concludes that gymnosperm and seed fern plants may have arisen separately along two different lines from a very early state.[37] It appears reasonable to believe that the groups of cycadophytes were each created.

Some gymnosperm plants bear their seeds upon leafy scales of "cones" and are thus called "conifers" (cone-bearers). The conifers also are an evolutionary conundrum since they have been a definite and separate group as long as the seed ferns.[38] Andrews believes that the Cordaite-conifer group has arisen independently of any other seed plant group.[39]

Another gymnosperm plant group is the Gnetales—an example of which is the present day Mormon Tea plant or *Ephedra* spp. Delevoryas indicates that little is known about the origin or evolution of the Gnetales group. *Ephedra-like* pollen is found as early as the Oklahoma Permian deposits. Andrews states that even in such early layers the pollen is clearly recognized as that of a gnetalean genus—Ephedripites.[40]

The ginkgos (e.g., the modern Maidenhair tree with its fan-shaped leaves) and the Taxales (evergreen shrubs such as our "Yew" trees) are other groups of gymnosperms. Concerning these groups, Andrews quotes Florin as stating that as far back as fossil material is found, the conifers, ginkgos, and Taxales are distinct and clearly differentiated from one another.[41] Delevoryas cites evidence to demonstrate that the Taxales have been a distinct group since the Jurassic times.[42] Wesley states that there is little likelihood that the single terminal seed of the Taxales is derived from the conifers.[43]

2. *Supposedly "advanced" and "primitive" characteristics occur in the same fossil plant.*

Only two examples of this second enigma will be considered, although others exist. The Upper Devonian fern-like plant *Racophyton zygopteroides* is primitive in many respects (e.g., no leaf blades present) but is quite advanced in that it presents an intricate three-dimensional system of branches (some bearing sporangia).[44]

Before Charles Beck's work of 1960, *Archaeopteris* spp. (with its long, primitive, fern-like leaves) was thought to be quite distinct from *Callixylon* sp. which had the advanced woody anatomy of the gymnosperms. In Beck's work, however, *Archaeopteris* spp. leaves are reported as attached to a *Callixylon* sp. stem![45] In woody anatomy *Archaeopteris* spp. is therefore as "advanced" as most gymnosperms, yet its leaves are fern-like.[46] Although evolutionists plead that it is possible for part of a plant to evolve more quickly than another part, it is presently postulated that the discovery of primitive and advanced features in the same fossil specimen is more easily and more adequately explained from the standpoint of non-evolutionary creationism.

3. *Modern forms frequently are identical or similar to remote fossil specimens.*

Changes in the non-vascular plants (e.g., fungi and algae) throughout geologic strata have been only slight. Frequently extant algae are quite similar to the fossil types. Also in the mosses and liverworts extant forms are similar to the fossil entities. Any evolutionary descent for mosses or liverworts is a puzzle.[47] The genus *Lycopodites* of the Paleozoic is like the *Lycopodium* or "ground pine" of today.[48] Plants with fan-shaped foliage like modern ginkgos have been found from the Upper Devonian to the present.[49]

A persistent and perhaps unanswerable question that faces the "living fossil" concept is, "Why did certain plants stop evolving long ago?"

4. *Where supposed phylogenies (family trees) are postulated, significant gaps occur.*

The evidence for gaps in supposed ancestral trees is so well recognized by both creationists and evolutionists that only two brief examples will be presented. For a review of literature pertaining to the gaps see Arthur Custance[50] and Paul Zimmerman.[51]

The arthrophytes in higher layers such as the Calamites (tree-like plants resembling the "horse-tail" of today) are supposed to have descended from a prototype something like *Protohynia janovii* of the Lower Devonian or *Calamophyton* spp. of the Middle Devonian. But Andrews believes there is a gap between these early supposedly ancestral plants and the later arthrophyte groups of the Carboniferous.[52]

The cone of coniferous gymnosperms is supposed to have originated from earlier plants which bore seeds on short-branched stalks. The supposed ancestral types such as *Cordaianthus* spp. bore their seeds on dwarf leafy branches. At the base or axis of each leaf on the dwarf branch, there arose a secondary branchlet. The dwarf branchlets were composed in turn of bracts (leaf-like structures)— some of which were sterile and some of which (the more terminal ones) bore seeds. The whole reproductive structure was thus a leafy branch with many branchlets, each branchlet bearing bracts and seeds. The branch is supposed to have lost bracts and seeds from the branchlets by evolution until only two seeds (and perhaps a bract) were left in the leaf axil—this then being a structure like the modern pine cone. Although Andrews himself believes such a series is clearly illustrated through the sequence of *Cordaianthus pseudofluitans* (many bracts and seeds on a branchlet) to *C. zeilleri* (many bracts but only four seeds per branchlet) to *Lebachia* spp. (one seed, many bracts per branchlet) to other forms that seem to approach the structure of a pine cone, he admits that there are noticeable gaps between these supposed linking stages.[53]

The gaps which set apart certain fossil groups are so distinct that the groups cannot be easily classified in *any* of the known taxonomic categories! The Noeggerathiales have both large and small spores borne in delicately fringed, cup-shaped sporophylls. Wesley admits that these fossil plants cannot be classified in any taxonomic category.[54] The system of gaps and distinct groups evident argues for the non-evolutionary and miraculous creation of discrete functioning organisms.

5. *Some of the anatomical characteristics thought to be earmarks of only one particular group or set of groups have been found distributed in other supposedly non-related groups.*

Fern-like fronds (leaves) show up in several distinct groups. Such leaf structure is seen in the true ferns, seed ferns, and in the puzzling *Archeopteris*.[55]

Stomata (with their associated guard cell apparati) appear on most of the land plants. Many of these groups are supposed to have arisen from the algae independently of other groups. Even bryophytes such as the moss sporangial epidermi and hornwort sporophytes manifest stomata. (The epidermis is a tissue usually of one cell thickness and covering the surface of plants. The sporophyte is the generation which bears the spores.) According to evolutionary thought, this necessarily implies that the guard cell-stomata complex arose by chance many times in otherwise independent lines! The same incredible idea must then apply to the other anatomical features which any of these polyphyletic groups may have in common such as tracheid cells.

Some plants bore their seeds completely enclosed by a fruity structure called a carpel. Although true carpels are evident in angiosperms only, carpel-like structures have been found in supposedly non-allied lines. On *Caytonia* sp. of the Mesozoic seed ferns, there are distinctly fruit-like bodies.[56] This must mean (according to recent evolutionary theories) that fruit-like structures arose at least twice by chance in independent lines! The distinct creation of identical components in different plants is a more adequate explanation of such phenomena.

The Pentoxylaceae are a fascinating group of gymnosperm plants which combine features that are characteristic of several other distinct groups. They have stomata like those of the Bennettitales, a vascular leaf anatomy somewhat like that of Cycads, and a branched ovule-bearing organ that is not quite like the Bennettitales or Cycads. Wesley concludes that these plants must stand apart as a distinct group combining characteristics of the Medullosaceae, Cycadales, and Bennettitales.[57]

6. *The entire problem of angiosperm ancestry has remained a complete mystery.*

Cycadeoidea dacotensis has been suggested as an ancestral working model for angiosperms because it was thought to bear a structure somewhat like a *Magnolia* flower. There was an ascending series of whorls of reproductive parts on a short branchlet that gave botanists the idea that this bennettitalean plant could be somewhat like the ancestor of flowering plants. The flower-like structure in question has a lower whorl or whorls of sterile bracts—thought to correspond to the sepals and petals of modern angiosperms. Above these there was what was thought to be a whorl of compound microsporangiate stalks, which were believed to unfold during growth, forming something like a whorl of stamens in a flower. Finally, there was a central ovule-bearing axis that certainly reminds one of the seed-bearing portion of a *Magnolia* flower. Delevoryas, however, has shown that Wieland's earlier reconstruction of 1906 was in error concerning the supposedly branched and stamen-like pollen-bearing organs. According to Delevoryas' latest work, these were not branched and stamen-like but formed a massive compound synangium with a fleshy distal sterile mass of tissue. This whole fused item is supposed to have fallen from the stalk as a unit—something quite unlike the supposed Magnolian descendant.[58] So, what looked like a perfectly good ancestor for the *Magnolia* flower (and is still portrayed as such in most recent textbooks) is now seen to have been something entirely different. Delevoryas, who brought about this brilliant corrective research, suggests that the history of the flowering plant still remains a mystery. As far as the fossil record gives indication, angiosperms were always angiosperms. This demonstration that the Bennettitales were probably not ancestral to flowering plants rocks the whole foundation of angiosperm taxonomy under the famous and much-revered Besseyan plan—since this plan assumed that *Magnolia* was primitive due to its bennettitalian similarities, and the willow was treated either as a much-reduced or advanced type!

A review of the evidence presented in these six propositions (and much other information) may be what led the famous botanist Heribert Nilsson to conclude after much research and study by saying:

> My attempts to demonstrate Evolution by an experiment carried on for more than 40 years, have completely failed. At least, I should hardly be accused of having started from a preconceived anti-evolutionary standpoint. . . .
>
> It may be firmly maintained that it is not even possible to make a caricature of an evolution out of paleo-biological facts. The fossil material is now so complete that it has been possible to construct new classes, and the lack of transitional series cannot be explained as being due to the scarcity of material. The deficiencies are real, they will never be filled.[59]

Those who propose biblical creationism as a plan of fossil interpretation are sometimes said to worship a "God-of-gaps." This is not entirely true, however, since creationism recognizes God as the author of natural laws also. Creationism simply recognizes the possibility of "miracle" in the creation "toolchest" and asks for no "God-of-gaps" alone, but suggests that it was a "God-of-groups" who created "After their kind." The fossil evidence supports the miraculous creation of distinct types. Such creation appears to be special, rapid, and non-evolutionary.

NOTES AND REFERENCES

1. Harry Rimmer, *The Harmony of Science and Scripture* (Grand Rapids, Mich.: Eerdmans Publishing Co., 1936), pp. 70-71.
2. Theodore Delevoryas, *Morphology and Evolution of Fossil Plants* (New York: Holt, Rinehart and Winston, 1962), p. 12.
3. Henry N. Andrews, Jr., *Studies in Paleobotany* (New York: John Wiley & Sons, 1961), p. 12.
4. P. A. Popov, "Fossil Fungi of the West-Siberian Plain and of the Yenisely Ridge," *Bot. Zhur.* (1962), 47(11):1596-1610.
5. David L. Dilcher, "Eocene Epiphyllous Fungi," *Science* (1963), 142 (3593):667-669.
6. *Evolution: Science Falsely So-Called* (Toronto, Ontario: International Christian Crusade, 1963), p. 26.
7. Alan Wesley, *The Status of Some Fossil Plants* (in *Advances of Botanical Research*, Vol. I [New York: Academic Press, 1963]), p. 11.
8. Delevoryas, *op. cit.*, p. 16.
9. *Ibid.*, p. 17.
10. Andrews, *op. cit.*, pp. 398-402; cf. Delevoryas, *op. cit.*, p. 18.
11. *Ibid.*, pp. 42-43; cf. Delevoryas, op. cit., pp. 25-31.
12. *Ibid.*, pp. 54-55; cf. Charles B. Beck, "*Ginkgophyton* (*Psygmophyllum*) with a Stem of Gymnospermic Structure," *Science* (1963), 141(3579): 431-433.
13. Delevoryas, *op. cit.*, p. 21.
14. Harold W. Clark, *The New Diluvialism* (Angwin, Calif.: Science Publications, 1946).
15. Henry M. Morris and John C. Whitcomb, Jr., *The Genesis Flood* (Philadelphia: Presbyterian and Reformed Publishing Co., 1961).
16. Delevoryas, *op. cit.*, p. 49.
17. Andrews, *op. cit.*, pp. 284-286; cf. Delevoryas, *op. cit.*, pp. 63-64.
18. Delevoryas, *op. cit.*, p. 69.
19. *Ibid.*, p. 79.
20. *Ibid.*, p. 72.
21. *Ibid.*, p. 76.
22. Andrews, *op. cit.*, p. 68; cf. Delevoryas, *op. cit.*, pp. 69, 70, 93; cf. also Dilcher, *op. cit.*
23. *Ibid.*, p. 94.
24. *Ibid.*
25. Delevoryas, *op. cit.*, p. 97.
26. Andrews, *op. cit.*, p. 159.
27. Delevoryas, *op. cit.*, p. 128.
28. Henry M. Andrews, "Early Seed Plants," *Science* (1963), 142(3594): 925-131.
29. Wendell H. Camp and Mary M. Hubbard, "On the Origins of the Ovule and Cupule in Lyginopterid Pteridosperms," *Amer. Jour. Bot.* (1963), 50(3):235-243; cf. Henry N. Andrews, Jr., *op. cit.*, pp. 157, 159; cf. also Delevoryas, *op. cit.*, pp. 168-169.

30. Henry M. Andrews, *op. cit.*
31. Camp and Hubbard, *op. cit.*
32. *Ibid.*; cf. Henry N. Andrews, Jr., *op. cit.*, pp. 154-155.
33. *Ibid.*
34. Henry M. Andrews, *op. cit.*
35. Delevoryas, *op. cit.*, p. 101.
36. Henry N. Andrews, Jr., *op. cit.*, p. 312.
37. *Ibid.*
38. Delevoryas, *op. cit.*, p. 149.
39. Henry N. Andrews, Jr., *op. cit.*, p. 315.
40. *Ibid.*, p. 460; cf. Delevoryas, *op. cit.*, p. 165.
41. *Ibid.*, p. 315.
42. Delevoryas, *op. cit.*, p. 163.
43. Wesley, *op. cit.*, p. 49.
44. Delevoryas, *op. cit.*, p. 92; cf. Henry N. Andrews, Jr., *op. cit.*, p. 64.
45. Charles B. Beck, *Ginkgophyton* (*Psygmophyllum*) with a Stem of Gymnospermic Structure," *Science* (1963), 141(3579):431-433.
46. *Ibid.*; cf. Camp and Hubbard, *op. cit.*
47. Henry N. Andrews, Jr., *op. cit.*, pp. 398, 406; cf. Wesley, *op. cit.*, pp. 5-6.
48. Delevoryas, *op. cit.*, p. 47.
49. Beck, *op. cit.*; cf. Henry N. Andrews, Jr., *op. cit.*, pp. 54-55.
50. Arthur C. Custance, *The Earth Before Man*, Part II, Doorway Papers, No. 20, Box 1283, Stn. B, Ottawa, Canada.
51. Paul A. Zimmerman, ed., *Darwin, Evolution, and Creation* (St. Louis, Mo.: Concordia Publishing House, 1959).
52. Henry N. Andrews, Jr., *op. cit.*, p. 285.
53. *Ibid.*, pp. 320-325.
54. Wesley, *op. cit.*, pp. 31-35.
55. Charles B. Beck, "Connection between *Archaeopteris* and *Callixylon*," *Science* (1963), 131(3512):1524-1525.
56. Delevoryas, *op. cit.*, p. 126; cf. Henry N. Andrews, Jr., *op. cit.*, pp. 176-179.
57. Wesley, *op. cit.*, pp. 49-52.
58. Theodore Delevoryas, "Investigations of North American Cycadeoids: Cones of Cycadeoidea," *Amer. Jour. Bot.* (Jan. 1963), 50(1):45-52; cf. same author, *op. cit.*, 134-171.
59. As quoted in Custance, *op. cit.*, p. 51.

Chapter 7

Genetic Evidence Clearly Indicates
Remarkable Stability of Genesis Kinds

1

THE PARADOX OF A CENTURY

WILLIAM J. TINKLE, PH.D.*

When the theory of organic evolution was young, and the known facts—few though they were—seemed to favor it, most people said the theory was absurd. With the passing of a century many facts have been learned, most of which oppose the theory, but now people say, "Science has proved evolution and we must agree." Has there been a greater paradox in a hundred years?

The boast of science is that it is founded upon ascertained facts; but it is evident that if the truth were known and appreciated this contradictory situation could not prevail. In the short time at our disposal let us look at some of the discoveries, bearing in mind that evolution does not mean simply change, but changing one-celled animals into vertebrates.

A common belief in medieval times was that life arises of itself from non-living matter. People thought it was natural for weeds to grow from soil, for rags and corn to generate mice, and for meat to generate maggots. Of course if this were true it would help the theory of evolution, for it would remove the necessity of a Creator to start the organic world. Charles Darwin, in the second edition of *The Origin of Species*, suggested that God may have created the first germs of life. But he did not include this statement in the later editions, probably because he no longer believed it, for in later life he stated that he believed God never made a revelation. Most evo-

---

*Former head of Biology Dept., Taylor University; retired and living at 118 West South Street, Eaton, Indiana; Secretary of the Creation Research Society

lutionists were either very agnostic about the beginning of life or else thought that it generated itself spontaneously.

In the latter part of the nineteenth century some very thorough experiments were performed by Redi, Spallanzani, Schulze, Tyndal, Pasteur, and others, which convinced the scientific world that life comes only from pre-existing life.

Notwithstanding this careful experimentation, there is a present belief that life did arise by chance combination of conditions in an ancient shallow sea and that it arose only once. It is true that amino acids have been synthesized by Miller from ammonia, methane, hydrogen, and water vapor, but amino acid is not alive. No one can predict what may be formed in the future, but the accomplishments of highly trained men are very different from the results of chance. Since man has such great ability he must have been planned and formed by God, just as the Bible states. At any rate, we should not forget that life has never been observed to rise of itself, even after much experimentation.

Another discovery which is unfavorable to the theory of evolution is that "acquired characters" are not inherited. These are changes in a plant or animal caused by the environment, by use or by disuse. Examples are increased size because of good nourishment or the reverse; firm muscles because of use; thick fur in response to cold; pale color of plants because of the lack of light, etc. No one doubts that such characters occur, but J. B. Lamarck and Charles Darwin claimed that they are passed on to the next generation.

Many experiments have been conducted to test this theory and they have failed to give positive results. For instance, a race horse six years of age may have greater speed than he had at three years, and this increased speed is an acquired character. The colts which he sired at six years of age have no greater speed than the ones he sired earlier. Regardless of changes in the parent, each young animal starts back at the base line of the hereditary potential of its parents.

A hundred years ago very little was known about genes, the hereditary factors which carry characters or traits from one generation to the next. Now, however, they are known to occur in each cell of a plant, animal, or person. They are the most important particles in the chromosomes; and if you have taken a course in botany or zoology you have looked at chromosomes under the microscope.

In the division of cells and in the formation of eggs and sperms it is necessary that new genes be formed from the old ones. A hundred years ago it was thought that the genes might be formed slightly different each time and so perform a gradual progressive change over a series of generations. But careful study has shown that nature takes great pains to make the new genes just like the old ones. This is a significant discovery which biologists know very well but others do not appreciate. If a gene changes at all it is by an accidental reorganization called a mutation, which occurs very rarely.

Of course, you can see that if mutations were of all kinds, good, bad, and indifferent, the changes might still occur as Darwin postulated, only more slowly. Mutation has been widely hailed as the method by which Amoeba might change to Homo if given plenty of time. But look at the following examples of this type of change: cattle without horns; calves with short legs, dying at birth; calves with abnormal jaws, living only a few hours; yellow mice, always dying as young embryos in the homozygous or pure form; creeper chickens, a mutation causing death in the pure form; in fruit flies, small wings, crumpled wings, no wings at all, black body, white eyes, eyes reduced to a bar, crooked spines, and many others; seedless grapes; seedless oranges; stringless green beans; barley that must be staked up to make it stand; among people, lack of color in hair, eyes, and skin; also, lack of enamel on the teeth. In addition to these changes in bodily form, mutation causes a lack of vigor in the plant or animal. Very, very few such changes have been found to confer any benefit upon an organism, and so you see that these recent studies have made it hard to visualize what kind of changes would transform moss to an apple tree, or an amoeba to man. Atomic fallout causes mutations in the human race, and no one thinks such changes will be a benefit.

Another remarkable discovery is that the theory of recapitulation has no foundation of objective facts. It is a wonder that it was not given up long ago, for the so-called gill slits in the human embryo never are accompanied by gills or primordia of gills and they never break through to make slits. They are simply a series of furrows between arches. The theory did not apply to plants, and the experimental embryologists, an active group, never found it useful. Yet it may be ten years before some teachers will cease to reiterate this big blunder, which Ehrlich and Holm say is "biological mythology."

The general form of a young embryo of man or pig or bird is far removed from the shape of a fish, for it has a large brain, a large heart but no legs, fins, or any kind of appendage until a later stage of development. In fact, the proportions are not like those of any mature, free-living animal. The heart is formed early because the embryo needs blood; the brain gets an early start because it is a complex organ and needs much time for its development. There still is purpose in the world and science is not harmed by recognizing it.

Still another anomaly for the doctrine of evolution is the fact that all the branches of the animal kingdom appear together in the Cambrian system of rocks. (Some geologists exclude the vertebrates but Dunbar says fish skeletons are present.) Below the Cambrian there are no fossils except a few worm burrows and seaweeds, and even they are doubted by some geologists. If all life developed gradually from simple cells, there should be simpler and still simpler fossils in the deeper rocks, down to the spicules of sponges and shells of the one-celled plants called diatoms. This situation was partly known a hundred years ago, but it was thought that such fossils would be found after further search. However, some geologists have spent the best years of their lives looking for fossils below the Cambrian, but all in vain.

When I visited the Grand Canyon of the Colorado River, I was fortunate enough to hear a lecture on the formation of that "big gully," as the cowboy called it. The lecturer said that the deepest fossil which they had found was a trilobite. This was an animal with a hard exoskeleton and many legs, resembling a crayfish or crab. After the lecture I asked the speaker why such a complex animal was the deepest, instead of something simpler. He replied quite truly, that they are found just that way.

The last discovery which I shall mention has not received the publicity which it deserves, but it is well recorded by different trained workers. It is that skeletons of the modern type of man, *Homo sapiens*, are fully as old as those of famous cave men and other peculiar types.

When Eugene Dubois found a skull cap, a femur, and three teeth in Java in 1891, naming the find *Pithecanthropus erectus*, this discovery received tremendous publicity. But the two skulls which he found at Wadjak, Java, of the same age, were not made public until twenty years later. Why? "They were not what he was looking for" and did not fit his theory of evolution. These Wadjak people are described as much like the present black men of Australia, whose skill is widely recognized.

There is no scientific reason why we should not claim that Wadjak man is our ancestor and *Pithecanthropus* a degenerate, extinct type. For Wadjak man represents the rule rather than the exception. In China, in southern Africa, at Kanjera, Africa, at Swanscombe, England, and at Fontechevade, France, the story is repeated: men of *Homo sapiens* type are found who lived as long ago as the peculiar and so-called "primitive" types.

Here, then, is the paradox: when the information—meager though it was—seemed to favor evolution, the masses of people shouted, "Absurd"; now that new discoveries make it a poor interpretation, they bow their heads sedately and say, "Of course we agree." One is reminded of a cartoon illustrating the popularity of General Dwight Eisenhower. When he returned from the Second World War he was tired and wanted to rest, but there was a popular demand that he run for President of the United States. The cartoon represented the boom as a tree: Eisenhower had taken an ax and cut the trunk quite in two, but still the tree stood erect. Likewise the factual support of evolution has been sundered, but still we hear that it is true. Certainly the theory is in unstable equilibrium, and how long will it stand?

Here is illustrated the power of repetition. For a hundred years the evolutionary story of impersonal, materialistic law has been reiterated in glittering generalities, omitting troublesome details, until people tired of making objections and acquiesced. Let us as Christians be just as persistent in proclaiming the truth that, "In the beginning God created the heavens and the earth"; and "God so loved the world that he gave his only begotten Son, that whosoever believeth on him should not perish but have everlasting life."

DISCOVERIES SINCE 1859
WHICH INVALIDATE THE EVOLUTION THEORY

Walter E. Lammerts, Ph.D.*

Creationists of the later part of the nineteenth century such as Louis Agassiz had far too rigid a concept of species, postulating that even varieties were created in the places to which they were adapted.

During his voyage with the *Beagle*, Charles Darwin quite correctly saw that this extreme and entirely unbiblical idea of creation held by scientists of his day was simply not true. He quite correctly reasoned that the various varieties of finches (then called species) of the Galapagos Islands all came from one or at most several species migrating from the mainland. Clearly they were not created in their various forms, each peculiar to a particular island. But in 1859 he carried this idea to the extreme of claiming that all *kinds* of plants and animals by the natural selection of beneficial variations evolved from one or a few original simple one-celled forms of life.

Molecular Evolution

Later scientists have extended this concept to include the idea of chemical evolution, various simple gases such as ammonia (NH_3) forming a sort of organic "soup" in the original "primitive" ocean. From this complex of amino acids, proteins, carbohydrates, and finally deoxyribose nucleic acid evolved. First, of course, only simple "naked" DNA molecules developed the power of reproduction, but finally these developed cell walls, united, and over a billion years or so evolved into the complex of life we see around us.

Actually, this idea of chemical evolution is but a refined version of spontaneous generation. It is the only alternative to belief in creation ex-nihilo. From 1500 to 1860, few scientists doubted it. Aristotle, Newton, William Harvey, Descartes, van Helmont, and Lamarck accepted spontaneous generation without question. Even many theologians

---

*Editor of the Creation Research Society quarterlies from 1964-1968; P. O. Box 496, Freedom, California 95019

such as the English Jesuit John Needham subscribed to this view.

Step by step in a great controversy that spread over two centuries, this belief was whittled away until nothing remained of it. First, Francisco Redi showed that when meat is placed under a screen so flies cannot lay eggs on it, maggots never develop. This was a serious blow to one of the basic proofs of spontaneous generation. Then Lazzaro Spallanzani showed that a nutritive broth sealed off from the air while boiling, never develops micro-organisms, and so never rots. Needham objected that the air above the broth had been vitiated, so could not support life.

Louis Pasteur, in 1860 by a simple modification of Spallanzani's experiment, showed the air was not at fault. He drew the neck of the flask out into a long S-shaped curve with its end open to the air. Thus, while molecules of air could pass freely back and forth, heavier particles of dust, bacteria, and molds in the air were trapped on the walls of the curved neck.

Even yet it was not easy to deal with so deeply ingrained common sense belief as that of spontaneous generation. Pasteur's greatest help in disproving it was a noisy and stubborn opponent named Felix Pouchet, whose arguments before the French Academy of Sciences drove Pasteur to more and more rigorous experiments. When he had finished this remarkable series not a shred remained of the belief in spontaneous generation.

As George Wald[1] puts it, we tell this story to beginning students of biology as though it represents a triumph of reason over mysticism. Actually it is very nearly the opposite. The reasonable view was to believe in spontaneous generation, the only alternative to belief in a single primary act of supernatural creation. There is no third position.

It was Wald's belief that a scientist has no choice but to approach the origin of life through a hypothesis of spontaneous generation. If one refuses to believe in a God with power to create ex nihilo, I heartily agree with Wald. He quite correctly states that Pasteur proved untenable the idea that living organisms now arise spontaneously under present conditions. He then endeavors to show that they *may* have so arisen under past conditions.

Naturally, as he says, "Time is the hero of the plot." Given time enough, even the "impossible" becomes possible. Actually, scientists such as Wald and Walter R. Hearn substitute time for power.

In discussing the possible spontaneous origin of life, Wald is more honest than most chemical evolutionists. He says that students of chemistry are usually told that when, in 1828, Friedrich Wöhler synthesized the first organic compound urea, he proved that organic compounds do not require living organisms to make them. Of course, it showed nothing of the kind. Organic chemists are alive! Wöhler merely showed that they (living organisms) can make organic compounds externally as well as internally.

Organic chemists now mix inorganic substances such as water vapor, methane (CH_4), ammonia (NH_3), and hydrogen together under the activation of an electric spark and find traces of glycine, alanine, and other simple amino acids. S. L. Miller, Sydney Fox, and Walter R. Hearn[2] are quite excited over these discoveries and believe as stated above that given time enough life would arise in the sea from such spontaneously generated simple amino acids. Actually these men are only demonstrating that intelligent beings can make organic compounds from inorganic compounds. The complexity of the chemical apparatus used is such as to be a bit unrealistic in terms of their postulated primeval world free of oxygen. The strange fact that our planet appears to be unique in having water so necessary to life is taken for granted by them. A complete discussion of this modern version of spontaneous generation is too involved, but reference to Zimmerman's paper, "The Spontaneous Generation of Life," to appear in a subsequent book, will show the many insurmountable problems involved.

There is no question but what evolution as a working hypothesis has much attraction to the modern "scientific" mind. At least the vocal majority of scientists believe it either in its entirety or in part. The question is, should the Church again make the same mistake as it did in adopting the pagan concepts of Ptolemaic astronomy taught by leading scientists from Ptolemy (100 A.D.) to Copernicus (1473)? There is considerable evidence that the concept of evolution has insidiously influenced the philosophy of not only biology, organic chemistry, geology, and paleontology, but such disciplines as anthropology, archeology, sociology, psychology, history, and even theology.

So then, what really is the evidence for Darwin's extrapolation of his undeniably true micro-evolutionary observations into the general theory of evolution?

Biological Variation

First, let us consider variation, natural selection of which, according to Darwin, developed new species. He considered variation as essentially *unlimited* with those individuals most fitted to the environment being naturally selected. Again, the following generation, the same *range* of variability would occur. Thus, in the classical case of the evolution of the giraffe, quoting Darwin,

> So under nature with the nascent giraffe the individuals which were the highest browsers and were able during dearths to reach even an inch or two above the others, will often have been preserved, for they will have roamed over the whole country in search of food. These slight proportional differences, due to the laws of growth and variation, are not of the slightest use or importance in most species. But it will have been otherwise with the nascent giraffe, considering its probable habits of life for those individuals which had one part or several parts of their bodies more elongated than usual, would generally have survived. These will have intercrossed and left offspring, either inheriting the same bodily peculiarities or *with a tendency* to vary again in in the same manner. By this process *long continued* combined with the *inherited effects* of increased use of parts (the longer neck) it seems to me certain that an ordinary hoofed quadruped might be converted into a giraffe[3]

It should be noted that Darwin assumes (1) continuous variation, i.e., each generation showing the same *range* in variation of neck length and (2) effects of continuous use (or disuse). In fact, he devised a scheme of pangenesis now disproven to explain this presumed inheritance of the effects of use or disuse.

J. B. Lamarck was the most noted proponent of the doctrine of the inheritance of acquired characters, i.e., changes in plants or animals due to the environment, use, or disuse. That such characteristics are acquired by individuals during their life is obvious. However, as the physical basis of heredity became better known, the possibility of inheriting environmental effects became increasingly difficult to believe. First, August Weiseman developed his germ plasma theory, "Das Keimplasma," in 1892. He clearly showed that reproductive cells, instead of being developed by gemmules assembled from various parts of the body as suggested by Darwin, formed a continuous line from generation to generation, developing only from germinal tissue. The body or somatic cells are then the result of germ cell activity. His views were clearly shown to be correct by proof developed from 1900 to 1930 that the chromosomes carry the genes or factors determining the characteristics of the body. Since they are protected during cell division and gamete formation from most *normal* environmental internal or external influences, acquired characteristics cannot of course be inherited. More recently proof that deoxyribose nucleic acid molecules (DNA) arranged in helical fashion actually form an information code by which the body develops according to a master template makes even clearer the reason why the effects of environment cannot be inherited.

Now what are the real laws governing the inheritance of variation? Working diligently in his garden the Austrian monk Gregor Mendel carefully crossed various strains of peas and found a definite statistical pattern governing the inheritance of such characteristics as tall vs. dwarf growth habit. Tall (TT) habit was dominant to dwarf (tt) so that the first generation hybrids (Tt) were all tall. The dwarf habit of growth did not show up until the second filial generation or F_2 when one fourth of the plants were dwarf in habit (tt). Such traits are called recessive and some are due to two facters so occur in only 1/16 of the F_2 population, and others due to three factors occurred in 1/64 of the F_2 plants. Later work has shown that most major factors such as tall have modifying factors. Accordingly, by selections slightly taller plants may be obtained. But the limits are soon reached and from then on selection is no longer effective, since the strain has been thus made true breeding or homozygous for all of them. Variability is then *definitely limited* instead of being unlimited as Darwin thought. This is quickly shown in breeding for such characteristics as long bud in roses, where the ultimate in bud length is achieved in 5 or 6 generations. Yield in corn is another example—corn breeders making phenomenal progress during the first 20 years.

But then these inbred lines of corn used to produce the famous high-yielding hybrid corn seed could no longer be further improved since all the major factors for high yield had already been accumulated. Now corn breeders' time is mostly spent in maintenance of these inbred lines and breeding for increased disease resistance, local adaptation, and other related problems. All of our experience shows that *contrary* to what Darwin believed, the variability potential of each species is definitely *limited*.

On the Nature of Mutations

What, then, do present day evolutionists appeal to for the mechanism of evolution? The answer is mutations, which occur with varying frequency in plants and animals. Actually, they are the result of a "mistake" in the process of gene reproduction or, more specifically, the duplication of the deoxyribose nucleic acid or DNA molecules which either are or house the genes which determine the characteristics of plants and animals. Various agencies such as cosmic radiation and chemical mutagens cause mutations, but there is considerable evidence that a basic percentage are spontaneous, i.e., the reproductive mechanism simply does not *perfectly* reduplicate itself each time.

Can these chance "mistakes" or defects really explain the origin of the complex variation we see around us? Elliot G. Watson, British zoologist writing for the *Saturday Evening Post*,[4] lists four examples of life histories that simply cannot be explained by orthodox evolution theories. Thus the coral reef crab has claws so small as to be useless as weapons. But their backward curving teeth grasp the slippery bodies of small sea anemones, detaching them carefully from their hold on the rocks without injury. They are then held close to the pirate crab's mouth and continue to operate their tentacles so as to capture small creatures. These the crab with his free front pair of walking legs removes as dainty tidbits, leaving those he dislikes for the anemones, which are finally released unharmed.

Are these adaptations to be explained by chance mutations? Did a chance modification of the claws due to a "mistake" in the duplication of some DNA molecule prompt some ancestral crab to detach an anemone for the mere fun of it and by chance hold it near its mouth? If so, the crab passed on to its offspring this behavior tendency, and so through natural selection the crab species developed their close association with various anemones, the species differing, of course, to make the problem more complex for each species of pirate crab. This, Watson says, he simply cannot accept, and I agree.

My scientific colleagues who are evolutionists make much of the undoubted fact that under unusual new environmental conditions some mutations are advantageous. Thus, when bacteria are catastrophically exposed to high levels of penicillin or streptomycin, most of them die. But occasionally one lives because of a mutation to tolerance of these antibiotics. In penicillin this resistance is a step by step phenomenon, i.e., by increasing dosage rate increasingly resistant strains appear. In streptomycin the change to maximum resistance is effected in one mutation. But Pratt and Dufrenoy[5] point out that these resistant types are lower in metabolic ratio and so are at a *disadvantage* in cultures free of antibiotics. Are we then to believe in the strange concept that complex forms of life evolved by constantly stressing organisms in such a catastrophic manner? There is certainly no evidence that penicillin- or streptomycin-resistant bacteria continuously grown in high-level antibiotic culture ever achieve a metabolic ratio superior to the original type.

Mutation merely increases the variability potential, thus enabling a species to survive what otherwise would be complete annihilation. But this variability potential is definitely limited. Again, my evolutionary colleagues argue that this only seems so because our time of observation is so short. But they for some reason fail to see that adaptation either by mutation or segregation of already existing variability (heterozygocity) *rapidly* occurs up to a certain level, and then stops.

Also, the *more* complex the organism the *less* chance there is for mutations to occur of advantage even under new environmental conditions. Thus, my own Neutron Radiation experiments with roses resulted in hundreds of mutations, some of possible horticultural value. However, *without exception* all were either weaker or more sterile than the variety irradiated. While a National Research Fellow at the California Institute of Technology, it was my privilege to see the wonderful array of mutations of the fruit fly *Drosophila melanogaster* obtained by Sturtevant, Bridges, and Dobzhansky, then working with the great Thomas Hunt Morgan, who first realized the experimental value of this "biological Cinderella." Though remarkable as chromosome markers in linkage studies, demonstrations of allelomorphism and other genetic problems, not one could be said to have a higher survival value than the normal type. Occasionally, as described by Timofeef-Ressovsky, some mutations such as eversae or singed have a slightly greater viability at higher temperatures.[6] But even these, if combined in one individual by crossbreeding and selection, are reduced in viability and if combined with a third mutation have a lower viability than normal even at the higher temperature. And most certainly to effect significant changes in a species such as to warrant classification of it as a new one, or place it in a different genus, would involve the accumulation of *many* mutations. The possibility of such accumulation most certainly *has not* been demonstrated.

Origin of Higher Chromosome Numbers

Much has been made of the voluminous experimentation attempting to show how species with higher chromosome numbers have been built up by what is called amphidiploidy. Before discussing this perhaps we should make clear what is meant by "species." Many are really only what Jens Clausen calls ecotypes or distinctive genetic or physiologic races. All have the same internal balance and there is no genetic obstacle to a free interchange of genes where such races meet and hybridize. The so-called snow Camellia C. *rusticana* found along the cold coastal mountain plateaus of northern Japan is really only a race of C. *japonica.*

Others are ecospecies and have the genetic balance so distinctivly intricate that genes of two ecospecies cannot *freely interchange* genes without seriously impairing the vitality of the hybrid offspring. The species of conservative taxonomists working along conventional lines are usually good ecospecies. Chromosomes pairing appears rather normal but marked sterility is observed when these are hybridized.

Cenospecies are those entirely unable to exchange genes with one another. The chromosomes do not form pairs at the reduction division even though sterile hybrids may occur. It is by the crossing of these cenospecies with subsequent doubling of the chromosome number that amphidiploidy is presumed to have occurred.

The question then is, how much evidence is there for the origin of cenospecies or compariums of them usually equivalent to "genera"?

When amphidiploids were first produced "it was tacitly assumed that simple doubling of the chromosome number would in some miraculous way render any sterile hybrid fertile and vigorous." [7] Forty-five years of cytogenetic research has shown this is simply not true, though many even recent research men seem unable to realize the limitations imposed. Successful amphidiploids arise only from vigorous interspecific hybrids. If they are to remain so during succeeding generations, the original balance must remain unchanged. This means that only interspecific hybrids between cenospecies of one comparium have a chance of being successful amphidiploids.

Perhaps the most famous one is Raphanobrassica hybrid, first produced by Karpenchenko in 1927.[8] As reported by him, a uniform F_3 population was obtained, all 36 plants being quite fertile, having $2n = 36$ chromosomes.

Richaria and Howard[9] in their later, more thorough and detailed studies obtained quite different results as follows: (1) The F_1 hybrids formed a variable number of bivalents at the reduction division, usually 2 to 3 per cell; (2) Many of the F_2 plants had less than 36 chromosomes, and those with 36 showed variable pairing at IM with univalents, and quadrivalents occurring. Seventeen to 19 chromosomes were found in the pollen mother cell nuclei and accordingly even in F_4 plants varied in chromosome number from 33 to 37 chromosomes. (3) The F_2 plants were only partially fertile and even in the F_4 fertility varied from five to 42 percent! Howard quite correctly believes that this formation of quadrivalents in F_2, F_3, and F_4 follows from the fact that bivalents are formed in F_1. In fact, Howard points out that Karpechenko's published F_1, IM figures show only 16 or 17 chromosomal bodies in some cases instead of 18 one would expect if no pairing occurred. As a result, 40 percent of the F_2 plants grown by Karpechenko were partially sterile, due to incomplete chromosome complement or loss of genes due to chromosomal fragmentation during the F_1 reduction division.

Another widely accepted amphidiploid is that of *Galeopsis artificial Tetrahit* reported by Arne Muntzing.[10] *Galeopsis pubescens* (n = 8) x *G. speciosa* (n = 8) when crossed gave an F_1 population of 7 plants. These mint species showed some chromosome homology, since five to eight pairs of chromosomes were observed at the reduction division. A diploid F_2 generation of 197 plants was grown. This segregated for many characteristics and had an average fertility of 22 percent. One F_2 plant was triploid and almost completely sterile. Hand pollination of this gave no seed, so it was left among the other F_2 plants. Also, one of the wild type *G. Tetrahit* plants was only 60 to 90 feet away as was *G. pubescens*. Now, only *one* seed was harvested from this sterile plant and it grew into the artificial Tetrahit which, as illustrated by Müntzing[11] is *identical* to *G. Tetrahit*. He suggests that a triploid egg cell of the F_2 hybrid was fertilized by a pollen nucleus of *G. pubescens,* i.e., 16 *G. speciosa* and 8 *G. pubescens* chromosomes from the F_2 and eight from G. *pubescens* resulted in the 16 II F_3 plant. Were this actually the case, one would expect some quadrivalents since five to eight II were found at F_1 1M. None are reported in Muntzing's cytological study. What, then, is the explanation of this hybrid?

A paper published by R. E. Clausen and Lammerts[12] disclosed that among hybrids of *Nicotiona digluta* x the recessive white *Nicotiona tabacum* ♂ , the unusual white plant was a haploid resulting from a pollen grain nucleus stimulating the cytoplasm of a *Nicotiona digluta* egg cell to grow into a plant even though the female nucleus did not function. Unusual diploid *Nicotiona tabacum* hybrids were similarly explained as due to the functioning of diploid pollen grains. Since then many similar cases have been found in rose and especially camellia hybridizing.

Thus, the Captain Rawes camellia is shown by Lammerts[13] to have so originated. Also, plants of C. *japonica* (n = 15) x C. *reticulata* (n = 45) which are practically identical with C. *reticulata* and have 45 pairs of chromosomes are clearly shown to be the result of a diploid merogony.

G. *artificial Tetrahit* also probably resulted from such a diploid pollen grain and so in reality was G. *Tetrahit!* Its identity of appearance to that species and lack of quadrivalent formation are thus explained. Also, and more important, the strange *reduction* in size of the F_3 flower is thus accounted for. As is well known, real amphidiploids combine the characteristics of their F_1 parents and do not so radically depart from them in appearance as does G. *artificial Tetrahit*.

Though I urged Arne Müntzing to repeat this cross and verify his conclusions, he never saw fit to do so. Since in science it is axiomatic that experiments should be made in such a way as to be verifiable, I cannot accept his claim of the experimental origin of artificial Tetrahit because of the much more likely explanation by diploid merogony.

I have gone into this case at considerable length since for some reason there has been a tendency to accept evidence for the experimental evolution of plant species which would not be acceptable in other, more exact sciences.

Thus, it is obvious that for any amphidiploid to qualify as a species (1) the original F_1 hybrids show no pairing, yet give a reasonable percentage of diploid gametes, (2) the experiment should insure conditions such that *only* self-fertilization could occur, and (3) fertility and vigor of the F_2 should be at least comparable to that of the diploid species.

Judged by these criteria, even Jens Clausen's cases of experimentally produced amphidiploids from crossing Layias and Madias leave much to be desired. All were either so sterile or weak that they could not compete under natural conditions with the parental species.

It does indeed appear that the tobacco of commerce, N. *tabacum,* originated from the hybridization of N. *sylvestris* x N. *tomentosiformis,* each of which has 12 pairs of chromosomes. The sterile F_1 has 24 unpaired chromosomes. Greenleaf[14] by decapitating the stems caused callous tissue by application of hetero-auxin. Shoots from this tissue had 24II of chromosomes like N. *tabacum.* Though most of them are female sterile, recently D. R. Cameron (successor to Dr.

R. E. Clausen) has obtained fertile ones. Jens Clausen suggests this synthesis must have occurred long before the discovery of America by Columbus. Since Indians undoubtedly must have chopped down old tobacco plants, the idea that naturally occurring hybrids so cut down developed fertile shoots from naturally developed callous tissue is not too far fetched. However, this sort of thing would certainly not occur *naturally* without man's intervention.

The many recently reported cases of amphidiploids produced by colchicine treatment such as Towner's Tagetes[15] involve such complicated procedures that surely the authors of these experiments cannot imply these would occur under natural conditions.

Toward a More Realistic Approach

Considerable lack of critical judgment has been shown by some cytologists who infer relationship of species from the observation of occasional loose pairing of chromosomes in the F_1 hybrids. As both McClintoch[16] and Lammerts[17] have clearly shown, pairs of chromosomes are frequently found in both haploid corn and *N. tabacum*. In the case of *N. tabacum* variety coral haploid as many as six bivalents or pairs were observed. Since *N. tabacum* has been shown to be the result of chromosome doubling of *N. sylvestris* x *N. tomentosiformis* as above described, these pairs certainly are not the result of homology. In fact, pachytene studies showed they were clearly the result of non-homologous association since unlike chromomeres were aligned together in paired strands. Also, and more important, strands often folded back on themselves to form pairs! As I state in the paper cited above, "homologous attraction of chromomeres is due to a regulatory mechanism in some way causing an orderly alignment of the threads when the cell as a whole is timed for synapsis. When true homologues are not present this tendency for two by two association expresses itself in part by non-homologous pairing."

In view of such clearly shown facts, why do cytogeneticists still infer relationship of species simply because occasional pairs of chromosomes are found? Clearly they are motivated by a preconceived concept of evolutionary divergence from a common ancestor. I am, of course, not referring to clear cut cases of regular pairing such as the Drosera type found in the hybrid of *N. tabacum* (24II) x *N. sylvestris* (12II), where 12II are regularly formed.

Fortunately, a trend toward a realistic approach is now evident. Thus, Lennart Johnson[18] gives an excellent appraisal of the chromosome pairing he finds in the intergeneric crosses of Oryzopsis, Indian Mountain Rice, and Stipa the Spear grass. He clearly shows that the number of pairs is *proportional* to the number of chromosomes involved. Accordingly, they must be due to non-homologous association of chromosomes. Relationship of the plants as expressed in homology of the chromosomes is thus not the cause of pairing in his and many other cases.

C. J. Bishop in his recent "Reviews in Genetics and Cytology I. Plant Breeding" [19] is quite candid in pointing out the failure of the older chromosome homology and pairing concepts to hold up as regards practical plant breeding. Thus, he says it was postulated that frequency of multivalent chromosome association was a major factor in determining the degree of fertility of the individual plant. Recent research has failed to reveal any *fully consistent relationship* between *chromosome association* and *plant fertility*. Some plants with regular bivalent formation may be quite infertile.

The possibility that some diploids with high chromosome numbers arose from the tendency of auto-tetraploids to progressively favor bivalent formation was suggested early by Müntzing.[20] The view that this is a slow progressive, development has not received general support. Recent discovery of a single gene controlling bivalent formation in wheat (Riley and Chapman, 1958) shows clearly that diploid behavior is genetically controlled and not the result of lack of homology, whatever that term has come to mean.

The human mind tends to think of species with higher chromosome numbers having risen from adding chromosomes of two species with lower number. As shown above, most such experimentally produced amphidiploids combining the chromosomes of the basic diploid species would hardly survive under natural conditions. Recently an increasing number of diploid monoploids or polyhaploids have been isolated from tetraploid lines. Several Hindu (Indian) students have recently found that certain forms of Rubus classified as species are really polyhaploid derivatives of octoploid species, i.e., a reduction to the tetraploid level.

Very possibly we may find that many so-called "species" are really derived from pre-existing complex species of higher chromosome number and in a sense are degenerate offspring of a formerly much more intricate species pattern.

Thus, a recent paper on the rainbow and cutthroat trout by Simon and Dollar[21] indicates that the rainbow trout with 60 chromosomes was rather recently developed from the cutthroat trout having 64 by two centric chromosome fusions involving a centromere shift. This occurred since the last glacial period of the Pleistocene since the species were not isolated until the continuity of the Snake River and thus North Pacific drainage with the now extinct Lake Bonneville ended. The Provo strand line indicates a date less than 55,000 years ago, even on the basis of the very questionable orthodox ecological dating techniques.

Harlan Lewis, in a recent paper on catastrophic selection,[22] comes to the conclusion that reorganization of the species chromosome genomes or makeup is a rapid process in which all the differences become consolidated within a few generations. In the genus *Clarkia,* which is his specialty, all the derivative diploid species are better adapted to xeric or dry conditions. The history of the genus is one of response to increasing aridity and change in seasonal distribution of rainfall. Lewis' concepts are in marked contrast to the usual evolutionary one which postulates that structural and quantitative changes in chromosomes accumulate as homozygotes one by one over a long period of time through random fixation or by selection of those with presumed slight selective advantage. He clearly proves that *Clarkia lingulata* is of recent origin. It has an additional chromosome not present in *C. biloba* (n = 8) homologous to parts of two chromosomes of *C. biloba.* In other words, part of the basic genome of *C. biloba* is duplicated in *C. lingulata* (n = 9). The genomes also differ by a large translocation and at least two paracentric inversions. Hence the hybrids between them are *always sterile.*

Lewis suggests interspecific hybridization or a mutator gene similar to that reported by Ives[23] in Drosophila as the mechanism of chromosome reorganization.

From the viewpoint of creationism and flood geology, Lewis' concepts are most interesting. Certainly there is abundant evidence that since the Flood great areas of the world, including much of the Pacific north and southwest have become increasingly arid. As mentioned later, Lake Lahontan, once a vast inland body of water, is completely dried up and Lake Bonneville has shrunk to the Great Salt Lake.

He does not, however, show how translocations or inversions became established. Dobzhansky has clearly shown that translocations in homozygous condition are inviable. Of four translocations involving the second and third chromosome of D. *melanogaster* only one could be established in homozygous or true breeding condition. It was definitely less vigorous than the wild type.[24] Muller earlier had reported the same thing, and work by Meta Suche Brown involving translocations between the third and fourth chromosomes resulted in her conclusion that "No completely fertile strain could be isolated." [25] Inversions are, of course, merely translocations within the same chromosome and involve breakages and resulting injury also.

We are thus left in the strange dilemma of wishing to believe that changes such as postulated by Lewis could occur, since it would make an explanation of how the world became repopulated by so many distinct and obviously adapted species much simpler. Similar adaptation of species of roses, apples, and other deciduous plants to the cold weather brought on by glaciation as a result of the Flood is quite obvious and must have been as Lewis postulates for Clarkia quite rapid, also.

Though not "scientific" in the usual sense, I suggest that we are constrained to believe that these reorganizations or transformations are the result of intelligent design. Those of us who believe in the power of God should have no difficulty in believing that following the Flood, as the surviving basic species repopulated the world, God used such mechanisms as translocation, inversion, and duplication as means to adapt species to the changed environment. This phenomenon is much like that in mankind where the languages were *suddenly* and *rapidly* developed following the confounding of tongues at the Tower of Babel. In mankind, little in the way of chromosome variation or cross sterility of races has as yet been demonstrated. The pattern, however, is much the same since the obvious physical, psychological, and adaptive features of human races are obviously fully as great or even more so than the one slight morphological difference separating *Clarkia biloba* from *C. lingula,* i.e., the much narrower shape of the petal!

Assumptions Involved in Age Estimates

The statement is so often made that our observational time scale is too short to verify evolution. Given several hundred thousand or a million years, changes on the specific or genetic level could easily be effected. It is very easy to appeal to such unverifiable assumptions. But science is, or should be, demonstrated facts, not imaginary possibilities. So often the statement is made, for example, that radioactive dating by observation of the half-life of uranium, actinium, and thorium as they give off alpha particles and slowly change through a series of radioactive chemicals to radium and finally to the stable lead 206, 207, and 208 prove that the earth is about 1.5 or more billion years old.[26] But surely a little reflection will show that several assumptions must be made before any conclusions from half-lives of radioactive elements have any meaning. Four of these are: (1) in the specimen of mineral used *only* uranium and none of its degeneration products were present at Time = 0; (2) no loss of uranium by leaching or loss of radon gas has occurred; (3) there was never in the past a time when the rate of alpha particle loss was much greater than now; and (4) in the creation of uranium the reactions went the whole way. Or stated more precisely, how can we be sure that in the build up of uranium from hydrogen nuclei as physicists now conceive of the creation of the elements some Lead 206 and radium did not simply remain as such instead of all being converted to uranium and then disintegrating giving the series of derivatives now used by the uniformitarian school of thought as being evidence of such great age? Morris and Whitcomb[37] give a thorough-going critique of radioactive dating in *The Genesis Flood*.

The same may be said of the so-called astronomical evidence of such a great age of the universe. The red shift is interpreted as indicating that various galaxies of stars are speeding away from each other, or the universe is supposed to be expanding at a speed close to that of light as regards the most distant stars. Some astrophysicists now consider this as merely a "tiring effect" resulting from light photons traveling such great distances. Also, it has recently been pointed out that much of the red shift effect may be simply due to the effect of dust particles in space distorting the quality of light observed. Finally, touching on this subject of astronomy in relation to time, we should remember that evidently water is a unique feature of the earth found nowhere else in the solar systm (Gen. 1:2). Thus, the data of Explorer II show that Venus, once considered the "watery planet," does not have any and so could not support life.

The Significance of "Let There Be Light"

The first spoken word of creation was "let there be light." As is now clear, light is only one form of energy. Most probably all forms of energy were called into use or being during this first creation day.

The various stars and galaxies were then created by conversion of energy into mass according to the formula

$$\frac{e(\text{energy})}{c(\text{speed of light squared})} = m \text{ or}$$

$$\frac{e}{(3 \times 10^{10}) \, (3 \times 10^{10})} = 1 \text{ gram of mass.}$$

Thus 9×10^{20} ergs of energy became 1 gram of mass. Since one joule $= 10^7$ ergs of energy, 9×10^{13} joules of energy were used up in the creation of only 1 gram of mass. In more commonly understood electrical terms, since one watt is equal to one joule per second, this may be expressed as 9×10^{13} watt second or 9×10^{10} kilowatt seconds. Dividing by 3600 seconds this gives 25×10^6 kilowatt hours of energy. Now Niagara Falls generates about 415 thousand kilowatts per hour or about 9960 thousand KW per day. If one uses a rough figure of 10,000 thousand (10^7) kilowats per day for Niagara Falls, it is startling to realize that the amount of energy used in the creation of only 1 gram of mass is almost equal to 2.5 times the amount of energy generated by Niagara Falls in one day! The creative effort involved in the creation of the universe really staggers even mathematical concepts of power.

Obviously all of the light photons connecting all of the various orbital centers making up the galaxies were also set up at this time, i.e., the whole universe was one vast system of light and energy, since one cannot from the viewpoint of physics conceive of visible light as distinct from other forms of energy. By the fourth day the conversion of energy into mass evidently reached a concentration in the various gravitational orbits high enough to "activate" the various systems of atomic furnaces we now recognize as the sun and stars. It should be emphasized that, however vast the universe may be, light photons from the most distant stars would be immediately visible since the stars were made by conversion of light into closed orbits of energy we call mass.

A crude analogy is that of filling a large tank with water under pressure through a hose several hundred feet long. Once the tank is full the flow immediately reverses when pressure is discontinued. No matter how long the hose, water pours out *immediately* at a rate determined by the tank pressure. Astronomers of the uniformitarian school would have us starting with an empty hose. Then, of course, the time taken by the water to travel through the hose would be a measure of the length of the hose. So they assume stars beginning to shine with no photons of light connecting them with the earth or other stars. But if the stars are conceived as being created by the flow of energy into them, then as soon as they begin to shine by virtue of this accumulated energy, a reversal in flow of light photons would immediately be visible here on the earth.

The creation account, by stating that the sun, moon, and stars were not activated until the fourth creation day, indirectly supports the Copernicus system of astronomy. For if, as Ptolemy assumed, the sun in its daily cycle around the earth caused night and day, how could there have been nights and days before the sun gave light? The answer, of course, is that the earth's rotation gives our diurnal cycles and always has since God said, "Let there be light." This light came directly from Him until the fourth day, by which time the sun was activated as suggested above.

Actually, many astro- and geo-physical facts indicate the universe and solar system is in the order of thousands of years old. Space allows mention of but five:

(1) Rapid disintegration of comets. Since they are part of the solar system, the maximum age of the comets would correspond to that of the solar system. Unless one adopts the strange theory of Whipple that a reservoir of comets exists far out on the edge of the gravitational field, for which no real evidence exists, there is no other conclusion.

(2) A great annual amount of meteoritic dust, 14,300,000 tons, settles to earth each year. So in the presumed five billion years, a layer 54 feet thick all over the earth should have accumulated. No such layer is found on the ocean floor. Identification would be easy since about 2.5 percent of a meteor is nickel in contrast to .008 percent in the rocks of the earth.

(3) Operation Mohole studies[28] shows that instead of an average of 18,480 feet of sediments on the ocean bottom expected after a billion years of erosion, only about 1,800 are found at the *maximum*.

(4) Tektites of glassy meteorites show maximum ages far less than 1,000,000 years, even granting the validity of the questionable argon method of age determination.

(5) Sulphates (SO_4) are being carried into the ocean at more than twice the rate of sodium and chlorine, yet there is more than seven times as much chlorine in the ocean as sulphate and four times as

much sodium.[29] Evidently, then, both sodium and chlorine were abundant at $T = 0$. Since sulphates are fully as soluble as salt, they must have been present, also. Then the earth must be considerably younger than the 10,670,000 years it would take to accumulate the sulphates were there none at $T = 0$.

Only by tying the biblical concept of an original creation with the various curses resulting in the transformation of many life forms, and ending in the final catstrophe of a world-wide Flood can we build an adequate explanation of the world we see around us. Whitcomb and Morris very effectively present the argument for a universal flood being the cause of the major portion of the fossil-bearing, water-deposited strata in their recent book, *The Genesis Flood*. The after effects lasted for thousands of years as the earth's interior basins such as Lake Lahontan and Bonneville gradually dried up. Now the Caspian Sea is drying up at a rate causing such alarm to Russian agriculturists that an entire river is being diverted so as to empty into it. Southern California, which enjoyed a winter rainfall in 1750-1850 great enough to fill the large Los Angeles and San Gabriel river channels, is now practically a desert! Undoubtedly following the Flood rainfall was so great in many areas as to cause deposition of stratified rock several hundred feet or more in depth in a hundred years. In fact, the major mistake made by Sir Charles Lyell was his assumption that the rate of erosion and deposition of sediment then occurring (1830-1850) was a constant one. We can well liken the imbalance caused by the world-wide flood catastrophe to that of starting the swinging of a large pendulum. As the years go by the arc of action and reaction gradually lessens. However, the earth is still not entirely recovered from the strains due to weight inequalities which frequently adjust themselves by earthquakes. Not only during the flood, but for a long time thereafter, great lava flows occurred. The glaciers which once covered the upper half of North America have shrunk to pitifully small remnants of their former grandeur. Several students of geophysics predict that all of them will be melted by 2040, thus causing sea coast towns such as London and New York to be hundreds of feet under water!

As we are learning more about the deoxynucleic acid patterns which govern heredity, we are learning how a few transformations were effected in bacteria. Only by a careful study of all the facts of science can we understand how God effected all these changes or, better stated, permitted them to come about. Though we can never

WHY NOT CREATION?

hope to make this a perfect world, we can by the grace of God make it a better one. As Christian research scientists we have a twofold duty. The first is to God in that our science should ever more clearly show the glorious complexity of His creation. Though marred by the evils caused by man's sins, it still has much of its original beauty and, when properly interpreted, will give us a better understanding of the glory of that "new heaven and earth" which will be our home when our Lord and Saviour returns. The second duty is to our fellow man in that we must endeavor to make our scientific efforts of value to him. Also, we of all Christians in this age of skepticism and doubt must constantly remember that God's glory is shown in his wonderful creation, and He expects us to reveal it to our fellow men during our work in the laboratories, in our scientific papers, and generally in our lives.

NOTES AND REFERENCES

1. George Wald, "The Origin of Life," *The Physics and Chemistry of Life* (New York: Simon and Schuster, 1955), pp. 5-13.
2. Walter R. Hearn, "Origin of Life," *Journal of the American Scientific Affiliation* (1961), 13:38-42.
3. Charles Darwin, *The Origin of Species* (Everyman's Library, 1859), p. 9.
4. Elliot G. Watson, "Hidden Heart of Nature," *Saturday Evening Post* (May 27, 1961), 284:32-33.
5. Robertson Pratt and Jean Dufrenoy, *Antibiotics*, 2nd ed (Philadelphia: Lippincott-Company, 1953), p. 343.
6. N. W. Timofeef-Ressovsky, "Uber die Vitalitet einiger germmutationen und ihrer Kombinationen bei Drosophila funebris und ihre Abhängigkiet vom "genotypichen" und vom ausserem Mileau." Zeitschrift für Ind. Abstam. und Verebungslehre, Vol. 66 (1934), pp. 319-344.
7. Jens Clausen, David D. Keck, and William D. Hiesey, "Experimental Studies on the Nature of Species. II Plant Evolution Through Amphidiploidy, with Examples from the Madiinae" (Washington, D. C.: Carnegie Institute of Washington, Publications 564, 1945), pp. 63-64.
8. G. D. Karpechenko, "Polyploid Hybrids of Raphanus *sativus* L. x Brassica *oleraceae* L.," *Bulletin Applied Bot. Genetics and Plant Breeding* (1927), 17:305-410.
9. H. W. Howard, "Fertility of Amphidiploids," *Journal Genetics* (1937), 16:239-273; cf. also R. H. Richaria, "Cytological Investigation of Hybrids," *Journal of Genetics* (1937), 39:19-44.
10. Arne Müntzing, "Uber chromosomenwermehrung in Galeopsis-Kreuzugen und ihre phylogenetische Bedeutung," *Hereditas* (1930b), 14:153-172; cf. by the same author, "Cytogenetic Investigations on Synthetic Galeopsis Tetrahit," *Hereditas* (1932), 16:105-154.
11. Müntzing, *ibid.*, 1930b.

12. R. E. Clausen and W. E. Lammerts, "Interspecific Hybridization in Nicotiana, X. Haploid and Diploid Merogony," *American Naturalist* (1929), 63:279-282.
13. W. E. Lammerts, "Captain Rawes Camellia—Its Probable Origin," *American Camellia Society Yearbook* (1959), 9:14.
14. Walter H. Greenleaf, "Sterile Amphidiploids: Their Possible Relation to the Origin of N *tabacum*," *American Naturalist* (1941), 75:394-399.
15. Joseph W. Towner, "Cytogenetic Studies on the Origin of Tagetes *patula* X. Meiosis and Morphology of Diploid and Allotetraploid T. *erecta* x T. *tenuifolia*," *American Journal of Botany* (1961), 48:743-751.
16. Barbara McClintock, "The Association of Non-homologous Parts of Chromosomes in Mid Prophase of Meiosis in Zea Mays Z. Zellforchung" (1933), 19:191-237.
17. W. E. Lammerts, "On the Nature of Chromosome Association in N. *tabacum* Haploids," *Cytologia* (1934), 16:38-50.
18. B. Lennart Johnson, "Natural Hybrids Between Orzopsis and Stipa. III. Oryzopsis Hymenoides x Stipa Pinetorum," *American Journal of Botany* (1963), 50:228-234.
19. C. J. Bishop, "Reviews in Genetics and Cytology I. Plant Breeding," *Canadian Journal of Genetics and Cytology*, V (1963), pp. 1-9.
20. Clausen, Keck, and Hiesey, *op. cit.*
21. Raymond C. Simon and Alexander M. Dollar, "Cytological Aspects of Speciation in Two North American Teleosts, Salmo Gairdneri and Salmo Clarki Lewisi," *Canadian Journal of Genetics and Cytology*, V (1963), pp. 43-49.
22. Harlan Lewis, "Catastrophic Selection as a Factor in Speciation," *Evolution*, XXVI (1962), pp. 257-271.
23. P. T. Ives, "The Importance of Mutation Rate Genes in Evolution," *Evolution*, IV (1950), pp. 236-252.
24. T. Dobzhansky, "Translocations Involving the Second and Fourth Chromosome of D. *melanogaster*," *Genetics*, XVI (1931), pp. 629-658.
25. Meta Suche Brown, "The Relation Between Chiasma Formation and Disjunction" (University of Texas Publication, No. 4032, 1940), pp. 11-64.
26. Robley D. Evans, *The Atomic Nucleus* (McGraw Hill Book Co., Inc., 1955), chap. 16, pp. 511-535.
27. Henry W. Morris and John C. Whitcomb, *The Genesis Flood* (Philadelphia: Presbyterian and Reformed Publishing Co., 1961).
28. Leonard Engel and editors of *Life* Magazine, *The Sea* (New York: Time, Inc., 1961), p. 178.
29. Dudley Joseph Whitney, "How Old Is the Earth? Some Conservative Factors," *Pan American Geologist*, 92:113-124.

Chapter 8

The Evidence from Biochemistry and DNA Studies for Creative Design

1

LIFE IN A TEST TUBE?

WAYNE F. FRAIR, PH.D.*

Introduction

While many were discussing the first of the human heart transplants in mid December, 1967, suddenly the popular presses made the electrifying announcement that life had been created in a test tube. In a speech the night before, President Johnson had made the statement that we were about to receive one of the "most important news stories you ever read."

Reports in the popular news media preceded by some weeks the formal written scientific report. Even though certain of the early articles possessed an extravagant character—especially in large print—they were on the whole remarkably accurate, probably because scientists themselves held a news conference to clarify what had been accomplished.

At the press conference, Nobel laureate Arthur Kornberg, presently of the Stanford University School of Medicine in California, and his associate, Mehran Goulian, a Stanford postdoctoral fellow, explained their research, done in cooperation with Robert L. Sinsheimer of California Institute of Technology.

Essentially the announcement was that biologically active DNA (deoxyribonucleic acid) from viruses had been synthesized in the laboratory. Actually they did not manufacture viral DNA starting only with simpler non-viral chemicals, since, as will be shown later, viral DNA was an essential part of their reaction mixture. Rather,

*Professor of Biology and Chairman of Department of Biology, Kings College, Briar Cliff Manor, New York 10510

they succeeded in transferring from the living cell to the "test tube" the chemicals necessary for reproduction of viral DNA.

This scientific advance is considered to be important because DNA constitutes the hereditary material or genes which give to living things those characteristics carried from generation to generation. DNA characteristically is found in all organisms with the exception of certain viruses whose genes consist of RNA (ribonucleic acid). A synthesis using infectious RNA had been performed two years previously by Sol Spiegelman and co-workers at the University of Illinois; and so this recent work, which made use of DNA viruses, was to some extent an extension of those prior results.

Important Factors of DNA Research

Investigator Kornberg has been engaged actively in molecular research with DNA synthesis for over a decade. In 1959 he shared a Nobel prize in physiology and medicine for discovering DNA polymerase, an enzyme which catalyzes the production of DNA. For this production to occur, there must be a DNA template, an energy source, and the necessary building blocks (nucleotide forerunners or precursors). However, the resulting polynucleotide (DNA) would not exhibit biological activity like the parent template molecule.

The current success in producing DNA molecules which would manifest biological reproductive activity is based on several important factors. These are (1) purification of DNA polymerase, (2) selection of an ideal DNA template, and (3) utilization of a new polynucleotide-joining enzyme.

The DNA polymerase used by the Kornberg team in early experiments contained contaminated enzymes (nucleases). After the synthetic DNA was produced in incubation mixtures containing the polymerase, the contaminating enzymes would cause breakages in the new DNA. Thus the reproductive activity of DNA was destroyed. When the degrading nucleases were removed from the mixture, the purified polymerase led to production of DNA capable of reproduction.

DNA Organization

Exactly how DNA in the chromosomes of plant and animal cells is organized and controlled is not yet well understood. However, studies have indicated that DNA in the cell nucleus acts as a template for production of RNA, which moves from the nucleus to the surrounding region (cytoplasm) of the cell. Here the RNA operates with the ribosomes and dictates the conformation of various proteins, including enzymes which are essential for life of the cell and the organism of which the cell is a part.

The type of DNA widely discovered in various animal, plant, and human cells consists of two strands twisted about each other to form a helical structure. DNA resembles a ladder which has been twisted so that the two sides are spiral-shaped. The strands are joined together at the region of the rungs by hydrogen bonds. Each strand is called a polymer (poly, many; mer, parts) because it is composed of many repeating structural units. Each of these units is a nucleotide and so each polymeric DNA strand popularly is termed a polynucleotide.

DNA contains four types of nucleotides. All four contain a phosphate group, sugar, and a base. The difference resides with the bases, which are named adenine, thymine, cystosine, and guanine.

The structures of polynucleotides have been determined by physical and chemical means because they are too small to be visible. An electron microscope has been used for photographing strands of DNA, but cannot reveal the nucleotide sequence. The width of a DNA helix is 2 millimicrons, and it would take more than 12 million of these helixes side by side to equal one inch.

DNA and Proteins

In addition to functioning as a template for RNA production, which leads to formation of vital proteins, DNA becomes a pattern for its own reproduction at appropriate times. When this happens, the two polynucleotide strands separate. The linear sequence of bases in each strand will determine which nucleotides will be required to reconstruct the double-stranded condition. Where there is an adenine base, a thymine-containing unit moves in so that thymine joins with the adenine. Where the template strand contains thymine, an adenine unit will join.

When reproduction is complete, adenine (A) will be joined to thymine (T), and cytosine (C) to guanine (G). (See Figure 1) These specific combinations constitute a four-letter genetic alphabet which is A-T, T-A, C-G, and G-C. The sequence of these "letters" distinguishes one organism genotypically from all the others. Proteins will be constructed according to the "orders" given by the arrangement of letters.

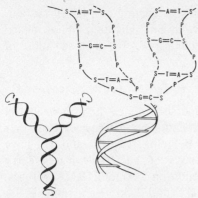

Proteins are composed of units known as amino acids, and they range in size from about 50 to 3,000 amino acids. It takes a sequence of three nucleotides to determine one amino acid. For production of a relatively small chain of 150 amino acids, a nucleotide sequence of 450 would be required. This sequence would constitute what popularly is termed a gene. It is necessary that the nucleotide sequence be preserved exactly in order that correct proteins be produced for maintenance of the life which is characteristic of each organism.

Figure 1. At left and bottom are diagrammatic views of the DNA helix. Above is a more detailed structure of DNA polynucleotide as it is reproducing. Each nucleotide is composed of Sugar, Phosphate, and a base, A, T, C, or G. (Courtesy Wiley & Sons. Inc.)

Minute Complexity Involved

Each organism contains within its genome not just a few genes, but in most cases thousands or millions. In the human body there are some 10 trillion cells, and each cell normally contains 46 chromosomes in its nucleus. Within the set of chromosomes of each cell, there are perhaps 3 million genes composed of nucleotide pairs numbering in the vicinity of 5 billion.

Cells of cows, mice, or corn each have a similar number. A single colon bacterium of *Escherichia coli*, which is about ½ micron (1/50,000 of an inch) wide and 2 microns long, has a single chromosome containing a single DNA molecule. The extended DNA molecule is about 1 millimeter long (or about 500 times the length of the *Escherichia coli* cell).

Each of these DNA molecules contains about 10 million nucleotide pairs, which constitute the thousands of genes giving the organism its structural and functional characteristics. It should be pointed out that not all genes are operating at one time, but each functions at appropriate times during an organism's life history. The proteins called *histones* seem to have an important role in *regulating* gene action.

Does all this minute complexity, with the coordination of operation necessary, point to a supernatural designer and sustainer? Those who accept the argument that design implies a designer say yes.

Others say they believe that life was self-creating and is self-sustaining. Both of these positions are based on individual philosophical ideas, which are not subject to rigorous proof. We shall say more of this later on.

Comparisons of DNA and RNA

In most organisms DNA is a double-stranded helical structure, but there is considerable variation found among viruses. The best-known DNA viruses, like smallpox, polyoma, T2, T4, and T6, have double-stranded DNA. Several groups of bacterial viruses carry their DNA in a single-stranded condition. Among RNA viruses, influenza, poliomyelitis, and bacterial virus F2 possess a single RNA strand, whereas, in the Reo viruses, RNA has been found in the double-helical form.

Even if the genetic information is carried normally on a single nucleotide sequence rather than a double one, the complementary replica strand can be produced at the appropriate time. So it appears that the important fact is that some type of nucleotide is present, whether it be RNA or DNA.

The structure of RNA is similar to DNA and differs from DNA in that (a) it normally possesses the base uracil instead of thymine, (b) carries an extra oxygen atom on each sugar portion, and (c) is usually single-stranded (whereas DNA is usually double-stranded).

The question whether nucleic acid (DNA or RNA) is required in all types of reproductive activity associated with living things still may be open; for there is suggestive evidence that certain disease conditions may be due to some type of "subviral" transmitting agent which is capable of reproduction. Scrapie, a disease of the nervous system, may be caused by such an agent.

Circular Viruses

The recent research of Goulian, Kornberg and Sinsheimer involved use of one of the smallest of the viruses. It is called ØX174 and carries a single strand of DNA in circular form.

Original evidence, which came primarily from electron microscopy, was interpreted to mean that DNA molecules were linear with two free ends. Now it appears that some DNA's can exist in either circular or linear form. The polyoma virus contains a circular double DNA, whereas ØX174 has the single circular strand, which remains circular during the time the complementary second strand is formed.

DNA circles are not confined to viruses as once thought, for even the *Escherichia coli* DNA molecule has been found in a circle. It has been suggested that the circular condition could have an important part to play in reproduction.

In order to understand the significance of the research of Kornberg's team in relation to life in general and the creation of "test tube" life in particular, it is necessary to understand reproductive processes, especially of the material they utilized.

Reproduction in Complex Forms

Most plants and animals with which we are familiar begin as a single cell, which divides and distributes its DNA equally to all daughter cells. The quantity of DNA in the sex cells (sperm and eggs) would be one half the amount in body cells. This is true for organisms such as birds, frogs, reptiles, mammals, and insects.

When speaking about creating life in a test tube, scientists usually are not thinking of anything as structurally complex as these. It is, however, possible to raise bird eggs in a glass incubator, frog eggs in a glass dish, and fruit flies in a bottle. Doing this involves the providing of an environment in which DNA can manifest its potentialities.

Creation of just a tiny fruit fly with its wings, eyes, legs, digestive tract, nervous system, reproductive system, muscular system, etc., involved proper alignment of some 10 millions of polynucleotide pairs in the DNA. Of course, not all forms of life are this complex, but even so, up to the present time, the closest approaches to the "making of life" of any kind have been limited to establishment of proper conditions in which DNA nucleotides could manifest their potentialities.

Bacteria and Viruses Considered

When we consider bacteria we find a group which largely is invisible without magnifying equipment. *Escherichia coli* is a good example. About 10,000 of them together on one plane would be required to form a spot large enough to be within the range of visibility of the unaided eye.

Bacteria reproduce asexually. When conditions are right for their multiplication, each cell splits to form two cells. Here again the nucleic acid is distributed equally to the resulting cells so that each has the same genetic material. As a result all cells so produced will manifest a similar phenotype—looking and acting like others of their species.

When we consider viruses, we find doubt about their being alive at all; for one of the characteristics of life involves the ability to reproduce. Viruses are not known to live outside of living cells except in the sense of surviving passage from cell to cell, for their activities go on *only within cells.*

It has been suggested that viruses, which are relatively simple structures, compose a link between nonliving and living substances. This does not appear likely because a virus lacks reproductive ability. Outside a living cell it is subject to forces which eventually will destroy it. Inside a cell its only function appears to be the supplying of information necessary for its own multiplication *at the cell's expense.*

So a virus may represent what was at one time a normal cellular constituent. Maybe as a result of some change it "escaped" from the cell's control while still requiring the cell for reproduction. Whether or not this is true, it does not seem likely that viruses existed prior to cells, since viruses need cells for their perpetuation.

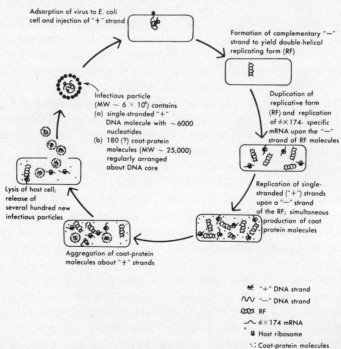

Figure 2. Life cycle of the ØX174 virus. This virus employs a circular DNA. The diagram shows only a small portion of the (+), (−), and (RF) circles. MW, relative weight of a single particle or molecule, the hydrogen atom being approximately one. (from Watson)

Variation, Reproduction of Viruses

Viruses show great variation in size and structural complexity; the largest virus approaches the size of very small bacteria. All viruses differ from cells in containing only DNA or RNA, whereas all cells have both DNA and RNA as discussed previously. The nucleic acid of viruses is in the center and is surrounded by a protein coat.

In order to reproduce, the virus must transfer at least its nucleic acid to the appropriate host cell. If the core is DNA, then the DNA will serve as a template for RNA, which works with the cellular machinery such as ribosomes and enzymes for producing the viral proteins. Also the DNA will serve as a template for its own replication.

If the viral core is RNA it will function directly in producing viral proteins and replicating more RNA. In both cases the specific nucleic acid core material and proper viral protein shell will be produced. These then join to form mature viral particles which will escape from the cell and attack more cells.

In addition to production of nucleic acid and coat protein, often one or many enzymes will be formed as well. In one way or another, these will be necessary for successful viral multiplication. For instance, if the cell has a heavy wall around it, the viruses could be trapped. Therefore many viruses have a gene coding for a cell-wall destroying enzyme which will cause the bacterial cell to lyse (or split open) at the appropriate time.

Life Cycle of a Virus

Before considering in some detail what Goulian, Kornberg, and Sinsheimer reported, it might be wise to discuss the normal life cycle of the virus they used, namely ØX174. (See Figure 2) The designation Ø indicates that this virus is a phage or bacteriophage (phage refers to eating or consuming). Phages destroy bacteria.

The phage, ØX174, is one of the smallest viruses and has a particle weight of only 6 million, which is the size of some very large protein molecules. The viral core consists of a single circular strand of DNA consisting of 5,500 nucleotide residues. This is 5 or 6 genes. Surrounding this DNA core is a coat of protein molecules.

The virus is adsorbed to the cell wall of a bacterium of *Escherichia coli*. The DNA, which is called a (+) strand, is injected and the protein coat remains outside the bacterial cell. Once the single (+)

strand of DNA is inside the cell, a complementary (—) strand of DNA is formed, thus producing a double-stranded helix. This double-stranded DNA is called a replicative form (RF).

The RF itself is duplicated, forming more RF. Also there is replication of specific ØX174 RNA molecules upon the RF molecules.

Then there is a replication of single-stranded (+) strands upon the (—) strands of the RF. At the same time, protein coat molecules are produced.

The protein coat molecules then aggregate around the (+) strands. Thus mature virus particles are formed.

The cell wall of the bacterium lyses and several hundred new infectious viral particles are released.

The new particles each in turn can infect a cell of *Escherichia coli*, and cause it to produce more viral DNA and viral protein and then to release several hundred more viruses. Thus the process continues.

Experiments Duplicated Viral Activity

The recent experiments were set up to duplicate *outside* the cell what normally happens inside. To prepare for the experiment, the researchers treated intact viruses with phenol in order to remove protein coats, thus leaving the pure DNA or what would serve as (+) strands or circles.

From *Escherichia coli*, DNA polymerase and polynucleotide-joining enzyme were obtained and purified. More *Escherichia coli* cells were broken (by a sonic method); the fluid was centrifuged and the supernatant boiled. This supernatant solution, therefore, contained the soluble heat-stable materials from the bacterial cell.

The incubation mixture in which the first DNA reproduction occurred was composed of the following: ØX DNA, four nucleotide precursors (deoxynucleoside triphosphates, purchased from an outside source), DNA polymerase, joining enzyme, DPN (a hydrogen carrier), boiled *Escherichia coli* extract, magnesium chloride, potassium phosphate buffer, mercaptoethanol, and albumin. Incubation time was 180 minutes at 25° C.

During incubation the natural ØX DNA (+) circles served as templates for formation of complementary (—) chains, the DNA polymerase catalyzing polymerization of the (—) chain. As the nucleotide precursors joined to become units in the new (—) polynucleotide chain, they underwent certain changes, including loss of some phosphate groups. The joining enzyme catalyzed the joining

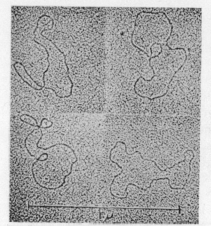

Figure 3. Electron micrographs of partially synthetic duplex circles. (from Goulian and Kornberg)

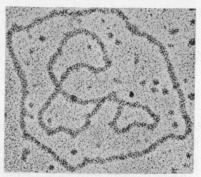

Figure 4. Two duplex circles of ØX174 DNA. One is extended, and the other is folded twice giving the appearance of 3 joined loops. Width of picture is approximately 500 millimicrons. Photo by Ron Davis of California Institute of Technology.

of opposite ends of the newly formed DNA (—) chain so that a duplex circle (RF) was complete (Figures 3 and 4). These circles were like RF isolated from infected *Escherichia coli* cells, except that the partly synthetic RF lacked supercoiling found in natural RF.

Duplex DNA Circles Produced

The new duplex circles were exposed to a pancreatic DN ase which broke one of them and led to their separation. The synthetic (—) strands could be separated from the (+) strands because in the incubation mixture thymine had been replaced by the unnatural, yet biologically active and heavier, bromouracil. When the material was centrifuged the bromouracil-containing (—) strands could be separated because of their greater density.

It was demonstrated by radioactive tests that the new (—) strands were not contaminated by (+) template strands. The (+) template material had been prepared with radioactive hydrogen (tritium, H^3), and nucleotide precursors used for the synthesis of the new (—) strands contained radioactive phosphorus.

The new (—) circles infected *Escherichia coli* cells. This had to be done using specially prepared *E. coli* since the DNA, which lacked the usual protein coat, was unable to penetrate normal bacterial cells. The specially prepared *E. coli* were without their cell walls and when they were thus altered DNA could enter. Under the laboratory conditions used in this research, bacterial cells without their walls are globular in shape and known as spheroplasts. The newly formed

DNA (—) circles infected spheroplasts and produced new intact viruses.

DNA Circles Infected Bacteria

The investigators also produced completely synthetic duplex circles by setting up an incubation mixture analogous to the one used previously. When the positive circles were separated, they could act as templates leading to the formation of RF within the *Escherichia coli* spheroplasts. Thus the researchers were able to perform an *in vitro* production of both infective (—) and (+) circles (Figure 5).

These experiments have demonstrated what might be occurring within the cells of *E. coli* after invasion by the ØX174 viral DNA. The investigators say it appears likely that the same enzymes utilized in their experiments are the ones used by infected *E. coli* cells to carry out the DNA polymerization and ligation of the ends of DNA strands. The enzymes they used were extracted from the *E. coli* bacteria, and the experimental environment with the boiled *E. coli* extract, etc., approximated conditions found inside *E. coli* cells.

Interpretation, Evaluation of Research

To refer to this recent research development as "production of life in a test tube" is plainly a dramatization of the research story. Scientists recognize the accomplishment not as the creation of a living organism, but rather as one enabling a DNA template to make a *copy of itself* in a "test tube" by a reproductive process normally occurring only within the bacterial cell.

However, the work does constitute the closest approach yet to what most of us think of when we say, "life in a test tube." The research establishes an important step forward in our understanding and control of life, and could lead to improved treatment of various diseases including cancer as well as man's gaining control over some hereditary conditions.

It probably is unwise to condemn the investigators involved in this recent project as recognition seekers. Even though their research may have been reported in extravagant terms, the men themselves are careful researchers. Their utilization of public media rather than only the technical press (in this case the December, 1967, issue of the *Proceedings of the National Academy of Sciences of the U.S.A.*) can be justified.

National funds channeled through government granting agencies

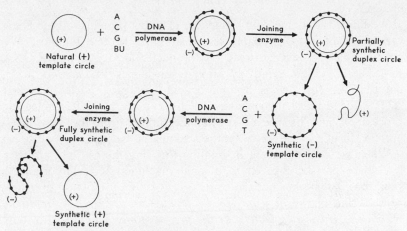

Figure 5. Enzymatic synthesis of viral ØX174 DNA. Both the synthetic (—) template circles and the synthetic (+) circles would infect bacterial cells, causing them to produce the appropriate complementary strands as well as the surrounding viral protein. Both duplex circles are considered replicative forms (RF). The letters A, C, G, BU, and T stand for the nucleotide precursors containing respectively adenine, cytosine, guanine, bromouracil, and thymine. (after Goulian, Kornberg, and Sinsheimer).

over the past seven years in support of Kornberg's research have amounted to about $2,000,000. Because these were public funds, the taxpayer who understands what is being done will be more willing to see his money used to support such basic research. Thus Kornberg decided that the cause of science would be advanced by general publicity. He said:

> I felt this work could be more easily interpreted for the public than some other things we have done. Lately I have become aware of the need for science to be better understood by the public, and I've had the feeling that we haven't always exploited our opportunities for gathering public support.

Most Investigators Cautious

Most scientific investigators dealing with phenomena associated with living things realize the complexity of life, and they realize the small part they actually are playing in clarifying some mechanistic details of how life maintains itself. We are increasing steadily our knowledge of the structure and function of DNA in reproducing itself and in producing RNA and the proteins necessary for life. But it should be pointed out that *all* living things, including the tiny ameba, possess hundreds and thousands of enzymes and almost none of the structure and stereo arrangement of these proteins even are known.

We know the amino acid sequences of a few proteins—these being various members of probably less than thirty protein families. We are not able, yet, even to read off the nucleotide sequences of DNA molecules. A few relatively simple substances like amino acids, polypeptides (or strings of amino acids), sugars, nucleotides and ATP (adenosine triphosphate, which is used in energy-releasing processes), and by use of special techniques even the very small protein, insulin, have been synthesized under laboratory conditions.

When we consider them in relation to living things, they are as a few spare parts compared to a giant machine. It is important to point out that because of the complexity of life, *production of a self-reproducing organism from simple precursors does not seem to be within the grasp of scientists at the present time.* This fact not only should challenge, but also should encourage a cautious optimism among those engaged in basic biological research.

Faith in God, DNA Considered

Some scientists have tried to use recent knowledge of DNA, RNA, and various phenomena of life to discredit faith in a supernatural being. Often the "god" of these individuals becomes the quest for truth. For some, science has become a religion which teaches men to worship products of the human mind.

On the other hand, there are those scientists, including myself, who have realized that there is a spiritual dimension beyond the millimicrons and cubic centimeters used in DNA and protein research. One day, some years ago while I was in graduate school, one of my associates told me in unforgettable terms what had happened to him at midnight the day before. He said he felt all of a sudden as though he had reached the top of his materialistic ladder. "There must be something beyond this," his very nature told him.

It seems to me that faith in God is logical. There are many philosophical arguments, which—true enough—do not prove His existence; yet, when taken together, they do show that faith in a supernatural God is *logical*. Also such faith is *satisfying*.

Speaking of God, St. Augustine said, "Thou hast made us for Thyself, and our hearts are restless till they find their rest in Thee." Some have said that God created man with an empty place that only He could fill. It is significant to me that belief in a supernatural being is found universally in all cultures, and as far as we know this always has been the case.

Relevance of Bible Indicated

The Bible indicates that the invisible things, from the time of creation, are seen and understood by the things that are made, and these point to God's power and deity (Rom. 1:20). The story is told that during the French Revolution, when some men were determined to remove churches, priests, Bibles, and everything that reminded people of God, a farmer laughed when told this. When asked why he laughed, the farmer pointed upward to the stars and said, "I was just wondering how you will get them down." Psalm 19:1 tells us that the heavens declare the glory of God.

The Bible indicates that Jesus Christ actually is the creator of Genesis 1:1 (see John 1:1, 14; Heb. 1:2; Col. 1:16), and it says in Colossians 1:17 that in Christ all things hold together. I think this can refer to the stuff of life. Modern physico-chemical studies have given us considerable knowledge of the attractive forces existing within molecules and of the bonds holding molecules together. I thank God for this knowledge, because with it we can understand better His creation.

There is something about looking at starry "diamonds" glistening in the night sky, which causes us to meditate on the greatness of the God who created them; but there is something about DNA and its operation which gives me a similar thrill. Here is evidence of the handiwork of a God concerned with intricacy.

The greatest complexity of which we presently are aware exists in living "protoplasm." It seems to me that the human brain (probably the most complex organ in existence), if anything, would lead one to at least suspect the existence of a Higher Power.

Those of use who have experienced this Higher Power, in the person of Jesus Christ in our lives, have the most for which to be thankful. We can and do participate in various phases of scientific research, and we are thankful to God for all the new knowledge He allows us to obtain. We are analyzing components of living things and we are synthesizing some; thus we are learning more of His creative activity.

Will it ever be possible—starting with simple chemicals—to put together something alive, and have it maintain itself and reproduce in a test tube (or outside of a test tube)? This question remains un-

282 WHY NOT CREATION?

answered. At any rate, as long as God ordains, we will go on researching and learning more about DNA and other aspects of His creation.

NOTES AND REFERENCES

1. M. Goulian and A. Kornberg, "Enzymatic Synthesis of DNA, XXII. Synthesis of Circular Replicative Form of Phage ØX174 DNA," *Proceedings National Academy of Sciences of U.S.A.* (1967), 58:1723-1730.
2. M. Goulian, A. Kornberg, and R. L. Sinsheimer, "Enzymatic Synthesis of DNA, XXIV. Synthesis of Infectious Phage ØX174 DNA," in *ibid.*, 2321-2328.
3. D. S. Greenberg, "The Synthesis of DNA: How They Spread the Good News," *Science* (1967), 158:1548-1550.
4. M. F. Singer, "*In Vitro* Synthesis of DNA: a Perspective on Research," in *ibid.*, 1550-1551.
5. J. D. Watson, *Molecular Biology of the Gene* (New York: W. A. Benjamin, 1965), p. 494.

CRITIQUE OF BIOCHEMICAL EVOLUTION

DUANE T. GISH, PH.D.*

In the field of biochemical evolution, we are in an area where the only debatable question is, could it have happened? There is no historical record available that may be examined to answer the question, did it happen? We must recognize, then, that one's conclusion on this matter will most likely be influenced chiefly by one's point of view rather than by the arguments presented. Indeed, we need have no illusion that evidence presented against the theory, no matter how powerful, will influence the conviction of avowed evolutionists that biochemical evolution has occurred. One of these avowed evolutionists, J. D. Bernal, has stated[1] that the earlier studies of the origin of life concentrated on establishing a case for it, but now the case no longer needs to be made; it can be accepted. He says that what interests us is not that it *could* happen, but precisely *how* it happened. Such statements as this may sound convincing to the uninformed, but even a quick survey of available information reveals how untrue and scientifically unsound such a statement is.

Melvin Calvin, who has engaged in considerable speculation on "evolution before life," has proclaimed, "We have no proof of evolution. We can only postulate some possible mechanisms for some of the simple steps that might lead from the chemical elements to chemical compounds that might agglomerate 'just so' and then become basic to life and reproduction processes."[2] In this chapter on evolution and information transfer,[3] which attempts to deal with the evolution of the more complex molecular systems, Alexander Rich is forced to a liberal use of such terms as "we postulate," "we imagine," "we theorize," "we could imagine," "let us imagine," and "we might imagine." Stanley Miller, in a paper[4] widely publicized and acclaimed, described the formation of a variety of organic compounds, including amino acids, in an apparatus containing methane, ammonia, hydrogen, and water, and energized by an electric dis-

*Upjohn Chemical Company, Kalamazoo, Michigan

charge. This demonstration has often been cited as evidence that early chemical evolution must have occurred, a chemical evolution that would have led to organic compounds which constituted the building blocks of complex molecules found in the living cell. It may be pointed out, first of all, that the significance of this demonstration is not really very great at all; it might even be termed trivial. Having placed a selected number of gasses in a closed system and supplied a source of energy we would be rather surprised had *not* such a variety of carbon-, oxygen-, and nitrogen-containing compounds been formed. Of considerable importance to the significance of this experiment is the answer to the question, did such a primitive atmosphere ever exist upon the earth? Such a reducing atmosphere has been postulated out of necessity, since it has been realized that reduced chemical compounds, which constitute the building blocks of molecules found in living systems, could not have arisen in an oxidizing atmosphere. It would have been thermodynamically impossible. Philip Abelson, Director of the Geophysical Laboratory, Carnegie Institution of Washington, in his paper[5] on the nature of the primitive atmosphere, has stated that an analysis of geologic evidence sharply limits the areas of permissible speculation concerning the nature of the primitive atmosphere and ocean. According to this evidence, the lowest oxidation state possible for carbon was carbon monoxide, and the evidence indicates further that the primitive atmosphere consisted chiefly of nitrogen and carbon monoxide, with hydrogen, carbon dioxide, and water present in lesser quantities. It is evident, then, that the basis for Miller's experiment did not exist.

Even though a basis for the origin of simple organic compounds, such as amino acids, sugars, pyrimidines and purines, could be established, the nature of processes that could have led to such complex molecules as proteins, polysaccharides and nucleic acids defies reasonable explanation. Oparin, in his book, *Origin of Life on Earth*,[6] has stated that "our knowledge of the primary formation of the lipids is therefore still scanty and unreliable." He states, concerning the origin of porphyrins, "certainly it is hard to tell at present to what extent analogous processes could have taken place under natural conditions independent of organisms." [7] In reference to nucleic acids he says "the question of the primary, abiogenic formation of compounds of phosphorus with organic substances is, however, extremely complicated and poorly understood." [8] Finally, he has stated "the problem of the primary development of proteins is extremely perplexing."[9] Since publication of this book, Fox and co-workers[10] have reported the polymerization of amino acids at temperatures of 170° to 180°, and Schramm and co-workers[11] have reported the polymerization of nucleotides when heated with a syrup of a polyphosphate ester. It is rather amusing to read these accounts, inasmuch as evolutionists have always claimed that chemical evolution of the more complex molecules took place in the "primordial soup of the primitive oceans," where such high temperatures and anhydrous conditions must be excluded.

Any natural process that might be imagined for the origin of proteins and nucleic acids would give rise to an infinitely complex mixture, with almost every conceivable sequence, stereoisomeric mixture, and chain length. Utter chaos would prevail. Any molecular species, once formed, would be subject to a wide variety of further reactions, and it is also certain that the rate of breakdown, such as hydrolysis, would exceed the rate of formation. For example, Howe[12] has pointed out that a pre-biologic earth, without a protective mantle of oxygen and ozone, would have been subjected to heavy doses of ultraviolet radiation in the region of 2,700 to 3,000 angstroms, radiation which breaks C-O, C-H, O-H bonds and others. Thus, amino acids, proteins, and nucleotides, if formed, would have been disrupted by such radiation.

One can imagine the tremendous quantity of a single molecular species that would be required to constitute even a concentration as low as 0.001 percent in a large body of water. Under these conditions, it is inconceivable how a single molecular species could ever have gained ascendency, let alone the complex mixture that would have been required for even the most primitive metabolism. The essential key to life is order and specificity. Each nucleic acid has a highly specific primary structure in the sequence of its component nucleotides. This specificity is the key to its function. It may dictate the structure of a protein, such as an enzyme, or it may regulate some biological activity. Before there was such specificity in structure, there could have been no function.

What natural processes could have brought such order out of chaos? What process could have selected a few nucleotides out of an almost infinite number of every conceivable sequence and ·chain length? What pressures could have forced their selection? In living processes, one way nucleotides express their function is by specifying protein structure, often stated in the terms, "one gene, one enzyme."

What function, then, could nucleotides have had before proteins arose? Assuming that nucleotides arose before proteins, or proteins before nucleotides, presents us with a dilemma. Nucleotides dictate the structure of proteins, but the synthesis of nucleotides is catalyzed by protein enzymes. Which, then, came first? The only reasonable answer is, neither. They both must have been present in their highly specific structure in order to have functioned and survived.

To bridge the gap between the molecular stage of evolution and the cellular, evolutionists have often resorted to the claim that there once existed molecules which were "autocatalytic like the virus." [13] In fact, Lindegren has stated[14] that the possibility that something similar to the viruses we now study was a stage in the evolution of more elaborate organisms is *"the basic hypothesis which directs the scientific activities of most of the foremost geneticists and biochemists of the present time."* It is utterly amazing to see such widespread acceptance of this view in the scientific community. It is a shocking display of ignorance concerning the nature and function of viruses and of their replication by the living cell.

Lindegren had the testimony[15] of N. W. Pirie, one of the world's authorities in the viral field, that viruses could never have played such a part. This has also been emphasized by Oparin,[16] among others. To say that a virus has the ability to reproduce itself is absolutely wrong. It has no autocatalytic ability whatsoever. Outside of the living cell, a virus is completely inactive, subject only to reactions that lead to its destruction. Even in the environment of the living cell, we cannot say that the virus reproduces itself. *The cell replicates the virus*, using the information supplied by the virus to produce copies of the viral nucleic acid and protein. The replication of the virus requires the action of a complex mixture of enzymes supplied by the cell, and other key components of the cell, such as soluble RNA and ribosomes, must be utilized. The energy required for viral synthesis, of course, must also be supplied by the cell. Since the sole function exhibited by the virus is that of supplying information for its replication, this in itself must presuppose the existence of an entity capable of utilizing that information, *an existence that must have pre-dated the virus*. It is possible that all viruses were at one time normal constituents of the cell, and which later suffered mutations. This mutation may have caused the exclusion of the constituent from its normal metabolic function in the cell, thus at the same time rendering it outside the control mechanism of the cell. Its structure, however, still remained capable of reproduction by the synthetic apparatus of the cell, this function of the cell being less discerning than the metabolic and control mechanisms of the cell.

No molecule capable of autocatalytic replication has yet been discovered, although, as already mentioned, such a molecule is often postulated by evolutionists. In light of present day knowledge, it can be emphatically stated that no such molecule exists nor has any molecule ever existed. We are now aware, at least in part, of the complex mechanism in the cell that is called into play to synthesize protein. The ultimate source of the information necessary for the replication of a protein molecule is believed to reside in the gene. Information in the gene is used to reproduce a messenger RNA. This synthesis, of course, requires the cooperation of the appropriate enzyme system and energy sources. The amino acids are activated via an intermediate complex with an activating enzyme, specific for each amino acid, and ATP. This complex reacts with soluble RNA (s-RNA), again specific for each amino acid, to give a complex of the amino acid with s-RNA. The AA-s-RNA complexes move to the microsomes, where they are laid down in the sequence specified by the messenger RNA.

The final step in the synthesis, the release of protein from the template, requires ATP, certain co-factors, and an enzyme. The picture outlined here, although a simplified one, gives some idea of the very complex system that must be called into play to synthesize a protein molecule. Furthermore, as Roberts has pointed out,[17] the system is quite sensitive to the spatial arrangement of the cellular structures. Disruption of the cell usually decreases the rate of protein synthesis by a factor of a thousand or more. *The organization of the synthesizing system appears to be of the greatest importance.* The protein synthesis accomplished with the reconstituted systems from *E. coli* and other cells represents only a residual trace of the protein synthesis occurring in the intact cell. These facts emphasize the tremendously complex and highly specific organization required to synthesize a single protein molecule in a living system. The abiogenic synthesis of a specific protein molecule is beyond the pale of our imagination.

The process by which correlated structures of an organism could have arisen by an evolutionary scheme has always been one of the insurmountable roadblocks in the theory of evolution. This roadblock would have been encountered far earlier in the evolutionary development of an organism, however. For on the gene level, itself, we see perfect and necessary correlation. This has been aptly stated by John Cairns:[18] "The bacterial chromosome has been shown to contain regions concerned solely with switching on and off the executive action of other regions; in turn, these 'operator' genes are controlled by 'regulator' genes. *It is the presence of such control mechanisms that converts what might be purposeless or even self-destructive activity into the ordered system we find in every living creature.*" We can see that the old saying, "one gene, one enzyme," can no longer apply, since for each enzyme several genes exist. Here again, as in the case of nucleic acid and protein, we can ask the question, which came first, the functional gene, the operator gene, or the regulator gene? How could the function of one be operative without the presence of the others. The conclusion must be that none ever existed independently, and that all must have come into existence simultaneously.

W. R. Hearn expressed his feelings, after attending a symposium on Genetic Mechanisms, that this was a poor time for the opposition to evolutionary ideas on the grounds that they "are only theories without empirical evidence or plausible mechanisms to back them up." [19] He pointed out that mutations are getting a lot less mysterious than they used to be and that the structures of biological macromolecules are now being determined. My reaction to recent advances have been just the opposite to that of Hearn's. As we begin to unravel the code of the DNA that constitutes the gene, and see there the tremendous degree of specificity in each tiny building block and the purposefulness of the overall plan, we see the opposite of chaos and of purposelessness, endless change. Indeed, what purpose, or what excuse for survival could such an organization have had without the presence of the living cell, in which its influence is expressed? And we must always remember that the DNA is not the master of the cell, it is the *servant* of the cell. Though we understand perfectly the chemical or physical basis of mutations, the nature of mutations remains unchanged. That is, as stated by W. R. Thompson,[20] all mutations are either useless, harmful, or lethal.

Even evolutionists admit that well over 99 percent of all mutations are harmful. Even if we were to admit that one out of every thousand mutations were useful, the stability of the genetic material would render the occurrence of a mutation so rare as to be incapable of effecting the change of one species into another. This is emphasized in the paper by W. J. Tinkle[21] in which the work of Muller is cited. His work, based upon experiments in Drosophila, permitted the estimate that the mean life of a gene (that is, the average time elapsing without change in any particular gene and its descendants) approximates 100,000 years. One can soon calculate the wait necessary for a favorable gene change, with a mutational rate of that nature, and with a frequency rate of a favorable change being one in one thousand or less!

Whether it be in the cry of a new-born babe, the beautifully correlated structure of the hummingbird, or in the marvelously correlated mechanism of functional gene, operator gene, regulator gene, messenger RNA, soluble RNA, ribosomal RNA, and the vast array of enzymes cooperating with them, we are witnesses to the fact that "the firmament showeth the handywork of God" (Ps. 19:1).

NOTES AND REFERENCES

1. J. D. Bernal, *Horizons in Biochemistry*, edited by M. Kasha and B. Pullman (New York: Academic Press, 1962), p. 11.
2. M. Calvin, as quoted in *Time* Magazine, Nov., 1958.
3. A. Rich, *Horizons in Biochemistry*, p. 103.
4. S. Miller, *J. Am. Chem. Soc.* (1955), 77:2351.
5. P. Abelson, *Abstracts 133rd National Meeting, Am. Chem. Soc.* (April, 1958), p. 53 C.
6. A. Oparin, *The Origin of Life on the Earth* (New York: Academic Press, Inc., 1957), p. 201.
7. *Ibid.*, p. 202.
8. *Ibid.*, p. 205.
9. *Ibid.*, p. 229.
10. S. Fox and J. Harada, *J. Am. Chem. Soc.* (1960), 82:3745.
11. G. Schramm, H. Grotsch, and W. Pollmann, *Angew. Chem.*, Inter. Ed. (1926), 1:1.
12. G. Howe, *J. Amer. Sci. Affil.* (1963), 15:124.
13. Oparin, *op. cit.*
14. C. Lindegren, *Nature* (1963), 197:566.
15. *Ibid.*
16. Oparin, *op. cit.*
17. R. Roberts, *Ann. N.Y. Acad. Sci.* (1960), 88:752.
18. J. Cairns, *Endeavor* (1963), 22:141.
19. W. Hearn, *J. Am. Sci. Affil.* (1962), 14:87.
20. W. Thompson, Intro., to *The Origin of Species*, C. Darwin (New York: E. P. Dutton and Co., Inc., 1956), p. 2.
21. W. J. Tinkle, *J. Amer. Sci. Affil.* (1961), 15:15.

3

IS DNA ONLY A MATERIAL CAUSE?

HAROLD ARMSTRONG, PH.D.*

The one thing that most distinguishes living beings is their ability to reproduce themselves. In so doing, they are, of course, carrying out God's command to "Be fruitful, and multiply . . " (Gen. 1:22).

It is true, perhaps, as has sometimes been remarked, that things which are not living, for instance, crystals, under suitable circumstances, may "grow." Be that as it may, certainly the things which are not living do not show the same striving to reproduce themselves; if the crystals ever received a commandment to multiply, they have not yet done much about it.

A second difference is that the living things are alike "after their kind" (Gen. 1:24); much more so than those that are not living. A snowflake, for instance, is a common crystal, or a collection of crystals. Whether or not it be true, as is so often said, that no two snowflakes are alike, certainly there is much variety among them, much more than there would be among bees in a swarm.

A third feature of living beings is nutrition. Metaphorically, it is true, we say that a fire is "fed"; we might say the same about a crystal growing from a solution. But any unprejudiced person would say that there is a difference; a living being uses its food in a discriminating way: some goes to its growth, some to maintenance, and some to act as fuel to keep life going. This is quite different from the "feeding" of a crystal in which material merely happens upon certain sites and sticks there. The crystal, in a sense, is an effect of the solution and of the circumstances; the living being, on the other hand, is in some way a cause.

This brings up a fourth point. The word "cause" suggests action with a purpose: the kind of action which we do as a result of thought. Thought, so far as we know, does not exist apart from life (not necessarily corporeal life); it might not be going too far to say

*Department of Physics, Queen's University, Kingston, Ontario, Canada

that life does not exist apart from the action with a purpose which, in us, would be considered as or related to thought.

Kinds of Causes

Since we have had to consider causes, let us look into that notion a little more. We may distinguish four kinds of cause, as Aristotle did: material, formal, efficient, and final.[1] Of a statue (to use Aristotle's own example), the material cause is the marble; the formal, the pattern of the finished statue, which was in the sculptor's mind before it was in the statue; the efficient, the sculptor and his tools; and the final, the sculptor's fee and his fame as an artist. We shall shortly use these distinctions profitably.

What we want to investigate is the notion that DNA is the "secret of life." First of all, what does such a statement mean? Presumably it means that it is the presence and activity of DNA that gives living beings their abilities. Is such a statement true? That is what we have to investigate.

Since the common theory has been discussed for several years, and is considered elsewhere in this *Annual,* there is no need to describe it at length here. It is enough to notice that molecules of DNA are supposed to be duplicated, an existing molecule acting as a template for a new one, as if, in the building of a house, a brick acted as a mold for making another brick. Thus, the appropriate proteins are built up. Also, enzymes are formed which somehow influence the larger features of the growing creature. The whole proposed "mechanism" is often spoken of as the "genetic code."

Objection to DNA As Code

Here an objection must be raised. So far, the word "code" is nothing more than a metaphor, and there are codes and codes. Until more has been said, nothing will really have been explained.

Is the "code" something like the Morse code? But this would require an intelligent being to read the code, and to do something about it with suitable organs. Is it like the punched cards of a Jacquard loom? This would require a mechanism to be operated by the code, a mechanism, moreover, much more complicated than the code, if our experience with automatic machines is at all applicable. (And if it is not, we are using words without meanings.)

The DNA would, it would seem, be considered in some sense a cause of the growing organism. But in what sense? Which of the four causes would it be? To elaborate on the distinctions between them, as Aristotle said,[2] "cause" means: (1) that from which, as an immanent material, a thing comes into being . . . (2) the form . . . , (3) that from which the change (here the production) first begins . . . , and (4) the end.

Of these we may remark that: (2) the form is immaterial, for "the soul is the place of forms," [3] (3) the efficient cause does not remain in the effect, and (4) the end is surely not DNA. It is true that someone once said that "a hen is an egg's way of producing another egg," but actually to believe such a thing is not only to put the cart before the horse, but also to mistake the cart for the horse.

So, the remaining possibility is that DNA is a material cause. Of course, a material, to be a material cause, need not be the only material, or even the one used in the greatest amount. A tiny amount of a crucial material may have a very large effect.

A striking example of this is the effect of indium or antimony, added to the extent of maybe only a few parts per million, on germanium for making transistors. Again, the design of a masonry structure might depend on the kind of mortar to be used; and an examination of old wooden buildings will show how their design was influenced by the use of pegs rather than nails.

Further Objections to DNA

Let us now consider some more objections to the notion that DNA could be an efficient or formal cause. (For this is what the common theory really means, although it is not put into these words. Supporters of this theory usually do not even consider finality.)

It has been common to imagine huge automatic machines, capable of many intricate tasks, and to say that living things are somehow like them.

Elsasser[4] has investigated this question, and points out that if a molecule of DNA, or a whole germ cell for that matter, somehow causes the whole organism, in the way alleged by the common theory, it must contain a tremendous amount of information. In fact, the information required could be stored only by assigning meanings to various dispositions of atoms. Even so, there would not be room for much redundancy (over-abundant, excessive amount) of information.

On the other hand, the disposition of individual atoms is (to say the least!) a very ephemeral thing. Any stability of information re-

EVIDENCE FROM BIOCHEMISTRY AND DNA STUDIES   293

quires enormous redundance, which, as we just saw, could not be fitted in. Thus, Elsasser concludes, any mechanistic theory which makes heredity depend on mechanically stored information simply will not work.

Another quite apt illustration may be drawn from the "degeneration of workmanship." Suppose that a man had a machine shop, equipped with new machines. Using those machines, he could build a second lot of machines, a second "generation" so to speak, nominally duplicating the first generation. But only nominally, for inevitably errors, tolerances, etc., will combine to make the second generation a little worse than the first.

And if the second generation of machines is used to build a third generation, it in turn will be yet worse, and so on. After a certain number of generations the machines would be so "bad" as to be almost useless.

It is hard to see how living things, if they depend on a material "code," would not undergo a similar degeneration. Now, though some degeneration, as expressed by mutation, does occur, the most harmful mutations are soon eliminated by natural selection.

Of course, machines do not degenerate from generation to generation, because the toolmaker intervenes. For instance, he can make a surface plate—a plane surface—independently of the accuracy of any machine. He does this by making three plates, and scraping them until any two will fit together over their whole surface. Then they are all truly plane. Notice, though, that he did this by referring to the form of the plane surface which was in his soul.

Another point which Elsasser has made is that if information be stored corporeally at all in living beings, it is stored in the softest and apparently most unstable parts. If a lobster, for instance, stores information, it is in the soft parts of his body, not in his shell.

Nor is the chemical storage of information, which has sometimes been suggested, in any better position. For most of the reactions in the body are close to equilibrium, and thus very subject to fluctuations.

Incidentally, the soft and delicate parts of the organism, in which information is supposed to be stored, are just those in which metabolism goes on most strongly. This means that the components are changed very frequently, which, again, does not fit in well with any corporeal storage of information. No one would print information needed permanently on the scratch pad beside the telephone.

Is Memory Encoded in DNA?

Heredity and the maintenance of the body during a being's life (so that, for instance, a man's fingerprints remain the same although his skin changes many times) would seem to be closely related. Memory, in the ordinary sense of the word, has at least some similarity to these things. So it has been suggested that memory is the encoding of experiences in DNA.

However, recently, this has been challenged. It had been reported that planaria, which had learned to do certain tasks, were fed to other planaria, which then showed the same abilities. But it now seems that nine laboratories, which have been trying to duplicate these alleged results, have been unable to do so.[5]

Moreover, mice, into whose brains had been injected drugs which inhibit the synthesis of RNA and protein, were still able to learn and to remember. In fact, there seem to be difficulties in the way of any theory of memory which makes it a purely corporeal thing.

No doubt the brain has something to do with memory. Yet, it seems that memory itself (as distinguished from the ability to act on memory) is not harmed by the removal of some of the brain. Moreover, memory itself does not seem to be localized in particular parts of the brain.[6]

It is, perhaps, not certain that memory, heredity, and the development of the individual are all connected. There is, though, one consideration which seems to point in that direction.

We ourselves, when we set out to make something, rely on memory; even if there is a pattern before us we have to remember how to read it, how to use the tools, and, indeed, even that we set out to make such and such a thing.

Now memory in this sense is certainly conditioned by the mind; we are not always thinking about how to read a blueprint, but can turn our attention to it when we wish. So an activity of the mind is involved here. And mind, in the strictest sense, seems to be incorporeal.

In support of this view, we can perhaps do no better than recall Aristotle's argument that as for corporeal functions, including the senses in so far as they are corporeal (and the same could be said of muscular activities), a strong exercise of the function leaves it impaired for a while. For instance, one is temporarily blinded by a strong light. But the exercise of the mind on something which is highly intelligible leaves it more, rather than less, able to deal with other matters.[7]

Examination of Experimental Data

So far, this discussion has been rather philosophical. Indeed, that is nothing to be ashamed of; for to discuss a thing philosophically is to try to know what we are talking about, and to talk sense about it. On the other hand, we can reason about anything only by starting from some premises, and if the question has to do with experimental facts some of the premises should come from experiment.

So let us consider some experimental facts. Many of these are collected in the writings of Commoner, who is one of the strong contenders against the view that the whole "secret of life" is contained in DNA.[8]

First of all, while we certainly should not underrate the humbler creatures, yet anyone would agree that a man is much more complicated than an amoeba. Now, as Commoner has pointed out, if the development of the creature is governed by DNA, it would be natural to *expect* the more complicated creature to have the larger amount of DNA.

Is this, in fact, what is found? It is not. Man's cells, for instance, contain about seven picograms of DNA each; but those of the African lungfish contain about 100 picograms, and the cells of Amphiuma, a primitive amphibian, about 168 picograms.[9]

On the other hand, there is a case in which two very similar species of insect, although morphologically indistinguishable, differ by 50 percent in the amount of DNA in their cells.[10] This would suggest that, at least in part, the function of DNA is something other than to serve as a "carrier of structural information."

Another fact pointing to this same conclusion is the evidence that the formation of DNA is itself a more involved thing than the copying of templates. The static specificity of DNA (i.e., its nucleotide sequence) is, it seems, regulated not only by the nucleotide sequence of the template, but also in part by the specificity of the polymerase enzymes which catalyze DNA synthesis.[11]

In other words, DNA, the supposed "vehicle of heredity," is itself influenced by environment as well as by heredity. Indeed, the sharply enhanced rate of mutation, which has been observed in bacteria under conditions of extreme thymine deprivation, suggests: (1) that an alteration in the nucleotide sequence of the DNA occurs under these conditions, and, thus, (2) that the specificity of the DNA synthesis may be partly controlled by the concentration of available free nucleotides.[12]

Experiments on Synthesis of DNA

Some experiments in which DNA is synthesized *in vitro* have a bearing on our question. Three things are involved: some DNA put in as a "primer"; the necessary enzyme, the DNA polymerase; and the necessary deoxynucleotides. Some experiments in which DNA primers from various sources were used along with polymerase from *Escherichia coli* showed that the nature of the resulting DNA was affected by the polymerase as well as by the primer.[13]

If the DNA primer and the enzyme are from the same organism the new DNA will be the same as the primer DNA within five percent. But, if the primer and the enzyme are from separate differing species of organisms, the disparity of sequence of the new DNA and the primer DNA is as much as 17.25 percent! The precision of protein synthesis also depends on *both* the DNA code and the specificity of the synthetic enzyme. Also the pH, magnesium content or concentration, and temperature affect the reaction system. As Commoner sums it all up, "Self-duplication and biochemical specificity is a property of an intact whole cell, which is an inheritably complex system, and not the property of one or another molecule. We can ignore this fact only at the price of self-delusion."

On the other hand, *in vivo* experiments have shown that the precision with which an intact *E. coli* cell is capable of regulating the specificity of the proteins which it synthesizes, depends not only on the specificity provided by the DNA genetic agent, but also on the amino-acyl RNA synthetase which is involved.[14]

DNA as Other Than Code

There are other observations which it is difficult to fit in with the notion of a "code," but which favor another interpretation. For a wide range of creatures, the amount of DNA in a cell is about proportional to the volume of the cell. (That is to say, the ratio of amount of DNA per cell to the volume of a typical cell is about the same for a wide variety of creatures.)

Moreover, the rates of consumption of oxygen, and of metabolism, are about inversely proportional to the amount of DNA per cell.[15] Commoner suggests that this is because—

DNA synthesis and the resultant sequestration of the catalytic nucleotides which are active in the oxidation electron transport system will tend to reduce the rate of catabolic degration of the metabolites. In turn, this may be expected to increase the relative proportion of the available metabolites which enter into the anabolic process and thereby contribute to the synthesis of cell substance . . . one may anticipate a positive correlation between the DNA content and the overall size characteristic of the mature cell and a negative correlation between DNA content and the cell's characteristic rate of oxidative metabolism.[16]

Which, in other words, means that DNA is here acting as some sort of material cause. On the other hand, as Commoner concludes, in another place, "The unique precision of the chemistry of intact biological appears to be conditioned, in some as yet unknown way, by the inherent structural organization of the cell." [17] To which one might add: "that is to say, by the form—the formal cause."

There are other points which might be mentioned. There seems to be evidence to show that in special cases certain features can be inherited independently of DNA. And more important, even though it were established that DNA somehow arranges the growth of cells, no one seems to have suggested a way in which it could control the pattern of a flower, say, or the structure of a bird's feathers. To say that is "by enzymes" is just to imitate the dear old lady who said that machinery works "with screws, somehow." Moreover, it is undoubtedly true that living beings, as they grow, adapt themselves to the circumstances to some extent. It is hard to see how this could be if their development were completely controlled by a "code," like the working of an automatic screw machine.

Conclusion

Now to conclude this discussion. Theoretical arguments and experimental evidence have been given to show that DNA is not the whole cause of life and of heredity. Indeed, anyone who holds the doctrine of the four causes would not have expected otherwise. And if anyone doubts that doctrine, it is suggested that he try to think of a case in which he knows that there are not the four causes (as disdinguished from not knowing what they are).

On the other hand, DNA seems to be a cause in some sense, and an immanent one. So it must be a material cause. But a very special and crucial material; hence it is not surprising that it has a great effect on the development of the creature.

But there must still be a formal cause, and that can be only in a soul, or that which stands in the same relation to a single cell as the soul does to the whole creature. (It is sufficient here to take the word "soul" in Aristotle's sense; the Christian sense includes and goes beyond that.)

The two other causes exist, but this argument is not especially concerned with them.

An account such as this, then, which satisfies the biology without doing violence to the metaphysics, seems to be what we set out to find.

NOTES AND REFERENCES

1. Aristotle, "Physics," Book 2, Chapter 3.
2. Aristotle, "Metaphysics," Book 5, Chapter 2.
3. Aristotle, "On the Soul," Book 3, Chapter 4.
4. W. M. Elsasser, *The Physical Foundations of Biology* (New York, Pergamon Press, 1958), pp. 120-160.
5. S. H. Barondes, of the Albert Einstein College of Medicine, at a recent meeting of the American Association for the Advancement of Science, at Washington, reported in the *Whig-Standard*, Kingston, Ontario, Canada, January 5, 1967, p. 8.
6. Elsasser, *op. cit.*, pp. 133, 137.
7. Aristotle, "On the Soul," Book 3, Chapter 4.
8. B. Commoner, *Nature* (June 6, 1964), 202:960-968, (Aug. 1, 1964), 203:486-491; cf. by the same author, *Clinical Pharmacology and Therapeutics* May and June, 1965), 6:273-278; cf. also, by the same author, *Science* (June 2, 1961), 133:1745-1748.
9. C. Vendrely, *Bull. Biol. France and Belg.* (1952), 86:1; cf. R. Vendrely and C. Vendrely, *C. R. Soc. Biol.* (1952), 235:444.; cf. also, A. E. Mirsky and H. Ris, *J. Gen. Physiol.* (1951), 34:451.
10. F. Schrader and S. Hughes-Schrader, *Chromosoma* (1952), 7:469.
11. H. K. Schachman, J. Adler, C. M. Radding, I. R. Lehman, and A. Kornberg, *J. Biol. Chem.* 1960), 235:3242; cf. J. Josse, A. D. Kaiser, and A. Kornberg, *J. Biol. Chem.* (1961), 236:864.
12. E. Chargaff, *Essays on Nucleic Acids* (Amsterdam: Elsevier, 1963); cf. L. R. Cavaliere and B. H. Rosenberg, *Ann. Rev. Biochem.* (1962), 31:247; cf. also R. Hendler, *Science* (1962), 142:402; B. Commoner, *Science* (1961), 133:1445, and by the same author, *Horizons in Biochemistry* (New York: Academic Press, 1962).
13. I. R. Lehman, S. B. Zimmerman, J. Adler, M. J. Bessman, E. S. Simms, and A. Kornberg, *Proc. U. S. Nat. Acad. Sci.* (1958), 44:1191.
14. W. E. Barnett and K. B. Jacobson, *Proc. U. S. Nat. Acad. Sci.* (1964), 51:642.
15. Commoner, *op. cit.*, Nature, Vol. 202.
16. *Ibid.*
17. Commoner, *op. cit., Clinical Pharmacology.*

MUTATIONS REVEAL THE GLORY OF GOD'S HANDIWORK

Walter E. Lammerts

For many years mutations, or suddenly appearing changes in either the appearance or behavior of individual organisms, have been considered the material basis of evolution. However, as more is learned about the exact nature of mutations, they seem to be less likely to be building blocks for the origin of even varieties, let alone species of plants. Indeed, cyto-genetic research, and especially molecular genetics, has revealed an ever-increasing complexity of the physical basis of inheritance called the "gene."

First Level of Investigation

The study of mutations has involved probably three levels of investigation. First, after their discovery by such pioneers as Hugo DeVries, there was the painstaking work of T. Hunt Morgan and his associates, Calvin Bridges and A. H. Sturtevant. These men patiently accumulated information on the naturally occurring changes, or mutations, in eye color, wing form, eye structure, bristle arrangement, and numerous other features of the fruit fly, *Drosophila melanogaster*.

Careful intercrosses and back-crosses showed that these mutations could be grouped into four linkage groups corresponding to the four chromosomes of the species. Within each chromosome the mutant genes were located serially, like beads on a string. The order of their sequence was determined by crossing-over studies; those far apart showing much recombination, while those close together, very little. As a result, "chromosome mapping" could be done with fair precision, though odd "clumping" of genes in certain areas remained puzzling. Similar detailed chromosome maps were made in corn, tomatoes, flour beetles, and various grains, such as wheat.

Meanwhile, the *process* of mutation was greatly speeded up by X-ray irradiation of the fruit fly. Muller first made this discovery in 1928. Here was a way by which biologists could, in a few years, obtain more mutations than Morgan and his associates found in a lifetime of patient observation. Thus quantitative studies as to the percentage of harmful versus neutral, or possibly advantageous, mutations could easily be made.

Here was the first disappointment for evolution-minded biologists, for most mutations found were harmful. In fact, only about one in a thousand seemed to be even neutral or showed *slight* advantage under laboratory methods of nutrient agar culture. Unfortunately, X-rays did not prove very effective as regards inducing variations in plants, though some success was obtained by pollen irradiation in such plants as corn.

Here, again, most mutations were semi-sterile types and proved to be the result of translocations, so that portions of chromosomes formerly separate were now attached, and, reciprocally, portions previously in one chromosome were transferred to another. These reciprocal translocations were in fact quite common and may schematically be represented as follows:

Chromosome 1	Chromosome 2
Translocated Chromosome 1	Translocated Chromosome 2

There was considerable enthusiasm for a while that translocated chromosomes might explain the origin of new chromosomal arrangements, but soon it was found that all were lethal when homozygous.

The era from 1920 to 1945 might well be termed the period of great discovery and freedom to speculate that biologists were finding the "real" physical basis of evolution. Mutations were considered by many biologists as really *new* entities, useful as building blocks, so to speak, by the process of natural selection.

Then came mathematical treatises, by such masters at the art as J. B. S. Haldane, R. A. Fischer, and Sewell Wright. They argued most convincingly that even though only one in a thousand mutations was advantageous to the extent of even a one percent advantage, these would slowly accumulate under the pressure of natural selection in a population and lead to evolutionary change.

Thus Patau showed that a mutation with a one percent advantage would increase according to the pattern shown in Figure 1. Increase from .01 percent to 0.1 percent of the population would occur only after 900,230 generations in a large population. Though millions of

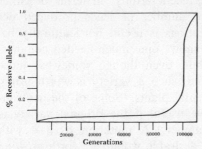

Figure 1. Showing very slow increase of a recessive mutation with advantage of 1 in 1000.

years would be needed to effect the transformation of the small five-toed, dog-sized Eohippus to the modern large one-toed horse, still geologists claimed abundant time was available, so all seemed well with the general theory.

Second Level of Investigation

Then came what might be called the second level of investigation. Population geneticists decided to study the actual way in which mutations did or did not accumulate under actual natural field conditions. And parallel to these intensive studies, other means of inducing mutations were conducted which involved use of gamma radiation, neutron radiation, and various mutagenic chemicals.

Thus, as I reported in the 1965 *Creation Research Society Annual*,[1] neutron irradiation of axillary leaf buds, or "budding eyes" of roses, was a highly effective way of obtaining mutations. In fact, more mutations were obtained by the irradiation of 50 rose "budding eyes" than one could find in a field of a million rose plants in a whole lifetime of patient searching for "sports."

Here was a splendid tool also for measuring the vigor and viability of mutations. For, as a measuring stick, so to speak, for calibration, we had the original unvarying variety easily propagated by budding. Accordingly, by rebudding the mutant forms *at the same time* as the original variety, and growing under comparable hothouse conditions, accurate comparison as to vigor, pollen fertility, and other characteristics could be made.

An interesting feature of this work is as follows: although some mutations showed useful horticultural variation, such as an increase in petal number, or loss of the unpopular magenta coloration, *all,* without exception, were weaker than the variety originally irradiated. This was true even with the remarkably vigorous variety, Queen Elizabeth. Some fairly vigorous and interesting coral and white mutations were obtained, but these failed commercially since they were not vigorous enough under varying garden conditions.

Similar results were obtained by other workers using gamma radiation, and it is now quite clear that mutations in plants are usually significantly weaker, or have a reduced fertility, in terms of either the percentage of good pollen or number of seeds produced per plant. Artificial induction of mutations is useful horticulturally because sometimes a mutation may show some much-needed commercially desirable characteristic. Thus, even though somewhat more difficult to grow or giving less seed, such a variety is worth using. This is particularly true of ornamental plants. Some of the neutron-induced rose variations may prove useful if the original variety is super-vigorous but lacks petal number. A mutation from it with enough petals to be commercially desirable would be worth growing even though less vigorous than certain overly vigorous types such as Queen Elizabeth.

In recent years, enthusiasm for demonstrating evolution by a study of induced mutations has about died out, since clear-cut cases of obviously advantageous mutations simply do not occur.

Meanwhile, such population geneticists as Band[2] were showing what natural selection can and cannot do. Her work was with fluctuations in naturally occurring outdoor populations of the fruit fly, *D. melanogaster*, so carefully studied under laboratory conditions from 1947 until 1962. One of her most remarkable conclusions was that natural selection does *not* increase the most viable or best true-breeding lines or homozygotes in natural populations!

Most pertinent were observations made following the unusually severe winter of 1960-61 at Amherst, Massachusetts. September temperatures were the highest on record, and samples were collected then. The 1962 collections were made during the driest season on record. The results of genetic analysis of variability and viability in 1961 and 1962 were compared to the more normal season of 1960 and the earlier ones of 1947-49. Her conclusions follow:

1) Natural selection is highly efficient in maintaining population fitness during stress as in the summer of 1962. The effects are shown only in the heterozygotes.

2) Stabilizing selection has led to the retention of most components of genetic diversity.

3) There is no evidence of improvement in viability of the homozygotes (those showing the mutation and breeding true for it).

4) No decrease in genetic load was shown. This is because most load components (recessive mutations) remain concealed in the random heterozygotes.

5) Hence, joint effects of directional selection and stabilization

are directed to the interaction of genes and gene complexes in the heterozygous condition.

6) A slight reduction in total genetic diversity resulted from stress conditions.

Band does not stress the most interesting conclusion: namely, that there is no evidence that selection has been primarily directed to the elimination of harmful variations or mutants. Neither do such variants appear to reduce the viability of the heterozygote. Her Figure 1 is fascinating in that it shows *no* improvement in average viability of the homozygotes mutations, or any reduction in the magnitude of the genetic load.

From the viewpoint of evolving new characteristics these conclusions are indeed pertinent. The only source of new and distinctive features leading possibly to species formation are mutations. These must gradually be accumulated in true breeding or homozygous conditions, since, of course, species and even varieties differ from each other in various traits which are *constant*.

Yet Band's research shows that even the most viable homozygotes do not increase in number. Furthermore *no improvement* in their viability occurs. Since even drastic mutations show no harmful effect if recessive in the heterozygous condition, there simply is no mechanism for eliminating them. Now the ratio of "harmful" to "useful" mutations is at least 1,000 to 1. Quite obviously, if a species really did evolve by natural selection, the genetic load of drastic or harmful mutations would become so high in a few hundred generations as to result in all offspring having some defect, because of chance mating of identical genotypes and resulting homozygosity. The fortunate fact that this is not yet true, in the human race or in most plant and animal species, argues strongly for the special creation of the species unit, and especially for its existence for a *relatively short time* instead of hundreds of thousands or millions of years.

Catastrophic Selection

With the discovery that strains of bacteria resistant to penicillin, aureomycin, or chloromycetin always showed up when these drugs were used to effect cures of various diseases, great enthusiasm was aroused for a while among evolution-minded biologists. Here at last was "proof" that beneficial mutations really did occur.

But enthusiasm was short lived, for it soon became clear that these mutations did not arise as a result of exposure to penicillin. Rather they seem to occur at a *constant rate*. Associated with the resistance, there always is a decrease in viability under *normal* conditions. Accordingly, under normal conditions, they are soon "swamped out"; and either are completely eliminated or are carried along as heterozygotes in a very small number of individual bacteria. Now most bacterial cells appear to be haploid, but there is increasing evidence that sexuality does occur; hence *some cells* are, for a time at least, diploid; hence heterozygosity does occur even in bacteria.

When a strain is exposed to antibiotics, either the mutation rate for these otherwise defective resistant mutations is so high that sooner or later one occurs, or an already established one is given the starting advantage of having no competitors. Soon the entire population is of the resistant type, and new medication is necessary. However, as soon as treatment is relaxed, the normal type bacteria take over, and the resistant strain is either eliminated or reduced to a minute fraction of a percentage of the population.

The story has been remarkably well presented as regards the housefly in a recent issue of *California Agriculture* in an article entitled "Housefly Resistance to Insecticides." [3] The conclusions on the housefly parallel those based upon studies of bacteria. Thus, the article author writes:

> It is now well established that the development of increased ability in insects to survive exposure is not *induced directly* by the insecticides themselves. These chemicals do not cause the genetic changes in insects; they only serve as selective agents, eliminating the more susceptible insects and enabling the more tolerant survivors to increase and fill the void created by destruction of susceptible individuals.

There are several fascinating observations:

1) Resistance to DDT and dieldrin continued at a high level *in an area where these sprays were used*, in spite of the flies not having been sprayed with either chemical for about ten years. In other words, once established, resistant strains maintained themselves without selection pressure.

2) Flies at a cattle feed lot and at a nearby poultry ranch showed little resistance to any organophosphates or carbonates, since they had not been sprayed very often with them. Yet *agricultural crops* in the area had been treated regularly. Evidently the resistant strain of flies, though able to maintain itself once established, is *incapable of spreading* through the whole range of species even in a given area

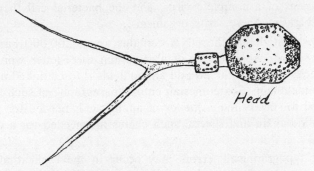

Figure 2. Diagrammatic representation of T-2 Bacteriophage magnified 500,000 diameters. Weighs 100
million times the hydrogen atom. Head has 1 chromosome with 200,000 base pairs (After electron
micrograph, Benzer, p. 71.)

such as Blythe, where this observation was made. Surely flies in the
nearby agricultural area became resistant from frequent spraying of
the crops, yet feed lots and poultry farms had a low level of resistance.
Also, in no instance were 100 percent of the flies, *even in the most
exposed areas*, resistant to the chemicals used.

Third Level of Investigation

An explanation of just why most mutations were harmful, or, once
established, tended to maintain themselves at various percentages of
the total natural population without further selection pressure, was so
far wanting. With the advent of molecular genetics the third level of
understanding has now been reached.

Thus Seymour Benzer[4] has found that the T_4 bacteriophage, which
infects the colon bacillus, is a most useful organism for mapping in
detail the molecular limits of gene structure. In a 20-minute experiment by use of a single test tube, a quantity of genetic data can be
obtained, which would require the entire human population of the
earth if such a complex organism were used for study!

Phages are virus organisms characterized by a hexagonal-looking
head and a complex tail, by which they attach themselves to the
bacillus wall (Figure 2). Within the head is a long-chain molecule
of DNA having a weight of about 100 million times that of hydrogen.
After attachment, the DNA alone moves into the bacillus cell and
takes over reorganization of the cell machinery to manufacture 100

or so copies of a complete virus, and the bacterial cell then bursts open, liberating these virus organisms.

It is estimated that the DNA contains about 200,000 base pairs. Each base pair is one letter of a minimum three-letter word which may specify which of the 20 odd amino acids is to be linked up into a polypeptide chain. Sometimes an entire "paragraph" of such "words" is needed to specify the *sequence* of amino acids needed for *just one* polypeptide chain and several such chains are needed for a complex protein.

Now "typographical" errors may occur in the replication of the DNA molecule. Transpositions, deletions, additions, or inversions may occur. As Seymour Benzer says, "In a daily newspaper the result is often humorous. In the DNA of living organisms, typographical errors are *never* funny and are often fatal" (emphasis added).

However, these "typographical" errors or mutations can be used to analyze a small portion of the information carried by a T_4 bacteriophage, and thus reveal the amazing complexity of not only the DNA code, but the very processes of cellular activity as well.

One group of mutants called rH mutants can be identified quite easily by the appearance of the plaques or clear regions they form on the surface of a culture in a glass dish where phage particles have multiplied and destroyed the bacterial cells. The shape and size of these plaques are hereditary characteristics of the phage that can be easily identified and scored. A plaque produced in several hours will contain about 10 million phage particles, the progeny of a single phage particle.

Now the T_4 phage can produce plaques on either host strain B or K. This standard form gives rise to rH mutants easily recognizable by a distinctive plaque on B cultures. But these mutants cannot form plaques on bacterial strain K. This is the "key" to the whole mapping technique used by Benzer; for an rH mutant can grow on bacterial strain K, if the cell is simultaneously infected with a particle of the standard type. The function of the standard type phage has been traced to a small portion of the T_4 phage genetic map known as the rH region.

As mentioned before, various different-appearing plaques or mutants arise spontaneously in this area. These may be crossed with each other by adding each of them to a liquid culture of B cells.

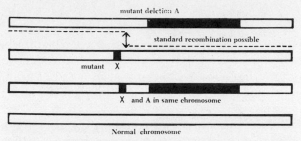

Figure 3. Showing how deletions are used to test location of mutants.

This gives an opportunity for the progeny to recombine portions of genetic information from either parent.

If the two mutants resulted from typographical errors in different parts of the DNA molecule, some individuals of the standard type will be regenerated. A sort of "crossing-over" occurs (see Figure 3). These reconstructed standards will produce plaques on the K strain, whereas the original mutants cannot. In this way one can detect a single recombination among billions of offspring. This allows the resolution of two rH mutants that are only *one base apart* in the DNA molecular chain.

The exact mechanism of recombination is not known. However, it seems that two defective DNA molecules may actually break apart to form one non-defective molecule, which then is replicated; or, in the course of replication, there may be "copy choice," such that only good portions of the two mutant molecules are "copied." This appears to me as granting quite a remarkable power of selectivity to some "curative" agency in the T_4 phage cell.

At any rate, the results of a long and elaborate study of hundreds of non-reverting rH mutants shows that *all* can be represented as containing deletions of one size or another in a single linear structure. By contrast, the rH mutants discussed above behave as if their alterations were localized at single points. By testing against the non-reverting segments at this particular area of the T_4 phage DNA molecule, all mutants located within a given segment will not recombine when tested against it (Figure 4).

By use of about 80 such non-reverting segment mutations, the rH point mutations may be assigned to the proper one. Finally, those localized in one small segmental deletion length or segment are tested against each other. Those showing recombination are obviously at

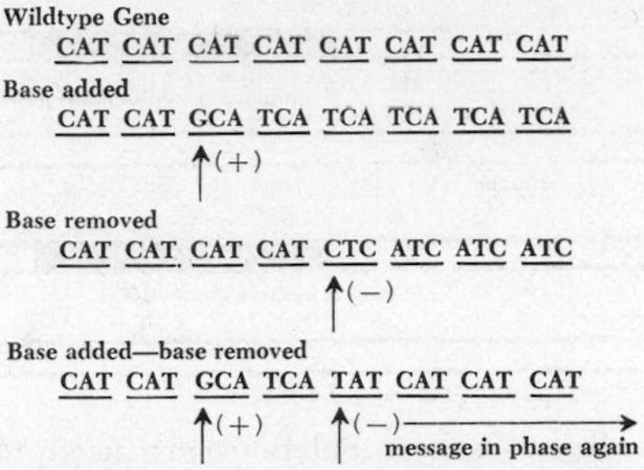

Wildtype Gene
CAT CAT CAT CAT CAT CAT CAT CAT
Base added
CAT CAT GCA TCA TCA TCA TCA TCA
⤒(+)

Base removed
CAT CAT CAT CAT CTC ATC ATC ATC
⤒(−)

Base added—base removed
CAT CAT GCA TCA TAT CAT CAT CAT
⤒(+)   ⤒(−)────────────→
              message in phase again

The imaginary message is CAT, CAT . . . Adding of
a base shifts the reading to TCA, TCA. Removing a
base makes it ATC, ATC. Addition and removal puts
the message in phase again. The reading is from left
to right in triplets of 3 nucleotide bases.

Figure 4. Showing effect of mutations.

different sites; and, then, each site is named after the mutant indicating its location. Finally, the *order* of the sites within a given segment can be established by measuring the recombination frequencies.

Of an estimated 350 sites in this small area, about 250 have been located, and only a hundred or so remain to be found. *All* are defective. Furthermore, certain chemicals, such as a 5-bromouracil, increase the mutation rate at certain sites by a factor of 10,000 or more, yet effect no change at other sites. All of these are also defective changes.

Where, then, are the "good" mutations, needed for evolutionary progression?

The reason for this state of affairs is clearly shown in a paper by F. H. C. Crick[5] in the *Scientific American* for October 1962. He shows that the sites discovered by Benzer correspond to changes in the DNA base nucleotides. Mostly, the defects are the result of adding or deleting one base, or at most a small group of bases, and are not merely the result of altering one of them. Such addition can be produced at random by compounds called acridines. Just how this chemical works is not fully understood. However, since the resulting changes can be combined or broken up, there seems little doubt as to the fact that they are additions or deletions.

As has been explained by Duane T. Gish,[6] the simplest code by which 20 amino acids could be specified involves at least three nucleotide pairs, or a triplet of "letters" such as ATT, GCA, TCG, ACC (A-adenine, C-cytosine, T-thymine, and G-guanine). The "message" evidently begins at a fixed point at one end of the gene, and is read three bases at a time. Then, if for some reason the reading starts at the wrong point, the message would fall into the wrong sets of three, and so would be incorrect. For each *correct* reading of the code there are two incorrect ones.

That is why the addition or deletion of a base in most parts of the gene makes it completely non-functional. The reading from that point onward would be totally wrong. Experimentally, this meant that if an additional base of plus mutation is combined with a plus, the combination is non-functional.

Likewise, a minus with a minus is non-functional. But if a plus is combined with a minus close to it, the function is restored. This is because, starting at one end of the rH region of the B cistron, or gene, the message would be read correctly until the extra mutation-causing base was reached. Then the message would not make "sense" until the location of the minus mutation or missing base is reached, after which the message would come back into phase or make "sense" again.

In other words, the function of the rH part of the B gene does not seem to be important. Accordingly, the message can be *"wrong"* for a short distance, and still be functional. But, if the distance is very long between the plus and minus mutations, the combination will not function. This is shown in Figure 4, adapted from Crick's paper.

Now, if only a sequence of three bases is needed to specify an amino acid, 64 could be specified instead of the actual 20 available. Offhand, it would seem that most "messages" are nonsense messages or triplets. However, the experimental results show that most of the 64 possible triplets, or codons, are not nonsense, but actually stand for amino-acids. Hence probably more than one codon can "call" for the same amino acid.

The picture emerging from the work of molecular genetists is a marvelously complex code which will stand mighty little in the way of alteration, either addition or subtraction, or change of *any* of the nucleotide bases. Only because the rH region is *relatively* unimportant in function was it possible to accumulate the large number of mutations, making possible the detailed analysis of this rather minute portion of the T_4 phage DNA molecule. Now evidently most portions of this molecule code message are so important that even a *short* portion out of phase causes a completely non-functional "message"; hence mutations do not survive.

The virus organism has only one chromosome; yet, "higher" animals, including man and, of course, all the plants except algae, have many chromosomes—each one made up of organized protein and DNA molecules. How did this organization come into being?

The only solution so far offered by evolution-minded molecular geneticists is a sort of molecular level "polyploidy." They picture an organism such as a bacterium, which has a single circular chromosome, as giving rise to one with two chromosomes. Then, presumably, mutations could accumulate in the "extra" chromosome, and be shielded by the normal genes of the original one. But, sooner or later, sexual union or conjugation of two bacteria would occur. Then, some of the resulting descendants would have only a pair of the "new" chromosomes, and no normal original genes to shield them from the possibility of having a lack of balance in the plus or minus mutations, which occurred during the time before conjugation.

Surely, it is stretching credulity a bit to picture these "new" chromosome pairs as having such a finely balanced set of plus and minus mutants as to have "correct" messages for all needed functions. In fact, it is difficult to see how any really new functions, such as the change from single-celled organisms like bacteria to even the simplest multicellular green algae, such as a *Protococcus*, could ever come about by accumulation of such defects as are so far reported by molecular geneticists.

It is true that the very nature of such experiments, as those of Benzer, where the K strain is used to reveal recombinations, would tend to concentrate attention on defective changes. Still, since these are picked up as changes in appearance of plaques on the B strain, *some* should be of a positive nature and grow on the K strain *better* than the standard type. Such seem never to have been found or at least remain unreported.

From the creation viewpoint, we could of course expect the DNA system to be a marvelously intricate one. Since designed to accomplish very complex tasks even in the "simplest" organism such as a T_4 phage virus, it obviously could stand little in the way of tinkering. In fact, in light of the picture of just how DNA, RNA, the ribosomes, and the cytoplasm interact to form the needed proteins, we cannot but marvel at the complexity of all these reactions taking place at one time in a single cell.

Surely, the ingenuity of man is taxed to find ways of experimentally solving the exact way in which even a "simple" type of phage operates. Should we not then be filled with a feeling of reverent awe at the glory of God's handiwork as shown by this revelation of the complex way in which His created organisms carry on their tasks? Truly the calling of a molecular biologist is a great one. Let us hope that some of our young creation-minded students approach this field, realizing that here they are coming close to seeing God at work as He daily maintains and preserves all creatures.

NOTES AND REFERENCES

1. Walter E. Lammerts, "Planned Induction of Commercially Desirable Variation in Roses by Neutron Radiation," *Creation Research Society Annual* (1965), pp. 39-48.
2. H. T. Band, "Natural Selection and Concealed Genetic Variability in a Natural Population of *D. melanogaster*," *Evolution*, 18:3, pp. 334-404.
3. C. P. Georghiou, *et al.*, "Housefly Resistance to Insecticides," *California Agriculture*, 19:10, pp. 8-10.
4. Seymour Benzer, "The Fine Structure of the Gene," *Scientific American*, January, 1962.
5. F. H. C. Crick, "The Genetic Code," *Scientific American*, October, 1962.
6. Duane T. Gish, "DNA: Its History and Potential," *Creation Research Society Annual* (1967), pp. 13-17.

5

DNA STUDIES IN RELATION TO CREATION CONCEPTS

JOHN J. GREBE, D.SC.*

Introduction

To discuss the new questions of science and the Bible requires some background considerations. Man's general concepts of the formation of the earth and the living organisms in relation to their environment are subject to continual revision. Scientists have learned more and developed more tools of research in the last forty years than in all time previous.

Once only organisms composed of millions and millions of atoms could be observed under a microscope. Now we can take pictures showing the pattern of position of single atoms. The behavior and details of an atom and its parts can be predicted with the precision associated with an automobile engine.

Most generally, discussions on the "theory" of evolution, or even the formation of the earth, are pros and cons about scientific inferences that have long since been superseded with facts. Similarly, Bible students often insist on reading into the simple and clear language of the Bible, interpretations based on information more than ten years old. How convenient it was that God must have done things to match their ideas!

Or, in another respect, it is particularly difficult to estimate ages, now that it is recognized how much radioactive decay is modified by cosmic rays. Cosmic rays are subject to action by the earth's magnetic field, and the amount of water in orbit around the earth. During the last reversal of the magnetic field, water and water-producing ions could not help but be swept down out of orbit. Such changes upset all radioactive dating, making isotope dating appear older in most cases.

With the above areas of misunderstanding out of the way, I want to assert that no one can point to a single fact of science, history, or

---

*Director of Research, Dow Chemical Company, Midland, Michigan (Ret); now living at 11604 - 114th Dr., Youngstown, Arizona 85363

archeology that conflicts with a literal reading of the Bible. We have asked avid evolutionists to come forth with factual evidence. We have seen only trivial misrepresentations of both science and the Bible. These have been well exposed in papers by Lammerts and others in various issues of the Creation Research Society publications.

Scientific Knowledge Incomplete

Lest someone think that the latest science is inferred to be complete in its knowledge of the Bible and God's creation, I must point out that Planck's length derived from Planck's constant (a very basic unit of real significance to science), is so small that the ratio of what we know of "inner space" to what we know is to be known, is much less than the proverbial drop in the bucket. It is less than one part in 10^{60}.

Even now scientists like G. G. Simpson of Harvard conclude:

> However, in my opinion nothing that has so far been learned about DNA has helped significantly to understand the nature of man or of any other whole organism. It certainly is necessary for such understanding to examine what is inherited, how it is expressed in the developing individual, how it evolves in populations, and so on. Up to now the triumphs of DNA research have had virtually no effect on our understanding of those subjects. In due course molecular biology will undoubtedly become more firmly connected with the biology of whole organisms and with evolution, and then it will become of greater concern for those more interested in the nature of man than in the nature of molecules.
>
> In fact at the level of molecular structure and interaction, information storage and transfer, energy transactions, and other defining characteristics of life, man is hardly significantly *different from a bacterium*—another illustration of the fact that that level of study is not particularly useful in considering the nature of men (emphasis added).[1]

and R. V. Eck concludes:

> Such ancient systems are extremely conservative because so many diverse later reactions have become intricately dependent on them that *they are no longer "free" to evolve.* A mutational change which might be beneficial in one way, in almost every case would be at a strong disadvantage in many other ways. When such a mutation occurred, the process of natural selection would therefore reject it. This conservative principle enables us to comprehend why ferredoxin from a living organism could still retain detectable details of its ancient origin.

Thus, in organisms still living there may exist biochemical relics of the era encompassing the *origin and evolution of the genetic mechanism*. Determination of the sequences of proteins such as ferredoxin and of nucleic acids such as transfer RNA, whose prototypes must have functioned at this early time should make possible a detailed reconstruction of the biochemical evolutionary events of this era (emphasis added).[2]

Top Scientists Concede Immutability of DNA

Many scientists recognize that the study of molecular biology lends no support to the evolutionist stand. Even now, they know that the DNA molecules of the various kinds of living beings are structurally all alike. Also, scientists know that DNA molecules are quite immutable and resist the conversion of one kind to another, in spite of observed mutations from radiation and variations according to Mendel's laws.

Some scientists look for new discoveries of the science of the future to try to explain unplanned and unguided deterministic "evolution" of the first DNA molecule with the genetic mechanism of any one living organism. There is no "Higher" or "Lower" any more.

The amoeba, the algae, or man each has a DNA code of the same atomic complexity, with about a million atoms each in the same kind of arrangement. Just think of the information written into the DNA slate of only about a million atoms. Man knows how to distinguish about 2,000 atoms, the various isotopes of our 100 natural and synthetic elements.

Only about ten of these are found in the DNA; and yet, each DNA code for man is nominally the same though we know that this structure—far too small to see under the optical microscope—has in it the information that differentiates you, your voice, your manner, your color combinations, your basic skills, your inherited susceptibility to various diseases, and of course also, your general appearance, from billions of other human beings.

It is comforting to know that there is at least a bucket full of spaces for factual observations for every drop we now have. Similarly, oceans of facts reach out into space from which our spacemen are recovering an ever-increasing number of pearls of wisdom. That immensity of space also contains facts to be discerned by new methods and apparatus. It is a grand new horizon for exploration, among facts and properties to which we are blind at the present. Certainly the average atom of the DNA must have associated with it no less than one millionth of the information to be coded. How is that possible?

While identical twins are as much alike as one can measure by all the tests known, ordinary twins and other persons differ from one another by at least 100 detectable variations. With at least 10 billion people past and present to differ from, one can safely say that there are a million million differences to be found among the million atoms making up the DNA of human beings, which are nominally alike as far as molecular structure and composition are concerned.

So each one of the million atoms of the DNA must somehow, on the average, help to convey one million traits and characteristics. While we know a lot about each element and isotope, a million properties are beyond our science by say 10,000 fold.

New Explanations Are Likely

All this would be a conundrum if we did not know that there is much more than this that is to be known, based on Planck's length, which is about 10^{20} (a hundred billion billion) times as small as the nucleus of the atom. Planck's length can be derived mechanically by accepting Maxwell's equations and Einstein's relativity and principle of equivalence (now a proven law), that matter is energy and vice versa.

If an electron and a positron are allowed to fall toward one another until they obtain the relativistic mass and density of a nucleus (which is also the threshold energy for electrons to interact with a nucleus for pair formation), then the separate charges moving at the velocity of light, produce a magnetic field equal to their new mass. Much heavier nuclei can also be explained this way. The gravitational constant can be derived from the attractions of such dipoles. Newton's laws of motion are also explained, since these charges rotate about one another at 0.91 times the velocity of light. A change in the velocity of displacement causes a relativistic increase in mass, exactly matching the requirements of Newton's laws. The separation of the paths of the charges become the distance of Planck's length and can obtain information in the pattern of their weave.

Therefore, we see that there are many steps available for defining details we could not possibly enumerate. Theoretically, the individual atom can carry in its nucleus—if composed of the required number of such couples of plus and minus charges (309 for each neutron, 308.5 for each proton)—more information than is in all the books of the biggest library.

The steps of differentiation are each small in energy content so that they are able to receive and transfer the information with the available electromagnetic power involved in thought. So we do not deal with the "extremely unlikely" in these concepts.

Statistics Show Odds Against Chance Assemblies

The DNA assembly uses only 20 out of 64 possible sub-assemblies. The basic units are called nucleotides. They are arranged in a spiral rope ladder-like structure, made of a purine, pyramidine, sugar, and phosphate unit, each group of four forming one of many rung sections.

The 15,000 or more atoms of the individual sub-assemblies, if left to chance as required by the evolutionary theory, would go together in any of 10^{87} different ways. (This is ten billion with 77 more ciphers behind it.) It is like throwing 15,000 dice at one time to determine what specific molecule to make; and then to test each one for the survival of the fittest until the one out of 10^{87} different possibilities is proven by the survival of the fittest to be the right one.

Just think, only 20 of these possible amino acids are actually used in nature to form, describe, and prescribe all the kinds of life known. And only a small amount of each individual cell of each living organism is made up of the DNA molecule. Theoretically, each cell could be multiplied and grown into the living whole just like growing a plant from a slip.

Now, let us try to locate, and hold for assembly, the sub-assemblies of 20 kinds out of the 10^{87} kinds that should form at random, if any did form. Lo and behold! The dice are loaded.

Not all the types of sub-assemblies expected at random are available in the same numbers. One of them is more than 10^{61} (100 billion plus 50 zeros behind it) times as predominant as the average because of its greater thermodynamic stability—as determined by well-established laws of equilibrium concentrations.

This is governed by the same kind of scientific facts as those used in the oil industry to get the best kind of much smaller petroleum molecules out of a refinery process. Even this predominant one is available only once in more than a thousand billion billion. But while you may want two of that predominant one, for finding each of the other units you have to wade through more than 10^{61} (more than 10 billion multiplied by itself six times).

Fortunately, one can find five more kinds of molecules that are used in the DNA for every 100,000 or so of the first. But then, the picking gets that much leaner for the other 14 kinds out of the 10^{87} possible ones, diluted by the predominant ones, which are there and reform in the equilibrium that must be maintained, if any of them are in position to form. Obviously, the creation of order out of random positions and rotations in each of the six degrees of freedom calls for the reversal of the laws of thermodynamics on a fantastic scale in addition to the required activation energies.

No wonder Einstein said about theistic evolution, "God does not throw dice," long before this extreme complexity was known. Nobel Laureate Dr. Harold C. Urey explained that there is not enough matter in the universe to make the many kinds of sub-assemblies that would form at random, if any do.

Let us now assume we have overcome the laws of chance generation which would call for the production of more than 10^{87} kinds of amino acids to pick and test from the survival of the fittest and to be put together in one specific way out of 4^{10000} alternate ways (yes, that is four multiplied by itself ten thousand times), for each and any one species. We find that this is for asexual reproduction.

Sexual reproduction requires that the same unique macro-molecular composition would appear (a) at the same place, (b) at the very same instant, (c) twice, (d) with exactly the correct temperature, (e) velocity, and (f) direction to meet and to stay together, (g) without interference from others for a long enough time to entwine together to make the first DNA pair in (h) a specific nutrient medium that is then protected somehow by, (i) a membrane, which permits (j) the RNA-smaller than DNA and (k) the hundreds of enzymes to (1) function together simultaneously (m) in a complex pattern of action, (n) somehow pre-trained or by "inherited" self-control.

Creation Required Specific Plans and Control of Individual Atoms

Now, if the exact kind and number of amino acid molecules were counted out and confined and somehow, *against the laws of nature*, also protected against "the survival of the fittest" in a thermodynamic equilibrium, one would still have only one chance out of 10^{31} (10 billion with 21 ciphers added) to obtain the one combination for any one species as a dead agglomerate.

WHY NOT CREATION?

To put life into this assemblage would be like expecting a fantastically large and complex organ to assemble itself from its parts; and then, somehow, start playing the most perfectly harmonious and varied music, new and original, continuously—all by itself. "Only metabolism" comparable to the chimney draft due to the sun would be available to furnish the energy. That organ represents merely a tiny part of the DNA code in a single cell of any one living organism.

Instruments are even now available that listen to this music for us in the form of electron spin resonance, Mossbauer effect, nuclear magnetic moment and resonance measurements. They detect the difference between the living and dead matter very easily.

The great fact so clearly established now is that this is the minimum organization for a living organism. It is as basic as the proof of Pasteur that only life begets life in answer to the notions about spontaneous generation of about a century ago.

Even now, this unsupported theory of spontaneous generation is still being promoted so that great scientists like Vannevar Bush have to define the problem of proving it all over again and point out the trivial support for such teachings. He states, "Science, when understood properly, makes man humble in his ignorance and smallness."[3]

All this says that it would be as near infinitely times as improbable to convert one kind into another by spontaneous generation, as it is for the first kind to form from the elements in the first place. Who would have predicted this from the coarse measurements of the past?

It is the new tools that show that each DNA code from that of the lowest to the highest organism differs, but also has the same atomic complexity. Even the data on the amino acid sequence for small proteins like the cytochrome C gene differs for each of the mammals. It is like having to use a different kind of oil in each car.

George G. Simpson, the leader in promoting evolutionary concepts in the United States, acknowledges that evolution requires the suspension or breaking of very basic, well-established thermodynamic laws, and as well: "It requires an attitude of hope if not of faith to *assume* that the *acquistion of organic adaptability* was *deterministic* or *inevitable*. . . ."[4]

He also recognizes that, granted macromolecules (by spontaneous generation) then: "The further organization of those molecules into cellular life would seem to have a far different, very much lower order of probability."[5] He points out additional hurdles and limitations of the theory, even mentions creation as an alternative to having hope and faith in long time intervals for chance and accidents to occur that are "so incredibly intricate" and "extremely unlikely."

Dr. Simpson also discusses the conditions that cause the fixity of species or kinds, but does not express it as positively as Thomas H. Jukes, who concludes a very learned review by saying: "One cannot imagine amino acids detaching themselves from a protein, combining with sRNA, and lining up in order to synthesize a messenger strand which would return to the nucleus to make a new gene." [6] Similarly Hinegardner and Engelberg regard the production of merely *a new enzyme* by the mutation of the genetic code—*incredible.*[7]

You can see from this that it would be much less of a miracle for God to create what He wants than to do that next to impossible job of selection and assembly called for by evolutionists. This says nothing about the RNA and enzymes that must be ready to do their job at the same time in cooperation with presupposed sustenance for metabolism.

Even before all these newly reported hurdles to spontaneous generation were understood, Simpson had arrived at the following conclusion: In spite of the information that there are likely to be at least 100,000,000 other planets in the universe as suitable for our type of life as the earth, it is extremely unlikely that life could have "evolved" by natural causes in any proposed time period to produce a being of some form that could plan and communicate. He would be the last to claim evolution as inevitable. You can then see why Simpson also allows for the possibility that it took a Superior Power.

Popular Notions Behind Current Science

While many top scientists are very active in pointing out that no facts of science contradict the Bible speaking for itself, it is important to state that the references cited were taken from reports that are written in the vein of evolutionary theory. However, top scientists generally try their best not to overstate their opinions. They show more respect for the marvels of nature than most theologians do, simply because good scientists know how to ask many and bigger questions than they can answer, while the novice does not know how little he knows.

Any indication of direction, pre-selection, or plan of action or design is strictly taboo, since only the test of the survival of the fittest may determine final use. A case in point is Dr. Christian B. Anfinsen, who just as much as disclaims evolution by saying, "We like to believe that Nature has been very wise and efficient in the design of the chemical compounds, however large and complicated, which make up the structure and machinery of living things."[8] Then he goes on to illustrate it.

Far from calling evolution a fact, he says, "It is unlikely that we shall ever have more than opinions regarding the origin of life." [9] This is the best kind of genuine testimony free of prejudice in favor of the Bible. While the DNA of some mammals differs from others by only two of these 20 sub-assemblies, man differs from others by 17. It would shock the old fashioned thinking of evolutionists on observations about a million times more coarse than now, to know their nearest DNA relatives.

On the other hand, the story of creation must have been written for the space age, as well as for the Hebrews, because it took until now to knock out of our heads the last of each successive generation of man's speculations about the formation of the earth, and all that was brought forth on it.

We just did not know enough facts to understand those specific words of Genesis One before this, so in our blindness some people condemned them to mythology. Nobel Laureate Glenn Seaborg, chairman of our Atomic Energy Commission reads it for what it says, in awe of the significance. Many scientists share this awe. Some would-be-scientists think they know better.

The men to be pitied most, however, are those biologists who have seen the ones who have shattered their image of evolution by the new science of molecular biology now earning so many Nobel prizes. They even try to ridicule it in top journals as one did in *Science*, by calling DNA—the holy trinity.

Basic Scientific Insights Result of Revelation

Even some of the tough theological points, long since ditched by modern rationalists and humanists, are now related to and explained by phenomena encountered in the physical sciences. A recent Nobel prize winner, for the discovery of the maser, Provost and Professor of Physics at M.I.T., Dr. Charles H. Townes, empasizes the role of faith and revelation. He stated:

> Einstein spent the last half of his life looking for a unity between gravitational and electromagnetic fields. Many physicists feel that he was on the wrong track, and no one yet knows whether he made any substantial progress. But he had faith in a great vision

of unity and order, and he worked intensively at it for thirty years or more. Einstein had to have the kind of dogged conviction that could have allowed him to say with Job, "Though he slay me, yet will I trust in him."

For lesser scientists, on lesser projects, there are frequent occasions when things just don't make sense and making order and understanding out of one's work seems almost hopeless. But still the scientist has faith that there is order to be found, and that either he or his colleagues will someday find it. . . .

Another common idea about the difference between science and religion is based on their methods of discovery. *Religion's discoveries often come by great revelations.* Scientific knowledge, in the popular mind, comes by logical deductions, or by the accumulation of data which is analyzed by established methods in order to draw generalizations called laws. But such a description of scientific discovery is a travesty on the real thing. *Most of the important scientific discoveries come about very differently and are much more closely akin to revelation.* The term itself is generally not used for scientific discovery, since we are in the habit of reserving revelation for the religious realm. In scientific circles one speaks of intuition, accidental discovery, or says simply that "he had a wonderful idea" (emphasis added).

If we compare how great scientific ideas arrive, they look remarkably like religious revelation viewed in a non-mystical way.

Think of Moses in the desert, long troubled and wondering about the problem of saving the children of Israel, when suddenly he had a revelation by the burning bush.

Consider some of the revelations of the new Testament. . . .

Similarly, the scientists, after hard work and much emotional and intellectual commitment to a troubling problem, sometimes suddenly see the answer. Such ideas much more often come during off-moments than while confronting data.

A striking and well-known example is the discovery of the benzene ring by Kékulé, who while musing at his fireside was led to the idea by a vision of snakes taking their tails in their mouths. We cannot yet describe the human process which leads to the creation of an important and substantially new scientific insight. *But it is clear that the great scientific discoveries, the real leaps, do not usually come from the so-called "scientific method," but rather more as did Kékulé's—with perhaps less picturesque imagery, but by revelations which are just as real* (emphasis added).[10]

This has been recorded for all branches of arts and music; and for physical sciences, particularly in the cases of Newton's theory of gravitation, Maxwell's theory of electromagnetism, Einstein's theory of relativity, Planck's theory of the quantum of action, and Heisenberg's uncertainty principle. All these have been established.

Townes continued:

> Can religious beliefs also be viewed as working hypotheses, tested and validated by experience? To some this may seem a secular and even an abhorrent view. In any case, it discards absolutism in religion. But I see no reason why the acceptance of religion on this basis should be objectionable. The validity of religious ideas must be and has been tested and judged through the ages by societies and by individual experience. Is there any great need for them to be more absolute than the law of gravity? The latter is a working hypothesis whose basis and permanency we do not know. But on our belief in it, as well as on many other complex scientific hypotheses, we risk our lives daily. . . .
>
> We must also expect paradoxes and not be surprised or unduly troubled by them. We know of paradoxes in physics, such as that concerning the nature of light, which have been resolved by deeper understanding. We know of some which are still unresolved. In the realm of religion, *we are troubled by the suffering around us and its apparent inconsistency with a God of love. Such paradoxes confronting science do not usually destroy our faith in science. They simply remind us of a limited understanding, and at times provide a key to learning more* (emphasis added).
>
> Perhaps there will be in the realm of religion cases of the uncertainty principle, which we now know is such a characteristic phenomenon of physics. If it is fundamentally impossible to determine accurately both the position and velocity of a particle, it should not surprise us if similar limitations occur in other aspects of our experience. This opposition in the precise determination of two quantities is also referred to as complementarity; position and velocity represent complementary aspects of a particle, only one of which can be measured precisely at any one time.
>
> Nils Bohr has already suggested that perception of man, or any living organism as a whole, and of his physical constitution represents this kind of complementarity. That is, the precise and close examination of the atomic makeup of man may of necessity blur our view of him as a living and spiritual being. In any case, there seems to be *no justification for the dogmatic position taken by some that the remarkable phenomenon of individual human personality can be expressed completely in terms of the presently known laws of behavior of atoms and molecules. Justice and*

love may also represent such complementarity. A completely loving approach and the simultaneous meting out of exact justice hardly seem consistent (emphasis added).[11]

But what loving parent has not appeared inconsistent to his child? God's well-defined purpose, and generally also that of the parent, is to mete out justice, "for your own good and to prepare you for much bigger and more important responsibilities of the future."

The late Dr. W. F. G. Swann, a great physicist and former director of the Bartol Research Foundation of the Franklin Institute, has left an expression of his views. After presenting proofs of purpose—design—plan—intelligence as evidenced in creation, he presents a challenge to any materialistic scientist.

Any materialistic scientist, who wants to claim evolution rather than admit the truth of the proofs of design, is challenged to present one or more items in any part of the creation which could be improved upon by the materialist, or by "chance." Near the close of his article, Dr. Swann wrote:

. . . as an end thought, I picture our very materialitic physicist who has designed his universe, and then, as a hell, is condemned to live in it.[12]

The materialistic physicist would surely forget some side effects, by which our great scientific technology has been plagued so very much. After writing that the existence of intelligence may be regarded as an observational fact, Swann explained,

And when I speak of intelligent design I mean the kind of design which is sufficiently like that which one of our engineers might have aspired to achieve; but so far beyond the powers of any living engineer to achieve, that it must, of necessity, leave mankind extremely humble in the estimation of his own powers.[13]

Recently, a most candid presentation of the best case noted so far for the evolutionary theory became available: *Chromosomes, Giant Molecules, and Evolution*, by Bruce Wallace.[14] I could point to many references for evidence for order, system, plan, direction, and efficiency in the author's use of genetic material; presented in an able way. For example, he states, "Is there any simpler solution to the problem of reproduction? I do not think that there is."[15] What a wonderful testimony for an all wise Creator!

Since when has anyone, anything, any happenstance, any shaking of dice or alphabet blocks come up with any admittedly more efficient solution when "there are literally billions of ways in which nucleic acid code words could have been assigned to the twenty amino acids."[16] Yes, there was one Source that overcame His own laws of nature like making water run uphill, to create energy and matter in fantastic simplicity and in beauty of complexity. Then He created the unique conditions and life on earth, allowing us very endowed creatures, in these last great years, to unravel some of the mysteries of that perfect order, unity, and efficiency of His creation.

Using the criteria presented by Dr. Wallace himself, as he wrote, "Search diligently for the adequate, reject the untestable—those are the recognized procedures of the laboratory, the classroom, the clinic, and the courtroom.." [17] The subject can best be closed with his words:

> At the very outset the following point was conceded: any person who is firmly and unalterably convinced that each of today's species of plants and animals arose by an act of special creation will find no evidence in this book that will compel him to change his mind. There simply is no such evidence, nor can there ever be. A Divine Being of infinite wisdom, we must all admit, could have created living forms in a manner that would have dribbled off as by-products all of these things we have gleaned as evidence for evolution. We can only say that He went about His task in a way that mimicked evolution in every detail; it is *unfortunate* that some event did not occur which would have clearly ruled out evolutionary theory (emphasis added).[18]

Fortunately, events have occurred which clearly do rule out this theory by the criteria presented. It is "untestable" because, "There simply is no such evidence, nor can there ever be."

Second, the laws of chance (which are well used by Dr. Wallace for his purpose of showing that it must be easier to modify an existing DNA code in a living cell than to start over from scratch) also show that they are not "adequate" to provide proof that any kind of DNA and its metabolism with RNA and enzymes in a nutrient medium protected by a membrane could possibly be formed by chance in the first place.

Just think how much less likely it is, that Wallace's most "simple solution to the problem of reproduction," "literally out of billions of ways," starting with the four bases available in a cell, would be produced by chance actions.

Finally, what is the probability of chance actions to go counter to well-established laws of thermodynamics? Being an honest scientist, Dr. Wallace does not claim this, nor have any other authorities. Not even the formation of only one new enzyme in a living cell is considered credible.[19]

Dr. Wallace also is true scientist enough to report the reason for such failures: "Each protein consists of tens, hundreds, or even thousands of amino-acid molecules attached to one another in a specified order; slight alterations in the sequence in which amino acids are strung together can destroy the biological function of a protein molecule." [20]

It is also well known that the mere insertion of the correct base unit in a reversed position leads to death. And yet there are those who have faith in *chance*, enough to believe the admittedly unprovable. Somehow accidental changes should suffice to provide the basis for a new species in one DNA strand of the many parallel strands and change the whole by a miracle.

Are we to believe that the same very complex accident can occur in the same position on all the DNA strands in both male and the female chromosomes which then "happen" to mate?

Still another way for producing a new variant could be by virgin birth. This is proven to occur under the most rigid laboratory conditions, among controlled strains of mammals used for research.

The chances would be enormously increased, but still, would be too hard to swallow. And yet, with direction, plan, and control, its occurrence is more likely, and may well be established through intensive research some day. Just to be able to produce a new, genetically perfect pair from the same flesh might open our eyes to the great depth of shared thoughts and feelings and the intimacy with the Creator of such a couple.

On the other hand, there are thousands of people, including the present writer, who experience and live by the guidance of the Creator, and have been privileged to see and live through critical turning points in their lives far ahead of the time of decision. Though blessed with enough adversity to keep them struggling, they carry on with that guidance that has not failed them. Since science has verified statement after statement in the Bible, then for us to accept as our personal Guide, our Creator, is a small act of faith indeed.

NOTES AND REFERENCES

1. G. G. Simpson, *Science* (April 22, 1966), pp. 472-478.
2. R. V. Eck, *Science* (April 15, 1966), pp. 363-366.
3. Vannebar Bush, *Fortune* Magazine (May, 1965).
4. G. G. Simpson, *Science* (February 21, 1964), 143:769-775.
5. *Ibid.*
6. Thomas H. Jukes, *American Scientist* (1965), 53:487-488.
7. Hinegardner and Engelberg, *Science* (May 22, 1964), p. 1031.
8. Christian B. Anfinsen, *The Molecular Basis of Evolution*, in the preface.
9. *Ibid.*
10. Charles H. Townes, "The Convergence of Science and Religion," *Think* (April, 1966).
11. *Ibid.*
12. W. F. G. Swann, "Blueprint of the Universe," *Science of Mind* (April, 1967), p. 16.
13. *Ibid.*, p. 13.
14. Bruce Wallace, *Chromosomes, Giant Molecules, and Evolution* (New York: W. W. Norton and Co., Inc., 1966).
15. *Ibid.*, p. 19.
16. *Ibid.*, p. 156.
17. *Ibid.*, p. 5.
18. *Ibid.*, p. 76.
19. Hinegardner and Engelberg, *Science* (May 22, 1964), p. 1031.
20. Wallace, *op. cit.*, p. 20.

Chapter 9

Botanical and Zoological Evidence

1

ANALYSIS OF SO-CALLED EVIDENCES OF EVOLUTION

WILBERT RUSCH, SR.

Introductory Observation

Before one begins to write in this semantic age of ours, it has become necessary to define terms—for instance, the term "creation." So I submit that in my opinion the theory of creation asserts that:

a) Organisms now living have descended from organisms of the same created kind, as referred to in Genesis;

b) within such created kinds, processes of change may have occurred and do occur to such an extent as to produce individuals differing in various degrees from their parents, yet never sufficiently different to constitute a new "kind" (for example, the various breeds of dogs, and the several races of men);

c) such physical changes, which are demonstrated to have appeared in organisms since their creation, have arisen through degeneration because of the Fall of Man or through natural causes which now continue to be in operation and which therefore can be studied experimentally.

I also should define the term "evolution." I am well aware of the fact that there are in both Standen and Kerkut references to two theories of evolution. However, in the majority of our present day science books, certainly those in the elementary, secondary, and undergraduate levels, the word evolution usually means what Kerkut and Standen both call the "general theory of evolution," that is, the theory that all the living forms in the world have arisen from a single source which itself came from an inorganic form. This is "amoeba to man" evolution and is the meaning of the word evolution as I am using the term in this presentation.

Now if it happens that more persons hold to one particular philosophy than another, that does not make the first philosophy true. It could actually be that the minority view may express the truth, with the majority view being false. So it is with evolution; the number who believe in it is no guarantee of its truth.

An honest person will accept items which have actual existence as facts. On this there should be no disagreement. But the hypotheses that are built on such facts, as well as the reconstruction of past events, are all legitimate grist for differences. As Dr. George once wrote, "Facts remain but theories crumble." [1] I might also point out that Dr. James Conant has said, "Statements about the past, predictions about the future, generalizations about what event will follow another, are all grist for the mill of the thoroughgoing sceptic." [2]

We find ourselves in a dilemma because those who subscribe to evolution take a body of facts and interpret them one way, while those who subscribe to creation take the same body of facts and interpret them another way. It is my contention that actually neither can be proven, both must be taken on faith.

And let me underline this last clause, *both* must be taken on faith. Evolution is not a fact, it is a theory. Recently the French biologist, Prof. Louis Bounoure, quoted Yves Delage, a late Sorbonne professor of zoology, as saying:

> I readily admit that no species has ever been known to engender another, and that there is no absolutely definite evidence that such a thing has taken place. Nonetheless, I *believe* evolution to be just as certain as if it had been objectively proved.[3]

Incidentally, Bounoure comments: "In short what science asks of us here is an act of faith, and it is in fact under the guise of a sort of revealed truth that the idea of evolution is generally put forward."

Dr. Bounoure, formerly president of the Biological Society of Strasburg, as well as Director of the Zoological Museum and still director of research at the National Center of Scientific Research in France, also wrote—"Evolutionism is a fairy tale for grown-ups. This theory has helped nothing in the progress of science. It is useless." In a later article on the same subject, Bounoure quoted from a present day Sorbonne professor of paleontology, Jean Pivateau, the admission that the science of facts as regards evolution "cannot accept any of the different theories which seek to explain evolution. It even finds itself in opposition with each one of these theories. There is something here which is both disappointing and disquieting." [4] More on this aspect will appear later.

At this point I must digress on the subject of quotes. The plaintive cry is often raised that a creationist may not use an evolutionist's statement as a support for a creationist's point of view. I submit that this complaint is invalid. For one thing, no reputable creationist attempts to portray an evolutionist as supporting the case of creation. This is not the intent of the quote. But if the evolutionist mentions a point in his writing that the creationist can use to his advantage, then by all the rules of evidence he is free to do so.

Certainly any piece of favorable evidence an attorney can pry out of a hostile witness is choice evidence indeed, and the attorney would be a fool not to make the most of it. Further, the dilemmas of evolution are often best presented by its proponents. They certainly can be trusted to minimize their difficulties, so I can scarcely be charged with exaggerating them. So, for the record, assume I quote from those of evolutionist persuasion, unless I identify the man's position as being otherwise. In this connection I would like to draw your attention to some words that W. R. Thompson wrote in 1956:

> As we know, there is a great divergence of opinion among biologists, not only about the causes of evolution but even about the actual process. This divergence exists because the evidence is unsatisfactory and does not permit any certain conclusions. It is therefore right and proper to draw the attention of the non-scientific public to the disagreements about evolution. But some recent remarks of evolutionsts show that they think this unreasonable. The situation where scientific men rally to the defense of a doctrine they are unable to define scientifically, much less demonstrate with scientific rigor, attempting to maintain its credit with the public by the suppression of criticism and the elimination of difficulties, is abnormal and undesirable in science.[5]

The statement that "everyone working in science accepts evolution as a fact" is often used as an argument for compelling the acceptance of evolution over against creation. I submit that this statement is not true, and I think that can be indicated by the known position of the following individuals:

Dr. Frank L. Marsh, professor of biology at Andrews University; Dr. Henry Morris, Professor of hydraulic engineering and head of the Civil Engineering Department, Virginia Polytechnic Institute; Dr. Walter E. Lammerts, in the past on the faculty of the University of California and for many years research director of Germain's, in addition to being the leading rose breeding authority on the west coast; Dr. Thomas Barnes, director of the Schellinger Research Laboratory, also on the faculty of Texas Western University; Dr. W. R. Thompson, former director of the Commonwealth Institute of Biological Control, Ottawa, Canada; Dr. J. J. Duyvenné de Wit, late head of the Zoology Department, Orange Free State University; Dr. John Moore, professor of science education, Michigan State University; Dr. Louis Wolfanger, professor of soil science, Michigan State University; Dr. Duane Gish, biochemist of the Upjohn Laboratories, Kalamazoo, Michigan; Dr. George Howe, professor of biology, Westmont College, California; and Dr. C.E.A. Turner, professor of chemistry, Surrey, England.

I am personally acquainted with all of these men and have been in correspondence with them many times. I am positive that each one in turn could name an equally large and possibly more impressive circle of men with whom they are acquainted and who also do not accept evolution as a fact. For example, Dr. Lammerts has told me that there are five friends of his who are all Ph.D.'s in nuclear physics on the staff of the Lawrence Radiation Laboratories, and who are involved in the government operation "Plowshare." All five of these men are creationists, although they are nuclear physicists.

To mention an additional few, I could add to this list the late Dr. L. Merson-Davies, gold medallist in geology, of England; the late Dr. Paul Lemoine, curator of the Natural History Museum, Paris, France; as well as Dr. Martin Lings, currently of the British Museum; and Professor Louis Bounoure of the National Center of Scientific Research, France.

Finally, I am in the unique position to know, as treasurer of the organization, that the Creation Research Society has more than 300 members who have earned Ph.D., M.D., or similar degrees in science and have signed a statement of belief in creation as opposed to evolution as voting members. Now I am willing to grant that this number may be in the minority, but that there is nobody working in the field of science of reputation who does not accept evolution as a fact is a statement I simply will not accept.

I think another valid question to be raised is, "Could books and articles on creation be scarce because the creationist view cannot get a fair hearing?" I ask the reader to judge from the following three examples. I feel that the situation is a little less biased in England, since I know that the *Journals of the Transactions of the Victoria Institute* are open to creationists' as well as evolutionists' viewpoints. Some recent studying I have been doing indicates that on the Continent, particularly in France and Germany, the question of evolution is even more open. Actually, the only two possibilities regarding the origin of the living world are development by transformisms (evolution) or creation by God.

The position of the science of today over against creation may best be demonstrated as follows:

(a) Dr. S. Zucherman once wrote:

> Either evolutionary change or miraculous divine intervention lies at the back of human intelligence. The second of these possibilities does not lend itself to scientific examination. It may be the correct explanation, but, from a scientific point of view, it cannot be legitimately resorted to in answer to the problem of man's dominantly successful behavior until all possibilities of more objective explanation thru morphological, physiological and psychological observation and experiment are exhausted.[6]

(b) Dr. W. R. Thompson recently wrote me that the chapter on evolution in his recently reissued work, *Science and Common Sense*,[7] would be much stronger against evolution were he to write it today. As he put it, at the time he wrote it the book had to be passed by a reader who had strong evolutionistic views, and therefore Thompson was forced to compromise to get the book published.

(c) The noted columnist, George Sokolsky, touched on another example when he wrote,

> So it appears from what can be learned about it that certain scientists, including leading astronomers, threatened Macmillan with a boycott of their textbooks if they did not rid themselves of Professor Velikovsky's book. Of course, what the learned and liberal professors wanted really was a total suppression of a book which opposes their dogma.[8]

Macmillan yielded to the threats, since they were an extensive publisher of textbooks, and transferred the publishing operations to Doubleday and Company, which does not publish science texts and therefore was immune to such a threat. Actually, Doubleday published all five of Velikovsky's works.

As a continuation of this story, I also refer the reader to John Larrabee's article in *Harper's* Magazine, entitled "Was Velikovsky

Right?" [9] I think this article ought to be required reading for all who maintain that scientists are completely objective, never biased, and thus not like the average human being. Larrabee points out that as early as 1950 Velikovsky predicted the high temperature of Venus, the radio emissions from Jupiter, as well as the phenomenon we know as the Van Allen radiation belts. For none of this has Velikovsky been given any credit on the basis of priority, nor have his predictions even been acknowledged in any of the descriptive writings on these matters.

Readers may be interested in a new work, edited by Alfred de Grazia, who is editor of the *American Behavioral Scieintist*. This book, *The Velikovsky Affair*,[10] documents the rising up in arms of the scientific establishment against Velikovsky's work as well as against the man personally. This, because his work launched an assault against the established theories of astronomy, biology, historical geology, and ancient history. It is interesting to read how such men as Harlow Shapley[11] and Fred Whipple[12] exerted pressure on first the publisher, Macmillan, and then Blakiston to prevent publication of the work. In addition to Velikovsky himself, casualties were James Putnam of Macmillan[13] and Gordon Atwater,[14] curator of the Hayden Planetarium, who were summarily dismissed from their posts for their support of Velikovsky's work.

There is an interesting paragraph that reads,

> Although American scientists and science editors continue to ignore—or rail against—Velikovsky's ideas, impersonal science itself continues to explode its own more conventional theories by turning up new evidence. Much new evidence tends to support Velikovsky; some of it is simply compatible with his views; up to now none of it has refuted them.[15]

To avoid misunderstanding, I should mention that Velikovsky is not a creationist, although considered a scientific heretic of the first magnitude.

In this country, almost all books dealing with creation that I know of have been published by religious book houses.

Evolution and Classification

The theory of evolution is based on a number of fundamental considerations. The first one I would like to consider briefly is classification or taxonomy. This argument runs along these lines: Since it is possible to classify organisms, it is held that all true classification should be genealogical. And so we have taxonomists reshuffling classifications of plants and animals in an effort to find new natural systems of classification. Then any current system of classification is held to be natural, and thus a proof of evolution.

Frankly, the fact that we can group living and fossil forms of life into some thirty animal phyla and some twenty-five plant divisions would be the last thing one should expect from an evolutionary development. While these major phyla and divisions aren't as clear cut as we might like them to be, nevertheless they are stable and recognizable entities. But a random evolutionary development should call for an enormous hodge-podge, rather than a small number of recognizable entities compared to total species number.

Furthermore, that we can arrange animals and plants into groups on the basis of resemblances should be no more significant for developmental history than that we can arrange elements into families. I have yet to hear a chemist propose that the halogen series evolved from fluorine to iodine, because it is possible to arrange them in this series.

We may also ask the question, "Why should the type form insect or cephalopod continue to be inherited in the face of random variations, if transformism be true?" Even in a lower hierarchical level, despite all repeated mutations, the majority of species and all genera are real entities. This was recognized by C. E. Davenport, who wrote,

> When I study thrips and wish to secure a species described fifty or more years ago as living in a certain composite plant in eastern Russia, then if I go to the designated locality and look in the designated species of flower, I will find the species with all the characters described fifty or 100 thrip generations ago. How is such an experience to be harmonized with universal mutations?[16]

Davenport says this is the heart of the problem of evolution.

The evolutionist says that when we find animals and nature grading in complexity of structure from a protozoan to a mammal at the other extreme, this proves that evolution from one cell to a multicellular form has taken place. The creationist says that a multiplicity of forms was part of the design of the creator. Both these statements are logical. Which one is correct? Since this is subjective evidence (animals and plants don't carry classification labels) an argument could be endless on this subject with no progress possible. I might quote the late Dr. Austin H. Clark, once curator of the U. S. National Museum, who wrote,

It is almost invariably assumed that animals with bodies composed of a single cell represent the primitive animals from which all others are derived. They are commonly supposed to have preceded all other animal types in their appearance. There is not the slightest basis for this assumption beyond the circumstance that in arithmetic—which is not zoology—the number one precedes the other numbers.[17]

Evolution and Comparative Anatomy

Much has been made of comparative anatomy as an argument for evolution. And again we reach an impasse. If a creationist and an evolutionist strolled through a museum, the latter would look at the specimens displayed and hold that structural similarity in mammals, for example, suggests that all forms have evolved from a common ancestor. Of course the former, seeing the same displays, would believe that the structural similarities suggest a common general design to meet a common environment created by God. Again there is no correct conclusion possible, since the evidence is subjective, to be bent depending on the belief of the individual using it.

However, a word of caution has to be injected here. To think of animals in terms of bones and dead bodies alone is not enough. Certainly, for example, the difference between cat and dog transcends the anatomical and physiological; the temperaments of the two animals are different and this also represents part of the innate difference between these two animals.

I would also like to point out the following fallacy. A scientist looks at an animal, names a certain bone, then looks at another animal and uses the same name for a corresponding part. He then postulates the bone is the same. Therefore the similarity is supposed to have phylogenetic significance, and he now uses this as evidence for evolution. Obviously the postulate of homology is a subjective one created by his own mind, which may or may not be correct.

Particularly in the case of the fossils are these two cautions necessary. Animal fossils are classified on the basis of skeletal parts solely, ignoring, of necessity, since they are absent, such characteristics as warmbloodedness, the number of heart chambers, red blood cell structure, presence or absence of a diaphragm, and the like.

Evolution and Vestigial Organs

A third proposed proof of evolution is vestigial organs. These are structures that are found in some animal or human organisms that are considered to have no use in the present form, but have had a use in previous forms and therefore represent a sort of "memory" of an evolutionary ancestor. Truly the fate of vestigial organs has been rather sad.

In the human being, there was once a long list of such organs that we considered as useless remnants of man's evolutionary past. Although this list once ran to well over a hundred, today most of the list has gone the way of all flesh. It seems odd to us today to find that such structures as tonsils, the parathyroids, the thymus, the pineal gland, the appendix, and the coccyx were all on this list. I might mention, incidentally, that certainly anyone who has suffered a broken coccyx is painfully aware of the fact that it serves as an anchorage for rectal muscles. Obviously if it is serving a useful function in the body it cannot be a vestigial remnant.

The appendix has now been admitted to play a part in the control of the intestinal flora, and again, since it has proven to have use, particularly in the light of recent observations made in connection with the growth of germ-free organisms, the appendix must be taken off the vestigial list. True, we can get along without our tonsils, and we can get along without our appendix, but we can also get along without one arm and one leg, and certainly nobody in his right mind would thereby class them as being vestigial.

In other animals, the claws on either side of the vent in certain boas and pythons as well as some other snakes have often been pointed to as useless relics of the hind legs of snake ancestors. But Dewar refers to A. K. Martin, who wrote "The Ways of Man and Beast in India," and who therein reports observing that these protuberances are of assistance in the movement of these snakes. Others have also referred to the fact that the spurs projecting from the python serve as a means of helping the animal anchor itself in movement through trees.

Two more examples should be mentioned, namely, whales with transitory teeth, and the semilunarfold in man. In man, the latter's main use is to collect foreign material that gets into the eyeball and collect this material into a sticky mass in the corner of the eye, where it can easily be removed and does no damage. This has been reported by E. P. Stibbe.[18]

With respect to the whales that have embryological teeth which never grow into teeth, Vialleton says,

Certain of these supposed vestigial organs deserve special examination, because they play a part that was unknown to Darwin. When he cited as truly vestigial organs the germs of teeth in the fetuses of whales devoid of teeth in the adult state, and those of the upper incisors in certain ruminants, the gums of which they never pierce, he forgot that these germs in mammals, where they are very large relative to the parts enclosing them, play a very important part in the formation of the bones of the jaws, to which they furnish a point on which these mold themselves. Thus these germs do have a function.[19]

Furthermore, Dr. John Cameron reports that he studied a microcephalic idiot of whom the jaws receded due to poor teeth development. He says, "In many of these individuals the teeth never develop at all. The cause of poorly developed jaws is due to a deficiency or actual failure of development of the dental germs." [20]

In his *Transformist Illusion,* Dewar insistently raises a rather pertinent question—namely, where are the nascent organs, those that are about to evolve into useful organs? No one other than Darwin has ever broached this subject. Logically, if new organs are in the process of being developed, then in some animal form we should find some incompletely developed organs which are on the way to develop into fully useful structures later, but at present have no function. Yet I have read absolutely nothing on this subject.

Evolution and Embryology

A fourth point is the evidence from embryology. Haeckel enunciated the Law of Recapitulation or Biogenetic Law in 1866. This is stated succinctly, "Ontogeny recapitulates phylogeny," or the development of the individual repeats the development of his race. Probably one of the main reasons for the lack of effectiveness of this law is that it does not apply to the plant world. This would then mean that since plants and animals are postulated as evolving from a common ancestor, this common ancestor gave rise to two lines of descendants—one following the Law of Recapitulation, the other not! De Beer and Swinton refer to the Law of Recapitulation as "a theory that in spite of its exposure, its effects continue to linger in the nooks and crannies of zoology."[21]

With respect to Sinnott and Wilson's position that some leaves would seem to recapitulate an ancestral trait, De Beer and Swinton say that the Biogenetic Law cannot be true in view of the frequency with which young foliage leaves are found to be more specialized than those formed at later stages. The embryologist Huettner gave a fairly accurate picture of the light in which it is viewed today when he said, "as a law, this principle has been questioned, it has been subjected to careful scrutiny and has been found wanting. There are too many exceptions to it. However, there is no doubt that it contains some truth and that it is of value to the student of embryology." [22]

Huettner proceeds further to point out some other difficulties. It became necessary to divide the characteristics developed in an embryo into primitive (palingenetic) and specialized (cenogenetic) characteristics. Then it developed that there was a problem in differentiating between the two. It is complained that the palingenetic traits are obscured and sometimes eliminated at the expense of the cenogenetic.

For example, there is never a true blastula or gastrula in the mammals. Also, organs do not develop in the proper order. In the earliest fishes found, there are teeth, but no tongue. But in the mammalian embryos, the tongue develops before the teeth. Huettner says that there are numerous cases of this type. It is known that environmental conditions will change the orderly sequence of differentiation in the embryo, which drives one to the conclusion that recapitulation is subject to change. All this leads Huettner to refuse to accept the recapitulation theory as a "law." It is also of interest to note that most crabs hatch out of a larval form known as Zoeas, which differ greatly from the adult form. Yet other crabs hatch out as miniature crabs. Where is the operation of the Biogenetic Law?

Along these same lines, embryologists who make phylogenies sometimes work at embarrassing cross purposes with paleontologists. In human development, it is noted that we find that most of the bones develop from embryonic cartilaginous foundations; for instance, those that develop into the ethmoid, sphenoid, occipitals, as well as the vertebra and the long bones of the fore limbs. This would seem to imply that cartilage is primitive and bone is more advanced. As one grows older, more and more cartilage is replaced by bone. Applied to phylogenies, this would mean that sharks, as cartilaginous fish, would be the precursors of the bony fish. Unfortunately, if you take the paleontological record on its face value, we find there, to our surprise, that the cartilaginous fish have developed apparently from the bony fish, since they occur later in the geological record.

In embryological development, simpler parts must be formed before more complicated ones. In small embryos, shape will be determined by physical forces, which play less and less a part in determining shape as size increases. Many apparent recapitulations may be only expressions of the fact that all animals are built out of the same kind of materials, such as carbohydrates, fats, proteins, etc. Often recapitulation is absurdly irrelevant. For instance, the respiratory surface develops late in an embryo, yet how could earlier forms have survived without it? The head size in the mammalian embryos is relatively enormous but very small in their ancestors.

Long ago, when I worked in embryology, it was pointed out at the time that the embryo has two types of organs: a) Those that do not function until after the child is born, of which the lungs are a good example. Hence we develop only one lung system. b) Organs which have a function during embryonic life as well as later, and hence change form, sometimes several times, to meet changing needs. I would consider the heart and the kidneys in this category. It might be said also that the embryo would seem to follow Maupertuis' postulate of least action.

Origin of Life Discussed

The question is often raised, "What about the ability of scientists to create life?" In these days we so often find a headline proclaiming "Scientists Create Life," only to discover that the progress towards this goal has been a crawl rather than an achievement. What is the true picture.

A theory that deals with the origin of life should start with the inorganic and wind up with at least a functioning cell. Intermediate steps of necessity would be proteins and deoxyribonucleic acids (DNA), as well as the ribonucleic acids (RNA). These are all molecules of tremendous size, but still organic molecules. They are not living, although associated with the growth and reproduction of living things.

Viruses are debatable organisms. F. Bawdin of England, noted virologist, holds that they are degenerate forms of life. Viruses are essentially a protein membrane enclosing a core of DNA. They multiply by invading the cells of an organism and using its cell constituents to produce additional viral units. One virus form that is useful to man invades bacteria and destroys them. These are known as bacteriophages or simply phages.

Stanley Miller first performed the experiment where H_2O, NH_3, and CH_4, when an electric spark was passed through the mixture, produced a soup of simple amino acids. More recently an electron beam has been passed through such a mixture and produced the simple ringed base adenine. This base, classed as a purine, occurs in RNA along with another purine, guanine, as well as pyrimidines such as cytosine, and uracil. Chemists then have also irradiated with ultraviolet light a mixture of H_2O, NH_3, and CH_4 to form HCHO, which has then been polymerized by further radiation to form ribose and deoxyribose. These sugars occur in a typical nucleotide molecule.

An inorganic phosphate has been heated with a mixture of uracil and ribose to link these two compounds together to form diuridilic acid, which is a double linked nucleotide molecule. However, doing this sort of thing in the laboratory under carefully controlled conditions, and having the same thing occur by chance in an open environment are two different things. Furthermore, these results are still a far cry from creating something living. These compounds are still organic chemicals, complex, yes; and this has been a beautiful job of synthesis, but not yet creating life.

Dr. Sol Spiegelman of the University of Illinois recently received a bacteriophage from Japan and isolated an RNA molecule from it. Then from another bacteriophage he also isolated a specific enzyme, replicase. When the two were placed in a nutrient material, other RNA's were produced. In this case, the enzyme can generate identical copies of added viral RNA. This new RNA can infect, by serving as the template for more virus. Each enzyme recognizes the genome for its own RNA and requires it as template for synthesis. However, the presence of more than one nuclease will break the whole procedure down. So this process is simply duplicating some cell chemistry. When Dr. Spiegelman was asked if he had created life in a test tube, he replied, "Only God can create life." [23] Another biochemist at the same time commented, "*If* we knew the chemical composition of each different molecule in the living cell and *if* we knew how they reacted, it would take us about 10 years to do what the living cell can do in 10 minutes."

But let's go back to the beginning of this discourse on the origin of life. Since the Urey-Miller experiment, it is practically stated as fact that the earth had a beginning atmosphere of H_2O, CH_4, and NH_3. But an interesting article in *Science*[24] would seem to negate this primordial atmosphere. Three investigators, Studier, Hayatsu, and Anders, examined meteorites that showed hydrocarbon traces. These meteorites were assumed to have come from either comets or asteroids, and so they set about examining the trapped gases within the bodies of these meteorites, on the assumption that these trapped gases might indicate the gases present when the hydrocarbons were formed. The results were not at all comforting to devotees of the Urey-Miller conditions. Examination indicated that rather than the presence of the required NH_3, which was totally lacking, N_2 was present.

Another surprising discovery was the overwhelming preponderance of aromatic rather than aliphatic hydrocarbons present. The carbohydrates and amino acids that were referred to before as being theoretical intermediates in the process of creating life, are all basically aliphatic compounds, or derived from them. None of these can be derived from aromatic compounds, so the presence of these latter would also seem to mitigate against a Urey-Miller atmosphere. There also was an absence of the heavier members of the methane series. To the authors, this evidence seemed to exclude a process such as the Urey-Miller one, as representing a solution to the origin of life in the past by natural processes.

I might add another piece of evidence against the Urey-Miller scheme, and that is the total absence of any evidence in the stratigraphic record of conditions other than those now pertaining. No matter how old the rocks are supposed to be, the pre-Cambrian sedimentaries and metamorphics are composed of fragments of older rocks which seem to be the same as those now present.

W. W. Rubey[25] in a discussion of Stanley Miller's paper on "Formation of Organic Compounds on Primitive Earth" was quoted as concluding that the ocean and the air were formed as products of degassing of the interior of the earth. Evidence for volcanic activity is found in the earliest rocks. Gases associated with present-day eruptions are H_2O, CO_2, N_2, CO, H_2, and S. Condensation of such a mixture would lead to an atmosphere of CO, N_2, H_2 and small amounts of HO_2 and CO_2. Where is Miller's NH_3, which is vital to his scheme?

So all this speculation becomes good clean honest fun, and the chemistry becomes examples of beautiful, clever synthesis of organic compounds with no life or near life yet having been created. Even if a system, classifiable as living, ever is synthesized, man will not have proved that this is the way that the first synthesis was executed.

He will only be mimicking the processes of nature, that is, he will be walking in the footsteps of the Creator.

Evolution and Paleontology

The question in many minds at the moment is probably, "What about geology and the fossil evidence? I think that at the beginning of this phase of my analysis I would submit that the question of the age of the earth is independent of the question of creation versus evolution, and I will so consider it. I know a number of individuals who will take the geological calendar as commonly presented today, but who nevertheless do not accept any part of the theory of evolution. One of the best examples was Douglas Dewar, recognized as one of the most effective proponents of creation.

In his *Transformist Illusion* he takes the geological calendar as real, but throughout the book he obviously will have no part of evolution. What is remarkable is that Dewar originally in his college years and for a while thereafter, was an evolutionist, but as he became more knowledgeable in the morphology and physiology of birds in India, he more and more was convinced of the fallacy of the theory of evolution. So by the time he returned to England he had become a prominent voice of the protest against evolution.

Fossils are facts of life. The shells and bony structures that have been uncovered are real, as are such things as tracks, imprints, casts, and molds. So they must be dealt with as actualities and not as figments of the imagination. However, the reader will bear in mind, that how they got to their resting place, under what circumstances they lived, as well as when they lived, are all subject to interpretation and difference of opinion.

A beautiful and complete series of fossil shells may by some be considered to provide an excellent evolutionary series in which one form grades into another. However, such a change in shell structure may be simply an indication of a change in environment, a more or less acid condition of the water. Dr. C. Emiliani has observed that temperature changes in the ocean will affect the coiling of a shell from right to left. I was present in a group in which Dr. Fagerstrom, of the University of Nebraska, reported that certain foraminiferan forms altered their shells in response to pH changes in the water they were living in.

So the very real question can be raised: Are these really evolutionary changes, or are they simply responses to environmental changes? What I wish to emphasize here is that the evidence from paleontology is not absolutely conclusive, and can never be so in itself, because it must always be incomplete, not only because it may be geologically imperfect at any given time, but because the picture it gives us of the organisms concerned is necessarily only a partial one.

Among the plants, the order of appearance of the fossils is anything but an order of progression from simplicity to complexity. In fact, in recent years, because of the development of palynology—the study of microfossils in the form of spores in the rocks—this picture has become even more complex. According to the evolutionary theory, we would expect to find liverworts and mosses following the algae as among most of the most primitive of plant forms, since they are the simplest of all plants that are considered to be archegoniate.

But unfortunately it has been observed that there is no geological evidence whatsoever that can make the delineation of the origin of bryophytes anything other than a hopeless one. This is probably the reason why in the various botany courses I have taken the subject of evolution usually hasn't even been mentioned.

Palynology involves the study of pollen grains—or spores—of plants. Often this is the only part of the plant remaining as a fossil. Spores are sculptured uniquely, so that they can be compared and identified as to genus in many cases.

Recent findings in this new field have thoroughly confused the evolutionary picture with respect to the plant world, in my opinion. Pollen grains have been found in Lower Devonian, Silurian, and Cambrian rocks, which would indicate the presence of vascular plants at the time of deposition of these rocks.

In addition to the presence of pollen grains, other difficulties have arisen. S. Leclercq of the University of Liege, Belgium, reports, "a marked discrepancy observed between two floras so close in geological time as the Middle and Lower Devonian is difficult to reconcile. The absence in Lower Devonian of plant impressions positively related to any of the very differentiated plants of the Middle Devonian is astonishing." [26]

Daniel I. Axelrod also reports that the oldest land plants now known are from the early Cambrian of the Baltic region.[27] Pointing out that the bulk of the unmetamorphosed Paleozoic and pre-Cambrian rocks are not continental but marine, Axelrod holds that few records of land plants would be expected in that period, at least as far as structures other than pollen grains would be concerned.

However, I would like to draw attention to the fact that the statements made by Axelrod relative to the distribution of the fossil plant forms and their environment apply with equal justice to the animal fauna. He points out the possibility that there were all sorts of land plants that were in existence that are not known as fossils because of the fact that the sedimentary terrestrial deposits are not available.

This, then, would imply that any missing terrestrial deposits, which might contain the structural fossils of plants, may also contain the fossils of land animals that once lived at the same time as such plant environments. Yet, said animals, according to all current paleontological theories, would not have been evolved at that time. The only problem is that animals do not leave pollen grains, whereas plants do.

It should be pointed out that nowhere do we find a complete record of deposition through all the geological ages. The complete geological record is made up by plugging in various segments of the record from various parts of the world so as to make up a whole geological column. But there is no locality where you can dig down and uncover a complete geological column from end to beginning. Actually, there is no locality where you can even dig down and uncover a complete series such as the horse from *Equus* at the top to *Eohippus* or *Hyracotherium* at the bottom. Such a series must be made by drawing together fossils from different states, yes, even from other continents.

While one committed to the theory of evolution might refuse to question a phylogenetic tree developed in this way, I submit it is still open to debate. May not many of these forms have lived contemporaneously at different localities, or must the only acceptable explanation be that they succeeded one another? The answer is not carried on labels engraved on the fossils.

Fossil Record Very Incomplete

If you look at the complete picture of life in the rocks, you find some rather peculiar things. Probably one of the most important is the sharp break that occurs between the oldest rocks, known as the pre-Cambrian, and the Cambrian rocks. Incidentally, all these fossils are aquatic. The first plants were algae on the basis of the remains. All the animals were invertebrates spread over all of the most important phyla, such as sponges, jellyfish, sea cucumbers, starfish, brachipods, mollusks, and crustaceans, as well as some worms.

Thus, of the great divisions of the animal kingdom, we find that all have been formed by the Cambrian period except the vertebrates, and these appeared in the next or Ordovician period. One very noticeable and important fact bearing on the theory of evolution is made evident. Amongst these earliest fossils we find that all the phyla appear in the rocks fully formed, i.e., possessing the complete bodily plan of construction typical of their phyla. For example, the earliest crustacea are undoubtedly crustacea, the earliest mollusks are undoubtedly mollusks, etc. As has been noted by any number of paleontologists, the phyla appeared separately, as it were, in most cases, giving among their fossils no indications of their origins from other phyla.

If evolution were true, then these phyla should have evolved one from the other in an increasing scheme of complexity and diversity. We should find them grading into one another, at least to a much greater degree than they do at present. We should find fossils which connect the phyla unmistakably, but to date none have been found in the early rocks. Even when we deal with the vertebrates, which supposedly appeared last among the animals, we can find no true connecting link with previous phyla. As a result there is no agreement regarding their origin.

A search of the literature in the last fifty years will show that the vertebrates have been derived from nearly every one of the invertebrate groups, except possibly the protozoa. I think this sudden appearance of all the phyla without any transitional forms is a most powerful reason for negating a theory of evolution from amoeba or unicellular form to all the various representative present forms. Arnold Lunn once wrote, "Faith is the substance of fossils hoped for, the evidence of links unseen." [28]

Simpson has said,

> The paleontological evidence for discontinuity consists of the frequent sudden appearance of new groups in the fossil record, a suddenness common to all taxonomic levels and nearly universal at high levels. Since the record is, and must always remain, incomplete, such evidence can never prove the discontinuity to be original. [29]

But this is certainly strongly suggested, if we are limiting ourselves to facts and not one theory. Actually, I would think that if the type of origin of new forms suggested by the known fossil record were to be named, it would of necessity be called origin by creation.

D. D. Davis, in 1949, commented on the gaps in the geological record. He held that the sudden emergence of new types, for example, families in order, has given real trouble of late. Davis mentions that many German morphologists question the validity of evolution, and both he and Simpson have mentioned such paleontologists as Schinde- wolf and Kuhn who have felt this way. Davis also said, the facts of paleontology conform equally well with other interpretations that have been discredited by neobiological work, for example, divine creation, innate developmental processes, Lamarckism, etc., and pale- ontology by itself can neither prove nor refute such ideas.[30] I agree, but let it be said that Davis still has faith in evolution.

Further, Oswald Spengler noted the following regarding the fossil record:

> There is no more conclusive refutation of Darwinism than that furnished by paleontology. Simple probability indicates that fossil hoards can only be test samples. Each sample, then, should rep- resent a different stage of evolution, and there ought to be merely "transitional" types, no definition and no species. Instead of this we find perfectly stable and unaltered forms persevering thru long ages, forms that have not developed themselves on the fitness principle, but appear suddenly and at once in their definitive shape; that do not thereafter evolve towards better adaptation, but become rarer and finally disappear, while different forms crop up again. What unfolds itself in ever-increasing richness of form is the great classes and kinds of beings which exist aboriginally and exist still, without transition types, in the grouping of today.[31]

Another difficulty of the fossil record is what might be termed "skipping." It was Dana who mentioned land snails of the Carboni- ferous period, which disappeared from the record, not to reappear till the Cretaceous period, after which they persisted into present times. Dana also mentioned scorpions of the Upper Silurian, which then disappeared until the Carboniferous. At this time they return in the fossil record, along with spiders, which both disappear after the Cretaceous, not to reappear until the Tertiary period.

In 1911, Smith mentioned the shrimp, *Anaspides,* which has not been found as a fossil in any rocks since the Carboniferous, but ap- peared in his day in mountain streams in remote Tasmania.

Finally, you may recall the coelacanth or lobe-finned fish, *Lati- meria,* which belongs to a group that was thought to have become extinct in the Devonian period. From the Devonian to the present day, not a single fossil of this form has been found in any rock. But by the end of 1958, nine had been found in the ocean off the island of Madagascar. Incidentally, its present apparent deep-water habitat ought to cause some rethinking of the formation of rocks that contain lobe-finned fossils.

Of the early Paleozoic, 90 percent of the rocks are depositions in shallow seas, with the remaining five percent those of coastal plains and deltas. We might well ask, where is the record of the land? What plants and what animals lived on the land at that time? In view of the findings of palynology regarding spores of vascular plants in the Cambrian, these become even more legitimate questions. But all the paleontological reconstructions seem to be confined to marine environments. Through the late Paleozoic, the percentage distribution isn't much different.

In the Mesozoic we find plenty of reptiles; and in these rocks we find a greater percentage of terrestrial deposits, which represent the environment of the reptiles. But does this necessarily mean that there were no reptile forms living through much of the Palezoic on the same land that was supporting the growth of the plants that produced the spores? I am fully aware that this is paleontological heresy.

Specific Points of Concern

I am bothered by the insistence on the principle "the present is the key to the past," and the principle of either uniformity or uniformitarianism. When I look at deposits such as the bone beds in western Nebraska, which consist of a remarkable number of various mammals whose bones have become completely disjointed and are one big jumbled mess that reaches a layer five to six feet thick, I ask myself, How could this have come about? I could add the islands of almost sheer bones that are described as existing in the sea north of Siberia. Include also the quick and sudden burial of lions and mammoths in Alaska, that are now being uncovered by gold-mining operations.

I am bothered by densely packed layers of shells alternating with almost completely fossil free layers that are found in the Greenhorn limestone in Kansas and Nebraska. Above all, I am disturbed by the cyclothen explanations that I read in all the geology books to explain the coal beds, and then I find innumerable cases of tree trunks fossilized or coalified, which pierce through successive layers in terms of tens of feet.[32] Despite the fact that catastrophism is ignored by most geologists, I am afraid that for me these instances and others that I could add spell catastrophe rather than slow, even deposition.

I am bothered when I read glib descriptions of equable paleoclimates over the whole world in terms of our present day solar relationships. I know that when you have a spherical body interposed in the path of parallel energy rays, you can't escape a climatic zonation due to the sphericity. There is some factor here that is not being taken into account.

I am disturbed when paleomagnetism is referred to airily, and complete reversals of the earth's magnetic field are postulated, which seem to be supported by sound evidence. But I ask myself what kind of circumstances brought this about, and, above all, what kind of associated phenomena have been completely left out of consideration? What force could have conceivably reversed the whole magnetic field of the earth? Now that we know that the radiation belts are involved in such a field, what kind of storms would have accompanied such a reversal?

Would the magnetic reversal take a measurable interval of time to occur? If so, would the midpoint represent a time of no shielding of the earth from cosmic ray bombardment from space? What would be the effect of such periods of no shielding on the radioactive time clocks, with respect to the rocks?

It will be interesting to read a final report on evaluation of fossils found in Cleveland shale during the construction of I-71. First reports indicate numerous anomalies, among them land plants deposited far from land, reptile-like parts when at the time of Cleveland shale deposition there supposedly were no reptiles, and index fossils misplaced by some millions of years.

Questions such as these and the failure to find reasonable answers drive me to suspend judgment on the picture that is painted in texts dealing with past conditions. I have no quarrel with the various rock layers as they are diagrammed in texts. If there has been drilling of wells along a line, then the cores would present factual evidence as to how this part of the earth's upper crust is composed. But I may be pardoned if I express considerable scepticism when a set of quite unnoticed activities is postulated as the means whereby these various layers were formed and laid down.

What About Human Evolution?

A final question in the minds of many is probably, What about human evolution? From the evolutionist's point of view, man has evolved from an ape form known as *Ramapithecus*. This has been found in India in the Siwalik Hills. Current opinion would seem to hold that this form is dated as Miocene. All the material that is available currently seems to be jaw and tooth material. From this point on to that rock level known as the Pleistocene, there is absolutely nothing to go on as far as fossil evidence is concerned.

In explanation, it is held that the habits of anthropoids do not favor fossilization. In this connection Ernest Mayr has some interesting things to say. For one, "Logically it is possible to conceive of a situation in which we would be certain that man has evolved [from the primates] but [we] would know nothing about the actual history of this evolution." [33]

From a standpoint of faith in evolution, Mayr says, "Our not very remote ancestors were animals, not men." [34] On the other hand, speaking from the scientific standpoint, Mayr also says, "Man's recent history is shot through with uncertainties." [35] And on another page, ". . . there is not merely one missing link [but a] whole series of grades of missing links in hominid history." [36]

Be that as it may, there has been a profound change in outlook on the subject of sequence of human fossils. All human fossils today are put into one genus, namely the genus *Homo*. This is correcting a rather unfortunate habit in the past that resulted in far more name forms than were justified. Dobzhansky says on this matter,

> A minor but rather annoying difficulty for a biologist, is the habit human paleontologists have of flattering their egos by naming each find a new species, if not a new genus. This causes not only a needless cluttering of the nomenclature but it is seriously misleading because treating as a species what is not a species beclouds some important issues.[37]

The result of the compression is that a common current classification groups all hominid fossils in the following three categories: (1) The first is *Homo transvaalensis*. This group is also sometimes referred to as *Australopithecus* species, either *africanus* or *robustus*.

(2) The second form is known as *Homo erectus*. This form has two varieties, one being *erectus* and the other *pekinensis*. (3) The final form is *Homo sapiens*. This form also has two varieties, one being *neanderthalensis* and the other *sapiens*.

Today these forms are all placed in the same genus—*Homo*—and referred to as hominids because they all show upright carriage, bipedal locomotion, and essentially human tooth and jaw structure. This question of what is a human being, particularly when you are dealing with just the skeletal parts, is somewhat of a problem. It should never be forgotten that paleontologists are dealing with a very incomplete organism.

Generally, it is arbitrarily assumed that if there is evidence of controlled use of fire and the use of tools accompanying the remains, then such remains ought to be classed as human. There are always the interesting questions, Were these tools and fire used by the fossil forms present, or were these used by another form which existed with the fossil form, but of whom there are no fossils as yet found? Behavior cannot be discerned in man's ancestry, for behavior leaves no bones.

Also, I think anthropologists are wary today of equating size of brain and quality. The brain size varies among all mammals. It certainly varies in human beings. The average capacity of the modern American is held to be about 1,400 cubic centimeters. And yet, Anatole France had a brain capacity of 1,000-1,200 cubic centimeters, depending on whom you are reading, while Jonathan Swift had a brain capacity twice as great. It is generally agreed today that the variation of *Homo sapiens* will run from somewhere close to 1,200 to about 1,500 cubic centimeters, whereas Neanderthal man ran as an average in excess of this, generally having a larger brain than modern man. His range, however, was from 1,300 to 1,425 cubic centimeters. *Homo erectus pekinensis* specimens range in brain capacity from 900 to 1,200 cubic centimeters, and *Homo erectus* runs from 770 to 1,000 cubic centimeters.

The brain case is considered to be a very human looking feature of the *Australopithecus* forms. The brow ridges are heavy, but no more so than in some human fossils and even a few modern skulls. The mastoid process is present, and it is conical as in man. This is considered to assist in anchoring the muscles that hold the skull erect and therefore it is assumed that the Australopithecines had a human rather than an ape-like neck. However, the brain size seems to have run about 450 to a speculative 600 cubic centimeters. If you take the 550 maximum which is the average estimate of most anthropologists, then you have what Vallois, the noted French anthropologist, calls a Rubicon. This 200 cubic centimeter gap has not been crossed by any fossils to date.

Not too long ago it was rather firmly held that there was a direct line of human evolution running from some unknown anthropoid precursor to the Australopithecines to Java and Peking man to Neanderthal to Cro-Magnon to modern man. This beautiful phylogenetic line has fallen by the wayside. Several factors have contributed to its demise. It has recently been admitted by Robinson, Leakey, and others that the Australopithecines can no longer be viewed as the oldest known relatives of *Homo sapiens* because more human (less brutalized) forms have been discovered who lived simultaneously with them. It was in 1963 that Dr. Leakey reported the find of a human pre-Zinjanthropus form, which he named *Homo habilis*. At that time he suggested that all works on anthropology would have to be rewritten, including his own, since *Homo habilis,* for practical purposes, was very similar to modern man.

Brown and Robinson discovered in 1949 some human remains in Swartkraus. These consisted of two mandibles. Dr. J. T. Robinson, of the Transvaal Museum at Pretoria, South Africa, has written an opinion of this discovery of *Telanthropus*, which claims them as a superior race, definitely human, which, after invading the sites where the more inferior South African Australopithecines lived, led to their extinction by more intelligent manufacture and use of weapons. Dr. R. J. Mason,[38] who is a research officer of the Archaeological Survey of the Republic of South Africa, is of similar opinion. Carleton Coon also refers to them as human.

One of the most fascinating developments also has been the finds of Neanderthals in the caves of Skhul and Tabun at Mt. Carmel. In Tabun you find more modern forms, apparently pre-dating the classical Neanderthal type. While the Tabun population was being specialized in a Neanderthal direction, the Skhul population was becoming less specialized. This has led the French paleontologist John Piveteau to state, "Being torn from the same layer as *Homo sapiens,* he [Neanderthal man] suffered, in his body, *a veritable regression*; but one recovers in the psychism of this physically degraded man the mark of his human origin" (italics added).[39]

In this same work, Piveteau makes a statement on page 50 which is being held by a number of other individuals, and has previously been referred to, namely that the dimensions of the brain cannot furnish any indication whatsoever as to its functioning. It should also be mentioned that the possibility exists that deleterious gene mutations and recombinations could bring about a decrease in brain size, even tending towards microcephaly. These would also bring about facial feature changes. Certainly these possibilities ought to be considered.

It might be supposed that if there really had been an evolving from simple to complex, from "amoeba to man," then we might also expect to find increasingly complex DNA structures. Such, however, is not the case. Tartar has observed that the genome of protozoa is evidently just as complex as that of metazoa. Higher organisms do not have larger or longer or more numerous chromosomes and hence, evidently, have not a corresponding greater number of genes.[40]

What are we then to do with this material on human evolution, of which I have given just the bare sketch? To deny the existence of the fossils is wrong. They do exist. However, we can look at these now, in the light of the evidence from the Neanderthal situation at Skhul and Tabun, and ask ourselves, Are these animals on the way to being men, or are these men who have been excessively brutalized and degenerated, actually, a sort of devolution, that resulted finally in extinction? This is the considered opinion of the late Dr. de Wit, formerly head of the Department of Zoology at the University of the Orange Free State in the Republic of South Africa.[41]

It is true that this overall application of the Neanderthal proposition is not subscribed to by the vast majority of the paleontologists. However, it might be pointed out that prior to the discoveries of Skhul and Tabun, any supposition that Neanderthal was a degenerate form of more modern human types would have been laughed out of existence. So we are faced again with the situation—here is the evidence. Which way shall it be interpreted?

NOTES AND REFERENCES

1. William H. George, *The Scientist in Action* (Random Scientific Book Club, 1938).
2. James B. Conant, *Science and Common Sense* (New Haven: Yale University Press, 1951), p. 37.
3. *Le Monde et la Vie* (October, 1963).

4. *Le Monde et la Vie* (March, 1964).
5. Charles Darwin, *Origin of Species*, Everyman's Library Edition (New York: E. P. Dutton and Co., 1956), p. xxii.
6. S. Zucherman, *Functional Activities of Man, Monkeys and Apes* (1933), p. 155.
7. W. R. Thompson, *Science and Common Sense* (Albany, N. Y.: Magi Books, Inc.).
8. *News Sentinel,* Editorial Page, Tuesday, July 11, 1950 (Fort Wayne, Ind.).
9. John Larrabee, "Was Velikovsky Right?" *Harpers* Magazine, August, 1963.
10. Alfred de Grazia, editor, *The Velikovsky Affair* (New Hyde Park, N. Y.: University Books, 1966).
11. *Ibid.,* pp. 20, 59.
12. *Ibid.,* p. 30.
13. *Ibid.*
14. *Ibid.,* p. 23.
15. *Ibid.,* p. 74.
16. *Smithsonian Treasury of Science,* Vol. II, p. 517.
17. Austin H. Clark, *Zoogenesis* (Baltimore: Williams and Wilkins, 1930), pp. 235-236.
18. E. P. Stibbe, *Journal of Anatomy* (1927-28), Vol. 72, pp. 159-172.
19. Vialleton, *Le Origine des etres vivants,* p. 164.
20. John Cameron, *Transactions of the Royal Society of Canada* (1918), Vol. 12, p. 179.
21. G. R. DeBeer and W. E. Swinton in chapter in *Studies in Fossil Vertebrates,* edited by T. S. Wastall (University of London: The Athlone Press, 1958).
22. A. F. Huettner, *Fundamentals of Comparative Embryology of the Vertebrates,* p. 48.
23. The Toledo *Blade,* Sept. 30, 1965, reported by Ray Bruner, Science Editor.
24. "Organic Compound in Carbonaceous Chondrites," *Science* (Sept. 24, 1965), p. 1455ff.
25. W. W. Rubey, *Annals of N. Y. Academy of Science* (September 30, 1957), Vol. 69, pp. 255-376.
26. S. Leclerq, "Evidence of Vascular Plants in the Cambrian," *Evolution* (June, 1956), Vol. 10, pp. 109-113.
27. Daniel I. Axelrod, "Evolution of the Psilophytales," *Evolution* (June, 1959), p. 264.
28. Arnold Lunn, *The Flight From Reason* (London: Eire and Spottisewood, 1931).
29. G. L. Jepson, E. Mayr, G. G. Simpson, editor, *Genetics, Paleontology and Evolution* (Princeton: Princeton University Press, 1949).
30. *Ibid.,* p. 64ff.
31. Oswald Spengler, *The Decline of the West* (New York: Knopf, 1932), Vol. II, p. 32 (Abridged edition, 1962, p. 231ff.).
32. Cf. N. A. Rupke, "Prolegomena to a Study of Cataclysmal Sedimentation," in chap. 5.

33. E. Mayr, *Animal Species and Evolution* (Cambridge, Mass: Belknap Press, 1963).
34. *Ibid.*, p. 287.
35. *Ibid.*, p. 168.
36. *Ibid.*, p. 637.
37. Theodosius Dobzhansky, *Mankind Evolving* (New Haven: Yale University Press, 1962), p. 171.
38. R. J. Mason, "The Sterkfontein Stone Artifacts and Their Makers," South African Archeological Bulletin No. 17, 1962, p. 109; cf. also J. T. Robinson, "Sterkfontein Stratigraphy and the Significance of the Extension Site," South African Archeological Bulletin No. 17, 1962, p. 87.
39. J. Piveteau, *Origine de L'homme* (Librarie Hachette, 1962), p. 99.
40. V. Tartar, *The Biology of Stentor* (New York: Paragon Press, 1961), p. 372.
41. J. J. Duyvené de Wit, "Reflections on the Architecture of the Organic World and the Origin of Man—A Critical Evaluation of the Transformist Principle," *Philosophia Reformata*, 29e Jaargang, 1964. This may be obtained from J. H. Kok N. V., Kampen, The Netherlands.

THE GALAPAGOS ISLAND FINCHES

Walter E. Lammerts

Introduction

Gregory and Goldman's *Biological Science* (Green version in B.S.C.S. series) gives an impression of a most remarkable adaptive variation in the Darwin finches of the Galapagos Islands.[1] Though somewhat more realistic, the B.S.C.S. Yellow version, *An Inquiry Into Life*, illustrates the same group.[2] Forms presumably resembling hummingbirds, woodpeckers, large and small seed crushers, and insect-eating types are shown as derived from a single pair of original birds.

It was my good fortune to be able to study the large collection of Darwin's finches at the California Academy of Science in the fall of 1965 and spring of 1966. The following is a report on the variations observed and measurements made.

Acknowledgments

I wish to acknowledge the kind cooperation of Dr. Robert F. Orr, ornithologist of the Academy, who permitted me to examine the specimens in this fine collection. He also showed me the remarkable range of variation in the collection of specimens of the song sparrow, *Melospiza melodia*.

Material and Methods

The California Academy of Science collection consists of 37 trays, each with about 100 specimens; some 3,700 well-preserved Darwin finches. I first made detailed measurements of the height, curvature, length, and breadth of each mandible of several specimens of each species. Overall length, breadth, and height of the body and wing measurements were taken. It was soon apparent that such a high correlation usually existed in these various measurements that only four will be reported in this paper, as follows:

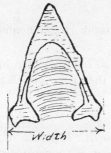

1) Length of bird from tip of bill to end of tail.
2) Height from belly to top of the back.
3) Total length of the bill.
4) Width of the ventral side of the lower mandible of the bill (Figure 1).

Figure 1. Typical Ventral view of lower mandible of *G. magnirostris*

All the specimens in each tray were first given a general examination, and then those which showed extremes in variation for curvature, width, and length of the bill were carefully measured. Then the various trays, *irrespective of their island of origin,* were compared both in general appearance and in detailed measurements. Unless otherwise mentioned, 25 specimens of each species and subspecies were measured.

Results of the Examination

The Darwin finches are a rather drab gray to brownish colored group of birds, except for the almost fully black dorsal plumage of the male of some species. The whole collection had an appearance of general uniformity. Only the *Certhidea* or the Warbler finches seemed truly distinctive.

Were it not for the historical importance of these finches as one of the "pillars" of evidence for the evolution of adaptive variations, I doubt if much attention would be given to them. A resumé of the collection may best be given by arbitrarily calling the tray containing the largest finches Tray 1. This is also the order from top to bottom in which they are filed in the collection. (Body measurements are given in centimeters, and bill in millimeters throughout.)

Tray No. 1

Tray No. 1 consisted entirely of specimens labeled *Geospiza magnirostris* from Culperrer, Wenman, Abingdon, Bindlo, Tower, and James Islands. This "species" has the largest bill and body. Much fluctuation in measurement was found, however.

Body variation: 3½-4 high x 14½-15 long. Bill variation: 13-18 wide x 19-20 long. Total of specimens measured—50.

The general impression was one of remarkable uniformity except for bill variation. The males were mostly black.

356 WHY NOT CREATION?

Tray No. 2

G. magnirostris from James, Jervis, Seymour, Indefatigable, Albemarle, and Barrington Islands.

Same range in variation shown except that one specimen had a bill only 13 mm. wide x 15 mm. long. Most of the males had black plumage. Total of 80 specimens measured.

Tray No. 3

All specimens were labeled *Geospiza fortis*. My first impression was that here we have a small version of *G. magnirostris*. The specimens were from Wenman, Abingdon, Bindloe, James, Jarvis, Daphne, and Seymour Islands.

Body variation—2.5-3 high x 11.5-15 long. Bill variation —9-11 x 10-15.

Tray No. 4

Also *G. fortis*. Mostly lighter gray forms from Seymour, Indefatigable, and Duncan Islands.

Body—2½-3 x 11-14½. Bill—9-12 x 11-15.

One specimen was as large as the smallest *G. magnirostris,* i.e.: 3½ cm. high x 14½ cm. long.

Tray No. 5

G. fortis from Duncan and Albemarle Islands. Many black colored males with mostly small bills. One had a bill 13 mm. x 15 mm., exactly similar in shape (curvature size and size of mandibles, 13 x 15 mm.) to the specimens in Tray No. 2, all of which were labled *G. magnirostris.*

Tray No. 6

G. fortis—specimens from Albemarle, Marborough, Barrington, and Chatham Islands. Some specimens had bills as large as 13 mm. wide and 18 mm. long. This bill was on a male 3 cm. high x 13 cm. long. There was also a great difference in the curvature of the bills. Thus one specimen, No. 5357, was much broader than No. 6270, as shown in Figure 2. There were many black-plumaged males in this collection.

Tray No. 7

G. fortis from Chatham, Hood, Gardner, Charles Islands.

Body—3½-3¾ high x 14-14½ long. Some birds were fully as large as *G. magnirostris* in this tray, both regarding body and size of bill.

Tray No. 8

G. fortis from Charles Island. There were many large specimens as Lack reported.[3] As he states it, "Where *G. magnirostris* is absent, *G. fortis* is large." But careful study failed to reveal any *difference* between these and *G. magnirostris, other than the label!*

Thus specimen No. 5260 had a bill 12 mm. x 17 mm. and a body 3.2 cm. wide x 12 cm. long. Others had bodies fully as large as the smaller *G. magnirostris*. The bill shape was often *identical* as may be seen in Figure 2. Though the bill of the specimen shown is slightly longer, many were *exactly* the same length and height.

Tray No. 9

All *G. fortis* from Charles Island. All were grayish-brown specimens and averaged large for the size of the species. One had a bill 13 mm. wide by 17 mm. long. Another (No. 5501) was 3 cm. x 14½ cm. with a bill 13 mm. x 18 mm.

Tray No. 10

All *G. fortis* from Charles Island. All except two black-colored males were gray colored on sides and belly and brownish above. One specimen, No. 6321, was 3.2 high and 14 long with a bill 13 mm. wide x 15 mm. long.

Tray No. 11

G. fortis from Charles, Champion, Gardner, and *G. fuliginosa fuliginosa* from James, Jervis, Seymour, and Indefatigable Islands. The *G. fortis* specimens were similar to those in Trays 8, 9, and 10. *G. fuliginosa fuliginosa*, however, had dimensions as follows:

Body—2.5 cm. high x 10 cm. long. Bill—7 mm. wide x 11 mm. long.

At first glance this seems a very sharp break in continuity. How-

Figure 2. Left: solid line, small *G. magnirostris;* broken line, large *G. fortis.* Right: large, intermediate, and small form of *G. fortis.*

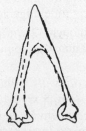

Figure 3. Solid line *G. conirostris*, broken line *G. scandens.* Ventral view of lower mandible adapted from Figure 61 of Bowman's article.

ever, one of the smaller *G. fortis* in Tray No. 3, No. 6189, had a body 2.5 cm. x 11.5 cm. and a bill 9 mm. x 12 mm.

Tray No. 12

G. fuliginosa, var. *fuliginosa* from Indefatigable, Duncan, Albemarle. Here a great variation in bill size and conformation occurs, as some were long and slender (5 mm. x 10 mm.), and others were wider (8 mm. x 13 mm.). About half were black-colored males and the rest were light gray to brownish females.

Tray No. 13

G. fuliginosa fuliginosa from Albemarle, Marborough, Brattle, and Barrington Islands. These had much coarser beaks but many were quite hooked, or rather showed great mandible curvature.

Tray No. 14

G. fuliginosa fulignosa from Chatham Island. Many males with black coloration. The specimens were more uniform than most.

Trays Nos. 15 and 16

Tray No. 15 was also *G. fuliginosa fuliginosa* from Chatham, Hood, Gardner, Charles Islands, and Tray 16 from Charles and Captive Islands.

Some beak variation, but body size was slightly smaller than that of Tray No. 11.

Further comparisons with *G. fortis* are as follows:

	Body	Bill
G. fuliginosa fuliginosa	2.6 x 11	8 x 10
Seymour Island (typical black male)		
Specimen No. 5781 (black male)	2.5 x .11	8 x 12
Specimen No. 6567 (Indefatigable)	2.5 x 11	9 x 11
G. fortis (typical black)	2.7 x 12	10 x 13
G. fortis Abingdon No. 5184	2.5 x 10.5	8 x 12
G. fortis Indefatigable No. 5187	2.5 x 12.5	10 x 12

So, although *G. fuliginosa fuliginosa averaged* smaller, complete intergradation was found.

Trays Nos. 17 and 18

All *G. difficilis.* Body variation—2.5-2.75 x 11-11.5 long. Bill variation—6-6.5 x 11-12.

The specimens in general had a more rufous colored tail but there was complete intergradation as regards this characteristic with that typical of *G. fuliginosa fuliginosa* and *magnirostris.*

Trays Nos. 19, 20, and 21

G. scandens from Abingdon, Albermarle, Bindloe, Charles, Chatham, Duncan, Indefatigable, Jervis, and Seymour Islands. At first glance these specimens seemed remarkably uniform for a long narrow bill, and I thought that here at last was a really distinctive species. The following are characteristic measurements: Bill—8 x 18; 9 x 20; 9 x 19; and 10 x 19. The body was rather uniform: 3½ cm. high x 14 cm. long. However, specimen No. 7173 had a bill 10 x 20 with a body 3½ x 13.

Trays Nos. 22, 23, and 24

G. conirostris conirostris from Culpepper, Hood, and Tower Islands. The body was 3-3.5 x 13.5-14 cm. and samples of bill measurements were as follows: 10 x 15, 10 x 17, 12 x 15 (identical to one specimen of *G. magnirostris* in both size and curvature of the bill), and 10 x 18 (identical to *G. scandens* in size and curvature of the bill).

The individuals of the species then are a connecting, intergrading link between *G. magnirostris* and *G. scandens*. Incidentally, this fact is also referred to by Bowman, who says, "It would seem, then, that in size and shape the bill of *G. conirostris* spans the morphological 'gap' between *G. magnirostris, G. fortis,* and *G. scandens.*" [4]

To be fair in my quotation from him I might also state that he considers *G. conirostris* unique in its structural plan of the mandibles and skull area. His discussion of these slight distinctions,[5] however, is not too convincing in view of the great variation shown. (For comparison of *typical* forms, see Figure 3, on page 357.)

Trays Nos. 25, 26, and part of 27

G. crassirostris: the plumage is generally more brownish and the males are black only on the head area. Otherwise this species is so similar in size to *G. magnirostris* that after a few preliminary measurements further study was not made. The bill also varied greatly such that identical measurements of length and width could easily be found in both "species."

Bowman, who is mightily impressed with minute skull differences, shows seventeen differences in his comparative analysis. It would seem that he is comparing the typical or perhaps average rather than those which show marked intergradation. A better comparison emphasizing the similarities is shown in his Figure 56, where variations in *G. magnirostris* are shown. Unfortunately, he does not show the marked and overlapping variation found in *G. crassirostris*.

Trays Nos. 27, 28, 29, 30, 31, 32, 33, and 34

Camarhynchus psitticula, habeli, and *affiinis* from Abingdon, Albermarle, Barrington, Bindlo, Charles, Duncan, Indefatigable, James, Jervis, Marborough, and Seymour Islands. All were predominantly gray in color, although much variation was found in coloration and some were as brown as *G. conirostris.* Again some *G. magnirostris* were fully as gray as specimens of the "genus" *Camarhynchus.*

	Body	Bill
C. habeli	3 x 12	9 x 13
C. psitticula	3 x 13	11 x 12
C. affinis	2.5 x 11	7 x 10
C. pauper	2.5 x 11	7 x 10
C. parvulus	2.5 x 10.5	7 x 7
	2.8 x 10.7	7 x 10
	2.8 x 12.5	7 x 10

These all intergraded and, except for the difference in species labels, would most certainly be considered as a variable group of light gray individuals of the same species.

Trays Nos. 35 and 36

Cactospiza pallida from Albermale, Chatham, Duncan, Indefatigable, James, Jervis, and Seymour Islands. All were very light gray, especially as regards the side and belly plumage coloration. The size was quite uniform, varying only slightly from a body of 2.5 x 12 and bill of 7 x 15.

Figure 4 shows a comparison of the typical *G. magnirostris* at the top, then *G. fortis, G. fuliginosa,* and *G. difficilis* compared to *G. scandens* on the right. All are males. The variation in color of bill is not significant, for color is a highly variable feature both intra- and interspecifically.

Figure 5 is a comparison of *G. fortis* at the top, then *G. conirostris* and *G. scandens* at the bottom. The upper two birds are females, the lower one a male. Note the variation in plumage color of background birds.

Discussion

If one were to remove all the species labels and arrange the Darwin finches from the largest to the smallest in body and bill size, complete

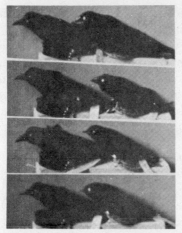

Figure 4. a) *G. scandens* (left) vs. *G. magnirostris* (right) b) *G. scandens* (left) vs. *G. fortis* (right) c) *G. scandens* (left) vs. *G. fuliginosa* (right) d) *G. scandens* (left) vs. *G. difficilis* (right). All specimens are black plumaged males.

intergradation would be found. The same is true of bill length and width. As mentioned above, there is complete intergradation of plumage coloration although the smaller birds tend to have lighter gray feathers.

The situation is exactly comparable to that of the song sparrow, *Melospiza melodia,* where one finds a comparable range in size of bird and bill. Here also the small desert forms are light gray in color.

Bowman works hard to show that there is a basic difference in skull configuration among *G. magnirostris, fortis,* and *conirostris.* However, his Figure 30 is not very convincing to me. For we must remember that the *broken* lines of *G. fortis* show the *variation* in skull size and the *solid* line of *G. magnirostris* upon which he places much confidence is only an average of many skull size measurements. Also, Figure 56 is quite revealing in showing the gradation. One cannot help but feel that the pattern of *distinction* exists more in the mind of Bowman than in the reality of specimens observed and so carefully measured.

If species are to be erected on such minute norms, then indeed we will be burdened with an almost infinite number of names.

It seems much more in line with reality to consider these birds as all in one species, broken up into various island forms as a result of chance arrangement of their original variability potential, as regards the rather minor variation in bill and body size, skull features, and plumage coloration. A Sewel Wright random variation pattern would give exactly this sort of thing. Presumably many pairs of finches from either Ecuador or even Central America happened to fly there and settle on these islands.

The *Certhidea* or Warbler finches are distinctive, though I doubt if the four species are more than merely color variations. *C. fuscus, becki, olivacea,* and *mentalis* were the labels shown on the various individuals in the collection. There was so much intergradation in color that it seemed rather strange to have different labels on these, all of which were rather similar in size.

Evidently a different original stock with quite a distinctive variability potential resulted in these Warbler finches, which, incidentally, are remarkably distinctive in feeding habits also. Present feeding habits are the *result* of the particular types of bills the individuals happened to have inherited. Most emphatically I cannot accept the idea that the variations in size of bill are "adaptive divergences" resulting from natural selection.

The various races now labeled as species and genera certainly exist and are not imaginary. But they are more comparable to the tribes of Indians existing in North America before Columbus discovered it, than to species, let alone genera. Ornithologists call attention to the fact that these forms remain distinct and have different song patterns. However, Orr reports that the *basic* song is the same. Again, this would be comparable to the various languages of the Indians—all variations of the same basic pattern.

Evidence as to the amount of natural hybridization is far from adequate. Possibly some of the intermediate forms, such as *G. conirostris rothschildi,* are really hybrids. Who really knows? Attempts so far to interbreed the so-called "species" in captivity have failed, according to Robert Bowman's assistant, Miss Cutler. However, she points out that mating even between *individuals* of the *same* species is difficult to achieve in cages.

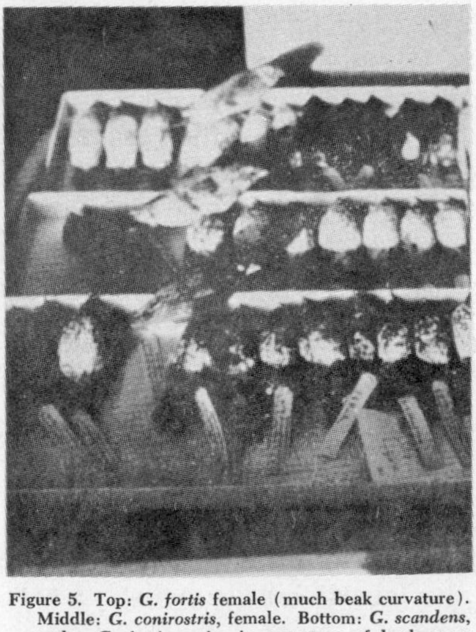

Figure 5. Top: *G. fortis* female (much beak curvature). Middle: *G. conirostris,* female. Bottom: *G. scandens,* male. *G. fortis* varies in curvature of beak some being identical to *G. conirost:is.*

One conclusion is certain, the entities called species are certainly not comparable in distinction to the basic species as in the genus *Rosa* or *Prunus* of the family Rosaceae. When it comes to genera, why would any ornithologist claim *Geospiza, Camarhynchus, Cactospiza,* and *Platyspiza* are comparable to the genera *Rosa, Rubus, Prunus, Fragaria* (Strawberry), or *Pyrus* (pear)? With all due respect to the importance of taking seriously subtle and not "easily recognized" differences, I submit that we are here considering variations on a totally different level.

This leads to an even more important question: Are not the families, genera, and species of *all* mammals and birds based on a lower order of diversity than those existing in plants?

Postscript on Needed Research

Familiar as I have to be in my work with a wide range of flowering plants, and especially the genera of the family Rosaceae and Compositae, it has for many years seemed to me that the families, genera, and species of vertebrates are based on characteristics which in plants would be classed as genera, species, and varieties. Furthermore, there is an undue emphasis on bone structure, as if this feature outweighed all other characteristics in establishing the validity and importance of the various distinctions.

This emphasis was understandable before we became aware of how the DNA system of inheritance works. But surely it must be apparent now that bone structure really has no more significance than such apparently ephemeral characteristics as color of the hair or indeed the fingerprint pattern of a foot or hand. For defects in the DNA code show up just as often in defective bone structure as in other parts of the body such as the brain. It is only the *relative permanence* of the bones in terms of time that has given them a *false importance* in the evaluation of resemblances and differences.

We must have a new look at vertebrate systematics in order to bring the classification of animals more in line with reality. On the basis of a world catastrophe we would expect air breathing creatures to be much more reduced in variety than plants or insects (which are preserved as eggs or pupae). Here the facts of nature are in accord with God's revelation in Genesis. For according to the inspired narrative, only representatives of the various *kinds* of animals and birds were preserved. Furthermore, the genetic potential of the clean animals and birds is recorded as being greater than that of the unclean ones, since three pairs of clean animals and only one pair of unclean animals were preserved.

Do we indeed now find greater diversity of clean than unclean animals? Lack of space forbids a complete analysis, but let us look at a few cases.

The horse is classified as unclean, and we have only *one living* species as compared with the dozen or more living before the Flood, ranging in size from the little five-toed, forest-dwelling *Eohippus* to the large, open plains and still living *Equus.* We have only two species of camels, yet many are recorded as fossils.

The hog is most interesting. *Mammals of the World*[6] lists five genera and nine species. The genus *Potomochoerus* has only one species *porcus* living in southern Africa, Madagascar, and Impalita Islands. It weighs 75 to 150 kg. and resembles the genus *Phacochoerus* and *Sus.* There is less hair on *Phacochoerus* and it has more teeth. The ears are more tufted than those of *Sus.* It is known as the European wild hog but is also living in North Africa, Asia, Japan, and the Malaysian Islands.

Frankly, I see little justification for placing *Sus* and *Potomochoerus* in different genera on the basis of differences such as tufting of the ears. *Sus* is credited with five species, but they certainly look remarkably similar to one another. *Sus salvanica* is often put in a separate sub-genus *Porcula* simply because it is small, weighing up to 75 kg. By contrast, the giant forest hog *Hylochoerus meinertzhayeni* weighs from 160 to 275 kg. It lives in the forests and bamboo jungles of Africa and looks like a great big *Sus.* It does not, however, have facial glands.

The wart hog, *Phacochoerus aethiopica,* is distinguished mainly by its warts, which are prominent only in the male. They are located on the side of the head and front of the eye.

The above differences seem simply the expression of heterozygosity for size, location of hair, and presence or absence of warts, often a heritable genetic defect.

There appears to be no basically distinctive pattern such as distinguishes the genus *Fragaria* (Strawberry) from the genus *Rosa* (Rose). I am not here claiming that all of these nine species of hogs came from only one ancestral pair, but rather that the distinctions compared to those defining the genera of the family Rosaceae are *relatively slight.* Careful breeding research may indeed show that all are capable of interbreeding and so, as domestic dogs, are really the result of segregation from an originally heterozygous pair. Mutations for other differences may well have also occurred during the *early phase* of their distribution and so added to the distinctions now observed as characteristic.

The case of the fifth genus *Babyrousa* with its single species *baburussa is* fascinating. Here we have a remarkable example of how an animal can continue to live *in spite of its obvious defects.* It lives in such odd places as the North Celebes, Togian Islands, the island of Burn, and Sula. This creature is almost entirely devoid of hair, and has a rough skin which is brownish grey, and hangs in loose folds as if reduced from twice its former weight. It now weighs about 90 kg. Most interesting is that the upper tusk grows through the top of the muzzle and then *curves backwards* and so is of no use as a weapon. Even the lower tusks are little used since they are not kept sharp. The young are not striped like most pigs.

Surely this creature should long ago have been eliminated were natural selection the potent agent for survival of the fittest as usually claimed. Genetically, it seems to be the result of malfunctioning of several DNA molecules which resulted in such an abnormal expression of ancestral *Sus* traits.

In birds we have many types of unclean kinds which are now represented by only a few species. Thus the Grebes of the world total 20. If comparable to Western ones I have seen (listed, incidentally, in Peterson's *A Field Guide to Western Birds*), they might well be reduced to as few as 10. The pelican is represented by only six species, two of which are in the West. There are only two eagles listed.

By contrast, among the clean animals we have dozens of species of grosbeaks, finches, sparrows, and buntings (Fringillids), tanagers (Thraupidae), meadowlarks, blackbirds, orioles (Icteridae), and warblers (Parulidae).

There does indeed seem to be a correlation in survival between the greater number of clean birds and animals saved and their present greater diversity, as compared to the single pair of unclean kinds saved and their present lack of variety. Careful research into this aspect of animal classification is needed.

This paper is presented mainly with the hope of arousing interest on the part of creation research oriented naturalists. It is admittedly only introductory to this vast subject of survival patterns. However, I believe it demonstrates that often the picture of genetic diversity given as the result of natural selection is, to put it mildly, exaggerated.

NOTES AND REFERENCES

1. *High School Biology* (Biological Sciences Curriculum Study—Green Version [Chicago: Rand McNally and Co., 1963]), p. 729.

2. *Biological Science: An Inquiry into Life* (Biological Sciences Curriculum Study—Yellow Version [New York: Harcourt, Brace and World, Inc., 1963]), p. 593.
3. David Lack, *Darwin's Finches* (An Essay on the General Biological Theory of Evolution). Harper Torchbooks No. TB 544 of The Science Library (New York: Harper and Brothers, 1961. First published in 1947).
4. Robert I. Bowman, *Morphological Differentiation and Adaptation in Galapagos Finches.* University of California Publications in Zoology (Berkeley, Calif.: University of California Press, 1961), p. 285.
5. *Ibid.*, p. 247.
6. *Mammals of the World* (Philadelphia: Johns Hopkins Press, 1964).

Chapter 10

Social Considerations

NEO-DARWINISM AND SOCIETY

JOHN N. MOORE, ED.D.*

Introduction

At a time when many scholars still write in optimistic manner regarding Western civilization (and even possible accommodations with communistic states), other scholars write about the dissolution of Western civilization as if there was once a Western tradition of a more or less fixed and complete body of belief and practice.

One such chronicler of changes in Western culture would be the late Professor Richard Weaver of the University of Chicago, who expressed himself on the dissolution of the West in 1948 in his book entitled, *Ideas Have Consequences.* On his first page Weaver wrote:

> In considering the world to which these matters are addressed, I have been chiefly impressed by the difficulty of getting certain initial facts admitted. This difficulty is due in part to the widely prevailing Whig theory of history, with its belief that the most advanced point in time represents the point of highest development, *aided no doubt by the theories of evolution* which suggest to the uncritical a kind of necessary passage from simple to complex. Yet the real trouble is found to lie deeper than this. It is the appalling problem, when one comes to actual cases, of getting men to distinguish between better and worse (emphasis added).[1]

Thus Weaver stated the position[2] that we must be ever conscious of avoiding the enticing point of view that present conditions are the best conditions, because we have "progressed" so far from previous undesirable, even primitive conditions. In other words, Weaver would call attention to the fact, as he saw matters, that we have not really progressed in Western civilization, and must objectively compare the

*Michigan State University, East Lansing, Michigan; now living at 1158 Marigold Avenue, East Lansing

repeatedly immoral inter-personal relationships of human beings, today, with those of past centuries, and so on back through recorded time. If we are completely honest with ourselves, we must admit that material advancement has far outstripped spiritual advancement.

Weaver felt there are too few modern thinkers who care to examine their lives. There are too few modern thinkers who will acknowledge the rebuke which comes of admitting that our present state *may be* a fallen state from that of Edenic innocence. Actually, one can assert that many, many so-called intelligent men, for at least four centuries, have been their own priests, and their own professors of ethics as well. The consequence has been an anarchy in "intellectual" circles which, today, threatens even that minimum consensus of value demonstrable as necessary for the continued existence of the political state.

Many people seem to be blind to the significance of a change, a profound change, which has occurred in the last four centuries, in man's conception of reality. Many intellectuals, who have not discovered that a world view is the most important aspect of man's ideas, will readily scoff at attempts to profit from experiences of those of the past. Such scoffers quite commonly turn to *argumentum ad hominem* in order to consciously or unconsciously discredit him who would look to the past for guidance in the present or for the future.

Nevertheless, careful analysis brings out the fact that it was the influence of proponents of the doctrine of nominalism which contributed immensely to changes in man's world view, i.e., his conceptions of reality. It must be remembered that the proponents of the doctrine of nominalism insisted that only particulars or individuals exist; and hence, nominalists denied that universals have a real existence. Experience, then, to the nominalists, is *the* source of knowledge.

The impact of nominalism tended to leave universal terms mere names serving our convenience to form labels. Thus the reality perceived by the intellect, or given by revelation, was banished from many intellectual circles. This brought about the practical result of positing that *the* reality is that which is perceived by the senses. In a word, the affirmation of sense perception as that which is real was a turning in the road toward modern empiricism.

But let us follow in skeletal outline Weaver's consideration of this train of circumstances in intellectual circles in the West since the development of nominalism. Changes have proceeded in accordance with perfect logic after the entrance by many thinkers of Western civilization upon a road completely dependent upon the viewpoint of reality which gave rise to modern empiricism. Actually, under this world view of reality, the pursuit of knowledge by observation and experiment as the only source of *real* knowledge became a map to give direction to, and be a basis for, formulation of policies of men. The great difficulties of today no doubt stem in part from this absolutizing of empirical knowledge.

Train of Circumstances

The denial of universals carries with it the denial of everything transcending experience, such as absolute truth, God, absolute moral values. The denial of everything transcending experience means inevitably the denial of truth entirely. Thus there is no truth toward which we seek, but only the immediate experience of the moment.

With the denial of absolute, objective truth, there is no escape from the relativism of the old Greek adage from Protagorus, "man the measure of all things." By such an adage men are convinced that they might realize themselves more fully in their autonomous intelligence.

The profoundness of such a change of belief made necessary, eventually, changes in every concept of man and there soon emerged a "new" doctrine of nature. Where once man's concept of nature had been regarded as imitating the thoughts of the creator God, and as imperfect representations of true reality known only by God, nature was looked upon as containing the principles of its own constitution and behavior. From this flowed the whole thesis of natural laws and even nature's God.

It follows that if physical nature is the totality of reality, and if man is of nature, it is impossible to think of man as suffering from constitutional evil or some original sin. Rather the defections of man must now be attributed to his simple ignorance or some kind of societal deprivation. Hence the clear deduction to the corollary of the natural goodness of man.

But there is more, because, if nature is a self-operating mechanism, and man is an intelligent animal adequate to his needs, then next in order is the elevation of man's intelligence. It became quite proper to regard as the highest intellectual vocation those methods whereby man interpreted data supplied by his senses; ergo, the careful study of nature known as science was above all philosophy—*the height* of human intelligence. From this position came the thinking of Hobbes and Locke and eighteenth century materialists and empiricists, who taught that man needed only to reason correctly upon evidence from nature.

By this time the religion of Western civilization began to seem ambiguous in dignity and meaning. One solution to the ambiguity was deism, which makes God the outcome of an intellectual reading of nature. But in denying antecedent truth, this religion left each man to make what he could of the world open to the senses; and "humanized" or "humanistic" religion followed at close marching order in these rapid changes of consequences to the world view based upon reality rooted in the senses alone.

The philosophy of materialism gained ascendency, and thus men soon found it necessary, in fact imperative, to explain man by his environment. Such an explanation was the work of Charles Darwin and others of the nineteenth century. According to the views of some analysts the very pervasive character of these changes is made manifest by the fact that several other students of nature, such as Alfred Wallace, T. H. Huxley, Asa Gray, Ernest Haeckel, were arriving at similar explanations in the field of biology when Darwin published his *Origin of Species* in 1859.

If man was ensconced firmly in nature, it became necessary at once to question the fundamental character of his motivation. If the question of human origin was decided in favor of scientific materialism, then biological necessity, issuing from the concepts of struggle for existence and survival of the fittest, became the cause of causes. With the acceptance of biological necessity as the basic cause of the molding of man entirely in consequence of environmental pressures, there follows a logical obligation to extend the same theory of causation to the institutions of man and human society.

Nineteenth century social philosophers were quick to use Darwin's formulations as powerful support for their thesis that human beings act always out of economic incentives. Therefore men like Karl Marx and the French socialists completed the abolishment of freedom of will on the part of the individual. Marx used dialectic materialism to reduce the full pageant of history to the economic endeavors of individuals and classes.

Consequently, man, as created in the divine image of God, was replaced by man as the wealth-seeking and wealth-consuming animal.

The ground was laid for the apparent imminent eclipse of the omnipotent God by the omnipotent political state, under the direction of the elite intellectual few who in their autonomy could eventually control nature, and man in nature.

Fairly recent consequences of change in world view include development of psychological behaviorism and psychoanalysis which deny freedom of will, the very existence of mind, and place in question such elementary means of direction of human conduct as instincts with the possible reduction of all motivation to naturalistic "drives" or "urges" of sexual behavior. Converts to this theory have been fewer in number than for other theories of man in nature, but they are only logical extensions of the thinking of those who embrace material causation.

Through means of psychological behaviorism man is left with nothing that transcends his experiences. He has no values and no morals; and his life becomes sheer practice without theory. Of course, modern man secretly hungers for truth, truth that will set him free, but he consoles himself with the thought that life should be experimental. Modern man feels he should try all ideas since he will acknowledge no basis or yardstick by which to evaluate any idea, except trial and error, which is strictly groping in the dark—an essentially *irrational* animal on the loose in nature.

Thus modern man concentrates on action, on doing, on method. He meets his problems with *ad hoc* policies. In net, modern man is pathetically susceptible to making all the mistakes of those who have gone before him simply because he does not know enough history, enough tested principles which approximate absolute truth; in short, transcendent values of the Word of God.

Hence the speechlessness of some men of culture is still extant in Western civilization when they are forced to witness the further rending of once transcending values of the worth of human life, full application of talents, sanctity of relations between male and female, and surrender of remnants of freedom of choice in exchange for decision-making by sycophants and self-less calculating machines.

Whether it is the rantings of the political demagogue or the uninhibited college or university student, the man of culture understands what is being done, but he cannot convey his understanding because he cannot convey the idea of sacrilege in the terms of materialism or scientific naturalism. As Weaver says:

His cries of *abeste profani* are not heard by those who in the exhileration of breaking some restraint feel that they are extending the boundaries of power and of knowledge.[3]

To bring this viewpoint even closer I will quote briefly from a letter which appeared in a post-humously published book in 1964. I refer to Whittaker Chambers' book, *Cold Friday*. Chambers was one intellectual who learned from the professors of his youth the materialistic world view, and then went all the way logically and became a Communist in full identification. Chambers knew of machinations of Communists in this country and was fully yielded to Communist Party discipline for a major part of his life. In writing about extant situations in 1954, he said:

I no longer believe that political solutions are possible for us. I am baffled by the way people still speak of the West as if it were at least a cultural unity against Communism though it is divided not only by a political, but by an invisible cleavage. On one side are the voiceless masses with their own subdivisions and fractures. On the other side is the enlightened, articulate elite which, to one degree or other, has rejected the religious roots of the civilization—the roots without which it is no longer Western civilization, but a new order of beliefs, attitudes and mandates. In short, this is the order of which Communism is one logical expression, originating not in Russia, but in the culture capitals of the West, reaching Russia by clandestine delivery via the old underground centers in Cracow, Vienna, Berne, Zurich, and Geneva. It is a Western body of belief that now threatens the West from Russia. As a body of Western beliefs, secular and rationalistic, the *intelligentsia of the West* share it, and *are therefore always committed to a secret emotional complicity with Communism* of which they dislike, not the Communism, but only what, by chances of history, Russia has specifically added to it—slave-labor camps, purges, MVD *et al.* And that, not because the Western intellectuals find them unjustifiable, but because they are afraid of being caught in them. If they could have Communism without the brutalities of ruling that the Russian experience bred, they have only marginal objections. Why should they object? What else is socialism but Communism with the claws retracted (emphasis added)?[4] [Note: Chambers said claws retracted, *not* removed!]

Chambers put the matter very boldly, very starkly. And now the introduction of this paper can be closed since a backdrop has been provided for what follows. But before proceeding, an assertion of the main thesis of this paper is in order. It is asserted categorically that presentation of evolution as fact, i.e., as observable, in educational institutions at any level across the surface of this globe, has been used by free-thinking scholars to implement a type of indoctrination of the intelligentsia of the various societies of Western civilization. The purpose of this paper is to develop this thesis with some documentation. Always the discussion of points presented is done against the backdrop provided in the Introduction regarding changes in the view of reality by many scholars of Western civilization.

Neo-Darwinism

Objective discourse is completely dependent upon clear definition of terms used. Responsibility for such definition rests in respectable circles of intellectual analysis with the author. Therefore, writing from the tradition of getting the facts, that is, the tradition of scientific method which I represent in the classroom, I wish to make abundantly clear my meaning in terms, such as Neo-Darwinism, evolution, and call attention to ambiguity of definition of terms.

According to some authors[5] a modern theory of evolutionary causation can be variously termed the *synthetic theory of evolution,* the *biological theory of evolution,* and the *theory of microevolution.* Darwin formulated his ideas on the causation of evolutionary change by using some combination of the concept of natural selection, concepts of Lamarck, and his invention to explain variation, which he discussed under the term pangenesis.

Thus Darwinism, which is the term used to refer loosely to Darwin's formulations by his successors, had to be modified when Gregor Mendel's cogitations on explanations of variation were available around the turn of the century. So for the last fifty to sixty years the terms *Neo-Darwinism,* and even *Modern Synthesis* have been in vogue to refer to organic evolution.

One can write quite properly today of a modern synthesis of ideas because Mendelian genetics and biochemical analysis of DNA and RNA have been added to the natural selection idea of Darwin with the omission of Lamarckian suggestions and Darwin's ideas of pangenesis. The above in this section is intended to point up the fact that modern theory on evolutionary causation is discussed under various terms.

What, then, is evolution? According to classical meaning and to usage which Darwin finally worked out in his last editions of *Origin of Species* and later publications, evolution is the idea that organisms have come into existence as the result of changes in pre-existing organisms.[6] Sometimes evolution is defined as transmutation of species,[7] but this carries the same meaning as the classical sense.

Or the concept of organic evolution may be represented as constituting the position embodied in these three propositions: (1) all living species are descended from different species that have lived in the past; (2) the differences that exist between living species have arisen slowly and gradually over long periods of time; and (3) the causes that have acted in the past to change one species into another continue to act today.[8] Clearly then, evolution involves the change of one species or form into another species or form.

It is true that many biologists will define evolution as any genetic change or modification. This is broad and raises the logical question, how does this definition differ from the meaning of the term variation? Ambiguity does obtain in the writings of some scientists and even in their oral presentations. At least one physical anthropologist admitted in private conversation that he used the terms "variation" and "evolution" in an equivocal manner. That is not the intent of the author of this paper.

Evolution shall be change of form or kind into another form or kind with *increasing* complexity. *Variation* shall be those changes of heredity or genetic character which are involved in modification within the limits of species or form. *Mutation* is understood to be the term used to refer to postulated changes of genetic material—the very elements of varietal modification.

Historical Interlude

We shall go on to some examination of the relation of the concept of evolution to specific areas of man's intellectual endeavors. But first let us return to the train of circumstances of change in concepts of reality, as drawn from Weaver's discourse in explanation of his title that ideas have consequences.

As that chain of circumstance was recited, I think we uncovered a crucial point to the main purpose of this paper on "Neo-Darwinism and Society." That crucial point was the effort by Charles Darwin and so many of his scientific contemporaries to explain man in his environment, to place sense-conscious man in his environment of sensual experience.

From the time of Darwin to the present, a type of indoctrination was implemented by free-thinking scholars. In fact, from Darwin's day to the present an acceleration in the process of such implementation can be identified. As followers of Darwin explained man in his physical environment—as just another animal—just the result of biological processes, then man became fully physical to them. That is, man was subsumed under the philosophy of materialism or positivism. Even his values, morals, and instincts, which Darwin still recognized, were resultants of biological processes.

Men of the mid-nineteenth century had been seeking explanations —explanatory systems—*some* system without God included. After 1845, great strides were made in formulation of fundamental theories relating to nature and the environment of man. It became a daring philosophical experiment, as Philip P. Wiener points out,[9] to study nature and make it intelligible *without leaning on a providential intelligence.* Man was going to go it *alone.*

Man found theories to provide explanations, on *his terms,* of his environment *and* his society. The theory of organic evolution was *the* theory, which was presented as new, but was really an old, old idea from the Greeks; in fact was a pre-Christian era idea. But nineteenth century materialists had prepared the way for re-acceptance of evolution.

In searching for explanations without God, ideas of "progress," of "development," of "perfection," (and *not* "degeneration," *not* "regeneration," *not* "justification by faith") had reached ascendency in men's thoughts, as Scoon brings out.[10]

Even the very old idea from the Greeks of spontaneous generation was considered; and, today, is used by scientists in a disguised form when they postulate regarding the origin of life. Some spontaneous synthesis of life is inherent in the writings of Oparin[11] and other men who write about possible protein synthesis in some original organic soup as their thinking partakes of a theory of *total* evolution, including the physical, as well as the biological.

Yes, evolutionary speculation had a popular audience because men were anxious to accept Darwin's way of seeing the world.[12] Intellectuals wanted to accept the Darwinian world-view. They had been influenced by the social philosopher, Herbert Spencer, who ranged widely in his writings on such subjects as sociology, psychology, biology, and ethics. In his discussion of these subjects, which were immensely interesting to independent, intelligent thinkers of his day, he infused these subjects broadly with evolutionary ideas.

And Thomas Huxley provided a means of compromise with religious people by coining the word agnosticism (which, somewhere, Engels called a "polite atheism"). Churchmen and believers were willing to compromise so as to be up to date with the latest explanations.[13] To compromise they yielded to the age-old attraction of a religion of justification by works. Justification by works, of course, is the essence of all natural, non-revealed religions and of all perversions of revealed religion. Therefore, such views can be shown to be just the reverse of the teachings of Jesus Christ, which are basic to Christianity. Even in the nineteenth century a topsy-turvy world view attracted so-called intelligent thinkers in Western civilization.

One historian, Bert J. Loewenberg,[14] has written as if evolution were a religion. He speaks of evolution being involved in the "conversion" of men of science, and "conversion" of vocal opinion, which suggests that truth is decided by the raising of hands—by taking a vote. Loewenberg refers even to the "infiltration" of evolution into every decision of scholarship. Yet, in 1959, Loewenberg penned this admission, "There were no incontrovertible facts attesting that one variety had been transmuted into another." [15] What kind of indoctrination occurred in the nineteenth century, which brought about dissemination of ideas, which conceivably are bearing fruit in this generation?

One feels safe in saying that people of Darwin's day had become accustomed to naturalistic explanations—naturalistic explanatory systems.[16] F. S. C. Northrop[17] has pointed out that Galileo and Newton had mathematized nature, and determinism was widely accepted because of man's successes in the physical sciences, wherein derived laws had come to replace Providence. As evolution was presented as fact, as observable, by Unitarians and free-thinkers, the evolutionary theory underscored an earlier faith in man alone, his acts and deeds being judged in the absence of God. Evolutionism had become then the formula of thought (the orthodoxy, the *Zeitgeist,* or the *Weltanschauung*) as surely as fixity of species had dominated earlier thinking.

Scoon[18] shows how extreme application of evolution as a fact, as observable, by Ernest Haeckel gave rise to an attempt to disprove three cardinal points of Christianity: the personality of God in Christ, the immortality of the soul, and freedom of will. Without question evolutionist Haeckel forcefully expressed a conviction in atheism. Dutch zoologist Jan Lever has written somewhere that at least three positions are possible in the conscious or unconscious philosophical presuppositions of the consistent evolutionist like Haeckel, or for that matter self-confessed atheist, Sir Julian Huxley. Generally speaking, at the root of the philosophy of evolutionism is a faith:

(a) that God does not exist, which is *atheism,* or

(b) that there was only an impersonal first cause, such as an explosion of a giant nucleus, with no further cause affecting the machinery of the world, which is a type of *deism,* or

(c) that nature itself is God, which is *pantheism.*

Each of these belief systems would involve a clear denial of a "personal God," that is, God in person. The conclusion is most logical that the belief of such as Julian Huxley in the origin of life from lifeless matter is *not* an idea reached *in*ductively. Such a belief quite clearly is a *de*duction from a "faith"; that is, a faith of atheism.

Yes, evolution was taken for granted as being factual, as being observable, and was used to counter the concept of fixity of species. Fixity of species involved the idea that there are as many species of plants and animals as appeared in pairs as a result of the Creator's work. Actually, fixity of species is no more than an idea of men of the sixteenth through eighteenth century.

Fixity of the species was not and *is not at all* biblical. Fixity of species was, and often still is, imputed wrongly to the Bible, because there is no mention at all of species as such in the Bible. Fixity of species is often represented by a row of straight arrows with arrowheads pointing upward. Since understanding of variation and change of species was the common result of studies of nature and artificial breeding under the influence of Darwin and his successors, then men thought they had destroyed part of the Holy Bible. Yet that Word only relates that each form shall bring forth "after its own kind," with absolutely no mention of evolution. But evolution was an explanatory system which suited the mind of men who wanted to be free of Providence.

The enthusiasm of evolutionists presented the tree of life to men. The tree of life of evolutionists is represented much as a main river and its tributaries—like the Mississippi River—is drawn on a map. Yet such a tree of life, with present forms having some common origin, is really not much more than the old chain of being of the Greeks.

Evolution, when presented as fact, as observable, was based upon the struggle for existence and survival of the fittest which almost every man knew from first-hand experience. Since reality *was* man's experience, then evolution was accepted as fact. Evolution was accepted as if it was observable because Darwin's massive collection of observations of nature made evolution seem so respectable, so plausible to sensuously oriented men of the nineteenth century.

In a recent publication Loewenberg presents the thesis that Darwinism was accepted fully as fact, as observable in the United States. His booklet, *Darwinism: Reaction or Reform?*[19] recounts permeation of the Darwinian synthesis into every sector of thought. What kind of indoctrination occurred in the United States? The years of 1859 to 1914 were proud years because the new age of science was followed by a new age of man. Because of Darwinism, there was a "new" *logic,* "new" *ethics,* "new" *psychology,* "new" *history,* "new" *philosophy,* and "new" *morality.* These changes in the area of ideation led to a "new" *sociology,* "new" *anthropology,* and "new" *economics.*

Darwinism was clutched to the bosom of Karl Marx and Friedrich Engels. These men wrote that Darwin had given them a basis in science, in biology, for their identification of the class struggle in society. They transferred the ideas of struggle for existence and survival of the fittest from biology to society.

In a recent article on "The Concept of Evolution," A. R. Manser[20] makes the point that it is impossible to understand why Darwin influenced the sociological theorists so profoundly, unless attention is given to the fact that Darwin's whole formulation constituted a type of sociology of nature. In fact, Manser suggests that perhaps Darwin should be called "Biology's Karl Marx rather than its Newton." Even now the dogmas of Marx and Engels are taught in Marxian biology presented to Communist intelligentsia.

Society

Now some attention should be given to the impact of evolution as fact, as observable, in specific fields of subject matter. Only a brief, sketchy treatment of three examples of consequences of the infiltration of the idea of evolution as factual, as observable, into the thinking circles of Western civilization, or more particularly in the United States, can be given. The degree to which infiltration of evolution occurred in the areas of (1) history, (2) economics, and (3) social studies and literature is immense. The impact on formulation of public policy as deduction from a materialistic world-view has been colossal.

History

As a *first* example of selected indoctrination by historians involving evolution, I want to refer to the work of Charles Beard. His work on an economic interpretation of the U. S. Constitution[21] could well be considered as an application to history of Darwinian concepts of struggle for existence and survival of the fittest. The thesis which Beard expounded was double-barreled:

a. The Constitution was the work of consolidated economic groups who were personally interested in the outcome of their labors.

b. The Constitution was put over in an undemocratic society by undemocratic methods for the express purposes of checking democratic majorities.

Let me note at the outset that Beard admitted that he had *not* done the necessary research and had only put on paper what he expected he would find. Yet his ideas were accepted as fact in 1913, and used to teach teachers who taught others that this country was founded as a result of class warfare. What kind of indoctrination occurred? And how is Beard's thesis understood today? Finally, after some forty or more years, his thesis is understood as not at all true; and with no basis in fact.

Beard's explanation has been carefully studied in regard to one colony after another. Finally the necessary research has been presented for use in academia. What a great deal of harmful indoctrination has occurred, until the book by Forrest McDonald, *We the People*,[22] appeared with careful treatment of land holdings and voting records of each of the thirteen colonies. And then there are the two specific works[23] by Robert Brown and Katherine Brown on similar close analyses of Massachusetts and Virginia. These researchers have destroyed Beard's expectations, and their results are just beginning to surmount the usual cultural lag in the publication field and the educational classroom.

Economics

To begin my *second* example of selected indoctrination by intellectuals who applied evolution to their field, I refer to statements made in the Introduction. After Darwin explained man as a physical being, as animal in nature, the next logical step was the extension of biological causation theory to the institutions of man and society. This Marx did as he reduced the whole sweep of man's history to the *economic* endeavors of individuals and classes. That Marx and Engels quickly accepted Darwin's formulations upon the reading of his *Origin of Species* is brought out by the following 1959 quotation from *Mainstream,* a journal very favorable to socialistic ideas:

> Darwin's *Origin of Species* was an exciting book to Marx and Engels. Here was the most concrete scientific confirmation of dialectics they had yet seen. . . . When Marx first read the *Origin* in 1860 he wrote to Engels: "This is the book which contains the basis in natural history of our view." And a few weeks later he wrote to Lassalle: "Darwin's book is very important and serves me as a basis in natural science for the class struggle in history. . . ."

> One striking difference in the thought of these two giants is that Marxism embraces Darwinism, leaving to biologists the working out of the innumerable controversial details. Darwinism stands apart, seemingly separable from Marxism. Yet it is evident to any objective observer, as it was to Wallace, that a theory of social evolution is required by the theory of biological evolution. And if one takes Darwin's thoroughly materialist stand, such a social science must be solidly against all forms of teleology and idealism. It is a most plausible thesis that as time goes on Marx and Darwin will appear ever closer together to those who study them, because the difference and separateness is trifling compared to all they had in common.[24]

Connections between Darwin, Marx and this country can readily be shown by denoting the impact of adherents of the Fabian Society in England. The Fabian Society was the initial work of Sidney and Beatrice Webb, who strove to implement Marxian theory in England. That Fabian Society members made an impact on the United States is documented in the Veritas Foundation publication, *Keynes at Harvard,*[25] which was sponsored by concerned alumni of Harvard University. Researchers of the Veritas Foundation have found that much of today's college youth shows thinking that reflects the following six premises:

1. The private enterprise system of the United States is full of basic contradictions and fundamental flaws which inevitably will relegate it to the scrap heap.

2. Manufacturers, merchants, bankers, and the host of corporate executives of the country are hopelessly reactionary and incapable of understanding the need of the "new order."

3. Thrift, savings, ownership, and accumulations of private prop-

erty are harmful to society and are not socially compatible with the "new order" which is rising out of the ashes of the "old capitalism."

4. Society is composed of classes and these classes are conspicuously banded together to protect their overall group interests.

5. The scope of government must be expanded to stand as a "third force," gradually expropriating or redistributing the wealth of existing capitalists through unrestricted powers of taxation and at the same time preventing the accumulation of any new capital.

6. College and university graduates can insure their personal future by attaching themselves to government bureaucracy, which is destined to expand indefinitely.

This is essentially the philosophy of John Maynard Keynes, who was very active in the Fabian Society and came to these shores to convince the then President Franklin D. Roosevelt that the United States should dispense with the gold standard and use printing press paper money. Interestingly enough, the exponents of the above type thinking, and members of the Fabian Society do their work under the guise of aiding free enterprise; yet, the shield or coat of arms of the Fabian Society shows a wolf in sheep's clothing. What a deception is represented by such a design! What kind of indoctrination has occurred in the classrooms at Harvard University when the above philosophy has been taught predominantly for about three decades? The reader is referred to *The Failure of the "New Economics"* by Henry Hazlitt[26] and *The Roots of Capitalism* by John Chamberlain[27] for clear writing on this subject matter area.

Social Studies and Literature

The *third* example of selected indoctrination by intellectuals involves consequences of accepting evolution as fact, as observable. in such areas of our culture as poetry, novels, drama, social studies, sociology, anthropology, and law. Of course "ideas have consequences," and one can wonder what has been wrought in our educational institutions in this country when one considers the research effort in *Cosmic Optimism* (A Study of the Interpretation of Evolution by American Poets from Emerson to Robinson) by Frederick W. Conner;[28] in *Darwinism in the English Novel* by Leo J. Henkin;[29] in *Evolution and Poetic Belief* by Georg Roppen;[30] in *Darwin Among the Poets* by Lionel Stevenson;[31] and finally in *Evolution, Marxian Biology, and the Social Scene* by Conrad Zirkle,[32] a botanist.

The latter book by Zirkle was published in 1958 and merits careful study. The author demonstrates how poetry has been used to make the concepts of evolution, struggle for existence, and survival of the fittest palatable to the cultured intellectual.

In the field of novels, Jack London was most effective and persuasive in winning acceptance of socialism, because he accepted the now discredited theory of inheritance of acquired characteristics by which he justified his socialism. The 1961 unpublished doctoral thesis of R. W. Carlson, *Jack London's Heroes: A Study of Evolutionary Thought,*[33] provides detailed perspective, and analysis in depth of London's use of evolutionary outlook and in turn Spencerian, Nietzschean, and Marxian outlook to shape his numerous fictional heroes. Of course the latter three outlooks were founded in each respect on some degree of materialistic, evolutionary world view.

Lastly, it can be shown that George Bernard Shaw through his dramatic works was very influential during his lifetime, and still is very instrumental in spreading Marxian biology among the intelligentsia. George Bernard Shaw was an outstanding member of the Fabian Society, and realized better than most other writers that the rationality of the Marxian doctrines depended upon certain biological postulates.

Conclusion

In conclusion, the main purpose of this paper should be re-stated. This paper was designed to develop a main thesis with some documentation. The main thesis of this paper dealt with the categorical assertion that presentation of evolution as fact, as observable reality, in educational institutions at any level across the surface of this globe has been used by free-thinking scholars to implement selected indoctrination of the intelligentsia of the various societies of Western civilization. For practical reasons brief discussions of points related to this assertion referred primarily to the United States against the backdrop of dissolution of the West as reviewed in the Introduction.

Evolution and the concept of struggle for existence have been instrumental in the hands of biologists, philosophers, educationalists, religionists, and many others in accelerating gross changes in Western civilization—as represented in this country. Evolution and Darwinism were accepted by materialistic thinkers as factual, and observable. Evolutionism even became a religion, an atheistic religion, for some as was pointed out in the instance of Ernest Haeckel and Julian Huxley, at least.

Yet—organic evolution *is not fact*, but only a guess. Is it not fraudulent and deceitful to present evolution as factual, as observable? Support for an affirmative answer to this question is clearly brought out by such scientists as G. A. Kerkut in *Implications of Evolution*,[34] David Lack in *Evolutionary Theory and Christian Belief* with subtitle: The Unresolved Conflict,[35] and by Henry Morris in *The Twilight of Evolution*.[36]

It can be stated firmly that absolutely no experimental evidence is known for evolution, when evolution is defined as development of one animal form from another (as reptile from amphibian), or one plant form from another (as angiosperms from cycads).

To teach organic evolution as fact, as observable, is to seriously misrepresent the state of current research. Further, such misrepresentation contributes strongly to selected indoctrination of young, formative minds. Ideas held by scientists relevant to possible animal group relationships have changed from one viewpoint to another viewpoint, and back again, over the past one hundred years.

Today, biologists are *again* considering (speculating) the possibility of animal forms coming from several or many different origins, rather than all forms traceable back to some single, simple animal origin. That the idea of several origins was entertained even by Charles Darwin is illustrated in a closing passage of his *Origin of Species:* "There is grandeur in this view of life, with its several powers, having been originally breathed by the Creator into a few forms or into one; . . ."[37]

With no difficulty at all one can demonstrate that several points of view (at least monophyletic versus polyphyletic)[38] are discussed in the scientific literature by those scientists willing to speculate on the subject of origins.

Such speculation about origins of living things goes quite beyond the bounds of adequately empirical, experimental scientific work. Scientists are limited properly to the observable and quantifiable. Hence attention to origins partakes necessarily of philosophical discourses based primarily upon circumstantial evidence.

Even so-called laboratory study of evolution is no more than examination of variation *within* one form or kind (such as bacteria, fruit flies, or moths). Evolutionists claim study of evolution in the laboratory *only* because they are addicted to using the terms "variation" and "evolution" in an *equivocal* manner.

Evolution is *no more than* a guess. Natural selection and evolutionary thought are *only theoretical*. No transmutation across basic kinds is known or demonstrable; and scientist after scientist attests to this situation. Yet, what kind of *selected* indoctrination occurs when teachers, professors, and textbooks writers present evolution and natural selection as factual, as observable?

Finally, we must recognize that the evolutionary philosophy, or Evolutionism, of such free-thinking intellectuals as Ernest Haeckel and Julian Huxley has been "fostered" by highly spurious science. True scientific principles and methods in the hands of true believers in the Word of God clearly expose evolution as very poor science. In point of fact, application of true methods of testability, repeatability, and experimental confirmation exposes evolution, when considered in precise meaning of change of one form or kind into another, as not even science. Therefore, true believers in the Word of God have nothing to fear from attacks on Genesis 1 and 2 from evolutionary atheistic philosophers.

But detachment of men and women from evolution, as a faith, is not as important as attachment of all who will respond to the Saviour. Most men of Western civilization have lost their way. On his own terms alone, Western man has sought the perfect organization of society by various means. That is, man has tried monarchy, oligarchy, democracy, socialism, fascist dictatorship, communist dictatorship, and even now is considering evolutionary humanism through controlled application of scientific technology. However, man's *changing* ways, in each instance tried, have fallen short of proffered promises, and men always falter over their own selfishness, the original sin.

Therefore, Christians would offer devotion to creationism to those who are lost, because Christ says, "I am the Way." To the mind of man which is steeped in error, Christ says, "I am the Truth." Christians know that Jesus Christ remains *constant* through the ages in offering salvation to those who answer His call for faithful acceptance. Only with His help can our good works with fellow human beings reach beyond the bounds of limited material dimensions. Only with His help can man be lifted to heights above supposed salvation through crass evolutionary humanism, which proponents offer as a "new" religion in place of worship of *the* God of the Trinity.

NOTES AND REFERENCES

1. Richard M. Weaver, *Ideas Have Consequences* (Chicago: University of Chicago Press, 1948), p. 1.
2. The following discourse in the Introduction is based upon pp. 1-7 of the Weaver book in *ibid.*
3. *Ibid.*, p. 26.
4. Whittaker Chambers, *Cold Friday* (New York: Random House, 1964), pp. 225, 226.
5. *Natural Science*, Vol. II (Michigan State University Press, Third [Revised] Edition, 1964), pp. 8-15 and 8-16.
6. *Ibid.*, p. 7-2.
7. *Ibid.*, p. 7-4.
8. *Ibid.*, p. 8-1.
9. Philip P. Wiener, *Evolution and the Founders of Pragmatism* (Cambridge, Mass.: Harvard University Press, 1949), pp. 8, 17.
10. Robert Scoon, "The Rise and Impact of Evolutionary Ideas," *Evolutionary Thought in America*, Stow Pearsons, editor (New York: George Braziller, Inc., 1956), p. 10.
11. A. I. Oparin, *The Origin of Life* (New York: Dover Publications, Inc., 1953).
12. Roy W. Carlson, "Jack London's Heroes: A Study of Evolutionary Thought." Unpublished Doctoral Dissertation, University of New Mexico, 1961, No. 61-5265, University Microfilms, Inc., Ann Arbor, Michigan, pp. 3, 27, 45, 46.
13. Windsor H. Roberts, "The Reaction of American Protestant Churches to the Darwinian Philosophy, 1860-1900." Published private edition, distributed by the University of Chicago Libraries, Chicago, Ill., 1938.
14. Bert J. Loewenberg, "Darwinism Comes to America, 1859-1900," *Mississippi Valley Historical Review* (December, 1941), Vol. 28, No. 3, pp. 340, 341.
15. Bert J. Lowenberg, "The Mosaic of Darwinian Thought," *Victorian Studies,* Darwin Anniversary Issue (Sept. 1959), Vol. III, p. 15. See also J. J. Duyvené DeWit, "Reflections on the Architecture of the Organic World and the Origin of Man" (A Critical Evaluation of the Transformist Principle), *Philosophia Reformata*, 29e Jaargang 1964.
16. Loewenberg, *op. cit.*, pp. 347-357.
17. F. S. C. Northrop, "Evolution in Its Relation to the Philosophy of Nature and the Philosophy of Culture," *Evolutionary Thought in America*, Stow Persons, editor (New York: George Braziller, Inc., 1956).
18. Scoon, *op. cit.*, p. 35.
19. Bert J. Loewenberg, *Darwinism: Reaction or Reform?* (New York: Holt, Rinehart and Winston, 1964), pp. 1, 15.
20. A. R. Manser, "The Concept of Evolution," *Philosophy* (Jan. 1965), pp. 21, 30.
21. Charles A. Beard, *An Economic Interpretation of the Constitution of the United States* (New York: Macmillan, 1913).

22. Forrest McDonald, *We the People* (The Economic Origins of the Constitution [Chicago: University of Chicago Press, 1958]).

23. Robert E. Brown, *Middle Class Democracy and the Revolution in Massachusetts, 1691-1780* (Ithaca, N. Y.: Cornell University Press, 1955); Robert E. and Katherine Brown, *Virginia, 1705-1786: Democracy or Aristocracy?* (East Lansing, Mich.: Michigan State University Press, 1964).

24. H. Selsam, "Charles Darwin and Karl Marx," *Mainstream* (June 1959), Vol. 12, No. 6, pp. 28, 36.

25. Veritas Foundation Staff Study, *Keynes at Harvard,* "Economic Deception as a Political Credo" (West Sayville, N. Y.: Veritas Foundation, 1960). See also Veritas Foundation Staff Study, *The Great Deceit* (Social Pseudo-Sciences [West Sayville, N. Y.: Veritas Foundation, 1964]); Anne Fremantle, *This Little Band of Prophets: The British Fabians,* No. 266, Mentor Books (New York: The New American Library, 1960); and Sister M. Margaret Patricia McCarran, *Fabianism in the Political Life of Britain, 1919-1931* (Chicago: The Heritage Foundation, Inc., 1954).

26. Henry Hazlitt, *The Failure of the "New Economics,"* "An Analysis of the Keynesian Fallacies" (New York: D. Van Nostrand Co., Inc., 1959).

27. John Chamberlain, *The Roots of Capitalism* (Princeton, N. J.: D. Van Nostrand Co., Inc., 1959).

28. Frederick W. Conner, *Cosmic Optimism* (A Study of the Interpretation of Evolution by American Poets from Emerson to Robinson [Gainesville, Fla.: University of Florida Press, 1949]).

29. Leo J. Henkin, *Darwinism in the English Novel* (New York: Corporate Press, Inc., 1940).

30. Georg Roppen, *Evolution and Poetic Belief* (Oslo, Norway: Oslo University Press, 1956).

31. Lionel Stevenson, *Darwin Among the Poets* (New York: Russell and Russell, 1963).

32. Conway Zirkle, *Evolution, Marxian Biology, and the Social Scene* (Philadelphia: University of Pennsylvania Press, 1958).

33. Carlson, *op. cit.*

34. G. A. Kerkut, *Implications of Evolution* (New York: Pergamon Press, 1960).

35. David Lack, *Evolutionary Theory and Christian Belief* (The Unresolved Conflict [London: Methuen and Co., Ltd., 1961]).

36. Henry Morris, *The Twilight of Evolution* (Grand Rapids, Mich.: Baker Book House, 1963).

37. Charles Darwin, *Origin of Species* (The Modern Library Edition), p. 374.

38. Even at the turn of the century examples of scientists supporting the idea of multiple origins can be found; in particular,

> . . . the assumption of monophyletic evolution of the whole kingdom of organic life is a delightful dream without any scientific support . . . it is impossible to trace back the chief types of the animal kingdom to one primitive form . . . Von Wettstein among the botanists, and, more particularly, Steinmann, Koken, and Diener among the palaeontologists, have recently come forward as champions of

the theory of polyphyletic evolution" (Erich Wasmann, entomologist, *Evolution* [London: Kegan, Paul, Trench, Truber and Co., 1909], pp. 15, 16).

Then, in 1935, Heribert Nilsson, botanist, concluded:

It is obvious that the investigations of the last three decades into the problem of the origin of species have not been able to show that a variational material capable of competition in the struggle for existence is formed by mutation. . . . We are forced to this conclusion that *the theory of evolution has not been verified by experimental investigations of the origin of species"* (emphasis Nilsson's [in journal *Hereditas,* Vol. 20, 1935, p. 236]).

But such thinking (speculating) has accelerated in the last decade as shown in the following eight quotations:

. . . although evolution finds wide tacit acceptance . . . , many people gravely doubt the validity of many of the more particular arguments by which it is customarily sustained . . . while it may be justified to believe that evolution affords a reasonable explanation of the facts of nature, it is not justifiable to maintain that no other explanation is possible or permissible" (Ronald Good, botanist, *Features of Evolution in the Flowering Plants* [London: Longmans, Green and Co., 1956], pp. 1, 2).

The surface of the land, the weathered superficial layers of the crust of the Earth, shallow continental basins and lagoons of the ocean, were the arenas in which life came into being on our planet *in the form of a multifarious host of germs* (R. L. Berg, biochemist, cited by A. I. Oparin and others, *The Origin of Life on the Earth* [New York: Pergamon Press, 1959], p. 171, emphasis added).

The difficulty of placing viruses, bacteria, certain "algae," sponges, and so on, in a fitting place in any taxonomic scheme based on a monophyletic hypothesis may stem from the possibility that the discontinuities are real and represent the existence of separate lines of descent from independent instances of neo-biogenesis (establishment of primitive organisms) at different times in the history of the earth down to the present (John Keosian, biochemist, in *Science,* Vol. 131, Feb. 19, 1960, p. 482).

It is worth paying serious attention to the concept that the invertebrates are polyphyletic, . . . One thing that does seem reasonably clear is that many of the groups such as the Amphibia, Reptilia, and Mammalia appear to be polyphyletic grades of organization. . . . On the other hand there is the theory that all the living forms in the world have arisen from a single source which itself came from an inorganic form . . . the evidence that supports it is not sufficiently strong to allow us to consider it as anything more than a working hypothesis (G. A. Kerkut, physiologist, *Implications of Evolution* [New York: Pergamon Press, 1960], pp. 152, 153, 157).

The palaeontological record as we know it today includes many examples of polyphyletic or parallel evolution in which the development of similar morphological features has been achieved in two or more independent lines (Loris S. Russell, palaeontologist, in *Evolution: Its Science and Doctrine*, edited by Thomas W. M. Cameron [University of Toronto Press, 1960], p. 10).

After quoting another researcher that as far back as fossil material is found, the conifers, ginkgos, and Taxales are distinct and clearly differentiated from one another, Henry N. Andrews, botanist, adds,

I am inclined to go a little farther than this and proffer the opinion that the ginkgophytes will ultimately be shown to have evolved as a distinct and independent line of seed plants (in *Studies in Paleobotany* [New York: John Wiley and Sons, Inc., 1961], p. 315; see also his statements on separate and independent origin of most other major groups of plants on pp. 159, 312, 398-402).

It is suggested that the major groups of animals arose polyphyletically, over a period of time, from a geographically widespread variety of prozoan eobionts which were evolving to explore the variety possible within a limited physico-chemical framework (J. R. Nursall, zoologist, in *Evolution*, Vol. 16, March, 1962, p. 122. See also his proposed polyphyletic or multiple origins scheme in diagram form on p. 121).

The great diversity of tracheophytes in Devonian times makes it tempting to believe that the Tracheophyta were polyphyletic, because even as early as that time the lycopod, spensopsid, and fern lines were distinct. Workers adhering to the polyphyletic point of view argue that because these lines are distinct as far back as they are known, they must have had independent sources. Other considerations, however, make it appear less likely that more than one group of ancestors are involved. . . . Probably the most convincing piece of evidence in favor of monophylesis is the nature of the life cycles of the tracheophytes (Theodore Delevoryas, *Morphology and Evolution of Fossil Plants* [New York: Holt, Rinehart and Winston, 1962], pp. 21, 22).